D1338640

This book is the first major study in English of a group of late twelfth-century religious enthusiasts, the early Humiliati, who were condemned by the Church as heretics in 1184 but – in a remarkable transition – were reconciled seventeen years later and went on to establish a highly successful religious order in north Italy.

The Humiliati have been accorded little attention in previous studies both because of the local nature of the order and because of its suppression in 1571, after one of their number made a disastrous attempt to murder Charles Borromeo. Using a combination of a wide range of sources, the nature of the early movement and its processes of institutional development are reconstructed. The book also includes a *Bullarium Humiliatorum*, a calendar of papal and episcopal letters and privileges, which will be of great use to scholars in the field.

FRANCES ANDREWS is Lecturer in Medieval History, University of St Andrews

Cambridge Studies in Medieval Life and Thought
Fourth Series

General Editor:
D. E. LUSCOMBE
Leverhulme Personal Research Professor of Medieval History, University of Sheffield

Advisory Editors:
CHRISTINE CARPENTER
Reader in Medieval English History, University of Cambridge, and Fellow of New Hall

ROSAMOND MCKITTERICK
Professor of Medieval History, University of Cambridge,
and Fellow of Newnham College

The series Cambridge Studies in Medieval Life and Thought was inaugurated by G. G. Coulton in 1921; Professor D. E. Luscombe now acts as General Editor of the Fourth Series, with Dr Christine Carpenter and Professor Rosamond McKitterick as Advisory Editors. The series brings together outstanding work by medieval scholars over a wide range of human endeavour extending from political economy to the history of ideas.

For a list of titles in the series, see end of book.

THE
EARLY HUMILIATI

FRANCES ANDREWS

CAMBRIDGE
UNIVERSITY PRESS

PUBLISHED BY THE PRESS SYNDICATE OF THE UNIVERSITY OF CAMBRIDGE
The Pitt Building, Trumpington Street, Cambridge, United Kingdom

CAMBRIDGE UNIVERSITY PRESS
The Edinburgh Building, Cambridge CB2 2RU, UK   http://www.cup.cam.ac.uk
40 West 20th Street, New York, NY 10011–4211, USA   http://www.cup.org
10 Stamford Road, Oakleigh, Melbourne 3166, Australia

© Frances Andrews 1999

This book is in copyright. Subject to statutory exception and
to the provisions of relevant collective licensing agreements,
no reproduction of any part may take place without
the written permission of Cambridge University Press.

First published 1999

Printed in the United Kingdom at the University Press, Cambridge

Typeset in 11/12pt Bembo   [CE]

A catalogue record for this book is available from the British Library

Library of Congress Cataloguing in Publication data

Andrews, Frances.
The early Humiliati / Frances Andrews.
p.   cm. – (Cambridge studies in medieval life and thought;
4th ser.)
Includes bibliographical references.
ISBN 0 521 59189 9
1. Humiliati.   I. Title.   II. Series.
BX3688.A53   1999
271'.79 – dc21   98–48328   CIP

ISBN 0 521 59189 9 hardback

CONTENTS

ACKNOWLEDGEMENTS

In the course of researching and writing this book I have benefited from the knowledge, support and guidance of a large number of friends and colleagues and it is a great pleasure to be able to acknowledge their assistance here. Above all, I should like to thank Brenda Bolton, whose enthusiasm proved infectious and whose confidence in the initial research provided great encouragement. Many other people have given either practical or moral support, or generously shared information and knowledge which has saved me from a number of errors. They include, in alphabetical order, Rob Bartlett, Nicole Bériou, Debra Birch, Alberto Castagnoli, Peter Clark, David d'Avray, John Doran, Christoph Egger, Christine Findlay, Robert Gibbs, Bernard Hamilton, David Luscombe, Seema Quraishi, Jonathan Riley-Smith and Connie Rousseau. In particular Peter Biller, John Hudson and Peter King generously read draft chapters and made many constructive suggestions. The mistakes which remain are, of course, of my own making.

In Italy I am indebted to Professors Maria Pia Alberzoni, Annamaria Ambrosioni, Maria Teresa Brolis, Giuseppina De Sandre Gasparini and Lorenzo Paolini, who gave both time and information generously and whose own works have provided inspiration; also to Daniela Castagnetti, Renata Crotti Pasi and Francesca Morelli who allowed me to see then unpublished work and to Alessandro Caretta in Lodi and all the unnamed archivists and librarians whose help was indispensable to a study such as this.

This project could not have happened without financial support from Westfield College, the Baring Foundation, London University, the British Academy, St Andrews University and the British School at Rome and I gratefully acknowledge their assistance. I would particularly like to thank Val Scott, Tommaso and Filomena Astolfi, Amanda Claridge and the BSR staff for making my year in Rome such fun. This book is dedicated to my family and to Louise Bourdua, with heartfelt thanks.

ABBREVIATIONS

See p. 253 for abbreviations used only in appendix 1.

AASS	*Acta Sanctorum*
ACA Milan	Archivio della curia arcivescovile, Milan
Ambrosiana	Biblioteca ambrosiana, Milan
ASBg	Archivio di stato, Bergamo
ASBr	Archivio di stato, Brescia
ASCo	Archivio di stato, Como
ASL	*Archivio storico lombardo*
ASMi	Archivio di stato, Milan
	Fondo pergamene
470/471 Brera	Buste 470 and 471. Sta Maria di Brera
526 Pta Vercellina	Busta 526 Umiliati di Porta Vercellina
385 Sta Caterina	Busta 385 Sta Caterina alla Chiusa
435 San Marco	Busta 435 San Marco
ASVat	Archivio segreto vaticano
Baldaria	Archivio della Cancelleria della Nunziatura Veneta. Monastero di San Giovanni Battista di Baldaria
ASVer	Archivio di stato, Verona
Ghiara	Fondo di Sta Maria della Ghiara
Beverara	Fondo di San Giovanni della Beverara
ASVic Ognissanti 1–2	Archivio di stato, Vicenza Fondo delle corporazioni soppresse. Monastero di Ognissanti buste 1 and 2
AVLodi	Archivio vescovile, Lodi
Bobbio	*Codice diplomatico del monastero di S. Colombano di Bobbio fino all'anno mccviii*, 3 vols., ed. C. Cipolla, Fonti per la storia d'Italia, 52–4 (Rome, 1918)

ix

List of abbreviations

Brera	Biblioteca nazionale di Brera, Milan
BF	*Bullarium franciscanum*, ed. J. H. Sbaralea, vols. I–IV, (Rome, 1759–68), ed. C. Eubel, vols. V–VII, (Rome, 1898–1904)
BSSS	Biblioteca della società storica subalpina
Casale	*Carte varie di Casale e monasteri del Monferrato. Cartari minori*, ed. E. Durando, BSSS, 42 (Pinerolo, 1908)
CDL	*Codice diplomatico laudense*, vols. I, II/I and II/II, *Lodi Nuovo*, ed. C. Vignati, Biblioteca historica italica, 2–4 (Milan, 1885)
Chrodegang	'Regula canonicorum secundum Dacherii recensionem', comp. J. P. Migne, *PL*, 89 (Paris, 1863), cols. 1058–96
DBI	*Dizionario biografico degli italiani*
DIP	*Dizionario degli istituti di perfezione*
Gesta	*Gesta Innocentii III Papae*, comp. J. P. Migne, *PL*, 214 (Paris, 1855), cols. xvii–ccxxviii
Grundmann	H. Grundmann, *Religiöse Bewegungen im Mittelalter* (Berlin, 1935, 2nd rev. edn. Darmstadt 1961); trans. S. Rowan, *Religious Movements in the Middle Ages* (Notre Dame, London, 1995)
Ivrea	*Carte dello Archivio vescovile d'Ivrea fino al 1313*, 2 vols., ed. F. Gabotto, BSSS, 5–6 (Pinerolo, 1900)
Maleczek, *Kardinalskolleg*	W. Maleczek, *Papst und Kardinalskolleg von 1191 bis 1216. Die Kardinäle unter Coelestin III. und Innocenz III.* (Rome, Vienna, 1984)
MGH	*Monumenta Germaniae historica*
Leges	*Leges, sectio III Concilia*, 3 vols., ed. A. Werminghoff *et al.* (Hanover, Leipzig, 1906–24)
SS	*Scriptores*, ed. G. H. Pertz *et al.* (Hanover, 1826–)
OBP	*Omnis boni principium*, ed. Zanoni (Milan, 1911), pp. 352–70
Oulx	*Le carte della prevostura d'Oulx raccolte e riordinate cronologicamente fino al 1300*, ed. G. Collino, BSSS, 45 (Pinerolo, 1908)
PL	*Patrologiae Latinae cursus completus*, comp. J. P. Migne, 221 vols. (Paris, 1844–64)

Potthast	A. Potthast, *Regesta pontificum romanorum*, 2 vols. (Graz, 1957)
RCM	Rule of Sta Croce Mortara, 'La regola dei Mortariensi', ed. V. Mosca, *Alberto, Patriarca di Gerusalemme*, Textus et studia historica Carmelitana, 20 (Rome, 1996), appendix 2, pp. 561–97
Register I–II, V–VII	Innocent III, *Die Register Innocenz III*, ed. O. Hageneder, A. Haidacher, W. Maleczek *et al.* (Graz, Cologne, Rome, Vienna, 1964–97); I *Pontifikatsjahr* 1198–9, II 1199–1200, V 1202–3, VI 1203–4, VII 1204–5
RIS	L. A. Muratori, *Rerum Italicarum Scriptores*, 25 vols. (Milan, 1723–51)
RSB	*The Rule of St Benedict*, ed. and trans. J. McCann (London, 1952)
RSCI	*Rivista di storia della chiesa in Italia*
S. Solutore	*Le carte dell'abbazia di S. Solutore di Torino. Carte varie relative a chiese e monasteri di Torino e territorio*, ed. F. Cognasso, BSSS, 44 (Pinerolo, 1908)
SCH	Studies in Church History
Sulle tracce	*Sulle tracce degli Umiliati*, ed. M. P. Alberzoni, A. Ambrosioni and A. Lucioni (Milan, 1997)
Vercelli, arcivescovile	*Le carte dello archivio arcivescovile di Vercelli*, ed. D. Arnoldi, BSSS, 85 (Pinerolo, 1917), pp. 205–452
Vercelli, capitolare	*Le carte dello archivio capitolare di Vercelli*, ed. D. Arnoldi, G. C. Faccio, F. Gabotto and G. Rocchi, 2 vols., BSSS, 70–1 (Pinerolo, 1912–14)
VHM	G. Tiraboschi, *Vetera Humiliatorum Monumenta annotationibus, ac dissertationibus prodromis illustrata*, 3 vols. (Milan, 1766–8)
Vitry *HO*	Jacques de Vitry, *The 'Historia occidentalis' of Jacques de Vitry: A Critical Edition*, ed. J. F. Hinnebusch, *Spicilegium Friburgense*, 17 (Freibourg, 1972)
Zanoni	L. Zanoni, *Gli umiliati nei loro rapporti con l'eresia, l'industria della lana ed i comuni nei secoli xii e xiii sulla scorta di documenti inediti* (Milan, 1911, reprinted 1971)

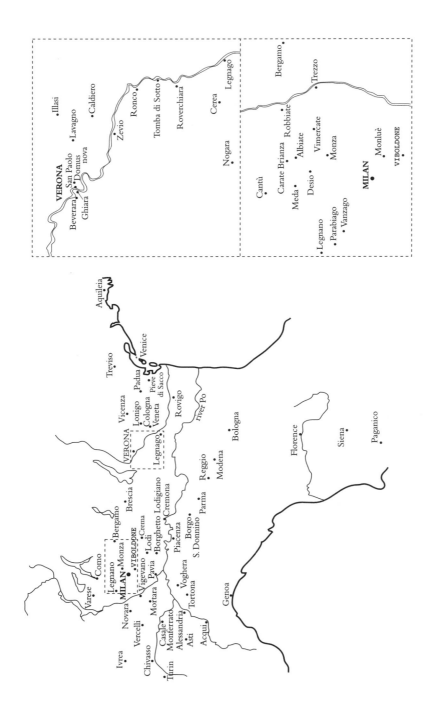

Key places mentioned in text

INTRODUCTION

Heresy lies in the eye of the beholder.[1]

The early Humiliati stood at a crossroads between tradition and novelty, orthodoxy and heresy. Latin Europe in the last decades of the twelfth century saw an outpouring of new forms of religious life which Marie-Dominique Chenu has described as an 'Evangelical Awakening': a renewed search for a more intense religious experience focused on the life of Christ and the apostles, as described in the Gospel: the *vita apostolica* and the model of the early Church, the *ecclesiae primitivae forma*.[2] The most successful of these new movements in the twelfth century, both numerically and historiographically, were the Cathars and Waldensians. The dualist faith of the Cathars took fast hold in the Languedoc and northern Italy and the Cathar Church was acquiring a clear organisational structure separate from that of the Church of Rome. The Waldensians came together in the 1170s as followers of Valdes of Lyons, a charismatic figure who attracted attention by his dramatic conversion to a life of poverty and preaching. When the English churchman and raconteur Walter Map encountered him and his followers at the papal Curia in 1179 he ridiculed their ignorance, but was sufficiently alarmed to observe 'they are making their first moves in the humblest manner because they cannot launch an attack. If we admit them, we shall be driven out.'[3] Both Cathars and Waldensians were considered heretics by men of the Church and were

---

[1] See Moore, 'New sects and secret meetings: association and authority in the eleventh and twelfth centuries', pp. 47–68 on the idea that anxiety (about new forms of religious life) lay in the eye of the clerical beholder.

[2] Chenu, *Nature, Man and Society in the Twelfth Century*, ch. 7; see also by the same author 'Moines, clercs, laïcs, au carrefour de la vie évangélique (xiie siècle)'.

[3] Walter Map, *De nugis curialium: Courtiers' Trifles*, ed. and trans. M. R. James, rev. C. N. L. Brooke and R. A. B. Mynors (Oxford, 1983), distinction 1, chapter 31, p. 127; trans. from *Heresies of the High Middle Ages*, Wakefield and Evans, p. 204.

caught in the broad net of the anathema declared in November 1184 by pope Lucius III sitting in council with Frederick I Barbarossa at Verona. Within a generation, the Waldensians had acquired a substantial body of members and, like the Cathars, were becoming doctrinally more remote from the orthodox Church.[4] The most successful movements in the early thirteenth century, by contrast, enjoyed the support of prelates and popes from the beginning. Francis and Dominic, charismatic preachers who took the meaning of the *vita apostolica* and the *ecclesiae primitivae forma* to new extremes, attracted vast followings and founded orders which were to dominate the pastoral and intellectual life of the thirteenth-century Church.

In this religious drama the Humiliati or 'humble ones' had only a walk-on part, limited first by geography and then by chronology. They first emerged in the 1170s on the north Italian plain between the foothills of the Alps and the Appennines, along the valley of the Po from modern-day Piemonte in the west to the edges of the Veneto in the east. The first references describe both groups of clerics living in community and lay men and women devoted to the religious life in small *ad hoc* associations promoting the catholic faith. In 1184 the Humiliati too, like the Cathars and Waldensians, were listed as heretics by Lucius III and Barbarossa, but by the turn of the century they were sufficiently established to approach the pope in search of approval. By this date, three distinct elements were recognisable: married or single lay men and women living a religious life while remaining in their own homes (later known as the Third order), male and female regulars living in common (the Second order), and clerics based in more formal communities (the First order). In 1201 these groups achieved recognition as three separate orders under one framework of authority.

By the mid-thirteenth century the *ordo Humiliatorum* had seen spectacular expansion. In 1278 Bonvesin da la Riva, himself a Humiliati Tertiary, recorded that there were over 200 houses of the regular 'Second' order and seven *canoniche* of the 'First', in the city and region of Milan alone.[5] His figures are not without problems, but the measure of success which they convey is undeniable. By the middle of the thirteenth century, the Humiliati had become a major presence in the religious, economic and administrative life of northern Italy.

In the following centuries, the order shrank in both size and prestige and in the 1500s the Humiliati were swept aside by the winds of change

---

[4] K. V. Selge, *Die ersten Waldenser, mit Edition der 'Liber Antiheresis' des Durandus von Osca*, 2 vols. (Berlin, 1967).

[5] Bonvesin da la Riva, *De magnalibus mediolani. Meraviglie di Milano*, pp. 81, 83. On Bonvesin, see A. S. Avalle, 'Bonvesin della Riva', *DBI*, XII (Rome, 1970), pp. 465–9.

in the Counter Reformation. The male orders were suppressed by Charles Borromeo and Pius V in 1571 with the bull *Quemadmodum solicitus pater*, the women (by this date Benedictine) left to fade out in a more dignified manner in the following centuries.

The experience of the Humiliati is unique. There are certainly points of comparison with the early experience of the Waldensians: both groups advocated a more active pastoral role for their members, both were condemned in 1184 at least in part because of their insistence on preaching without authority. Like the Humiliati, two groups of former Waldensians, led by Durand of Huesca and Bernard Prim, returned to orthodox obedience during the pontificate of Innocent III (1198–1216). Since the early sources for the Humiliati are sporadic and fragmentary and we are so much better informed about the actions and teachings of the early Waldensians, historians have found it logical to assimilate the two groups. But the parallels, although beguiling, are also restrictive. The reason why we do not have the same type and quality of early sources for the Humiliati is symptomatic. In part this is the result of the fate of the movement centuries later and the dispersal and loss of documentary sources, but it is also because they attracted less attention, fitting relatively smoothly into the religious and ecclesiastical life of northern Italy.

This book sets out to explore the reasons for the unique experience of the Humiliati, tracing their history from the earliest records in the 1170s to the height of their success in the mid-thirteenth century. When we look beyond, though never forgetting, the heretic label, to explore the evidence for the development of the *ordo Humiliatorum* and the relations of this group of religious enthusiasts with the local communities with whom they lived, both ecclesiastical and lay, we find a very different experience from that of even the reconciled Waldensians. In this process the Humiliati can be seen to have as much in common with confraternal groups and with the new and exciting orthodoxies of the thirteenth century, the Franciscans and Dominicans above all, as they do with heretics such as the Waldensians.

The book opens with a preliminary historiographical survey intended to illustrate the issues and debates of present and past research on the Humiliati and clarify the starting point for this study. This is followed by a case-by-case examination of the twelfth-century evidence for the Humiliati, both before and after 1184. Those concerned with the general framework rather than specific local examples may wish to limit their reading of this chapter to the opening pages and the conclusions which explore the impact of the condemnation and the nature of relations between the new movement and prelates in these years.

Chapter 3 then focuses on the process of approval at the turn of the century, examining the careers of the individuals involved on both sides of the negotiations, so as to establish a context for the actions of Innocent III and assess the contribution of both the Humiliati themselves and the prelates of the north Italian Church. Chapter 4 outlines the norms established for the order in 1201 and then illustrates the development of observance in the following years by consideration of dispensations on oath-taking, fasting and diet.

The next three chapters (5, 6 and 7) examine the evidence from the first decades of the thirteenth century for the development of the *ordo Humiliatorum*, defined in organisational terms as a network of houses bound by observance of a common rule and centralised administration. Chapter 5 analyses the nature, size and geographical catchment areas of houses, the presence of women, evidence for institutional security, the structural framework and the roles of superiors, both male and female. A pre-condition for the existence of an order was a common sense of identity or participation in a community and, although it is often elusive of illustration, examination of ties between different houses and communities helps to throw some light on this area. Local, city-wide or regional links between houses are therefore examined in some detail.

Chapter 6 uses professions of faith to consider the development of the vows and ritual for entry into the First and Second orders of the Humiliati. These records provide a unique insight into variations in practice, the evolution of uniform, regular observance, and once more, the emergence of a common identity as an order. They also furnish invaluable information about methods of recruitment and the experience of individuals entering the communities.

Chapter 7 returns to the evidence of papal letters to trace uniform observance, papal visitation and the impact of changes introduced in 1246 on the development of an *ordo Humiliatorum*. In particular it explores the activities of the first Master General, Beltramus of Brescia, using the settlement of disputes as a guide to the exercise of authority in the order. Finally, chapter 8 is a first attempt to place the Humiliati of the First and Second orders into a wider pastoral and ecclesiastical context, analysing the development of their pastoral rights, and their involvement in the business of death as well as their relations with other ecclesiastics in the region, both secular and regular.

This book is not intended as a general history of the early Humiliati. Research is still continuing in too many areas to make that as yet a realistic project. It is first necessary to understand the Humiliati as a movement outside and then as an order within the Church. That is the aim of this book. Only once this has been established can the question of their involvement in industry and communal government or their relations with the 'ordinary' people of northern Italy be appraised.

The geographical boundaries of this study are as far as possible those of the early Humiliati themselves in northern and later in central Italy. A conscious attempt has been made to use a variety of sources from across this area in order to complement rather than duplicate the spate of local studies being produced in northern Italy. Evidence for the area of Verona is, however, particularly prolific and has provided the opportunity for greater consideration of some aspects of practice (in particular professions of faith) than elsewhere. This also serves to counter a previous tendency to focus on Milan, certainly the Humiliati city *par excellence*, but not by any means the only one.

The chronological limitations of this study are dictated first by the surviving documents (the earliest date to the 1170s) and second by the nature of my approach. It is intended to explore the transition of a movement into an order. Consideration of a relatively long time span is therefore necessary; however, I have not generally gone beyond the 1270s. In those years a new and different epoch in the history of the Humiliati begins, marked by a protracted dispute with the bishops of Milan, Como and Brescia which led to the negotiation of a new status for the order, entirely free from episcopal intervention.

Heresy lies in the eye of the beholder. Whether the Humiliati should be seen as heretics or not was decided in two ways in this period: condemnation in 1184, reconciliation in 1201. In the 1990s, the Humiliati form a standard part of the undergraduate syllabus for the study of heresy, not religious orders. It is the intention of this book to make a plea for a reversal of that picture; to see the Humiliati as they saw themselves, fighting to defend the religious life in the bustle and tension of the north.

Chapter 1

TRADITION AND HISTORY

. . . una discreta fioritura di studi . . .

Volpe

POINTS OF DEPARTURE

Two weighty works are essential in the hand baggage of any student of the early Humiliati. The first, and still irreplaceable, is the three-volume *Vetera Humiliatorum Monumenta*, published in the 1760s by a young Jesuit scholar, Girolamo Tiraboschi (1731–94), better known to posterity as the author of a monumental history of Italian literature.[1] Tiraboschi taught rhetoric at the Brera Academy in Milan, which had acquired the site, name and archives of a prominent house of the Humiliati.[2] This gave him easy access to a mass of documentation, including the *Bullarium Humiliatorum*, a substantial collection of papal letters and privileges addressed to the order.[3] Many of these he published in the *Monumenta*, together with material unearthed in other archives in Milan and through correspondence with archivists and scholars all over northern Italy in a manner reminiscent of the working practices of the Bollandists and Maurists.[4] The resulting volumes include an extensive collection of documentation concerning the history of the order down to the sixteenth century, to which Tiraboschi added a careful critique in the form of seven lengthy dissertations.[5]

The second study, and one cast in a very different style, is a volume published in 1911 by Luigi Zanoni: *Gli umiliati nei loro rapporti con l'eresia, l'industria della lana ed i comuni nei secoli xii e xiii sulla scorta di*

---

[1] G. Tiraboschi, *Storia della letteratura italiana*, 11 vols. (Modena, 1772–95).
[2] A. Scotti, *Brera 1776–1815. Nascita e sviluppo di una istituzione culturale milanese* (Milan, 1979).
[3] Brera AD XVII.
[4] See, for example, his correspondence with canon Bartoli of Novara in Balosso, 'Gli Umiliati nel Novarese', 86–90.
[5] See below, p. 21.

6

documenti inediti.[6] Zanoni was a star student of the Milanese historian Gioacchino Volpe who later wrote a brief but revealing description of the work being undertaken by this group in the early decades of the twentieth century, relating it to the distinctive political and ecclesiastical climate of the times. The atmosphere, he wrote, had been dominated by christian socialism and opposition to the establishment, characteristics which evoked parallels with Valdes and Francis. He saw it as a time when many people lived between orthodoxy and heresy, with the threat of spiritual sanctions hanging over them. The controversy engendered had influenced the writing of history: 'There was at that time a notable flowering of studies dedicated to the religious or socio-ecclesiastical life, within which there were currents stirred by the tumultuous air beating from outside.'[7] Such studies were particularly being undertaken by young priests and Volpe praised, among others, the excellent work on the Humiliati by Luigi Zanoni, many of whose conclusions he shared.[8]

Zanoni was one of the scholars appointed to the Ambrosiana library in Milan, which holds in its archives manuscripts of the early chronicles of the order and seventeenth-century studies, as well as notarial documentation.[9] Like Tiraboschi, Zanoni thus had direct access to some of the sources for his work, but he too extended his research beyond the immediate confines of his own institution to other archives in Milan and elsewhere. In the extensive appendices to his volume he published documents which Tiraboschi either had not found or had not considered worthy of inclusion. These included transcripts of the rule of the First and Second orders, fifteenth-century chronicles of the order and extensive notarial material, illustrating in particular his interest in the communities of Tertiaries and Humiliati involvement in the wool trade and city administration.[10]

The approaches of Tiraboschi and Zanoni, separated by 145 years, were naturally very different, reflecting changes in historical writing and in the north Italian Church. Tiraboschi was a young Jesuit, writing in Latin and producing astute and systematic statements on the growth and extent of the Humiliati order in a work crowded with cautious detail, but also with telling insights. Zanoni was another young priest, but, perhaps prompted by the climate of opposition to the establishment

---

[6] Zanoni [The Humiliati and their relations with heresy, the wool industry and the communes in the twelfth and thirteenth centuries, on the basis of unpublished documents]; L. Zanoni, 'Gli origini degli Umiliati', *Civiltà Cattolica*, 62 (1911), 433–43, 670–80, summarises his arguments concerning their origins.

[7] Volpe, *Movimenti religiosi*, pp. xiii–xiv.   [8] *Ibid.*, and p. 55; below, p. 29.

[9] A. Paredi, 'Storia dell'Ambrosiana', *L'Ambrosiana* (Milan, 1967), part i.

[10] Zanoni, pp. 267–370.

bubbling around him, sought parallel themes in the lives of the people he studied. In the process he and another young contemporary, Antonino De Stefano, swept away some of the fabulous accretions to the history of the Humiliati which Tiraboschi's caution had made him reluctant to remove. These fables are nonetheless instructive, reflecting as they do the concerns of the Humiliati and those around them. They also furnish a context for the works of Tiraboschi and his successors and a background to the historiography of the Humiliati in the twentieth century from which the present study derives.

THE FOURTEENTH CENTURY

The first surviving attempts at a retrospective account of the origins of the Humiliati are the early fourteenth-century writings of two Dominicans, a circumstance not without significance in view of the association between the two orders during the thirteenth century, though neither author devoted substantial space to the theme. The Bolognese Francesco Pipino (died after 1328) made little more than passing reference to the beginnings of the Humiliati in a general chronicle, while the Milanese Galvano Fiamma (1283–c. 1344) inserted short but differing passages concerning the Humiliati or the actions of Guy *de Porta Orientale*, an early figure linked with them, in three related works.[11] Of these accounts the earliest is probably that of Pipino, a writer deservedly better known for a translation of Marco Polo's account of his travels in the East. Pipino's chronicle covers the years 754–1314 and is highly derivative, employing a wide range of sources, but none is given for the brief entry on the Humiliati and there is no need to assume anything more than common knowledge, perhaps acquired through association with members of the order. He records that Innocent gave the Third order their rule in the last year of the reign of Henry VI (which he identifies as 1199, thereby misdating emperor and approval), but projects the history of the order further back, correctly asserting that they had assumed the habit long before this date and remarking that this was before the Friars Minor or Preacher had appeared.[12] There is nothing contentious here, but he goes on to describe the Tertiaries as the founders of the First and Second orders, a point which may have

---

[11] *Chronicon fratris Francisci Pipini*, ed. Muratori, cited Zanoni, pp. 11–12 and n. 1; Galvano Fiamma, *Chronicon extravagans et chronicon maius (ad an. 1216)*, pp. 506–773; *Manipulus florum*, col. 632. There is no full edition of Galvano's third history, the *Galvagnana*, Brera AE X 10, fo. 70v, but see now Alberzoni, 'San Bernardo e gli Umiliati', pp. 96–124, who includes the text of the relevant passage, p. 103 n. 22; on Pipino and Fiamma, see Kaeppeli, *Scriptores ordinis praedicatorum medii aevii*, I, pp. 392–5; II, pp. 6–10.

[12] *Chronicon fratris Francisci Pipini*, col. 633.

been of particular concern to the Tertiaries in the fourteenth century, as will become clear.

Fiamma, by contrast, was a prolific and much more imaginative writer, and in his discussion of the Humiliati he made some surprising claims.[13] In all three accounts he associated Guy *de Porta Orientale* with Bernard of Clairvaux in the foundation of the Cistercian house of Chiaravalle Milanese in 1135. In the earliest (the *Galvagnana*, written between 1329 and 1340), he then described the 'building' of the *convenio sancti Bernardi* of the Third order of the brethren in the Porta Orientale of Milan by this same Guy and its confirmation by Innocent III, from whose title its name derived.[14] These brethren subsequently founded the order of the Humiliati and carried out visitation of them.

In his second account, the *Manipulus florum*, Fiamma maintained that on his way back through Milan, Bernard himself organised the 'order of St Bernard', now known as the *fratres de Conegio* and whose first house had been built by Guy in the Porta Orientale (a community of Humiliati Tertiaries when Fiamma was writing). He claimed that Guy, who assisted Bernard on that occasion, also went to Rome to receive confirmation of this order from Innocent III and he repeated the association of the name with the pope's title and the role of the Tertiaries as founders and visitors of the First and Second orders. In this version he added that they were exempt from communal taxes in Milan, a detail which enhances the impression that Fiamma was particularly concerned with the fate of the Tertiaries.

As Tiraboschi and Zanoni were well aware, there are some serious problems with Fiamma's account. Acknowledging that the work included fables, Tiraboschi threw doubt on the double role of Guy, pointing out that had he assisted Bernard in 1135 he would have been rather too old to visit Innocent III in 1201.[15] However, he did not reject Fiamma's testimony entirely, arguing instead that 'he mixed truth with the falsehood'.[16] Zanoni was less cautious, dismissing Fiamma as a 'credulous compiler', as many later historians have done (J. K. Hyde described Fiamma as a 'nasty plagiarist').[17] The energy of this dismissal is attractive and it is obvious that Fiamma's history of the origins of the Tertiaries is not entirely trustworthy. However, nor is it simply

---

[13] See also Andrews, '*Principium et origo ordinis*: the Humiliati and their origins', pp. 149–61.

[14] *Galvagnana*, Brera AE X 10, fo. 70v: 'ab Innocentio tertio dictus est ordo tertius'. For the dates see V. Hunecke, 'Die kirchenpolitischen Exkurse in den Chroniken des Galvaneus Flamma OP (1283–ca. 1344)', *Deutsches Archiv für Erforschung des Mittelalters*, 25 (1969), 111–208, 119–28; see also Alberzoni, 'San Bernardo e gli Umiliati', p. 116 n. 44.

[15] *VHM* I, p. 45.   [16] *VHM* II, p. 36. Also below, p. 22.

[17] Zanoni, pp. 11, 14; J. K. Hyde, 'Medieval descriptions of cities', *Bulletin of the John Rylands Library*, 48:2 (1966), 308–40, 336.

gratuitous fabrication. His explanation of the name Tertiary as a reflection of the numerical designation of the pope who approved their rule is undoubtedly fabulous. Yet it may also reflect a partisan purpose, since it would forestall any argument that the name depended on their being third in a descending succession, thereby defending the status of the Tertiaries against other Humiliati, particularly clerics, who might claim precedence or special privilege. The claim to early visitation rights over the First and Second orders points to a similar propaganda purpose, while mention of their tax-exempt status renews a theme running through papal correspondence from the time of Innocent III onwards.

The fabulous elements in Fiamma's writing should make us wary, but should not lead us to reject the whole account out of hand. As he perhaps intended, it makes sometimes entertaining reading and yet allows an insight into the preoccupations of the fourteenth-century Tertiaries. Tiraboschi's conclusion that Fiamma 'mixed truth with the falsehood' is almost certainly the right one. This point is perhaps confirmed by recent studies illustrating something of a cult of Bernard among the later Humiliati and the possibilities of a link at one remove between Bernard and Guy *de Porta Orientale*.

The evidence for each point is circumstantial. Bernard was by no means the only saint venerated by the later members of the order and indeed was not listed by a fifteenth-century Humiliati chronicler, John of Brera. Nor can a Bernardine tradition be traced back to the twelfth century. Yet there is sufficient evidence in the form of altar, house and church dedications and artistic patronage to argue that by the fourteenth century members of the order may have cherished particular devotion to Bernard[18] and may have found it easy to believe in an early association of their order with this great monastic leader. This may in turn be linked with notarial evidence showing that Guy *de Porta Orientale*, who was summoned by Innocent III in 1201, was the son of a man bearing the same name who had died in June 1174 and who would have been of the appropriate age to assist Bernard in 1135.[19] Whether or not this did indeed happen, the association with Bernard fits well with contemporary descriptions of the saint's encounter with penitents when he visited Milan, and his attempts to regulate groups of faithful lay people suspected of heresy by encouraging them to come together in fraternities.[20] Fiamma, or those from whom he got the tale, conflated

[18] Spinelli, 'La diffusione del culto di San Bernardo', pp. 193–215, pp. 203–4 and n. 29, p. 207 n. 36.
[19] Alberzoni, 'San Bernardo e gli Umiliati', p. 110 n. 27.
[20] Landulf of St Paul, 'Historia mediolanensis', pp. 46–7; *VHM* I, p. 37; Spinelli, 'La diffusione del culto di San Bernardo', pp. 114–15.

episodes at a distance of several generations, constructing an account which could only add lustre to the prestige of the Tertiaries, status which they greatly needed.

Already in the 1240s there had been disputes over the precedence of clerics in the house of San Michele in Alessandria, and in 1272 the Tertiaries had been excluded from the General Chapter of the order. By the fourteenth century the number of Tertiaries seems to have been in serious decline for, although their survival in small numbers is still recorded by the fifteenth-century chronicler John of Brera, they appear to have disappeared from Milan as early as the 1360s.[21] Fiamma's account may well reflect the desire of Tertiaries to emphasise their primordial role in such a way as to revitalise their movement and re-establish their position.

This suggestion that close association with members of the Third order caused Fiamma to reflect their anxieties in his writings is reinforced by a clause inserted not long after his death in a hospital foundation charter drawn up in the new archiepiscopal palace in Milan in 1346.[22] The hospital was established by the Tertiaries of the seven *convenia* of the city and suburbs.[23] It was to be dedicated to St Benedict and St Bernard and built using money and property given by all seven communities. The text of the charter does not claim any other than titular association with Bernard, but repeats the association of the name of the Tertiaries with Innocent III. It asserts that the original members of the order were nobles involved in the vanities and delights of the world who, being brought low, were divinely inspired to abase themselves by adopting a humble life and dress and were thus first and especially called Humiliati. The other two orders arose from the Tertiaries and, although their regular observances differed in many things, they were called Humiliati in their likeness.[24]

There are clear parallels here with Fiamma's account, in particular in the association of the Tertiary name with Innocent III. Once more, what matters to the author of this charter is the primacy and noble origins of the Third order. The tactic employed to promote these ideas differs, however, from that of Fiamma. Any explicit claims to association with Bernard are omitted in favour of documentable association

---

[21] Zanoni, p. 140 and see below, p. 13.

[22] Zanoni, pp. 287–91; Alberzoni, 'San Bernardo e gli Umiliati', pp. 125–8.

[23] The Senedogo, Porta Orientale, Porta Nuova, Porta Cumana, Porta Vercellina, Porta Ticino and Porta Romana.

[24] Zanoni, p. 288: 'se ad vitam et habitum humilem humiliantes fuerunt fratres humiliati primitus et specialiter nominati . . . ex predicto suo Humiliatorum primevo ordine tertio nuncupato processerunt alii duo fratrum ordines, ab eis in multis observantiis regularibus differentes, qui tamen ad ipsorum instar similiter Humiliati vocantur'.

with Innocent III, whose instructions concerning alms-giving in his letter laying out the rule for the Third order are repeated in the charter.[25] This text provides a literal explanation of the name of the order in that of nobles brought low; however, it fails to explain the reasons for this humiliation. The gap would be filled in a later re-elaboration of the tale.

The accounts of Pipino and Fiamma and the 1346 charter reflect the interests and concerns of the fourteenth-century Tertiaries, keen to emphasise their primacy in view of the increasing difficulties they faced. Yet what is perhaps most surprising is the lack of an account authored by any member of the order at this date, unless it be the 1346 charter. Nor is there any evidence of an interest in the past on the part of members of the First or Second orders, except when concerned to overrule some of the strictures of the founding members.[26] Only in the fifteenth century was a Humiliati brother finally to turn his attention to writing a full-scale chronicle of the order. The result echoes some of the themes of the earlier accounts, but reveals a rather different choice of emphases.

JOHN OF BRERA, CHRONICLER OF THE ORDER

John of Brera, as his name suggests, was a brother in the house of the Humiliati of the Brera in Milan where Tiraboschi was later to work. He completed his *Chronicon ordinis Humiliatorum* in 1419, followed by an abridged *Excerptum* in 1421.[27] Nothing more is known of John, although it has been suggested that he should be identified with the John of Marliano responsible for a collection of papal privileges compiled between 1408 and 1435, a suggestion which certainly fits with his use of privileges in the chronicle.[28]

The relatively late date for this first Humiliati-authored chronicle contrasts strikingly with the numerous accounts produced by their near contemporaries the Franciscans and Dominicans from the 1230s and even earlier. This may reflect a desire on the part of the first members of the order to distance themselves from their unfortunate early history,

---

[25] Appendix I, 7; see also p. 104.   [26] Below, p. 129.

[27] *Chronicon*: Ambrosiana V 9 sup. (a copy compiled 1536–54), *VHM* III, pp. 229–86; *Excerptum*: Ambrosiana G 302 inf. (fifteenth century), Zanoni, pp. 336–44; Ambrosiana G 301 inf. is a seventeenth-century copy made on the orders of cardinal Frederick Borromeo before the Ambrosiana acquired G 302 inf. (received in 1802); Castiglioni, 'L'ordine degli Umiliati in tre codici illustrati dell'Ambrosiana', p. 8. For Federico Borromeo's own interest in the Humiliati, see Wickham Legg, 'The divine service in the sixteenth century', pp. 294–5.

[28] Mercati, 'Due ricerche per la storia degli Umiliati', pp. 177–8, 193; the collection of sixty-eight bulls is now Brera AF IX II A2.

whilst by the fifteenth century changed circumstances may have made an account both more necessary and more desirable. Unwanted outside intervention and the declining circumstances of the order which, according to the chronicler, had shrunk to just thirty-three male and twenty female houses surely inspired John to seek to improve the reputation of the order, underlining its venerable and glorious past.[29]

John's chronicle includes catalogues of the houses of the order, lists of saints and superiors, as well as details of privileges and constitutional changes. He did not give special prominence to any connection with Bernard. Instead he presented two other accounts of the origins of the order and these, together with the 'Bernard story', were to form the backbone of historical writing on the Humiliati until the early twentieth century. Analysis of them was central to the approaches of both Tiraboschi and Zanoni.

Exile

The first of John's accounts provides an explanation for the origins and 'humble' name of the order in terms of exile. The original outline of the story portrayed a group of noble Lombards, mostly from Milan and Como, sent into exile in Germany by the pious emperor Henry II (1002–24), who suspected their intentions lest they conspire against the empire. After some time in exile, as the narrative explains, they were inflamed by the Holy Spirit to lay aside all worldly pomp and promised to serve God with humility, reflecting that one cannot otherwise ascend to heaven. They put aside their rich clothes and adopted humble dress, wearing robes of ash-coloured, undyed cloth (*baratino*) and came together, agreeing that should God aid them to return home, they would persevere in their devotions. Hearing of this, the emperor called them to him and enquired whether they were indeed given to the religious life as their habits suggested. On replying that this was so, the exiles won imperial permission to return home. Inducing their families to share their new way of life, they began working as merchants and wool-workers and multiplied 'like fish', both within *Lombardia* and beyond. These were the first of the Tertiaries, who, as the chronicler notes, were few in number by his day.[30]

This version appears to be an elaboration of the account given in the foundation charter of the hospital of St Benedict and St Bernard in 1346. Like that account, it identified the first Humiliati as nobles, but enlarged upon the reasons for their conversion and the origins of the

---

[29] John of Brera, *Chronicon*, ch. 3, p. 231. [30] *Ibid.*, chs. 1–3, p. 230.

new order. In doing so it illustrated the origins of the emphasis on humility and labour, both important elements in the later order. It also provided a neat association of the order with none other than the emperor himself. Whether the exile was a traditional tale or invented anew by John, it assigned to the Humiliati a glorious and venerable past which might enable them to contend with the new and expanding orders of the early fifteenth century.

John was living in the community of the Brera, as Tiraboschi was to do 350 years later, and his purpose in writing was very personally associated with the community in which he lived. Although his account of the exile made explicit reference to the Third order and he accepted their greater antiquity, he also placed his own house very early in the history of the order. This chronology was constructed on the basis of a record of a land purchase concerning the community which he had read and shown to other members of the order and which he (mistakenly) dated to 1036.[31] Such venerable age justified the undoubted prestige of the Brera in the later order.

St John of Meda

The second foundation story recounted by John of Brera took a further step in filling the gaps in the written history of the early order: the lack of a known and saintly founder. That close ties with a founder mattered is easily demonstrated by reference to the frequent efforts of individual Franciscan houses to claim foundation by St Francis or St Anthony, even when extremely implausible. Association with a saintly founder conferred honour and venerability on any community.[32]

John drew on a brief and anonymous *Vita* to describe the foundation of the First order by a saintly priest, John of Meda, in the first half of the twelfth century.[33] In four chapters he detailed the early twelfth-century foundation of an oratory at Rondineto near Como for men and women and then related several miracle stories, the most prominent of which again allowed him to underline the importance of his own community. Thus, while staying at the Brera during a preaching journey to Milan, John of Meda was visited by an angelic figure who provided him with enough money to buy abundant food for the whole community.[34] He also died there in 1159 and when his body was carried back to Como a healing miracle took place as it passed through the city.[35]

---

[31] *Ibid.*, ch. 10, p. 236. On the correct date of this document, see below, pp. 21, 23.
[32] See, for example, A. Sartori, *La provincia del Santo dei frati minori conventuali* (Padua, 1958), p. 224.
[33] Anonymous, 'Vita de S. Joanne de Meda', ed. Suyskens, pp. 343–60.
[34] John of Brera, *Chronicon*, chs. 10–11, pp. 236–7.   [35] *Ibid.*, ch. 12, pp. 237–8.

Whether or not John of Brera is to be identified with the privilege compiler, John of Marliano, his text reveals that he was familiar with the papal letters approving the order in 1201, and in the preface to his chronicle he fits the different elements into a wider chronology, though he omits John of Meda here. The exile becomes the 'beginning and origin of the order', followed by the second age marked by the issuing of privileges for the order by Innocent III in 1201 and the approval of the rule *Omnis boni principium*, which he mysteriously attributes to all three orders, although it was clearly not intended for lay people living in their own homes.[36] Finally, the third age had begun with the confirmation of the first Master General in 1246, and the later exemption of the order from diocesan authority.[37] This tripartite chronology established the venerable antiquity of the Humiliati, linked them to a saintly founder and yet showed sensitivity to the importance of documentary evidence, which was used extensively. It also neatly avoided any direct reference to heresy.

The passage on the first Master General reveals John's other purpose in writing, since it gave him an opportunity to contest the legitimacy of events in his own day. He observed that in 1246 the Master had been elected by the three orders of the Humiliati and that such elections had been conducted regularly until twenty years earlier, since when they had been obstructed. John does not give a precise date or name the cause of the problem, which was the action of pope Boniface IX in appointing Andrea Visconti as both provost of Viboldone and Master General of the order in 1401, but he warns that those responsible would ultimately face judgement.[38] His purpose in writing was thus two pronged: both to lend glory to the past of his order and improve its reputation and to appeal to that past as a means of opposing what he considered to be undesirable outside interference in his own day.

LATER WRITERS

Whether or not it was first compiled by John of Brera, the exile story in particular became widely popular with later writers, who subjected it to continual minor modifications. John of Brera himself set the precedent for this by giving two slightly differing versions of the story. As we have seen, in his *Chronicon* of 1419 he dated the exile to 1017 and identified

---

[36] On the rule see ch. 4.
[37] John of Brera, *Chronicon*, preface, pp. 229–30; see below, pp. 206, 237.
[38] John of Brera, *Chronicon*, preface, p. 230; Spinelli, 'La diffusione del culto di San Bernardo', p. 205 n. 33.

the emperor as Henry II (1002–24).[39] However, in his 1421 *Excerptum* the emperor intended may have been Conrad II (1024–39), for he wrote only that the exile had taken place 'before 1036 AD', a date no doubt based on the Brera document which he believed dated to that year.[40]

The potential for variation of this story was realised in the numerous fifteenth- and sixteenth-century works which mentioned the Humiliati. These ranged from ecclesiastical chronicles (including one by another member of the order, Marco Bossi of Florence) to popular city histories, including that of Milan by Benedetto Corio and general works such as the encyclopaedic and widely published *De inventoribus rerum* of Polydore Vergil.[41] Each author gave their personal adaptation of the tale. As early as 1483 an Augustinian writer from Bergamo, Giacomo Filippo Foresti (1434–1520), ignored the 1036 document in his *Supplementum supplementi chronicarum* to make a chronologically more convincing association of the exile with the conflict with Barbarossa in the 1160s and 1170s. Variations on the eleventh-century version nonetheless remained popular and the fact of the exile itself was widely disseminated.[42]

In 1571 the male houses of the order were suppressed and the closing years of the sixteenth century produced a new element in accounts of the Humiliati, as studies of the two protagonists of the suppression, cardinal Charles Borromeo and pope Pius V, began to appear.[43] In his *Vita* of Borromeo published in 1592, Carlo Bascapè, the General of the Barnabite order, with whom Borromeo had considered uniting the Humiliati, was understandably more interested in the disastrous final years than in the origins of the movement, as was his fellow Barnabite, Giovanni Gabuzio, who published a *Vita* of Pius V in 1605.[44] Both writers concentrated on the dramatic circumstances surrounding an assassination attempt on Borromeo by a member of the order, Gerolamo Donato, known as 'il Farina'. As cardinal archbishop of Milan Borromeo had been appointed Protector of the Humiliati in 1560. He had made energetic attempts to reform the much reduced order, but his

---

[39] John of Brera, *Chronicon*, ch. 1. p. 230.   [40] John of Brera, *Excerptum*, ch. 2, p. 336.

[41] B. Corio, *Historia continente da lorigine di Milano tutti li gesti, fatti e detti preclari, e le cose memorande milanesi in fino al tempo di esso autore* (Milan, 1503), ed. A. Butti and L. Ferrario (Milan, 1855–7); P. Vergil, *De inventoribus rerum* (Venice, 1499–1521).

[42] For details of these works and others see Andrews, 'The early Humiliati: the development of an order c. 1176–c. 1270', pp. 31–43.

[43] The bull of suppression is *Quemadmodum solicitus pater*, in *Bullarum diplomatum et privilegiorum sanctorum romanorum pontificum*, VII, pp. 885–8.

[44] C. Bascapè, *De vita et rebus gestis caroli SRE cardinalis tituli S. Praxedis archiepiscopi mediolani* (Milan, 1592), book II, 10–12; G. A. Gabuzio, *De vita et rebus gestis Pii V pont. max.* (Rome, 1605), pp. 116–18.

methods had provoked an angry response from some of the Humiliati. This rose to such a pitch that Farina determined to shoot Borromeo with an arquebus on the night of 26 October 1569, while the cardinal was at prayer with his family and servants in a chapel of the archiepiscopal palace. The attempt failed and this was attributed to miraculous intervention: the bullet had glanced off the cardinal's back, leaving him unharmed. The episode was later cited in Borromeo's canonisation process. The consequences for the Humiliati were disastrous. Farina and three accomplices were executed in August 1570 and the male orders were suppressed in 1571.[45]

The reputation of the Humiliati could hardly have reached a lower ebb than in the late sixteenth and early seventeenth centuries. In 1606, Jacques Auguste Thou published a history of his times typical of contemporary attitudes. Although he dismissed the early history of the Humiliati in five or six lines, he found space for some select inaccuracies, claiming that pope Lucius III (1181–5) had been responsible for approving the order (when Lucius was the pope who had condemned the Humiliati) and suggesting that he gave them the rule of St Benedict, a mistake perhaps based on knowledge of more recent practice and the Benedictine observance of the surviving nuns.[46] Thou was on firmer ground with more contemporary history and wrote a detailed account of the corrupt practices and libidinous behaviour of the last members of the order and the attempt on Borromeo's life, which were undoubtedly of much greater concern to his audience.[47]

Yet the seventeenth century also saw the beginnings of more critical interest in the early history of the Humiliati. The same techniques of incisive scholarship which were being developed in Belgium by John Bolland, his students and assistants, Jesuits working on the lives of the saints, were also applied to the Humiliati. At the request of cardinal Frederick Borromeo, founder of the Ambrosiana library, Pietro Puricelli (1589–1659), archpriest of the collegiate church of San Lorenzo in Milan and an early *letterato* of the Ambrosiana, set out to make a systematic study of the documentary evidence for the history of the Humiliati held in that library and elsewhere. Puricelli certainly seems to have had no difficulty in obtaining material and was in regular correspondence with some of the surviving Humiliati sisters. His manu-

---

[45] See Castiglioni, 'L'ordine degli Umiliati', pp. 27–35; L. Anfosso, *Storia dell'archibugiata tirata al cardinale Borromeo in Milano la sera del 26 ottobre 1669* (Milan, 1913); Besozzi, 'L'ultimo preposito degli Umiliati di Cannobio', pp. 423–38. The events surrounding the attempt on Borromeo's life still provoke strong feeling: O. Clizio, *Il frate che sparò a san Carlo* (Arona, 1984, 2nd edn. 1990), was sold with a publicity flyer 'peccato che fallì il colpo! [Pity he missed!]'.

[46] *VHM* I, p. 87.

[47] J. A. Thou, *Historia sui temporis* (Paris, 1606), pp. 768–70.

script *Historia ordinis Humiliatorum* contains translations and transcripts of the constitutions and rule of the order, numerous early documents and even the painstakingly prepared parchment copies of vows taken by sisters who had joined the order in the 1560s.[48] Puricelli did not, however, use this material to challenge earlier accounts of the origins. He was no doubt unwilling to discredit the sisters' treasured traditions, if indeed he himself harboured any doubts. A second manuscript, the *Sacri Humiliatorum ordinis monimenta* [sic], which contains Puricelli's outline for the planned history, shows that, true to his times, the author was more interested in the use of the Humiliati breviary, the Ambrosian rite and the details of the suppression of the male houses, than in the early chronology of the order.[49] Although this work was never completed or published, his endorsement of 1017 as the correct date for the origins of the Humiliati was to be imitated by numerous other writers, including his close contemporary and friend, the Benedictine Placido Puccinelli who was briefly master of the novices at the ex-Humiliati house of Gessate near Milan and wrote both a history of that house and a chronicle of the whole order.[50]

Puricelli's chronology was destined to set the background to most serious scholarship until the early twentieth century, but the seventeenth century also produced a series of antiquarian studies which dealt with the early history of the Humiliati in the context of city histories. The most notable of these were the works of Pietro Maria Campi (1569–1649) and Primo Luigi Tatti (1616–87). Campi was a canon of the major church of Sant'Antonino in Piacenza and wished to highlight the religious and cultural patrimony of his home town.[51] He included documentation on many matters, which makes his volumes still essential reading, as much has since been lost. For the Humiliati he nonetheless came to the ingenious conclusion that the evidence which he had come across for their origins in the twelfth century must in fact refer to a reform of the order, since he 'knew' from the works of Corio and others, that it had originally been founded in the early eleventh century.[52]

Tatti, who became superior of the Gallio College in Como run by

---

[48] Ambrosiana C 74 inf. edited in 1677 by the Ambrosiana prefect Pietro Paolo Bosca.

[49] Ambrosiana S 89 sup. The outline, fos. 67r–74v, is followed by a draft of the general preface, fos. 75r–77v.

[50] *Cronica delle venerande memorie della congregazione umiliata*, Ambrosiana D 88 inf. and H 205 inf., a seventeenth-century copy; S. Schenone, 'La vita e le opere di Placido Puccinelli. Cenni per una biografia', *ASL*, 114 (1988), 319–34, 333–4.

[51] See S. Ditchfield, *Liturgy, Sanctity and History in Tridentine Italy: Pietro Maria Campi and the Preservation of the Particular* (Cambridge, 1995), p. 11.

[52] Campi, *Dell'historia ecclesiastica di Piacenza*, I, p. 320.

Somaschi fathers on the site of the early Humiliati house of Rondineto, was equally concerned to promote the reputation of his home town. Perhaps because of the associations with his own college, his real interest lay with John of Meda, whose *Vita* he also apparently wrote.[53] He was particularly concerned to prove that the saint was from Como, since other writers had claimed that he came from Milan.[54] He gave a series of reasons for his assertion, none of which need interest us here, except to observe that he refrains from mentioning those whom he calls 'our writers', as he knows the Milanese would consider them partial, a reminder of the extreme *campanilismo* of these authors.[55]

In the eighteenth century the tradition of writings by authors with personal or local reasons for interest in the early Humiliati continued. Another Barnabite, Francesco Luigi Barelli, included the Barbarossa version of the exile story within a history of his own order.[56] There were also the beginnings of some serious attempts at revision. The French writer Pierre Helyot, a Franciscan Tertiary, sought to obtain original source material, writing to the Ambrosiana library in Milan for information. He accepted Fiamma's account of Bernard's role in giving the Humiliati a rule in the 1130s and thus rejected John of Brera's date for the origins of the order, arguing that they could not have been without a rule for over a hundred years. He then suggested that the true date for the beginnings of the order was 1117, when Henry V (1111–25) forced several Lombard towns to recognise him as rightful sovereign after the death of countess Matilda in 1115. Thus it was possible to accept both the connection with St Bernard in the 1130s and the role of John of Meda in founding the First order.[57]

Perhaps it was inevitable that Helyot's approach, which moved far outside the bounds of received opinion, should provoke strong criticism. Giuseppe Sassi, who worked at the Ambrosiana from 1703 and may have known of Helyot's correspondence at the beginning of the century, had read his work and set out to disprove his theories. Although Sassi refers only to an *auctor gallice*, no scholar can have been in doubt that Helyot was the French author whose eight volumes had

[53] The preface to P. L. Tatti, *Degli annali sacri di Como*, 3 vols. (Como, 1663–1735), refers to this work, published in 1677, but I have been unable to locate it.
[54] P. Morigi, *Historia dell'origine di tutte le religioni* (Venice, 1569), p. 34.
[55] Tatti, *Degli annali sacri di Como*, II, p. 376.
[56] F. L. Barelli, *Memorie dell'origine, fondazione, avanzamenti, successi ed uomini illustri in lettere e in santità della congregazione de' clerici regolari di S. Paolo chiamati volgarmente Barnabiti* (Bologna, 1703), p. 321, no. 19; p. 326, no. 28.
[57] P. Helyot, *Histoire des ordres monastiques, religieux et militaires et des congrégations séculières de l'un et de l'autre sexe*, 8 vols. (Paris, 1714–19), VI, pp. 152–65.

created 'a fog he now wished to dispel'.[58] Sassi foreshadowed the work of Tiraboschi in his survey of the evidence (as well as in the strong criticism of Helyot). He relied on Puricelli's conclusions to show that the origins of the order had indeed been in 1017 and went on to argue that there could be no basis for the connection with Bernard, pointing out that the accounts of Bernard's life make no mention of it.[59]

Nicolò Sormani (died c. 1777), another scholar from the Ambrosiana, dedicated two studies to the Humiliati. The first was apparently reproduced in very small numbers, being intended mainly for surviving nuns of the order in Varese who had requested that he provide them with information about their institution.[60] However, thirty years later, discovering that his original work was almost impossible to find, Sormani produced a shorter version as the second section of an account of Milanese saints.[61] His purpose was to exhort: the history of the Humiliati might serve both for spiritual benefit and, in recounting their fall, as a warning never to trust too much in one's own greatness. To accomplish this aim he made extensive use of early manuscript sources and chronicles, providing a catalogue of the privileges received from the time of Innocent III and of the saints and houses of the order.[62] He frequently cited the fifteenth-century chronicles by members of the order and the widely circulated chronicle of Antonino Pierozzi, the saintly archbishop of Florence (1446–59), who had suggested rather sourly that the exiles had simply made a virtue out of necessity.[63] Sormani followed several earlier historians, placing the exile and origins of the Tertiary Humiliati in 1017, followed by the Second order in 1034 and the First order founded by John of Meda in 1119.[64] He described their involvement in agriculture and commerce as intended to enable them to endow churches, hospitals and holy places and to promote public affairs without fraud or dishonesty, 'for the good of the prince and his subjects'.[65] The Humiliati were thus awarded a central and very worldly role in the furtherance of good government, and he even associated them with the beginnings of the statutes of Milan.[66] He gave translations of the rules and papal privileges held in the Ambrosiana and

---

[58] G. A. Sassi, *Historia literario-typographica mediolanensis* (Milan, 1745), cols. 247–58.

[59] Both the 'Vita prima sancti Bernardi', compiled by three authors c. 1155/56 and revised by 1174, and the 'Vita secunda' (c. 1170), include accounts of Bernard's visit to Milan, *PL*, 185, cols. 273–80, 469–524, esp. cols. 499–501.

[60] N. Sormani, *Breve storia degli Umiliati col testo de' codici manoscritti e diplomi* (Milan, 1739); see also Longoni, 'Origini degli Umiliati a Monza', 21.

[61] Sormani, 'L'origine de'laici regolari, cioè Umiliati', pp. 145–96.

[62] *Ibid.*, pp. 175–89.

[63] A. Pierozzi (Sant'Antonino), *Chronicon* (Florence, 1484), 2, fo. 178.

[64] Sormani, 'L'origine de' laici regolari, cioè Umiliati', pp. 151, 153–4.

[65] *Ibid.*, p. 149.   [66] *Ibid.*

cathedral archives and discussed the history of the Second and First orders, alleging that the communities of the Second order called themselves 'houses' not monasteries to distinguish themselves from the Benedictines, from whose rule they had adopted many practices.[67] He also emphasised the separation between men and women in the houses of the Second order.[68]

Two near contemporaries made extensive use of Sormani's work. One of these was Gian Battista Biancolini, who wrote a seven-volume history of the churches of Verona, in the tradition of the work of Campi and Tatti of the previous century. Biancolini quoted long passages from Sormani's translations of key texts, but also provided editions of Veronese material not previously published.[69] Giorgio Giulini (1717–80), who became official historian of Milan, also made frequent use of Sormani's work and its conclusions in his study of that city.[70] Both authors' careful transcripts from local archives have yet to be supplanted.[71] Both also accepted the conclusion that the origins of the Tertiaries lay in 1017 but, following Sormani, Giulini used persuasive palaeographical grounds to dismiss as a forgery the document of 1036 which John of Brera and Puricelli had adopted as early proof for the existence of the Brera.[72]

Girolamo Tiraboschi

As this survey has shown, Tiraboschi was by no means working in a vacuum. Zanoni was later to demonstrate in particular how closely he followed Puricelli's work.[73] Indeed, in his preface Tiraboschi himself paid due tribute to Puricelli's authority on the subject of the Humiliati, and he frequently preferred his judgement over that of others.[74] Like many of his predecessors he also had personal reasons for his interest in the order, since he was living and working on the site of one of their houses. However, in spite of some dependence on Puricelli and close contacts with Giulini, whose opinions he valued to the point of inserting one of his letters in his text, Tiraboschi's work on the Humiliati outshone anything thus far attempted, both in scale and in the quality and depth of his investigation.[75]

---

[67] *Ibid.*, pp. 153, 157–74.   [68] *Ibid.*, p. 154.
[69] Biancolini, *Notizie storiche delle chiese di Verona*, VI, pp. 190–211.
[70] Giulini, *Memorie spettanti alla storia . . . di Milano*, III, p. 283, VII, p. 409, VIII, p. 32.
[71] See appendix I.
[72] Giulini, *Memorie spettanti alla storia . . . di Milano*, III, p. 283; John of Brera, *Chronicon*, ch. 10, p. 236, and above p. 14.
[73] Zanoni, pp. 253–5.   [74] *VHM* I, p. 20 and preface (n.p.).
[75] *Ibid.*, pp. 395–400 (Giulini's letter).

Initially at least, the concerns of his numerous predecessors determined the areas which Tiraboschi considered. In his first *dissertatio* he examined the bases for the conclusions of earlier writers and, like Sassi, was particularly critical of Helyot.[76] He accepted the eleventh-century origins for the Humiliati, dating the exile to 1014 and the return to 1019 and associating it with Henry II (emperor 1002–24).[77] However, he did so only after consideration of all the alternatives and on the basis of meticulous examination of the fifteenth-century chronicles. He also sought to elucidate the eleventh-century political context, examining the activities of Henry I and the failed attempt by Marquis Hubert and Arduin of Ivrea to oppose imperial rule.[78]

In his second *dissertatio*, Tiraboschi discussed the foundation of the First and Second orders and the roles of St Bernard and John of Meda. His consideration of the involvement of Bernard illustrates his methods well.[79] He first underlined earlier writers' dependence on Fiamma's account, noting that the only dissenter had been Sassi. The fallibility and errors of Fiamma's work were then emphasised and he queried why only the Tertiaries should have taken their name from Innocent III, since the First and Second orders had also been approved by him.[80] Tiraboschi pointed to the lack of information in other sources, including the lives of St Bernard (as Sassi had done) and the fifteenth-century chronicles of the order, and concluded that a passage referring to Bernard in John of Brera's 1419 chronicle had been interpolated by a later hand.[81] He argued for the lack of any cult of Bernard within the order, as he was not included in the list of Humiliati saints given by John of Brera, although other people's saints, including Homobono of Cremona, had been adopted.[82] He dismissed arguments concerning the use of seals with an effigy of Bernard, noting that Manni had already shown that this was not the exclusive motif of all houses, since Faenza had used a simple cross.[83] Finally, he produced what he considered his strongest argument: the lack of any reference to Bernard in Innocent III's letter of 1201 approving the Third order. Surely Bernard would have been mentioned if the Humiliati way of life had been dictated by him.[84] Tiraboschi does not conclude his argument by dismissing any link between Bernard and the Third order, but remains cautious,

---

[76] *Ibid.*, pp. 12–15.   [77] *Ibid.*, p. 19.

[78] *Ibid.*, pp. 15–17; Tabacco, 'La storia politica e sociale', p. 126.

[79] See also Alberzoni, 'San Bernardo e gli Umiliati', pp. 97–9.

[80] *VHM* I, p. 33.   [81] *Ibid.*, p. 39.

[82] John of Brera, *Chronicon*, ch. 39, pp. 285–6.

[83] Manni, *Osservazioni sopra i sigilli antichi*, VII, sigillum 8. Four seals now in the Museo Nazionale, Florence, are discussed in Bascapè, 'Insegne e sigilli dell'ordine degli umiliati', pp. 93–4.

[84] *VHM* I, pp. 42–3; a point underlined by recent work showing how much this pope admired

suggesting that although Bernard did not give the Humiliati a rule, his example and many sermons might have led them to adopt a holier and more perfect way of life.[85]

The remainder of Tiraboschi's second *Dissertatio* deals with the last of the evidence concerning the origins of the Humiliati. After considering the involvement of Guy *de Porta Orientale*, he set out to date the beginning of the Second order. Following Giulini's work, he established convincingly, by noting the inaccuracies of the dating and the reference to individuals known to have been alive in the fourteenth century, that the document presented by John of Brera as proof for the existence of the Brera in the eleventh century dated to 1307.[86] He concluded that the origins of the Brera and of the Second order lay in the 1130s (1136–7) and not before.[87] Finally and more briefly, he examined the role of John of Meda in the foundation of the First order, suggesting a date of c. 1129 for the foundation of Rondineto and 1140 for the beginning of his order.[88]

The remaining chapters of Tiraboschi's study provide a comprehensive survey of other traditional aspects of the history of a religious order: their rule, privileges, great men, office-holders, a catalogue of houses and in this case, the suppression of the order. However, it is his publication of documents, including John of Brera's original chronicle, the constitutions and in particular papal and episcopal letters, which makes Tiraboschi's work still essential for any student of the Humiliati. Although not exhaustive, the series of letters and privileges he published includes the first edition of the fundamental three approving the order in 1201. These are not in the *Patrologia Latina* as the registers for the fourth year of Innocent III's pontificate (1201–2) do not survive.[89]

In the wake of Tiraboschi

During the nineteenth century the lines of research laid down by Tiraboschi and his predecessors were not seriously challenged, although an early attempt to reinterpret the evidence had already been made by the Cistercian abbot of Sant'Ambrogio in Milan, Angelo Fumagalli (1728–1804). With strong historical sense, Fumagalli had placed the

---

Bernard and the Cistercians: B. M. Bolton, 'The Cistercians and the aftermath of the second crusade', *The Second Crusade and the Cistercians*, ed. M. Gervers (New York, 1992), pp. 131–40.
[85] *VHM* I, p. 43.
[86] *Ibid.*, pp. 51–5. He used similar techniques to demolish the claim for an eleventh-century origin for Rondineto inserted in John of Brera's 1419 chronicle by Giorgio Lurasca, a sixteenth-century provost of Viboldone.
[87] *VHM* I, pp. 56–9.   [88] *Ibid.*, pp. 73, 196–212.
[89] Appendix I, 7–9; Pasztor, 'Studi e problemi relativi ai registri di Innocenzo III', pp. 287–304.

beginnings of the order in the late twelfth century, had rejected the exile story and the role of Bernard and had drawn attention to the writings of Jacques de Vitry on the origins of the name as describing those who demonstrated great humility both in word and in deed.[90] However, Fumagalli was a lone voice and the account of the eleventh-century exile was still widely circulated, even appearing romanticised and illustrated in a mid-nineteenth-century collection of Italian folk tales.[91] This undoubtedly reflected an awareness of the traditional nature of the tale rather than any claim to historical accuracy, but rejection of the historicity of the exile began to be generally accepted only in the first years of the twentieth century, when the early history of the Humiliati was substantially revised in line with the evidence of the contemporary documents available.

The task of revision was undertaken initially by Antonino De Stefano, who in 1906 convincingly established that the origins of the order lay sometime around 1170. He based his argument on the grounds that the first documents collected by Tiraboschi are all later than 1170, that the near contemporary Anonymous Chronicle of Laon dates the origins to 1178–9[92] and that the most reliable source, pope Innocent III, makes no reference to a remote origin for the order.[93] De Stefano intended to expand what was originally a brief article into a complete study of the order, but was preempted by Luigi Zanoni. Nonetheless, it is his work in this field which marks the point of departure generally accepted by recent historians. The exile story was now accepted as an attempt by members of the order to give the Humiliati the kind of historical and 'noble' significance enjoyed by the great religious orders.

De Stefano also queried the historical basis for the existence of John of Meda. Already in the sixteenth century some details of the *Vita* appear to have been questioned. Zanoni was to record the marginal annotations on a copy of John of Brera's *Chronicon*, marking as false the accounts of the saint's visit to the Brera and his death in 1159.[94] Earlier writers, as we have seen, had suggested that he must have lived in the second half of the twelfth century, not the first, in order to fit him in with the Barbarossa version of the exile story.[95] Nonetheless, no one had seriously doubted his existence or sanctity and John of Meda had

---

[90] A. Fumagalli, *Delle antichità Longobardico-Milanesi*, 4 vols. (Milan, 1792–3), IV, pp. 141, 152–61; Vitry, *HO*, p. 144.

[91] D. Carutti, 'Erberto e Guido, ossia l'origine degli Umiliati', *Tradizioni italiane*, ed. A. Brofferio, 4 vols. (Turin, 1847–50), I, pp. 609–38.

[92] On the date see below, p. 39 and n. 5.

[93] De Stefano, 'Le origini dell'ordine degli Umiliati', pp. 851–9.

[94] Zanoni, p. 251.   [95] Above, pp. 16, 19.

won his place in the *Acta sanctorum*.[96] Suyskens, who edited the *Vita*, doubted whether John had been canonised, but accepted his saintly title, recalling all those who were not canonised but who were venerated as saints.[97] De Stefano however, apparently unaware of a statue of John placed over the door of the Humiliati church at Viboldone in the façade completed in 1348 (if this identification is correct), argued that the earliest references to John were in martyrologies from the fifteenth century or in the *Vita*, which he dismissed as an apologia made up of *topoi* and devoid of historical details.[98] In 1910, a local historian Antonio Giussani rejected this, countering that the existence of John was documented by the survival of his sarcophagus in the church of Rondineto, described during a pastoral visit by bishop Feliciano Ninguarda in 1592.[99] Zanoni, who accepted Giussani's contention, though perhaps without knowing his work, also argued that the persistent tradition of the order and the tomb then in the Gallio College, which he dated to the thirteenth century, showed that John of Meda had at least existed.[100] However, he accepted that a tradition desirous of a patron of the stature of a saint such as Francis or Dominic had transformed John from a worthy of the order into a saint deserving of their praise. In 1927 De Stefano returned to the subject, noting that the earliest reference to the tomb was Ninguarda's account of 1592, when it was found to be empty, evidence which he considered conclusive proof that John had never existed.[101] De Stefano's conclusions, in particular that the *Vita* had 'nothing to do with history', would be considered too drastic by modern students of saints' lives.[102] Nor is the record of an empty tomb reliable evidence, however. There seems to be no twelfth- or thirteenth-century source for John of Meda's cult and without new evidence, analysis of his early role must remain unresolved.[103]

The works of De Stefano and Zanoni marked a clear break with the past, closing the agenda for debate unwittingly established by Galvano Fiamma and John of Brera in the fourteenth and fifteenth centuries. Many new questions which they raised are still topical, and brief

---

[96] Anonymous, 'Vita de S. Joanne', pp. 358–60.   [97] *Ibid.*, p. 346.

[98] The inscription dating the façade is published in Gatti Perer, 'Gli affreschi trecenteschi', p. 126; De Stefano, 'Le origini dell'ordine degli Umiliati', pp. 858–9.

[99] A. Giussani, 'Il sarcofago di san Giovanni da Meda', 93–114.

[100] Zanoni, p. 2; nothing of the tomb now remains.

[101] De Stefano, 'Delle origini e della natura del primitivo movimento degli Umiliati', pp. 31–75, pp. 43–5.

[102] See for example A. Vauchez, *La sainteté en occident aux derniers siècles du moyen age d'après les procès de canonisation et les documents hagiographiques* (Rome, 1981).

[103] On the possibility that he should be identified with James of Rondineto, see now Alberzoni, 'Giacomo di Rondineto. Contributo per una biografia', pp.152–3.

elucidation of their arguments will serve to clarify the point of departure for this study.[104]

Heretical origins and the response of the papacy

Tiraboschi had assumed that early references to the Humiliati as heretics were a mistake, but De Stefano and Zanoni both sought to link the first Humiliati with contemporary heretical movements.[105] In 1906 De Stefano argued that the early Humiliati derived from the Waldensians. He based his arguments on the concordance of their ideals and customs such as abstaining from oath-taking and litigation and on the similarity of the early history of the two groups as shown in texts such as the Anonymous Chronicle of Laon.[106] He also pointed to the close ties between northern Italy and southern France, where Waldensianism had originated, and suggested that the Humiliati's origins should be associated with the passage of Valdes through *Lombardia* in 1179.[107]

This argument was rejected by Zanoni, on the basis that while the pope gave the Waldensians (restricted) permission to preach, this was specifically prohibited to the early Humiliati. He also observed correctly that the Brera house could be documented before 1179 and that therefore the guiding spirit of the order could not have been Valdes.[108] Zanoni claimed instead that the inspiration for the Humiliati lay with the Cathars, who were certainly active in Milan in the late twelfth and early thirteenth centuries, and he alluded to the similarity of their ideals concerning poverty, oath-taking and work. Finally, on the basis of four documents from the late twelfth and early thirteenth centuries, he argued that the term 'Patarine', which in his view was the Lombard name for Cathars by this date, was occasionally applied to the Humiliati, proving to his satisfaction that this was the group from which they sprang.[109]

Developing an idea first proposed by Felice Tocco, Zanoni then posited a split in the Humiliati between the orthodox, who were to become the 'authorised' order, and those who chose not to return to the Church and perhaps even formed the core of the movement of the Lombard Poor.[110] This provided an explanation for two references to

---

[104] See also K.-V. Selge, 'Humiliaten', *Theologische Realenzyklopädie*, 15 (Berlin, 1986), pp. 691–6; Paolini, 'Le Umiliate al lavoro. Appunti fra storiografia e storia', pp. 230–2.

[105] *VHM* I, p. 79. [106] Below, p. 39.

[107] De Stefano, 'Le origini dell'ordine degli Umiliati', pp. 859–65.

[108] Zanoni, pp. 32–4. [109] *Ibid.*, pp. 39–41.

[110] Zanoni, pp. 64–93, esp. pp. 69, 81–4. He cites, p. 83 n. 1, a review by Felice Tocco of E. Montet, *Histoire littéraire des vaudois du Piémont d'après les manuscrits originaux* (Paris-Geneva, 1855), but fails to note where this review was published. I have been unable to trace it.

the Humiliati as heretics after 1201, and has been widely adopted.[111]
The idea of a split was particularly attractive to catholic historians
wishing to underline the distinction between the heterodox and an
orthodox and acceptable majority. Thus the Capuchin friar, Ilarino da
Milano, would later write of the 'heterodox Humiliati' in the same
breath as of both Cathars and Waldensians.[112] In 1927 De Stefano
reiterated his arguments in favour of a Waldensian connection, arguing
that there was no evidence that the Humiliati were dualists, in his view
a definitive refutation of Zanoni's argument in favour of a Cathar
source.[113]

In the 1930s Herbert Grundmann, whose study of medieval religious
movements retains such authority sixty years later that it has recently
been translated into English, recognised similarities with both Cathars
and Waldensians on issues such as oath-taking and accepted that some
Humiliati may have chosen to join the Lombard Poor.[114] Grundmann's
main concern however, was to investigate the origins and nature of the
response of the papacy. Careful examination of Innocent's letters of
1201 led him to conclude that the issues at stake were those of oath-
taking and the right to preach and that the Curia was concerned to be as
accommodating as possible to the Humiliati. A clear distinction
between preaching on the articles of the faith and preaching on morality
was thereby established and a lay group was given permission to choose
its own preachers for the first time, two developments which Grundmann considered unprecedented and of great importance for the
future.[115]

In 1945 Ilarino da Milano rejected the claims for the heretical
associations of the 'orthodox' Humiliati presented by De Stefano and
Zanoni. Like Zanoni, he pointed out that the Humiliati pre-dated the
Waldensians and that, unlike them, the fundamental basis of their
religious life was not poverty, but the choice of a humble state and
dedication to artisan work.[116] Although he admitted that they were
perhaps stimulated by heretical asceticism, he dismissed links with the
Cathar heresy and concluded that the Humiliati were orthodox in
origin and sprang from the vitality of catholic spirituality, thereby
rejecting Grundmann's view of the origins of both orthodox and
heterodox religious movements as an organic whole.[117]

---

[111] Below, p. 63; for an example of this view see Leff, *Heresy in the Later Middle Ages*, II, p. 449.
[112] Da Milano, 'L'eresia di Ugo Speroni'.
[113] De Stefano, 'Delle origini e della natura del primitivo movimento degli Umiliati', p. 53.
[114] Grundmann, pp. 80, 89.   [115] *Ibid.*, p. 82.
[116] Da Milano, 'L'eresia di Ugo Speroni', pp. 454–6.
[117] Views later summarised in I. da Milano, 'Umiliati', cols. 754–6; see also Selge, 'Die Armut in

The early Humiliati

Grundmann's study had sought to establish the religious quality of the Humiliati movement, centred on observance of the *vita apostolica*, the nature of the papal response and their return to the Church in 1201. His work formed the background to the analysis of the late Michele Maccarrone, who, as a canon of San Pietro in Rome, was particularly concerned to clarify the role of Innocent III in bringing the movement back into the Church, underlining what he identified as the pope's original wish to bring them together into one uniform order.[118] The work of Brenda Bolton, important in drawing the attention of an English-speaking audience to the subject, follows similar themes.[119]

Writing slightly later than Maccarrone, Rolf Zerfaß, whose main concern was lay preaching, rejected Grundmann's analysis of the unprecedented nature of the authorisation given to the Humiliati. He concentrated on the approval of the Third order, examining the precedents for such lay prayer fraternities (*Gebetsverbrüderungen*) and argued that, whether or not he had intended to, Innocent never authorised lay public preaching.[120] In his view, because of the suspicious and nervous church hierarchy, the pope was now forbidding debate usually allowed to the laity to 'strengthen themselves as brothers in faith'. Such debate would, Zerfaß claimed, 'in quieter times never have been denied to the Christian faithful'.[121] Zerfaß's view has not achieved wide currency, but following the ideas of Grundmann, most recent writers recognise a common source of inspiration for Waldensians and Humiliati (as for the Mendicants), summarised by Giovanni Miccoli as the 'Patarine-evangelical' or 'pauperist-evangelical' background to both heretical and reform movements.[122]

Finally and with great significance for future study, Maria Pia Alberzoni has identified problems with previous readings of the papal letters of 1199–1201. This has led her to begin to reappraise the terms of the approval of the order, providing new particulars which will be discussed in detail below.[123]

den nichtrechtgläubigen religiösen Bewegungen', p. 203 n. 36; da Milano, 'Il "Liber supra stella" del piacentino Salvo Burci', pp. 122–35.
[118] Maccarrone, 'Riforma e sviluppo della vita religiosa con Innocenzo III', p. 47 and *Studi*, pp. 284–90.
[119] Bolton, 'Innocent III's treatment of the Humiliati', pp. 73–82 and 'Tradition and temerity', pp. 79–91.
[120] He used the work of Meersseman, later collected as 'Ordo fraternitatis'. *Confraternite e pietà dei laici nel medioevo*.
[121] Zerfaß, *Der Streit um die Laienpredigt*, pp. 205–10.
[122] Miccoli, 'La storia religiosa', p. 609; see for example Merlo, *Tensioni religiose agli inizi del duecento*.
[123] Alberzoni, 'Gli inizi degli Umiliati'; below, pp. 69–71.

28

Social origins and motivation

Other closely related themes much debated in this century include the social origins and motivation of the early members of the movement. For Zanoni the organisation of the Humiliati was part of the class struggle. Employing the vocabulary of nineteenth-century social conflict, he described the organisation of the Humiliati as the only way for the humblest salaried workers to unite against the exploitation of 'capitalist' merchants.[124] He quoted the Dominican Humbert of Romans on their life of labour, and concluded that the formation of religious fraternities by groups such as the Humiliati was intended as an escape for the urban 'proletariat', the first form of proletarian resistance against industrialism.[125]

These views were shared by Ellen Scott Davison, whose work was the first study of the Humiliati in English. She placed the Humiliati in the context of the failures of the Church and the 'quickening of religious life, the renewal of faith in the conquering power of the individual'.[126] In her view, it was inevitable that new reform movements should be lay and independent of the Church. She made some provocative (and undocumentable) claims, arguing that the 'early Humiliati *made no attempt to follow the monastic life*' to which they were opposed because of its distortion 'of Christ's teaching *by breaking the unity of the home*' (my italics),[127] or that the early Humiliati 'had refused all possessions', while the members of the Second order 'were *communists*' (my italics again) because they held property in common.[128] Although her work is also a useful survey of the sources, it has been ignored by most historians of the Humiliati, who have almost all been based in Italy and have wisely concentrated on material easily available there.

As we have seen, Volpe, in his study of religious movements and heretical sects, also explicitly shared his student Zanoni's approach.[129] He described the Humiliati as 'very largely poor people', from the 'low working classes' and saw their history as an 'ascent from humble manual labour to an almost capitalistic organisation of the wool industry'.[130]

---

[124] Zanoni, p. 166; discussed in Selge, 'Die Armut in den nichtrechtgläubigen religiösen Bewegungen', p. 200 n. 29.

[125] Zanoni, pp. 64, 160–1.

[126] Scott Davison, *Forerunners of Saint Francis and Other Studies*, p. 168.

[127] *Ibid.*, p. 182.   [128] *Ibid.*, p. 197.

[129] Above, p. 7; on Volpe, whose career spanned eight decades, see O. Capitani, 'Gioacchino Volpe, storico del medioevo', *Medioevo passato prossimo. Appunti storiografici. Tra due guerre e molte crisi* (Bologna, 1979), pp. 191–209; first published in *Studi romagnoli*, 22 (1971), 319–34.

[130] Volpe, *Movimenti religiosi*, p. 55.

Coulton, too, accepted Zanoni's analysis of the origins of the Humiliati and contrasted them with monasticism which was 'too self-centred and too far aloof from the multitudes that needed salvation'.[131]

Grundmann exposed the inconsistencies in this purely social analysis, observing that even Zanoni had had to accept that the religious factor was the fundamental root of the movement.[132] He noted that the accounts of contemporaries record the entry of rich citizens and nobles into Humiliati communities and suggested that the profession of voluntary poverty and *humilitas*, central to their proposed way of life, would have had little value had it arisen from pre-existing indigence.[133]

Grundmann's social analysis has not always been accepted and was indeed dismissed in the 1970s by Freed who, working from material on the friars, pointed out that the social origins of the leaders of a movement need not be identical with those of their followers and that a systematic examination of the identity of documentable friars (and by extension, Humiliati) was necessary.[134] Whether explicitly or not, however, Grundmann's emphasis on the importance of religious motivation has frequently informed the approach of historians writing both on the Humiliati in particular and more generally on heretical movements, where there has been a strong tendency to emphasise the role of religious impulses. According to Violante, speaking at the Royaumont conference on Heresy and Society in the early 1960s, 'social conditions are important essentially in so far as they influence opportunities for propaganda and diffusion of heresies and the means of defence for heretics against persecution', but 'the profound reasons for the rise and success of heretical movements must always be sought in a general consideration of the religious history of the epoch'.[135] Raoul Manselli's contribution at the same conference reveals a similar emphasis: 'by contrast to Volpe, I wish above all to underline that the heretics of Italian cities were responding first of all to a religious and spiritual need'.[136]

Grundmann's emphasis on religious motivation is also to be found in many of the more recent works which make specific reference to the Humiliati, though it has not acquired exclusive authority. Ilarino da Milano had accepted his refutation of Zanoni's arguments on social origins, but identified the Humiliati as members of the industrial

---

[131] Coulton, *Five Centuries of Religion*, II, p. 114.
[132] Grundmann, pp. 160–1, referring to Zanoni, pp. 87, 169.
[133] Grundmann, pp. 160–1, 168.
[134] Freed, *The Friars and German Society*, pp. 110–11.
[135] Violante, 'Hérésies urbaines et hérésies rurales en Italie du 11e au 13e siècle', pp. 194–5.
[136] R. Manselli, 'Les hérétiques dans la société Italienne du 13e siècle', *Hérésies et sociétés dans l'europe pré-industrielle, 11e–18e siècles*, ed. J. Le Goff (Paris, 1968), pp. 199–202.

bourgeoisie and emphasised their humility rather than poverty.[137] By contrast, Barbieri's work on the economic function of the order describes them as labourers transformed into merchants after papal recognition in 1201.[138] Brenda Bolton has proposed as an alternative that the First order was 'mainly aristocratic', while there was also a 'strong lower-class base' and 'some of the Tertiaries were clearly artisans'.[139] Kurt-Victor Selge has queried Zanoni's analysis of the Humiliati as a response to early capitalism,[140] while Lester Little, who sees the Humiliati as an example, alongside the Waldensians, Beguines and Cathars, of a 'sensitive response to the profit economy', concentrates mainly on the position of the Tertiaries. He recognises that there were some noble members, but again swings the balance of interpretation back towards Zanoni's approach, arguing that 'many of the Humiliati were living on the margins of society' and that some at least had turned to them because, in lieu of a guild, they offered 'economic and social security [for workers otherwise] completely at the mercy of the merchants'.[141] In a similar vein, Enrico Guidoni has returned to Zanoni's account of the proletarian origins of the order and later acquisition of entrepreneurial status.[142]

In 1991 Steven Epstein wrote 'at the present time no answer exists to the question, who were the original Humiliati?'[143] and it is certainly the case that local studies of their social origins in notarial archives have yielded varying results. Guerrini, in an analysis of the order at Brescia, had accepted Zanoni's interpretation of the Humiliati as a 'gesture of protest by the proletariat' and concluded that the earliest members there had been the humble dependants of religious institutions: tenants (*livellari*), gardeners and peasants as well as burghers (*burgenses*), united by their catholic and orthodox traditions in the face of the heresy of the aristocracy.[144] By contrast, De Sandre Gasparini, working from a careful re-examination of the archival sources, has argued that the Humiliati in Verona derived 'at least in good measure, from the "middle class" which was expanding . . . notaries, artisans, the odd merchant . . . "new" people'.[145] Brolis, working on similar lines on Bergamo, has

[137] Da Milano, 'L'eresia di Ugo Speroni', p. 454.
[138] Barbieri, 'La funzione economica degli Umiliati'.
[139] Bolton, 'Innocent III's treatment of the Humiliati', p. 79; see also her 'The poverty of the Humiliati', p. 57 and *The Medieval Reformation*, pp. 95–6.
[140] Selge *et al.*, 'Verbali delle sedute', p. 42.
[141] Little, *Religious Poverty and the Profit Economy*, pp. 113–20.
[142] Guidoni, *La città dal medioevo al rinascimento*, pp. 164–5.
[143] Epstein, *Wage Labour and Guilds*, p. 93.
[144] Guerrini, 'Gli Umiliati a Brescia', pp. 193–4, 198.
[145] De Sandre Gasparini, 'Movimenti evangelici a Verona', p. 154; on the idea of a middle class see G. Constable, 'Was there a medieval middle class?', *Portraits of Medieval and Renaissance Living:*

reached only slightly different conclusions. Pointing to a wider spectrum than that presented by De Sandre Gasparini, she argues that the Humiliati of Bergamo included both members of the most modest levels, 'small tenants and *massari* of the bishop' and individuals 'of means and culture' who possessed property, came from the families of lawyers and judges and knew how to manage money.[146] This great flowering of studies has not yet reached any definitive conclusions; however, in a recent summary Lorenzo Paolini has accepted that recruits from the lower and middle ranks of society seem to prevail, but notes that members of wealthy families, citizen and noble, are frequently mentioned. He lists examples from Milan, Brescia and Bergamo, adding that the list could easily be much extended.[147] Most recently, Alberzoni has again underlined this last aspect, using the notarial records for the Brera house in Milan to demonstrate that as the decades passed, this community attracted increasing numbers of male recruits from the city nobility and families involved in government. Similar assessment for women is not possible since if listed at all in such records, they are not accorded a second name.[148] Seven years after Epstein's statement, we have a slightly better idea of who the Humiliati were, however vague: membership ranged across the classes but included quite large numbers of the 'middling group'. Yet Paolini's cautious approach must be borne in mind, in particular when he points out that the social composition of houses is never homogeneous and varies from *domus* to *domus*, from countryside to city, inside the walls and out and (as Alberzoni has neatly demonstrated) diachronically in the same community.[149] The absence of information about women only adds to the need for circumspection.

Involvement in industry, finance and communal administration

Other themes of particular concern to Zanoni and more recent historians include Humiliati participation in the wool industry, in financial affairs and in communal administration. Extensive evidence for their role in these areas was integral to Zanoni's social and economic approach to the movement. Thus, for example, he dedicated a long section to their successes as wool-workers. He noted the demand for their services elsewhere, the appearance of trade in a new 'type' of cloth, the *panni humiliati*, recorded in Genoa, and their role as *mercatores*,

---

Essays in Memory of David Herlihy, ed. S. K. Cohn and S. A. Epstein (Ann Arbor, 1996), pp. 301–23.

[146] Brolis, *Gli Umiliati a Bergamo*, pp. 102–10.

[147] Paolini, 'Le Umiliate al lavoro', p. 234 and n. 12.

[148] Alberzoni, '"Sub eadem clausura sequestrati"', pp. 81–4.

[149] Paolini, 'Le Umiliate al lavoro', p. 234.

whose appearance in the notarial records he identified as marking the achievement of prosperity.[150] As evidence for their wool-working techniques he used the rough manuscript illuminations of John of Brera's 1421 *Excerptum*, produced decades after the end of wool-working in the order.[151]

Although remarking on the poverty of the sources, Zanoni also investigated their financial abilities, skills which had not been lost on contemporaries, as demonstrated by the late thirteenth-century Franciscan chronicler and wit Salimbene de Adam's account of them driving a hard bargain with Roland, bishop of Spoleto.[152] The evidence for *commenda* contracts from Genoa in the 1230s or from the Brera in Milan for sales which Zanoni saw as loans disguised to avoid the sin of usury, fitted well with his commercial view of the order. This led him to argue that the oblation of some adults or even whole families gave the houses involved 'an excellent deal, acquiring in one go a precious capital sum', while also arguing that the function of their houses was 'eminently social', providing an opportunity for young people to learn a skill before returning to the world.[153] Zanoni also recognised that the acquisition of capital led to the purchase of landed property, such that according to a late fifteenth-century chronicle of the order, in the fourteenth century Bernabò Visconti had prohibited further purchases of land on their part, fearing lest they should acquire most of Milan through their purchases.[154]

Zanoni explored in detail the nature of relations between the Humiliati and communal governments. He argued that the early papal letters on the problems of communal taxation and the imposition of military service on the Tertiaries reflected a policy of shouting loudly so that a bad situation would not get any worse (*di chi a buon conto getta alte strida, perché il male non ingrossi*). By mid century it was the intervention of cardinal legates, in particular Octavian *degli Ubaldini* and Gregory *de Montelongo*, which contributed to the worsening of relations between clerics and commune and the increasing imposition of taxes, forced loans and even confiscation of property.[155]

Finally, using city statutes, Zanoni examined the reasons for the choice of Humiliati, particularly from regular communities, as communal office-holders. He argued that they were favoured as men not

---

[150] Zanoni, pp. 145–85.
[151] Ambrosiana G 301 inf.; for colour reproductions, see *L'Abbazia di Viboldone*, pp. 16, 18 and 19.
[152] Salimbene de Adam, *Chronicon*, pp. 865–6; see also below, p. 167, n. 174.
[153] Zanoni, pp. 191–2.
[154] Marco Bossi, *Chronicon sui Humiliatorum ordinis*, pp. 345–52; discussed Zanoni, p. 195.
[155] *Ibid.*, pp. 203–15.

associated with any party, so as to put an end to the enmity of the different factions, as for example in their role as scrutineers for communal elections in Cremona.[156] However, Zanoni once again remained true to his financial approach. Although he accepted that the Humiliati were involved in some communal tasks to ensure against fraud, he concluded that members of such orders were chosen as communal treasurers and tax and toll collectors because the capital of the house to which they belonged could be used as a reserve, guaranteeing against any losses and, at the same time, allowing the commune to save on the expenses of tax collection.[157] He recognised that some Humiliati found the work of toll collection distasteful, as witnessed for example by papal letters reporting the departure of members of the order to avoid such tasks, but there were also benefits for the Humiliati: they received a stipend, shared some of the fines, enjoyed access to large amounts of capital and were accorded 'that esteem which men in all periods accord to gold and those who handle it'.[158]

Zanoni's study remains fundamental on these themes, although, as with other aspects of his work, its fiercely economic and commercial emphasis has been subject to some modification. The nature of the notarial archives, often dispersed or lost after the suppression of the order in 1571, has once again made the piecing together of further evidence slow and haphazard. Local studies such as those on Cremona re-echo Zanoni's emphasis on the increasing financial and administrative role of the Humiliati during the thirteenth century.[159] Epstein, writing on guilds and commerce, dedicates ten pages to the wool-working activities of Humiliati in Genoa and their relations with the wool guild. He comments that 'the one certainty remains that this urban religious movement was from its earliest stages associated with the wool-cloth industry',[160] an understandable, if restricted, approach when viewed from the vantage point of the Genoese material, but less convincing for some other cities. Recent studies of Bergamo, Modena and Pavia, among others, have produced further evidence to broaden the picture.[161] Thus we find Humiliati acting as overseers for the commune of Bergamo in the building of a new bridge at Almenno in

[156] *Ibid.*, p. 218.   [157] *Ibid.*, pp. 219–20, 237.
[158] *Ibid.*, p. 241 and citing Innocent IV (appendix I, 70).
[159] Giunta, 'Gli Umiliati di Cremona'; *Le pergamene degli Umiliati di Cremona*; on the Cremona records see now D. Graffigna, '"Carte Umiliate" da Cremona a Palermo', *Sulle tracce*, pp. 101–13.
[160] Epstein, *Wage Labour and Guilds*, p. 93.
[161] Brolis, *Gli Umiliati a Bergamo*, pp. 141–89; Romagnoli, 'Gli Umiliati a Modena', pp. 510–16; Crotti Pasi, 'Gli Umiliati a Pavia nei secoli xii e xiii'; Dr Crotti Pasi kindly allowed me to see an early copy of her article, now in *Sulle tracce*, pp. 317–42, to which all footnotes will refer.

1250.[162] Paolini, while recognising the difficulties and in particular the provisional nature of any conclusions, has outlined their attitudes to work, which he defines as central to Humiliati spirituality.[163] He recognises that not all houses were involved in the production of wool cloth and suggests that recruitment may have been favoured both by the variety of work and by continuity between activities in Humiliati houses and those of secular life.[164] Nonetheless, he concentrates on the wool industry, pushing the evidence to its limits, as Zanoni had done by using the fifteenth-century illuminations of John of Brera's work to examine the methods, the divisions of labour and the involvement of Humiliati women in the process.[165]

In addition to wool-working, recent studies have placed greater emphasis on the Humiliati's involvement in agriculture and the acquisition of landed property.[166] Their charitable activities, such as the administration of hospitals, have also been re-examined and, in a recent analysis, Alberzoni proposed a new interpretation of some of their monetary dealings, linking them with the charitable provision of financial support to help individuals escape the risks of usury.[167]

Settlement patterns and the distribution of houses

Although Tiraboschi undertook a systematic discussion of Humiliati houses city by city, settlement patterns still await an extensive synthesis of the scope of that undertaken by Pellegrini for the Franciscans.[168] Guidoni has attempted a first analysis and a number of smaller catalogues are beginning to address these issues in detail.[169] These reveal a far greater number of houses than previously recognised and have led to

---

[162] Brolis, '"Superstantes pontis de Lemen"', pp. 9–16.

[163] Paolini, 'Le Umiliate al lavoro', pp. 236–42. For early studies of the Humiliati and work, see Manselli, 'Gli Umiliati, lavoratori di lana'. The provisional nature of conclusions is particularly pertinent in view of the project on the Humiliati in *Lombardia* led by Professor Ambrosioni in Milan (assisted by Professor M. P. Alberzoni) and the ongoing work by Professors De Sandre Gasparini in the Veneto, Andenna in Brescia, Cracco and Merlo in Piemonte, and Paolini himself in Emilia-Romagna (and their students). See Andrews, 'The second generation of the "Sambin Revolution"', pp. 141–2; see now also A. Ambrosioni, 'Umiliate/Umiliati', *DIP*, IX (Rome, 1997), cols. 1489–1507; E. Mercatili Indelicato, 'Per una riconsiderazione del lavoro presso gli Umiliati. Il caso di Lodi', pp. 111–75.

[164] Paolini, 'Le Umiliate al lavoro', pp. 247–8.   [165] *Ibid.*, pp. 254–65.

[166] Bolcati and Lomastro Tognato, 'Una *religio nova* nel duecento vicentino: gli Umiliati'.

[167] Alberzoni, 'L'esperienza caritativa presso gli Umiliati'.

[168] Pellegrini, *Insediamenti francescani nell'Italia del duecento*.

[169] Guidoni, *La città dal medioevo al rinascimento*, pp. 159–85; see also, for example, the works of De Sandre Gasparini, Brolis, Longoni, Romagnoli and Crotti Pasi cited above and Arizza and Longatti, 'Gli Umiliati in diocesi di Como'; Menant, 'Les monastères bénédictins du diocèse de Crémone. Répertoire'; Spinelli, 'Gli Umiliati in Emilia-Romagna'; Longoni, 'Gli Umiliati in Brianza'; Mambretti, 'Note sugli insediamenti Umiliati nel territorio di Vimercate'; Besozzi, 'Le case degli Umiliati nell'Alto Seprio'; Brolis reports, *Gli Umiliati a Bergamo*, p. 26 n. 12, that

some debate about the question of rural or city origins for the movement as a whole, as part of a wider discussion concerning the location of
popular movements and heresy. Following Zanoni, Violante applied the
question to the early Humiliati, arguing that they were essentially city
based, but that many houses had originated in the countryside and later
transferred to cities, or that the movement was founded by recently
immigrant 'peasants'.[170] More recent work has examined the problem
through consideration of the names of Humiliati communities, which
were often associated with places in the contado of towns.[171] However,
no analysis can be conclusive until far more is known about the precise
topographical distribution and chronology of houses, something which
the numerous local studies of recent years begin to render within our
grasp.

SUMMARY

Research into the Humiliati in the twentieth century has tended to
address a set range of key questions: their heretical beginnings and
return to the Church under Innocent III, their social origins and
motivation, involvement in the wool trade and finance, and the physical
distribution, size and nature of their communities. The area under
investigation has gradually expanded outwards from a largely Milanese
core with other pockets of interest, to a wider view of the movement
across the whole of northern Italy. However, despite previous attempts
to provide a broad picture and early local studies, much work on the
Humiliati has remained essentially Milanocentric. By virtue of its
ecclesiastical and commercial importance in the area, Milan was a
natural focus for the Humiliati. With, or in place of Como, it was seen
as the city of origin of the nobles in the exile story. The four main
houses entrusted with responsibility for the order in 1201 were not far
from the city and Milan itself had certainly become a focus for the
administration of the order by the mid-thirteenth century. However,
there is a real need to fit Milan into its context. The many studies which
should counteract this emphasis by providing information on other
towns and areas have sometimes appeared local, even 'campanilistic' in
spirit, so that contacts between houses and similarities of experience are

Lucioni is at present preparing a new map of Lombard settlements. See now also various articles
in *Sulle tracce*.

[170] Violante, 'La chiesa bresciana nel medioevo', pp. 1079–82; Violante, 'Hérésies urbaines et
hérésies rurales en Italie', p. 179; see also Zanoni, pp. 196–9.

[171] Spinelli, 'Nota sul problema dell'ubicazione delle "domus" degli Umiliati', though his work
on Bergamo has largely been superseded by Brolis, *Gli Umiliati a Bergamo*, pp. 23–101; see also
Merlo, *Eretici ed eresie medievali*, p. 59.

occasionally missed because the material is not drawn together. The most recent contribution, a collection of essays on the Humiliati in *Lombardia*, includes articles on Lodi and Brescia in greater detail than in the past, but these are still treated in isolation from other cities and regions.[172]

By contrast, studies based on the accounts of contemporary observers and papal records, such as those of Grundmann and Maccarrone, have tended to treat the Humiliati as a homogeneous unit, about which general statements could easily be made. What will be attempted here is a balance between the two approaches, using the papal and notarial evidence together to trace both the forces for regionalism and variation and the impetus for unity in the development of an *ordo Humiliatorum*.

[172] See G. Archetti, 'Gli Umiliati e i vescovi alla fine del duecento. Il caso bresciano', and E. Mercatili Indelicato, 'Per una storia degli Umiliati nella diocesi di Lodi. Le case di S. Cristoforo e di Ognissanti nel xiii secolo', *Sulle tracce*, pp. 267–314, 343–492.

Chapter 2

THE BEGINNINGS OF THE HUMILIATI:
THE TWELFTH-CENTURY EVIDENCE

. . . et pro fide catholica se opponentes . . .

Universal Chronicle of Laon

The 'prehistory' of the Humiliati, before papal approval of the order in 1201, has recently been characterised as a time of fluidity about which little is known and which is difficult to define.[1] This case is made on strong grounds: the sources are extremely sporadic and of varying value, and the picture they convey is often one of transience, both before 1201 and well into the new century. Yet careful examination of the early material, some of which has long been known,[2] but much of which has only recently come to light, does allow us some insight into their early experience. As we shall see, this suggests that while there may have been some confusion about the early identity of the Humiliati, the heretical status of the early movement should not be overemphasised. Many of the communities included a strong clerical element and were much closer to the establishment of the Church than previous accounts have recognised. The impact of condemnation in the 1180s was to make the Humiliati sensitive about the use of the name and is reflected in cautious (but not absolute) silence, not persecution.

BETWEEN ORTHODOXY AND HERESY

The documented period in the wilderness for the Humiliati covers some twenty-five years, from the first references to their activities in the mid-1170s to the procedures leading to papal approval of the order which began in 1199–1200. However, the construction of communities

---

[1] De Sandre Gasparini, *La Vita religiosa nella marca veronese-trevigiana tra XII e XIV secolo*, p. 48. 'Prehistory' was perhaps first coined for the Humiliati by Zerfaß, *Der Streit um die Laienpredigt*, p. 205.

[2] Zanoni, p. 8 n. 3.

and documentary record often mark a point of arrival rather than of departure,[3] so their history can probably be projected back to the early 1170s, if not before. An important source for these years is a brief entry in the Anonymous Universal Chronicle of Laon, a work which continues down to the year 1219 and was almost certainly authored by a Premonstratensian canon.[4] In one short section this makes an implicit link between the Waldensians and the Humiliati. It describes Valdes of Lyons' meeting with Alexander III and his later lapse into disobedience over the issue of preaching and goes on immediately to portray the manner of life of the Humiliati and their reaction to papal restriction:

In the year of grace 1178 [=1179?[5]] . . . At that time there were certain citizens [*cives*] of Lombard towns [*civitates*] who lived at home with their families, chose a distinctive form of religious life [*quendam modum religiose vivendi*], refrained from lies, oaths and law suits, were satisfied with plain clothing, and argued for the catholic faith [*pro fide catholica se opponentes*]. They approached the pope and besought him to confirm their way of life [*propositum*]. This the pope granted them, provided that they did all things humbly and decently, but he expressly forbade them to hold private meetings [*conventicula*] or to presume to preach in public. But spurning the apostolic command, they became disobedient, for which they suffered excommunication. They called themselves Humiliati because they did not use coloured cloth for clothing, but restricted themselves to plain dress.[6]

This account enables us to divide the early years of the movement into an initial orthodox phase during which individuals calling themselves Humiliati and living a particularly humble lifestyle promoted the catholic faith, followed by a period of heresy subsequent to their excommunication for disobedience. They had approached the pope with some kind of proposal for a distinctive religious life, perhaps like Valdes at the Third Lateran Council in 1179,[7] but had not been able to accept the limitations on their activities required by the pope.

The excommunication of the Humiliati was determined in *Ad abolendam*, a wide-ranging decree intended 'to eradicate the depravity of heresy which in modern times has begun to spread in many parts of the world'. The bull was issued by pope Lucius III (1181–5) together with the emperor Frederick Barbarossa at the council of Verona in

[3] Cracco, 'Premessa', p. 4.
[4] Anonymous of Laon, *Chronicon universale*, pp. 449–50; on the question of authorship see the editor's introduction, p. 442.
[5] The correct date depends on whether we accept that the Humiliati approached Alexander at the Lateran Council which opened on 5 March 1179 in the modern calendar, 1178 in the Easter calendar in use in Laon in this period; below, p. 47.
[6] Translation adapted from *Heresies of the High Middle Ages*, trans. Wakefield and Evans, pp. 158–9.
[7] Selge, 'Humiliaten', p. 692.

November 1184. It first condemned every heresy, 'by whatever name it is known' and then went on to single out certain groups so as to ensure that none should escape:

We decree that Cathars and Patarines and those who mendaciously assume the false name of Humiliati or Poor of Lyons, Passagines, Josephines and Arnaldists, be subject to perpetual anathema. [8]

The Humiliati and Poor of Lyons are once more linked together in this text, as they are implicitly in the account of the chronicler of Laon. Contemporaries clearly associated the two groups in their minds and more recent historians have also linked them, particularly in the context of early Waldensian history, where interpretation of this passage was long the subject of debate. Some writers claimed that only those who improperly called themselves humble (Humiliati) or Poor of Lyons were condemned, or that this applied only to Passagines and Josephines who did so.[9] They thus concluded that the true Poor of Lyons and Humiliati were not anathematised, and were not heretics. However, other sources leave no doubt that the Humiliati were in fact intended. They are included in two lists of heretics dating to the end of the twelfth century. In a letter probably sent in the 1190s to accompany his *Tractatus de fide*, Peter of Blois (c. 1135–1211) lists them with Publicani, Patarines, and *Cruciati* and attributes heretical doubts about infant baptism, the clergy, the eucharist and conjugal relations to all four groups.[10] There is no other evidence to link the Humiliati in particular with these trademark heretical ideas, but the condemnation is clear and at much the same time the continuator of the annals of Melk in Austria gives a list based on *Ad abolendam* which, while fusing the name of the Humiliati with the Poor of Lyons (*Humiliatos pauperes*), nonetheless

---

[8] Appendix I, 2: 'Catharos et Patarinos et eos, qui se Humiliatos vel Pauperes de Lugduno falso nomine metiuntur, Passaginos, Iosephinos, Arnaldistas perpetuo decernimus anathemati subiacere.' On the Josephines see da Milano, 'L'eresia di Ugo Speroni', 457–60. On the Passagines, who advocated an especially literal observance of the Old Testament, see Manselli, *Il secolo xii. Religione popolare ed eresia*, pp. 295–301.

[9] See Gonnet, 'Sul concilio di Verona', 21–30.

[10] Peter of Blois, *The Later Letters of Peter of Blois*, ed. E. Reven, Auctores Britannici medii aevii, 13 (Oxford, 1993), letter 77 p. 326 lines 69–73: 'Isti sunt quos publicanos, paterinos, humiliatos, cruciatos, sive aliis nominibus censent, qui nec in parvulis baptismum credunt nec in sacerdotibus gratiam spiritus sancti, nec in sacrificio altaris corporis et sanguinis dominici veritatem; in laicis vero fidelibus detestantur consortium copule coniugalis.' I am grateful to Professor David Luscombe for drawing my attention to this passage; on Peter of Blois, see R. W. Southern, *Medieval Humanism and Other Studies* (Oxford, 1970), pp. 105–32 and 'The necessity for two Peters of Blois', *Intellectual Life in the Middle Ages: Essays Presented to Margaret Gibson*, ed. L. Smith and B. Ward (London, 1992), pp. 103–18; on the sect of the Publicani, see *Heresies of the High Middle Ages*, trans. Wakefield and Evans, esp. p. 723 n. 3.

confirms that they were condemned by pope and emperor.[11] Innocent III's correspondence in 1199–1201 corroborates the same point in several ways. The letters refer variously to the fact that the Humiliati had not yet returned to the Church, the scandal that had been engendered and the need to correct those in error. They also aptly cite the parables of the prodigal son and the lost sheep.[12]

The most alarming error of the Humiliati was certainly to insist on preaching without authority, which the text of *Ad abolendam* goes on specifically to condemn: 'all those who when either prohibited or not sent, without authority from the apostolic see or the bishop of the place, shall presume to preach in public or privately, shall be judged heretics'.[13] As the Chronicle of Laon records, the Humiliati did indeed meet privately, holding closed meetings (*conventicula*) which by their very nature, could not always be controlled.[14] Ecclesiastical nervousness about such activities with regard to the Humiliati is confirmed by the account of another Premonstratensian canon, Burchard of Ursberg, writing some decades later, c. 1215–30, but recording his experiences on two trips to Rome in 1198 and 1210.[15] Burchard wrote that the Humiliati and Poor of Lyons, 'two sects which had arisen in Italy and still survived', had been 'listed . . . among heretics, because superstitious doctrines and observances were found among them and because in secret sermons which they usually delivered in hidden places, they denigrated the Church of God and the priesthood'.[16] In the following sentence, he turns to criticism of the group led by Bernard Prim whom he encountered at the Curia in 1210, but he returns to the Humiliati with renewed vigour later in the same passage. He accuses them of 'thrusting their sickle into the harvest of others'[17] by preaching to the

---

[11] 'Annales Mellicenses, Continuatio zwetlensis altera', p. 542: 'Imperator invitatus in Italiam, a Lucio Romano pontifice et Lombardis honeste suscipitur . . . ubi etiam ipse et pontifex Romanus hereticos diversarum sectarum, Arnoldinos, Paterinos, Publicanos, Humiliatos pauperes deleverunt et Catzarios pravissimi dogmatis secundum gradus religionis sue, quorum alii Credentes, alii Perfecti nuncupantur, qui totam Ytaliam commaculaverant, persecuntur, et papa eos excommunicavit; imperator vero tam res quam personas ipsorum imperiali banno subiecit.'

[12] Appendix I, 4: 'et Humiliatos, qui nondum redierunt ad mandatum apostolice sedis', 8: 'de filio prodigo . . . de centesima ove perdita et reducta . . . errantes etiam revocare'; below, pp. 66–73.

[13] Appendix I, 2: 'omnes qui vel prohibiti vel non missi, praeter auctoritatem ab apostolica sede vel ab episcopo loci susceptam, publice vel privatim praedicare praesumpserint . . . haereticos iudicaverint'.

[14] See Moore, 'New sects and secret meetings: association and authority in the eleventh and twelfth centuries', p. 60.

[15] See Neel, 'The historical work of Burchard of Ursberg, 6: Burchard's life and his historiographical achievement', 6, 35.

[16] Burchard of Ursberg, *Chronicon*, p. 377; translations adapted from *Heresies of the High Middle Ages*, trans. Wakefield and Evans, pp. 228–30.

[17] Close to Deuteronomy 23:25.

41

people without the authority or licence of prelates, seeking to direct their lives and hear confessions and once more 'disparaging the ministry of the priesthood'. The Humiliati are described as rough (*rudes*) and illiterate, doing manual work and preaching, accepting the necessities of life from their believers.[18] Burchard had been in Rome at the very beginning of the pontificate of Innocent III and his account might therefore be endorsed as a reflection of opinion in Rome in 1198. As with the remainder of his chronicle, however, his polemical purpose should be borne in mind. In 1198 Burchard was still a young man, not yet a cleric and his outlook was strongly anti-papal.[19] He was not close to the Curia or well informed on attitudes there either in 1198 or later: although he appears to have a broad understanding of the different groups, he mistakenly implies that the Waldensians led by Bernard Prim remained outside the Church and seems unaware that the Humiliati had been accepted into the Church by Innocent III.[20] Moreover, in this passage his chief interest was in the two new orders, symptoms of a new age, the Friars Minor and Friars Preacher.[21] His aim was to portray the mendicant orders as part of papal action to correct earlier difficulties by supplanting the Waldensians and the Humiliati. The Humiliati thus play the role of a dangerous sect contrasted as strongly as possible with the friars. Their alleged rawness and illiteracy is introduced in order to contrast it with the scholarship and professionalism of the Dominicans.[22] They are denigrated in order to underline the virtue of the mendicants. In view of this context, the account cannot be taken at face value as a source for the Humiliati or for widely held attitudes towards them. Some historians have assumed that all heresies in this period were anti-clerical,[23] but there is no other evidence to substantiate Burchard's claims that the early Humiliati disparaged the priesthood or set out to challenge the clergy. Nonetheless, he does give some clues to their activities which match those of other sources discussed here, suggesting that they were actively preaching and involved in pastoral care, themes to which I shall return.[24]

The second reason for naming the Humiliati among those to be

---

[18] Burchard of Ursberg, *Chronicon*, p. 377.

[19] *Ibid.*, p. 366: 'Ego quoque, in minori aetate et seculari vita constitutus adhuc, eo tempore constitutus Romae'.

[20] This does not seem to fit with Little's view of Burchard's 'broad historical vision'; see Little, *Religious Poverty and the Profit Economy*, pp. 167–8.

[21] Neel, 'The historical work of Burchard of Ursberg, 4: Burchard as historian', 251.

[22] Burchard, *Chronicon*, pp. 366–77; Grundmann, p. 114.

[23] See for example, E. Delaruelle, 'Dévotion populaire et hérésie au moyen âge', *Hérésies et sociétés dans l'Europe pré-industrielle 11e–18e siècles*, ed. J. Le Goff (Paris, 1968), pp. 147–55, p. 153.

[24] See below, ch. 8.

condemned was their refusal to take oaths. Again it is the later papal letters which make this clear, going to great lengths to explain that swearing oaths was necessary in some circumstances.[25] That this issue was particularly momentous is also confirmed by the comments of later canon lawyers. For example, Tancred of Bologna, writing c. 1210–15 in a gloss on *Ad abolendam* in the *Compilatio prima*, omits all reference to preaching and argues that their only sin had been to condemn oaths or oath-takers. The same point was also made by his colleague Johannes Teutonicus, working at Bologna c. 1213–18, in a gloss on *Olim causa*, a decretal in the *Compilatio tertia* (the first universally accepted decretal collection), which refers to a Humiliati community in the area of Tortona.[26]

The full text of *Ad abolendam* directs bishops or their representatives actively to seek out heretics in their dioceses and to require those in areas where heretics are reputed to live to swear that, should they know of such heretics or people who hold secret meetings or differ in life or custom from the common life of the faithful,[27] they will declare it to the bishop or archdeacon. Almost certainly prompted by this exhortation, members of the local Church hierarchy in Verona did indeed hunt out and condemn the early Humiliati. In 1199 Innocent III complained to the bishop about the excommunication by the archpriest of the diocese of those who had not yet returned to the Church and who were called Humiliati against their will, yet were in the pope's eyes not heretics but fully orthodox.[28] Whereas the anonymous chronicler of Laon had identified the group as calling *themselves* Humiliati (because of their plain dress), Innocent's letter shows there is now reluctance to use the name. Indeed, avoidance of the term in official correspondence until 1211, when it was first used by the papal legate, Gerard *de Sesso*,[29] suggests that the name bore at least pejorative, if not heretical associations (not unlike the use of 'beguine' in northern Europe) and that even though there are no other documented examples of a prelate taking action against them, the condemnation was taking effect. Even after approval in 1201 the negative connotations of the name continued, as the expulsion of 'Humiliati' from Cerea in 1203 and Faenza in 1206 demonstrates.[30] Yet, as we might expect, the impact of condemnation often depended on local factors[31] and was not consistent. Examination

---

[25] See below, pp. 100–104, 106, 108.   [26] See below, pp. 64–5.

[27] Appendix I, 2: 'seu a communi conversatione fidelium vita et moribus dissidentes'.

[28] Appendix I, 4; see also below, pp. 67–8.   [29] Appendix I, *16; *VHM* I, p. 61.

[30] On Cerea see 'Statuti rurali veronesi', ed. Cipolla, p. 344; on Faenza, appendix I, 11 and p. 63.

[31] A point made by Leff, *Heresy in the Later Middle Ages* I, p. 40.

of the early evidence for the appearance of the Humiliati in the notarial archives will serve to illustrate this point.

THE EARLY EVIDENCE

The sources for the Humiliati are particularly sparse in the twelfth century. What continuity there is in the archives is only to be found from the 1220s. However, studies concentrating on topographically restricted areas have produced sporadic references from the twelfth century which, when combined, help to construct a clearer picture. In some cases this involves the use of accounts by modern writers whose reliability needs to be ascertained. Ronchetti, writing in the early nineteenth century, claimed that the Humiliati entered Bergamo before 1171, on the basis of a judgement given in a late fourteenth-century dispute. The Humiliati and a lay hospital order, the Crociferi,[32] had both been claiming precedence in processions and the case was referred to the bishop, who decided that the Humiliati should go first since they had entered the city earlier. As the Crociferi were 'known' to have entered Bergamo in 1171 (in fact they are documented at least from 1160),[33] this gave Ronchetti a date before 1171 for the arrival of the Humiliati.[34] As well as his chronological oversight, Ronchetti failed to give a source for his claim and Brolis, probably correctly, chose to ignore it in her study of the Humiliati in the city (where the first records are otherwise thirteenth century). Yet, in most cases where it can be tested, the work of such *eruditi* proves reliable and, since they often recorded documents which are now lost, without their evidence the history of the Humiliati in any period would be very much less complete. This chapter will thus examine each case on its merits before attempting to draw conclusions across a wider spectrum.

The Milanese houses: Viboldone

In the eighteenth century Tiraboschi uncovered what have remained the earliest documented references to Humiliati houses, those of Viboldone and the Brera in Milan.[35] The evidence is to be found in brief entries in chronicles and in contracts drawn up as settlements or property deals involving the nascent communities.

The first reference to Viboldone is in the anonymous Lesser Annals

---

[32] Vinken, 'Croisiers', *Dictionnaire de spiritualité ascétique et mystique, doctrine et histoire*, II (Paris, 1953), cols. 2561–76.
[33] Brolis, *Gli Umiliati a Bergamo*, p. 31 n. 23.
[34] Ronchetti, *Memorie istoriche*, III, p. 220. [35] *VHM* I, pp. 325–34.

of Milan. This describes the building of a church about 9 kilometres from Milan and close to the Via Emilia, a location which would facilitate communications and trade, as well perhaps as hospitality, though the fertility of the land and the proximity of the monastery of Chiaravalle may have been just as important.[36] The entry in the Annals is made under the year 1176, and is thereby associated with momentous events in Milanese history:

> In the year of our Lord 1176 in the month of April, Galdinus, archbishop of Milan died. In the same year the church of Viboldone was built. And in the same year the emperor Frederick was defeated by the Milanese at Legnano.[37]

A similar pattern of events is presented by the chronicle of Goffredus da Bussero:

> In the year of our Lord [1176] on 5 February, the church of San Pietro Viboldone was built and on 29 May, the emperor Frederick was defeated by the Milanese between Legnano and Borsano.[38]

Goffredus' account is not contemporary: he was born in 1220 and he is sometimes somewhat unreliable in his chronology, even dating the entry of the Franciscans in Milan and the canonisation of St Dominic to 1195.[39] However, other evidence suggests that the chronology for Viboldone is sound. In December 1322 an *Instrumentum transactionis* was drawn up recording transactions between the provost and brothers of Viboldone and the provost and canons of the *pieve* (or baptismal church) of San Giuliano, in whose district Viboldone stood.[40] This includes a copy of a charter of 4 February 1176, when the new community stipulated an agreement with the provost of San Giuliano. Although it is a late copy, it appears to be a reliable duplicate of the original since the details of individuals mentioned match contemporary records. The list of witnesses includes Alberic da Soresina of the Milanese cathedral chapter and the jurist Anselm dell'Orto, who was frequently employed as a delegate and counsellor by archbishops Galdinus (1166–76) and Algisius (1177–85). Also present as a guarantor (*fideiussio*) was John da Busnate, who had held the office of Consul of Justice in 1172 and may have been related to the earliest documented member of the

---

[36] See, albeit with caution, since the chronology is occasionally faulty, Marrucci, 'Il territorio e il complesso di Viboldone', p. 66.

[37] 'Annales mediolanenses minores', pp. 392–9.

[38] Goffredus da Bussero, *Chronicon*, p. 241.   [39] *Ibid.*, p. 242.

[40] *Instrumentum transactionis inter praepositum et canonicos S. Iuliani ex una, et praepositum et fratres domus de Vicoboldono ex altera* (18 December 1322). Discovered by Baldassare Oltrocchio in the hands of the provost of Viboldone, it was communicated to Tiraboschi, *VHM* I, p. 195; on the later copies in the Archivio della prepositura di San Giuliano Milanese, see Tagliabue, 'Gli Umiliati a Viboldone', pp. 11, 30 n. 17.

community, Obizo da Busnate (though Obizo is known only through the *Instrumentum transactionis*).[41] The agreement was formalised in the house of the archdeacon of Milan, Hubert Crivelli (later archbishop and pope as Urban III, 1185–7), and in the presence of Crivelli himself. Guy *de Porta Orientale*, acting as guarantor 'on behalf of the congregation of the brothers of the church of San Pietro, which is to be built in Viboldone', underwrote a payment (*fictum*) promised to the provost, 'for the restoration of tithes and first fruits and oblations which the said church of San Giuliano had in that place'.[42] Such an agreement fits well with contemporary attempts to stem opposition to monastic ownership of tithes and to avoid disputes by providing compensation with money or land to the owner of the tithe.[43]

It has been suggested that, as well as enjoying this early cooperation from the archdeacon of Milan, the Humiliati of Viboldone found a direct source of inspiration in the life of the archbishop himself, Galdinus della Sala, who was to be revered as a saint by the Milanese.[44] Galdinus' episcopacy covered the years of the city's rebirth after the disastrous defeat of 1162 and he therefore holds a special place in the history of the Ambrosian Church, although he did not live to see the triumph over Barbarossa at Legnano. He was one of the few prelates of his time to oppose heretics actively: according to tradition, he died in the pulpit, having just preached a sermon confuting the errors of the Cathars, an activity which the Humiliati were themselves to undertake.[45] Partial confirmation of a link between Galdinus and the Humiliati is provided by the *Instrumentum transactionis* of 1322, which records Galdinus' involvement in promoting the new community by giving his consent to lay cession of tithes to Viboldone.[46] However, the suggestion of more than administrative links between the archbishop and the new community cannot be definitively confirmed. More important here is the resoundingly orthodox nature of this young community, demonstrated by the full collaboration it received from

---

[41] Tagliabue, 'Gli Umiliati a Viboldone', pp. 15, 31, nn. 37–9.

[42] *VHM* II, p. 117: 'ex parte congregationis fratrum Ecclesie Sancti Petri, quae debet aedificari in loco Vicoboldono . . . pro restauratione decimae et Primitiae et oblationum, quas ipsa Ecclesia S. Iuliani habebat in suprascripto loco'.

[43] Constable, *Monastic Tithes*, p. 271.

[44] S. Latuada, *Vita di S Galdino* (Milan, 1735), pp. 63–6, among others; *VHM* I, p. 81; Gruber, 'Die Humiliaten im alten Tessin', p. 286; see also 'De S. Galdino S.R.E Cardinale', ed. Henskens, pp. 593–9; E. Cattaneo, 'Galdino della Sala cardinale arcivescovo di Milano', *Raccolta di studi in onore di S. Mocha Onory. Contributi dell'Istituto di Storia Medioevale*, II (Milan, 1972), pp. 356–83 (now also in *La chiesa di Ambrogio. Studi di storia e di liturgia* (Milan, 1984), pp. 49–76).

[45] Cattaneo, 'Galdino della Sala', p. 374 n. 76; on Humiliati activity against heretics, see the comments in Vitry, *HO*, 28, p. 146.

[46] *VHM* I, p. 333.

the local Church hierarchy, in the persons of the archdeacon and leading clerics, whether or not Galdinus himself was directly involved. Furthermore, the community's church was dedicated to St Peter, the 'papal saint', surely at least a claim to orthodoxy, although its significance was perhaps provocative in this fiercely Ambrosian context.[47] Most important of all, the community also received papal protection from Alexander III (1159–81), in a bull which does not survive but is referred to in a later privilege[48] and may have been issued at the time of the visit to the pope recorded by the Chronicle of Laon, perhaps at the third Lateran Council and possibly including a party from Viboldone itself.[49]

Viboldone's success seems to have been assured for, again according to the *Instrumentum transactionis*, in July 1181 Obizo da Busnate, described as a 'canon of the aforesaid church of San Pietro', was among those present when the community of Viboldone (*illi de Vicoboldono*) paid 83½ of the 105 lire of compensation agreed upon five years earlier. They agreed to hand over the remaining 21½ lire once they had purchased 'all other things which are in that place of Viboldone'. The sum paid suggests that most of the *pieve* was now in their hands and already exempt from tithes.[50]

Viboldone did not suffer as a result of the condemnation of those who called themselves Humiliati in 1184. In April 1186, only two years after *Ad abolendam*, Hubert Crivelli, now pope Urban III, issued *Religiosam vitam degentibus*, renewing Viboldone's privilege of papal protection.[51] The bull was issued at Verona, and may have formed part of Urban's attempts to win support in the north,[52] suggesting that the community was important or strategic enough to be worth courting. It is undersigned by thirteen cardinals, including Gratian, cardinal deacon of SS Cosma e Damiano, who was to be called upon to examine the order by Innocent III in 1200–1.[53] Although he refers to the rule of Benedict with regard to the election of superiors,[54] in other respects many of the clauses in Urban's privilege reflect standard practice, as well as closely resembling points to be used by Innocent III when approving

---

[47] On the importance attached to using the Ambrosian rite, see for example, appendix I, *10, archbishop Philip 'de Lampugnano's' letter c. 1201, authorising the Brera to build a church and have a priest to celebrate the divine office as long as he were 'Ambrosian': 'a quocumque presbitero *dum tamen ambroxiano* recipiendi'.

[48] Appendix I, 3: 'ad exemplar felicis recordationis Alexandri Papae praedecessoris nostri'.

[49] Anonymous of Laon, *Chronicon universale*, pp. 449–50.

[50] Tagliabue, 'Gli Umiliati a Viboldone', pp. 15, 31 n. 40.

[51] On this type of bull, see Dubois, 'Les ordres religieux au xiie siècle', 283–309.

[52] Ambrosioni, 'Monasteri e canoniche nella politica di Urbano III', p. 615.

[53] Appendix I, 3; below pp. 92–3.

[54] See below, ch. 4, on the rule of the order.

the order in 1201. He confirmed their ownership of property[55] and exempted them from the payment of tithes on the labour of their own hands or the food of their animals, the same concession given to the Second order in 1201, when Viboldone obtained the right to receive tithes itself, as did all houses of the First order.[56] Urban allowed them to accept both laity and clerics and forbade transfer to another house unless to achieve a stricter regime.[57] More remarkably, he also allowed them freedom to provide burial for any who might choose to be buried there, unless they had been excommunicated and as long as it did not damage the rights of the church from which the body came. Finally, and most importantly, the privilege was addressed to the brothers professed to the regular life (*regulari vita professis*), indicating that this was a canonical community, professing a rule.[58]

The two privileges for Viboldone appear to be unique among the Humiliati until 1201, but that of 1186 confirms that, in the eyes of this pope at least, there was no association between the familiar and well-established religious community not far from the gates of Milan and the mendacious heretics calling themselves *Humiliati* condemned by his immediate predecessor. Yet, although the name was not used, there can be little doubt that this was a Humiliati community. The association with Guy *de Porta Orientale*, who had been present in 1176,[59] was repeated in Innocent III's letters of 1200 and 1201.[60] Lanfranc, the provost of Viboldone, was one of those addressed by Innocent III when writing to the order during the negotiations over their return to the Church in 1200, and in *Non omni spiritui* of 16 June 1201 Innocent was to confirm his position as one of the four principal provosts of the new order, with authority over the other houses.[61]

The Brera

Close ties with the local Church hierarchy are also to be found in the earliest known document referring to the double community of men and women at the Brera in Milan. The document, which is again concerned with tithes, is exceptionally informative about the nature of

---

[55] Innocent III's letter in 1201, appendix 1, 9, further confirms Viboldone's possessions, naming rural property in a place identified only as *ad montem*.

[56] On the development of tithe concessions see Constable, *Monastic Tithes*, p. 306.

[57] Appendix 1, 3: 'nisi obtentu arctioris religionis discedere'.

[58] Ambrosioni, 'Monasteri e canoniche nella politica di Urbano III', p. 615; Tagliabue, 'Gli Umiliati a Viboldone', p. 15.

[59] Tagliabue, 'Gli Umiliati a Viboldone', p. 12 argues that the presence of Guy was 'indisputable proof' of Viboldone's Humiliati identity.

[60] Appendix 1, 5 and 7; below, pp. 77–80.   [61] Appendix 1, 5 and 9; below, pp. 107–8.

the new community at such an early date.[62] In November 1178, in the house of Algisius, treasurer (*cimiliarcha*) of Milan, and in his presence, Martin, priest of the church of San Giovanni *qui dicitur quattuor faties* (in the Porta Comacina), Henry, John and Otto *veglones* of the church of Sta Maria *yemalis* (the winter basilica) and Rugoro and Tettavillanus of San Michele gave up tithes on land in the *braida* or *brera* which had once belonged to Guercius *de Badaglio*.[63] The land had now been purchased by Suzo Bagutano, Iohannibellus *de Arcuri* and Peter *de Sologno*, on behalf of 'the religious men' who were to live there.[64] In return for five silver lire of Milan, the tithe was surrendered to William, priest of the church of Sant'Ilario, who had been sent to receive it by archbishop Algisius. On behalf of the archbishop, William then granted the tithes to Suzo Bagutanus as the representative of the men and women living in a house built on the land and 'who are humbled for God' (*sunt humiliati per deum*).[65] This identification is confirmed by a note written on the verso of the document, in a contemporary hand, if not actually by the same scribe, which describes the property as belonging to the Humiliati: 'on the land of the Humiliati of the brera known as Guercius *de badaglio's*'.[66] By 1178 there was thus a recently established house for both men and women on a site near one of the main gates of the city of Milan. Once again the new community enjoyed the support of an archbishop who wished to favour novel means to promote religious enthusiasm in his province.[67]

Zanoni argued that a reference in 1186 to Patarines living in the area of the Brera referred to the Humiliati.[68] Acting on behalf of his relative Giacominus, Ambrose Cagapisto, a member of a prominent local family

---

[62] The original identified by Alberzoni is now Milan, Trivulziana, fondo belgioioso cartella 291, 7 November 1178; *VHM* II, pp. 119–22.

[63] On *veglones*, lay office-holders in the church of Milan, see Du Cange, *Glossarium*, s.v; on Guercio *de badaglio* or *da Baggio*, who gave his name to the suburb of Milan near the Porta Comacina, see Corsi, 'Note sulla famiglia da Baggio (secoli ix–xiii)', pp. 166–204. Guercio was already deceased in 1153; see *Pergamene milanesi dei secoli XII e XIII*, XII, pp. 70–2.

[64] Milan, Trivulziana, fondo belgioioso cartella 291 (7 November 1178); *VHM* II, pp. 120–1: 'que est in braida que fuit de guertio de badaglio . . . ad partem religiosorum hominum que habitare debebant in illa terra'.

[65] *Ibid.*, 'illorum hominum et feminarum qui et que sunt humiliati per deum ad domum illam que edificata est super predictam terram'.

[66] Trivulziana, fondo belgioioso cartella 291 (7 November 1178), verso: 'Cartam finis quam fecerunt Martino presbiter ecclesie sancti iohannis qui dicitur quattuor faties [and five others] . . . de decima quam habebant super terram humiliatorum de braida qui dicitur guertii de badaglio et eorum heredum soluendo solitu fictum omni anno'.

[67] See Alberzoni, 'Nel conflitto tra papato e impero, da Galdino della Sala a Guglielmo da Rizolio (1166–1241)', p. 231.

[68] Zanoni, pp. 40–1.

long associated with Sant'Eusebio and with links with the Brera,[69] paid rent to Albert, priest of Sant'Eusebio, for two houses situated in the *Braida Guercii*, both of which included *patarini* amongst their neighbours. Zanoni observed that the Humiliati were occasionally called Patarines, in his view the Lombard name for Cathars, and called to witness Jacques de Vitry's letter written in 1216 which observed that 'malicious and secular men' called the Humiliati 'Patarines'.[70] Zanoni thus concluded that the Humiliati sprang from the Patarine and Cathar tradition of Milan.[71] Yet there is no reason to suppose that there could not have been both Humiliati and Patarines in the same area of Milan in 1186; the city was after all notorious as a den of heretics (*fovea hereticorum*).[72]

Apart from the 1186 document, the Brera disappears from the records until 1198. This is probably the result of poor record survival, but it is possible that there was a deliberate decision to keep a low profile. The next document recording the community, dating from February 1198, certainly shows continuity of personnel, since it again refers to Suzo Bagutanus acting as their representative in the purchase of land neighbouring their existing properties.[73] This time he is accorded the title of prelate, and acts on behalf of the 'congregation of the brethren of the Brera' (*congregatio fratrum de Braida*), terminology which suggests a more formal structure for the community, but the Humiliati name is not used.

Both the Brera and Viboldone communities were thus involved in acquiring property and tithes before they received official papal approval of their order in 1201. They also enjoyed good relations with local churchmen and their lay neighbours who sold them both land and tithes, though the cordiality of ecclesiastics may have been maintained by avoiding the name. These are the best documented of the early Humiliati communities and reveal the greatest continuity, but their close ties with the ecclesiastical hierarchy were not unique, as other early references to Humiliati individuals or communities reveal.

The situation outside Milan

In 1180 the Humiliati were associated with a strategically important hospital and church 'near the water called Bardonezza' between

[69] Andenna, 'Una famiglia milanese di "cives" proprietari terrieri nella pieve di Cesano Boscone. I Cagapisto', pp. 641–86; see *Pergamene milanesi dei secoli XII e XIII*, XII, pp. 63–72 for links between the Cagapisto family and Sant'Eusebio from 1135; see also below, p. 226.

[70] Jacques de Vitry, *Lettres*, p. 72: 'qui a maliciosis et secularibus hominibus Patareni nuncupantur'.

[71] Zanoni, pp. 41, 267–8; above, p. 26; see also Bolton, 'Sources', p. 132.

[72] Jacques de Vitry, *Lettres*, p. 72. [73] *VHM* II, pp. 126–7.

Piacenza and Pavia on the *strata romea*, the pilgrim and trade route to Rome. Bardonezza lay physically within the limits of the diocese of Pavia, but belonged to Piacenza, a point which was not always accepted by the Pavians.[74] According to an early seventeenth-century copy of a charter, in February 1180 Tedald, bishop of Piacenza (1167–92), placed the administration of this hospital and church in the hands of Peter Cabacia, a *humiliatus* and *conversus* of the hospital.[75] This was done in response to a petition and prayers from the Humiliati and for the 'support of the poor, the church and the hospital'.[76] It has been suggested that the Humiliati may have been brought in to resolve the precarious financial situation with which the hospital had been faced at least since 1164, when the minister had been forced to take on a debt of almost 24 Pavian lire.[77] The assumption was presumably that the Humiliati had already acquired the monetary skills with which they are associated in the thirteenth century and were brought in as financial consultants. If so, this is a remarkable example of financial wizardry, for the solution must have been very quickly found: the administration by a *humiliatus* and presence of others seems to have been extremely short lived. Just eight years later, in 1188 bishop Tedald is recorded receiving the hospital back from Arduin, Bethlemite preceptor and proctor in *Lombardia* and the March.[78]

Another account of an early Humiliati community, in Piacenza itself, again survives only because recorded by a seventeenth-century anti-quarian, this time the Piacentine historian Pietro Maria Campi, on the basis of a document then in the cathedral archives of Piacenza, but since lost. Where comparison is possible, Campi's work appears reliable: he cites an archive and his account of the earlier Bardonezza charter matches the edition now available in the work of Storti. His edition is thus very likely to be accurate. Once more the document describes the Humiliati enjoying the support of bishop Tedald. In September 1180, with his consent, Ardengus Vicedomino and Trecco Zematio gave land between the churches of San Salvatore and San Paolo, for the building

[74] *Il 'registrum magnum' del comune di Piacenza*, I, no. 166, pp. 368–74 (31 March 1202): peace agreement between Piacenza, Pavia and Milan. The commune of Pavia undertakes not to obstruct the bishop of Piacenza's spiritual rights over the hospital: p. 373: 'Et commune Papie non impediet episcopo Placentie spiritualia hospitalis Bardonezie'.
[75] First noted by Campi, *Dell'historia ecclesiastica di Piacenza*, II, p. 52 cols. 1–2; discussed by Tiraboschi, *VHM* I, p. 95; see now Storti, *Arena Po*, pp. 43–52, 120–1.
[76] Storti, *Arena Po*, p. 121: 'ad peticionem et preces humiliatorum et sustentacionem pauperum, ecclesiam et hospitale'.
[77] *Ibid.*, pp. 45–6.
[78] *Ibid.*, pp. 122–3; R. W. Emery, 'Bethlemites', *New Catholic Encyclopaedia* (New York, London, 1967), II, pp. 374–5; *Il 'registrum magnum' del comune di Piacenza*, I, no. 212, pp. 443–4 (9 March 1188).

of a Humiliati house, hospital and church to be dedicated to Sta Maria *de Bethlehem*, later called Sant'Anna.[79] Tiraboschi linked this settlement to the Third order, since Tertiaries in Piacenza were to be mentioned in the papal letter of 7 June 1201 *Incumbit nobis*.[80] The earliest record found in a recent study of the town, however, dates to 9 May 1250 when the 'Minister of the new house of the Humiliati' near San Savino sold some property.[81] The use here of the title 'Minister' usually associated with superiors of the Third order, might uphold Tiraboschi's argument that the early reference was also to Tertiaries in Piacenza. In the interim, however, there had certainly been other Humiliati present in the city, since a record of 1235 refers to a Humiliati provost visiting the house of the twelve apostles there.[82] Any assessment of the nature of the early community must, however, remain purely speculative, if it ever took shape.

In 1182 in Pavia bishop Lanfranc Beccari (d. 1198) gave the Humiliati the church of Sta Maria Maddalena in the countryside near the river Vernavola. Once again our knowledge of the concession is based on the description of a seventeenth-century scholar, Gerolamo Bossi, who described a charter then in the possession of a signor Bigoni.[83] The bishop gave the Humiliati the church of Sta Maria Maddalena, but retained the right to ordain their clerics and confirm the provost, obliged them to attend synods, receive constitutions and pay a cense of one pound of pepper on the feast of St Thomas. It is a concession which once more implies the existence of a well-integrated community, not simply enjoying good relations with local ecclesiastics, but a part of their establishment, enjoying the same rights and carrying the same responsibilities as secular clerics would have done in an equivalent position.

Unfortunately, nothing more is known of the church of Sta Maria Maddalena *presso Vernavola*, nor of the Humiliati community there, which may suggest that bishop Lanfranc's experiment was not successful. However, another early Humiliati community near Pavia, first recorded in 1183 at *Vigalono* or Vialone (recently identified as on the right bank of the Olona on the old road towards Lodi) is much better documented and was to become one of the four principal provostures

---

[79] Campi, *Dell' historia ecclesiastica di Piacenza*, II, p. 53 col. 2.

[80] *VHM* II, pp. 95–6; below, appendix I, 7.

[81] Racine, *Plaisance du xème à la fin du xiiième siècle*, II, pp. 825, 826 and 831 n. 68: 'Minister domus nove Umiliatorum [sic] posita aput rivum S. Savini'.

[82] See below, p. 164.

[83] Cited Zanoni, p. 8 n. 3 and Crotti Pasi, 'Gli Umiliati a Pavia', p. 318.

of the order in 1201.[84] On 20 May 1183, six men, all described as ministers and including donnus Trancherius son of John *de Braida* and a priest, Hubert, sold some land on behalf of the '*mansio* [hostel] of the Humiliati of Pavia at Vialone'. The sale was made in order to pay for lands purchased nearer to their *mansio*, in the neighbouring territories of Sant'Alessio and of Vialone itself, 'so as to be useful to the same *mansio*' (*pro utilitate ipsius mansionis*).[85] The evidence for a policy of property acquisition similar to that at Viboldone, and even consolidation of their properties, as well as the important reference to a priest, certainly implies an expanding and respectable community.

A fleeting record of an early Humiliati presence comes from Frassineto Po, near the confluence of the rivers Po and Sesia in modern-day Piemonte, and pre-dates other known records for the area considerably. On 8 December 1183, the abbot of the Cistercian monastery of Rivalta Scrivia and the provost of the church of Sant'Ambrogio in Frassineto Po reached agreement concerning a house in Frassineto which 'had once been of the Humiliati' and which had recently been given to the Cistercians at Rivalta.[86] The use of the building had already passed out of the control of those named as Humiliati, perhaps quite some time before this agreement was stipulated as may be implied by the use of *quondam fuerat* (*que quondam fuerat Humiliatorum*), and no later records for the Humiliati at Frassineto have so far been found.

A second reference from this area can only be dated approximately between 1183 and 1193, the years of the episcopacy of bishop Hugh of Tortona, but it suggests that there may have been a more substantial community of Humiliati here. The evidence comes from *Olim causam*, a letter of 1200 issued by Innocent III in settlement of a dispute and included in later decretal collections.[87] The dispute did not involve the Humiliati directly, but a concession made by the bishop at their request allowing them to build a hospital and oratory in *loco Calventiae*. The Humiliati were to pay 3 shillings yearly to the bishop and accept the investiture of their superiors from him, to whom they still owed obedience (*obedientia manualis*) and who retained lordship (*dominium*). The site had previously been occupied by the Templars and on hearing of the concession made by the bishop, the Master of the Templars in *Lombardia* went to the house and took away the church furnishings,

---

[84] See Crotti Pasi, 'Gli Umiliati a Pavia', pp. 319–21.

[85] The document, which survives in two twelfth-century copies in the Archivio di stato Milan, is published in E. Barbieri, *Notariato e documento notarile a Pavia (secoli xi–xiv)*, (Florence, 1990), appendix 1, pp. 194–7, with comments on the relationship between the two texts, p. 84 and a photograph of the original charter, table 17; cited Crotti Pasi, 'Gli Umiliati a Pavia', p. 320.

[86] Merlo, 'Tra "vecchio" e "nuovo" monachesimo (metà xii–metà xiii secolo)', pp. 458–9.

[87] Appendix 1, 6.

books and equipment from the house and ninety sheep. This did not mean that all the Templars were happy to leave and the papal letter later records their forced removal by the bishop. Although the Humiliati are otherwise undocumented in the area of Tortona until 1232,[88] the concession suggests both that the bishop was discriminating in favour of the Humiliati and that there may have been a considerable community, including clerics, ready to officiate at the church from which the Templars removed their property.[89] Perhaps the Humiliati were planning to keep sheep as the Templars had done. If so this is the closest we get to linking the twelfth-century Humiliati with the wool industry for which in some areas they later became famous.

From Tortona we move north to Como, where the fifteenth-century chroniclers claimed that John of Meda founded the mother-house of the First order some time in the mid-twelfth century.[90] By contrast the earliest extant documentary reference is to the community of Rondineto in 1189. In the *Addenda* to his third volume, Tiraboschi published a partial transcript of a document recording that on Tuesday 14 July 1236, in the cloisters of the Dominican church of Sant'Eustorgio in Milan, brother Stephen, Dominican provincial prior in *Lombardia* and papal visitor of exempt houses and of the Humiliati, entrusted the priest Giroldus of Rondineto with the administration and prelacy of the house of Sta Maria di Ronco Martano *de Valbixaria*.[91] He thus confirmed the election made on Monday 5 May of that year by Domina Herena *de Pirovano*, Domina Prudentia and Domina Riccha, sisters in the Ronco house, who chose Giroldus as pastor, rector and provost of their congregation. The text of Stephen's grant records that forty-seven years earlier, on 2 June 1189, Martin *de Inzago*, minister and *conversus* of the church of Sta Maria and his brother John, also a *conversus*, had given the church and house to brother James Rusca and an otherwise unidentified Michael, representatives of the men and women of the congregation and fraternity of 'Rondineto' (*congregatio et fraternitas de Rondanario*).[92] That this had indeed long been held by the Humiliati is corroborated by Innocent III's letter to the First order in 1201, when he confirmed their ownership of property, including 'the church, estate and other possessions in Ronco Martano and in Valle Bissaria, with all things pertaining to them, which are all known to belong to the house of Rondineto'.[93]

---

[88] Below, p. 227.   [89] On this dispute, see also below, p. 86.
[90] Above, ch. 1.   [91] Below, pp. 107, 142, 164, 205.
[92] *VHM* III, pp. 303–5; original now lost; see also below, p. 74; the origins of the name (now Rondineto), perhaps lie in the proximity to Lake Como: *arundinetum*, full of reeds; Giussani, 'Il sarcofago di San Giovanni da Meda', 98.
[93] *VHM* II, p. 141; III, pp. 303–5.

In 1198 brother James was still acting as superior of the community, and according to Tiraboschi, was described as 'provost of the fraternity and church of Rondineto' and as 'provost of the *mansio* of Rondineto'.[94] Such titles suggest he was a cleric, as the terms of approval were to require all provosts to be, and evidence for his career after 1201 confirms this view.[95] He was almost certainly the James of Rondineto who was to go to the Curia as one of the representatives of the Humiliati to seek Innocent III's approval at the turn of the century.[96] Rondineto had surely reached a high level of administrative and patrimonial security, if it felt both confident and wealthy enough to make representations to the pope.

The remaining twelfth-century records for the Humiliati again date from the 1190s, but two of these are not well documented. As recently as 1977 Meersseman, in his study of fraternities, stated unequivocally that the Humiliati were present in Vicenza on 1 April 1190, but gave no source for his claim and went on to list the earliest documents, which date only to 1209.[97] Similarly, material concerning the church of Sta Margherita di Morigallo in Genoa, recorded as a Humiliati church from March 1192 in a recent catalogue of Ligurian monasteries, awaits further confirmation.[98] However, the documentary status of the final references to the Humiliati so far known from their wilderness years is clear cut. In the first, dated December 1193, a citizen of Milan, Andriottus of Santa Maria, his wife Donzella and his mother Tantebella sold some land in the rural *borgo* of Vimercate to Peter of Cuniolo and Ambrose Imperii, both from Vimercate. Peter and Ambrose were acting on behalf of the brothers and sisters 'who are called Humiliati' (*qui appellantur humiliati*) and who were living in a common house (*casa communi*) in Vimercate.[99] Once more we find a clearly identified group, living the common life and involved in the acquisition of property.

The last community documented before the approach to the Curia provides a context for Lanfranc of Lodi, another of the representatives sent to seek Innocent III's approval. His house was San Cristoforo in

---

[94] *VHM* II, p. 22: 'prepositus fraternitatis et ecclesie de Rondenario . . . prepositus mansionis de rundenara'; Morelli, 'La casa di Rondineto', pp. 10*–11*; Dr Morelli kindly allowed me to consult her own copy of her text; on James, see now Alberzoni, 'Giacomo di Rondineto', pp. 117–62.

[95] Below, pp. 74–7.   [96] *VHM* II, p. 22.

[97] Meersseman, '*Ordo fraternitatis*', I, p. 325; my own research in the Vicenza archive has so far produced no document to confirm Meersseman's statement.

[98] Maiolino and Varaldo, 'Diocesi di Genova', pp. 93–151, scheda 37, pp. 128–9; the document cited was stipulated by the notary Guglielmo Cassinese, but makes no reference to the Humiliati: 'Guglielmo Cassinese (1190–1192)', ed. Hall, Krueger and Reynolds, II, no. 1784.

[99] The document is transcribed in Mambretti, 'Note sugli insediamenti Umiliati nel territorio di Vimercate', appendix 1.

Lodi which is first documented in 1195. In that year, Sotius *de Campo Longo* left 40 shillings for his soul to the 'church of San Cristoforo of the Humiliati'.[100] Three years later, in December 1198, Albert Niger left a share in tithes from Fançago to the *canonica* of San Cristoforo.[101] Here we have a community with its own church receiving legacies for the souls of testators. It is even called a *canonica*, though in the 1198 document, unlike that of 1195, the name Humiliati has disappeared.[102] While the nature of the documents means that no individual member of the community is named, and hence none is identified as a canon, it would be taking minimalism to extremes to argue that there were no clerics here or that this is not a Humiliati community. Its superior was to be the last of the four established as a senior provost just two and a half years later, in June 1201.

CONCLUSIONS

First of all, there are numerous limitations. The evidence presented here is fragmentary and may well be supplemented in future. The dispersal of the Humiliati's own records means that often the only way of tracing them is to sift laboriously through the documentation of other communities in search of their neighbours and other outside contacts in the hope that these may be the Humiliati.

Second, some of these sources may reflect later revisions, in particular the early fourteenth-century copy of transactions concerning Viboldone, where the use of the term *canonicus* to describe Obizo in 1181 may fulfil fourteenth-century expectations rather than the terminology of the 1180s. Nonetheless I am inclined to accept the reliability of these editions and those of the later antiquarians, because where it has been possible to check other examples of their work against originals (as in the case of Campi's work on Piacenza), I have not found any insertions of anachronistic material or more than very minor mistranscriptions.

Third, we must not assume that all of the 'Humiliati' communities mentioned here are directly associated with the later order. Some undoubtedly were: Viboldone, Vialone, Lodi, Rondineto and later the Brera all became important in the order after 1201. Viboldone was to host the first recorded General Chapter in 1256,[103] while notaries from the Brera later prepared copies of an important papal letter for commu-

---

[100] Appendix III, 1.   [101] Appendix III, 2.
[102] It was to return: ASMi, 187 Lodi, San Domenico (1250): 'in canonica sancti Christofori de humiliatis'.
[103] Below, pp. 214–15.

nities elsewhere,[104] and all these houses appear in later catalogues of the order.[105] In some cases this continuity can also be observed in the experience of individuals who may be traced both before and after approval: thus James Rusca of Rondineto is documented from 1189 until 1218, and members of his family were still associated with the house in the 1230s, though James himself had left by 1217.[106] Guy *de Porta Orientale* can be associated with the order from 1178 until 1209[107] and Iohannibellus, who was one of the representatives of the Brera community in Milan in their purchase of land in November 1178, may well be the same man to whom archbishop Philip *de Lampugnano* addressed a letter for the community c. 1201.[108] Isolated references are, however, more problematic and hint at greater transience or even confusion. In 1184 the compilers of the *Ad abolendam* decree clearly thought that they could identify a recognisable group by using the term Humiliati. Bishop Tedald and Peter Cabacia, or at least the notary who drew up the document for Bardonezza in 1180, also obviously assumed that the description 'Humiliati' was a suitable one, as did Ardengus Vicedomino and Trecco Zematio in Piacenza. However, it is interesting that in both these cases the sources hint at associations with the Bethlemites: at Bardonezza the hospital was later handed to them, while at Piacenza the proposed church was to be dedicated to 'Sta Maria *de Bethlehem*'.[109] It is just possible, therefore, that the name Humiliati was used here for communities administratively linked to a different order. This was certainly the case later for a community of women described as 'the white ladies' (*domine albe*), living together near the church of Sant'Eustorgio in Milan, given to the Dominicans in 1220.[110] These women requested and obtained permission to transfer to the Dominicans in the first half of the thirteenth century[111] but continued to use the Humiliati name long after they had adopted the Dominican rule.[112] Similar confusion about identities could easily be listed for elsewhere.[113]

---

[104] See appendix I, 59.

[105] On the 1298 catalogue, used by Tiraboschi as the basis for his list of houses (*VHM* I, pp. 313–94 and II, pp. 1–115) and the other catalogues (1288 and 1344, *VHM* III, pp. 265–7, 270–3 and 273–85), see now Broggi, 'Il catalogo del 1298', pp. 3–44.

[106] 'Le carte di Sta Maria Vecchia di Como', 16 (1217), 17 (1217), 19 (1230), 21 (1232); see also Alberzoni, 'Giacomo di Rondineto', p. 150 and below, pp. 74–7.

[107] Below, p. 77–80.   [108] Appendix I, ★10.   [109] Above, p. 52.

[110] L. Airaghi, 'La basilica di Sant'Eustorgio in Milano da canonica a convento Domenicano', *Aevum*, 55 (1981), 294–325.

[111] Alberzoni, 'Un mendicante di fronte alla vita della chiesa nella seconda metà del duecento. Motivi religiosi nella cronica di Salimbene', pp. 7–34, p. 21 n. 54.

[112] Zanoni, p. 63; Balosso, 'Gli Umiliati nel Novarese', p. 79, lists other fifteenth-century examples of the name being applied to Franciscan and Dominican sisters.

[113] For example Rigon, 'Penitenti e laici devoti fra mondo monastico-canonicale e ordini mendicanti: qualche esempio in area veneta e mantovana', pp. 59, 63 n. 54.

This lack of a monopoly on the name Humiliati or a clearly defined membership and identity underlines the dangers of over-rigid categorisation in writing the history of the early Humiliati, as of many other nascent religious movements. It seems unlikely that there was a single source for the different experiments described here. The houses are often placed on rivers or major routes: some are referred to as *mansiones* (hostels or staging posts). Ideas and names certainly travelled along such routes, but the concrete evidence for links between houses is non-existent before the approach to the Curia, and such links need not necessarily be projected back much before that date. Where the references are to communities at a distance from Milan, Lodi and Como, whence the delegates to the Curia came, such as the elusive building at Frassineto Po, any formal links seem extremely unlikely. Indeed, where only one reference is available and a Humiliati presence is not confirmed later when the documentation becomes more prolific, it is very difficult to state whether or not groups or individuals felt that they belonged to a particular movement, or identified with groups in other areas who used (or were given) the same name.[114] Some were probably what would later be termed Tertiaries, living in their own homes and leading a life of religious devotion which earned them the name Humiliati. Yet even in the thirteenth century, when the term had attained the status of a more or less official title, random references to otherwise undocumented communities remain difficult either to identify as heretics, or to pin to the 'authorised' order, particularly in view of the mobility of houses.[115] Moreover, other evidence confirms the continuing importance of local experience and variety long after the papal approval of 1201.[116] Even in movements with a clearly recognisable founder, such as the Franciscans, not all similar experiences can or should be associated directly with the actions of the single founder. This has been recognised in the recent adoption of the term *minoritismo* to describe the infinity of similar experiences inspired by the 'Franciscan' ideal of *minoritas*, but not originating from Francis himself or his order.[117] Perhaps a similarly flexible term such as *umiliatismo* might be a helpful way to consider those individuals and groups for which there are only isolated references and, after 1201, no evidence of ties with the 'official' order. These would include those on both sides of the limits of

---

[114] da Milano, 'Il "Liber supra stella" del piacentino Salvo Burci', pp. 90–146, illustrates some of the difficulties of identification in the *arruffio* of late twelfth-century sects.

[115] Alberzoni, 'Il monastero di Sant'Ambrogio e i movimenti religiosi del xiii secolo', pp. 165–213, p. 199.

[116] Below, chs. 5–7.

[117] Cracco gives a useful account of the distinction in his 'Premessa' to *Minoritismo e centri veneti nel duecento*, pp. 3–7.

orthodoxy imposed in 1201.[118] They were inspired, to a greater or lesser extent, by similar ideals of *humilitas* as the 'official' Humiliati, or at least they were perceived to be so by those keeping the records, most often the notaries of their commercial transactions.

The problem of notarial perceptions needs to be addressed, since notarial records tend to present a rather different view of the Humiliati from that given in papal letters or in the narrative accounts written by ecclesiastics. The chronicler of Laon, as we have seen, described them as living at home with their families, following a distinctive form of religious life, refraining from lies, oaths and law suits and wearing plain clothing. He also noted their private meetings and preaching in public in defiance of a papal prohibition. The author understandably empha-sised the novel and newsworthy aspects of the new movement, and such activities were also described by Burchard of Ursberg and, with much greater enthusiasm, by Jacques de Vitry in his *Historia occidentalis*, based on his experience of the Humiliati in Milan when passing through in 1216.[119]

By contrast, the picture of the early Humiliati given in the notarial records appears far more traditional. Of course, the activities described in the Chronicle of Laon are not of a kind to be recorded in notarial archives, which generally deal with commercial or administrative transactions: in this case the acquisition of property, the administration of churches, compensation for secular clerics and the concession of rights and revenues such as tithes. By the same token, these details were hardly worthy of comment to the chroniclers, because part of the everyday business of the Church; yet they need emphasising here. Historians, like the contemporary chroniclers, have tended to underline the 'novel' aspects of the new movement, their heretical links, the involvement of the laity in preaching the religious life, the distinctive nature of their new communities. Yet much of the evidence presented here shows a far more 'establishment' experience. Before the condem-nation of 1184 and in at least two cases *after* that date, bishops and senior ecclesiastics, even two popes, were involved in promoting the new communities: giving them the control of churches in Piacenza and Pavia, perhaps hospitals in Bardonezza and Tortona, allowing them the revenue from tithes, as at Viboldone and the Brera, even taking them into the protection of the Church. Elsewhere the direct involvement and support of the secular hierarchy is not so apparent, but the

---

[118] A similar idea was already hinted at by Tiraboschi who, when discussing later examples of nuns who followed the rule of St Augustine, but were called Humiliati, suggested this must be understood 'lato . . . sensu'; *VHM* I, p. 366.

[119] Below, pp. 136, 188–9.

communities clearly possessed churches, as at Rondineto and San Cristoforo Lodi.[120] The lay presence was undoubtedly important in the new movement, and their preaching and rejection of oaths led the Humiliati into conflict with the Curia, as the Chronicle of Laon suggests. Yet, although the priest at Vialone in 1183 is the only one specifically so titled, the involvement with the administration of churches clearly required the presence of other clerics. This is also confirmed by documents such as the concession to Sta Maria Maddalena, requiring the community to accept episcopal constitutions and to attend diocesan synods. One thing these records do prove is that the bishops who approved these grants and the notaries who recorded the transactions found nothing incongruous in calling a group of clerics administering a church Humiliati. The name was never an exclusively lay term and the involvement of priests and clerics early in the history of the movement deserves greater attention. Perhaps because it was easier to distance himself from the dubious early history, the fifteenth-century chronicler John of Brera followed the fourteenth-century Tertiaries in arguing that it had been lay nobles who had founded the movement. This had clear advantages, conferring noble status and providing an unembarrassing explanation for the name. It also put a safe distance between his own clerical status and the condition of the founders of the order who, as he politely put it, were to encounter 'murmurings about them' which led them to seek papal approval.[121] It may well be that the very first Humiliati were indeed lay people. But the extant documents, however sporadic, suggest that there was always a mixture, with a strong clerical element, and that it was this part of the movement which took the lead in approaching the Curia.

These sources also enable us to say something about other aspects of the early movement, including the type and location of houses and the nature of their attitude to poverty. The majority of the communities identified are not city based: the exceptions are the Brera in Milan, San Cristoforo, Lodi and the house planned in Piacenza. The remainder are all situated in very small centres or on major routes, gainsaying the Chronicle of Laon's description of the first Humiliati as *cives* from the *civitates* of *Lombardia*, but at least provisionally supporting Violante's hunch that the movement began in the countryside.[122] These docu-

---

[120] This corrects Guerrini, who argued that the early Humiliati had no chapels or churches of their own; Guerrini, 'Gli Umiliati a Brescia', p. 194.

[121] John of Brera, *Chronicon*, 16, p. 241: 'contra Humiliatos tunc murmurabatur quoniam ipsi in aliquibus errabant'.

[122] Violante, 'Hérésies urbaines et hérésies rurales en Italie', p. 179, and above, p. 36.

ments also reveal that double communities were common and perhaps that some were acquiring increasing organisational stability even in these pre-approval years. Notarial terminology is not a reliable standard, but it is intriguing that the 'men and women living in a house' at the Brera in the winter of 1178 had twenty years later become a *congregatio fratrum* headed by a prelate and engaged in consolidating their ownership of the land around their house, as also occurred at Vialone and Viboldone. This evidence confirms the reflections of previous writers on the 1201 letters: the Humiliati ideal of poverty here seems closer to the traditional monastic and canonical concept of property in common, enabling the individual to be poor, than to any literal interpretation of apostolic poverty.[123] These were religious men and women devoted to humility for God (*Humiliati per Deum*), but buying property to support their communities, as well as administering churches and caring for the sick in hospitals. This was not the abject poverty embraced by Francis of Assisi and his early followers. Was it this moderation which made them easy to integrate with the local secular clergy?

However we answer that question, the Humiliati certainly did fall foul of the ecclesiastical hierarchy and the evidence presented here throws light on the impact of the 1184 decree. Statistics are notoriously unreliable as a measure of medieval phenomena and with such a small sample would be almost meaningless. Although there are perhaps slightly more references to the Humiliati before the 1184 watershed, which might indicate that communities such as Bardonezza were lost as a result of the condemnation, the lack of references could well be because of accidents of survival. Zanoni may be right to assume that the references to Patarines in the area of the Brera in 1186 indicated Humiliati, catching them in the same blanket condemnation this term had acquired, but there was in any case certainly some reluctance to use the name Humiliati after 1184. The failure to do so in 1198 when Suzo Bagutanus purchased land on behalf of the *congregatio* of the Brera is symptomatic, and in the same year Albert Niger's will lacks the earlier suffix *de humiliatis* for the church of San Cristoforo in Lodi. Of particular importance in this context is a reference in the letter sent by Innocent III in 1199 to bishop Adelard of Verona (1188–1214).[124] The pope complains about the treatment of the Humiliati by an archpriest in the diocese of Verona and states that the Humiliati are so-called although the name was unwanted (*qui, licet inviti, a populo Humiliati dicuntur*). His avoidance of the name in the letters of approval in 1201 and in all his

---

[123] Bolton, 'The poverty of the Humiliati', *passim*.
[124] Appendix I, 4; on Adelard see D. Cervato, *Adelardo cardinale, vescovo di Verona (1188–1214) e legato pontificio in terra santa (1189–1191)* (Verona, 1991).

correspondence concerning the order until 1214, seems to reflect a similar sensitivity.[125] Combined with the fall in the number of references to the Humiliati in the 1190s, it seems clear that *Ad abolendam* was gradually taking effect, and that the stricture included in that decree against the mendacious assumption of the name Humiliati had had a direct impact on the name itself. One way to avoid condemnation was to avoid use of any specific name at all. This view is supported by the dramatic contrast between the number of references in the pre-approval phase under discussion here (little more than a dozen) and the large number of houses and communities addressed by Innocent III in 1201. In those letters Innocent refers specifically to Tertiaries in nine places (Milan, Monza, Como, Pavia, Brescia, Bergamo, Piacenza, Lodi and Cremona), to members of the 'monastic' Second order in eight (Milan, Monza, Marlano, Vico, Zerbeto, Pavia, Bergamo and Brescia) and to the four First order houses of Rondineto, Viboldone, Vialone and Lodi.[126] Clearly many Second and Third order communities have escaped all but this papal record, and it may be that discretion had been considered the better part of valour so that the name was avoided while communities continued to flourish.

This argument cannot be conclusive, but it underlines the point that the heretical nature of the pre-approval Humiliati should not be overemphasised. They did not err in matters of dogma, but were condemned for their refusal to stop preaching and holding private meetings and for their attitude to oath-taking. Unlike the Waldensians, there is no evidence for other unorthodox beliefs and practices developing after rejection by the Church. Their attitude to preaching and oath-taking did, of course, make them heretics, but as we should perhaps expect in the north of Italy, where heresy was rife and resistance to prosecuting it even rifer, such activities did not often lead to active persecution, particularly before the imposition of the papal inquisition, realised under pope Gregory IX (1227–41).[127] The example of Verona is the only case of persecution recorded for the Humiliati during the twelfth century and was perhaps the product of special circumstances. The decree *Ad abolendam* was issued there and may have been particularly familiar to local ecclesiastics, who acted upon it. The bishop, Adelard, had attended the council as a canon of the cathedral and had been created cardinal priest of San Marcello by Lucius III in

---

[125] The first papal letter to use the title is Appendix I, 17 (1214).

[126] Appendix I, 7–9; on the identity of Vico and Zerbeto as perhaps in Como, see Alberzoni, ' "Sub eadem clausura sequestrati" ', n. 37.

[127] See Diehl, 'Overcoming reluctance to prosecute heresy in thirteenth-century Italy', pp. 47–66.

1185[128] an indication perhaps that he identified with that pope's policies, though Urban III had also been appointed to the cardinalate by Lucius and acted as a general legate in *Lombardia* in 1184, but seems to have taken a very different stance, at least in his attitude to the Humiliati.[129] The archpriest of whom Innocent complained in 1199 may also have been the archpriest responsible for ordering the expulsion of 'Humiliati and Cathars' from Cerea in the diocese in 1203.[130] Persecution may thus have been the response of a small group and even here the impact cannot have been disastrous, since the first reference to a Humiliati community in Verona dates from 1204, and shows a well-established community, hardly suffering from the ill effects of recent persecution.[131]

The use of the name Humiliati to describe heretics was also to recur in a papal letter for Faenza of December 1206, five years after the order was approved. Earlier that year heretics in the city had been identified as 'poor of Lyons, or even Patarines',[132] but the Patarines were now replaced by the Humiliati: 'Humiliati, Poor of Lyons, or any sectaries of heretical depravity' were to be expelled from the city.[133] The use of the name and the link with heretical depravity need not, however, prove a split in the original movement of the Humiliati. Rather, it may reflect one of two things: either continuing echoes of the text of *Ad abolendam*, where the Humiliati and the Poor of Lyons had been coupled in a list simply intended to identify all 'depraved heretics', or perhaps simple confirmation that the *umiliatismo* of these years included groups on both sides of the orthodox divide.

Elsewhere, the absence of references to the Humiliati in the mid-1190s, and perhaps a reluctance to use the name, suggest that *humiliatus* had become a pejorative epithet, associated with heresy. Perhaps it was this which led the Humiliati to turn to the new pope, Innocent III, and try to silence those who were 'beginning to murmur' against them.

---

[128] He resigned the *titulus* in 1188 on becoming bishop of Verona, but continued to call himself cardinal of the Roman Church; see Robinson, *The Papacy 1073–1198: Continuity and Innovation*, p. 91.

[129] *Ibid.*, p. 168.   [130] See p. 43.

[131] De Sandre Gasparini, 'Movimenti evangelici', 154.

[132] *PL*, 215, cols. 819–20.

[133] Appendix I, 11: 'humiliatos pauperes de Lugduno, seu quoslibet pravitatis haereticae sectatores ...'; see also Bolton, 'Sources', p. 132.

Chapter 3

QUIA IN NULLO PECCABANT: THE INSPECTION AND APPROVAL OF THE HUMILIATI 1199–1201

Today the Humiliati have been received by the Church because they sinned in nothing, except in that they condemned oath-takers.

Tancred.[1]

This gloss on the text of *Ad abolendam* in the *Compilatio prima* sums up the position of the Humiliati at the end of the process of ratification to which they submitted themselves in the first years of the pontificate of Innocent III. It was produced by the canonist Tancred of Bologna (c. 1185–c. 1236), early in the second decade of the thirteenth century (c. 1210–15) and reflects the view of a man well acquainted with Innocent's actions and decisions. He was also responsible for the 'ordinary' gloss on the *Compilatio tertia*, the collection of Innocent's early decretals prepared by Petrus Beneventanus in 1209–10 which, under the title on the restitution of spoils, included *Olim causam*, Innocent's Decretal referring to the Humiliati in Tortona.[2] The same assessment of the Humiliati as once condemned but now accepted is also found in an early (c. 1210) and rather cryptic gloss on *Compilatio tertia* by Tancred's teacher in Bologna, John of Wales (fl. 1210–15).[3] John, however, makes no reference to oath-taking, so this element may have originated with Tancred. It is again found in the slightly later work of another Bolognese canonist, Johannes Teutonicus (c. 1170–1245), who wrote his own gloss on the same Decretal in *Compilatio tertia*

---

[1] Gloss on 1 Comp. 5.6.11 (=X.5.7.9) s.v. 'Humiliati', Admont, Stiftsbibliothek Ms. 22, fo. 72va: 'hodie humiliati ab ecclesia sunt recepti. quia in nullo peccabant. nisi quia iurantes comdempnabant. tancredus'; identical in second recension, Vat lat. 1377 fo. 84vb.

[2] *Olim causam*, 3 Comp. 2.6.2 (X.2.13.12), Appendix 1, 6; see also Brundage, *Medieval Canon Law*, pp. 227–8.

[3] John of Wales, Gloss on 3 Comp. 2.6.2 (=X.2.13.12) s.v. 'Humiliati' (first layer of glosses), Munich, Bayerische Staatsbibliothek. Clm 3879, fo. 187va: 'Humiliati: ar[gumentum] istarum sectam non reprobari, vel supple olim'.

c. 1213–18.[4] Since these men were living and working in northern Italy, they would have been familiar with members of the new order, as many in their audiences must have been. Their writings reflect the approach of canonistic technicians at work producing up-to-date glosses for the classroom, but also provide an insight into contemporary under- standing of where the problem for the Humiliati had lain. Their attitude to oath-taking, not preaching, is picked out as the cause of sin. This reflects the emphasis of Innocent III's letters to the Humiliati, which include long and detailed disquisitions on the need for oath-taking. The canonists' silence over the question of preaching, which had been of particular concern to the drafters of *Ad abolendam* and to the anonymous chronicler of Laon, suggests that by this date Innocent's acceptance of the legitimacy of lay exhortation had not provoked controversy among these lawyers or their audiences.[5]

The process which led to this resolution of the status of the Humiliati, recognition of their orthodoxy and acceptance into the Church had taken over two years to complete. The first Humiliati representatives probably approached the Curia of pope Innocent III in 1198–9 and seem to have returned there in 1200. Their petitions led to careful examination of their proposed way of life (*proposita*) by two papally instituted delegations, whose conclusions were in turn examined and corrected by the pope himself before he issued letters approving the three strands of the new order in June 1201.

The key importance of this process has been recognised in previous studies which, in underlining the novel aspects of the treatment accorded to the new order, have drawn out the significance of the distinction which Innocent recognised between new evangelical groups such as the Humiliati and doctrinal heretics such as the Cathars.[6] Yet of greater interest here is the contribution of the Humiliati leaders themselves, and the reasons for Innocent's choice of particular local churchmen to examine their proposal. After briefly delineating the process itself, this chapter will consider the role of these individuals and their relations, both with each other and with the papacy, and assess the potential contribution of these men to the new order which emerged. Since the sources are fragmentary and often detached from the Humi- liati themselves, whose original proposals do not survive (except in so

---

[4] Gloss on 3 Comp. 2.6.2 (=X.2.13.12) s.v. 'Humiliati', *Johannis Teutonici apparatus glossarum in compilationem tertiam*: 'Set uerum est quod tempore Lucii fuerunt excommunicati, set postea tempore Clementis fuerunt recepti, quia non errabant nisi quod dampnabant iurantes'; see also Brundage, *Medieval Canon Law*, pp. 219–20.

[5] On oaths, see below, pp. 130–2.

[6] Grundmann, p. 73; Maccarone, *Studi*, pp. 284–90; Bolton, 'Innocent III's treatment of the Humiliati', pp. 75–6; Zanoni's work on this has been almost entirely superseded by these studies.

far as they may be discerned from the texts of the papal letters), the contribution of any one party cannot always be established. Nonetheless, as we might expect, close examination of the process demonstrates that developments such as the return of the Humiliati to the Church were as much a result of activity in the provinces as of new policy decisions imposed from Rome. As other episodes in the pontificate of Innocent III show, papal enthusiasm alone was insufficient to carry a project through. What mattered was that the men chosen to carry out his plans were receptive to the pope's ideas, knowledgeable concerning the circumstances in which they were to operate and capable of imposing their will in the localities.

THE LETTERS AND FIRST CONTACTS

The essential chronology for the re-acceptance of the Humiliati into the Church is disclosed in five surviving papal letters. No correspondence on the Humiliati side is extant in the papal records or, apparently, elsewhere.[7] The sequence can therefore be considered complete only in so far as the papal letters seem to develop a logical pattern. Further letters are referred to and we must assume that there were still others, unless the individuals involved were present at the Curia.

In the first letter, *Licet in agro*, of December 1199, Innocent instructs bishop Adelard of Verona to re-examine the members of the movement in his diocese and, if at all possible, to welcome them back into the Church.[8] This is followed in December 1200 by *Licet multitudini credentium*, addressed to the Humiliati themselves, which first mentions their appeal to the papacy and Innocent's delegation of the case to a group of prelates.[9] Finally and most importantly, come the letters of 7, 12 and 16 June 1201: *Incumbit nobis*, *Diligentiam pii patris* and *Non omni spiritui*, which authorise the three strands of the new order, specify certain regulations and detail the processes leading to this approval.[10] Innocent records that after the Humiliati first approached the Curia, he had instituted an enquiry to be undertaken by Albert, bishop of Vercelli, and the Cistercian abbots Peter of Lucedio and S[imon?] of Cerreto. After initial examination and correction of the Humiliati proposals on the pope's behalf, Albert and Peter had sent him a revised version some time before December 1200 (the abbot of Cerreto had died before the case was begun). In the Curia the revisions were re-appraised by a

---

[7] There seems no need to accept Bolton's suggestion, 'Sources', p. 127, that there may have been a 'systematic destruction of Humiliati writings', as there is no evidence for such large-scale hostility.

[8] Appendix I, 4.   [9] Appendix I, 5.   [10] Appendix I, 7–9.

second and higher-ranking group composed of Peter Capuanus, cardinal priest of San Marcello (promoted December 1200), Gratian,
cardinal deacon of SS Cosma e Damiano, and brother Rainier, almost
certainly Rainier of Ponza, the pope's confessor. Finally, Innocent
examined and corrected the proposals himself, before giving his
approval in the summer of 1201.

The most conspicuous point to emerge from examination of these
letters is Innocent's enthusiasm for the Humiliati.[11] The *narratio* of *Licet
in agro* of 1199 to Adelard of Verona reveals that earlier in that year, or
in the previous year, an archpriest in the diocese of Verona, perhaps
believing that he was acting on the authority of a papal letter, had
promulgated a sentence of excommunication against the Humiliati
together with Cathars, Arnaldists and Poor of Lyons. Innocent's
reaction is symptomatic of his support. He pointed out that in his earlier
letter (now no longer extant) he had in fact wished to establish a
distinction between groups like the Humiliati and heretics such as the
Cathars.[12] He accepted the need for vigilance, repeating the call of *Ad
abolendam* 'to eradicate the depravity of heresy', but warned pastors to
beware 'lest they condemn the innocuous or absolve the poisonous',
underlining that it was not his intention 'to condemn the innocuous
along with those who do harm'.[13] Most importantly of all, he also
reminded the bishop that the Humiliati had already sworn obedience 'in
his [Adelard's] hands', showing that some members of the movement in
the diocese of Verona had already sought, and found, reconciliation.[14]

Innocent's attitude was not unlike the policy of Alexander III
towards potential heretics. Alexander had recommended that enquiries
be made 'from people who will know about their manner of life and
their beliefs' and that these should be reported to him.[15] A similar
investigation had been required by the drafters of *Ad abolendam*.[16]
Innocent was thus elaborating on established practice in instructing
Adelard to call the Humiliati themselves back to his presence and
enquire both of them and of others concerning their life and doctrines.

---

[11] Bolton, 'Innocent III's treatment of the Humiliati', pp. 75–6.

[12] On the possibility that the earlier letter had been sent to numerous northern towns as a
statement of 'policy' see Grundmann, pp. 72–3.

[13] Appendix I, 4: 'Similiter etiam licet ad abolendam hereticam pravitatem invigilare debet
sollicitudo pastoris, sollicite tamen debet attendere, ne vel dampnet innoxios vel nocentes
absolvat . . . Quia vero non est nostre intentionis innoxios cum nocentibus condempnare.'
Compare Appendix I, 2.

[14] Appendix I, 4: 'qui etiam in manibus tuis stare mandatis ecclesie iuraverunt'.

[15] See Alexander to Henry, archbishop of Rheims and his colleagues, discussed in Moore, *The
Birth of Popular Heresy*, pp. 80–4; Grundmann, pp. 74–5; Bolton, 'Tradition and temerity', pp.
84–6.

[16] See above, p. 43.

If they were found to be free of error he was to lift the sentence of excommunication and declare them to be 'catholic'. If on the other hand he should find anything heretical in their beliefs or behaviour, yet they were prepared to withdraw from error, then, having caused them publicly to refute their errors and swear an oath 'as it was usual to require from such individuals', he was to give them the benefit of absolution.[17] No mention is made of the possibility that the Humiliati might be unrepentant, refusing to swear or to bow to their bishop's authority, yet as we have seen, the later canonists' glosses suggest that rejection of oaths was acknowledged as their one record-worthy sin.

Alexander III had preferred to risk absolving the guilty than punishing the innocent, warning the archbishop of Rheims against excessive harshness in discipline: '"Be not over just" for "he that violently blows his nose brings out blood."'[18] Innocent III was more inclined than his predecessor to encourage vigorous action against heresy while rewarding orthodoxy. Yet here Innocent advocated caution and careful thought before labelling individuals as heretics. The reasons for Innocent's apparent faith in the orthodoxy of the Humiliati at this early stage are not obvious. He states that, like the other groups condemned by the archpriest, the Humiliati had 'not yet returned to the mandate of the apostolic See', but it is possible that they had already visited him or perhaps even one of his predecessors by this time.[19] John of Brera dates the visit to 1199, his late fifteenth-century successor Marco Bossi dates it to 1198, while a mysterious reference by the canon lawyer Johannes Teutonicus attributes the acceptance of the Humiliati to a Clement, presumably pope Clement III (1187–91).[20] Although essentially inaccurate, since the Humiliati were certainly not given approval before 1199–1200, it is just possible that Johannes or his amanuensis was recording a misunderstood or vaguely remembered earlier visit to the Curia by members of the movement, which might explain Innocent's confidence and enthusiasm. Yet had they indeed approached Innocent himself or a predecessor, it is strange that he made no reference to it and did not ask Adelard to await the response of the Curia. While their heretical character should not be overemphasised, there is no evidence that the Humiliati had yet changed their attitude to either preaching or oath-taking, the grounds for their condemnation in 1184. Yet in the case of Verona, Innocent was not simply withholding judgement

---

[17] Appendix I, 4.   [18] Cited in Moore, *The Birth of Popular Heresy*, p. 84.
[19] As acknowledged by Grundmann, p. 75; Maccarrone, *Studi*, p. 285; Bolton, 'Innocent III's treatment of the Humiliati', p. 74; Alberzoni, 'Gli inizi degli Umiliati', p. 200.
[20] John of Brera, *Excerptum*, 23, p. 341; Marco Bossi, *Chronicon sui humiliatorum ordinis*, pp. 350–1; for Johannes Teutonicus, see above, n. 4.

pending further investigation. Adelard was given the straightforward alternative of declaring the Humiliati catholic or accepting a public refutation of their errors. The pope may have known more about the encounter between Adelard and the Humiliati than the letter reveals and was perhaps encouraged by the knowledge that they had sworn obedience in the bishop's hands. Or his knowledge may have been more immediate. While still a cardinal, Innocent had been concerned with the problem of heresy, as revealed in a letter sent to Henry VI in 1195–6 exhorting him to take action.[21] He had also spent time in north Italy in the 1180s and it is very likely that he knew of the numerous well-integrated communities among the Humiliati which had received the early support of northern churchmen.[22] He now took the opportunities afforded by his office to acknowledge their desire to belong to the Church and willingness to compromise and be corrected.

Whether or not the Humiliati had visited the Curia before his letter to Adelard, some of the details of the negotiations which did eventually take place can now be clarified on the basis of a recent re-examination of the extant text in the Vatican Registers of *Licet multitudini credentium*, the next letter concerning the Humiliati. The transcript in the *Patrologia Latina* omitted crucial information about the addressees of the letter, who can now be shown to have included members of all three strands of the order as they were to be approved in the following year:

L[anfranc] provost of Viboldone, T[rancherius?] provost of Vialone, the chapters of Rondineto and San Cristoforo Lodi and all the brethren of the same profession, the chapter of the Brera and all the brethren of the same profession, and with them, Guy *de Porta Orientale* and all the brethren of his profession with him.[23]

The identity of these three strands as belonging to the First, Second and Third orders respectively is confirmed by later sources. Thus the three separate groups were defined before the intervention of the second delegation and cannot have been determined, as was previously believed, either by the Curia or by Innocent. Rather, they may have been devised by the Humiliati themselves and, as Grundmann argued, reflect the simple sociological distinctions between the types of people involved in the early movement.[24] What they now sought from

---

[21] Maleczek, 'Ein Brief des Kardinals Lothar', pp. 564–76.

[22] On Innocent's earlier career, see Moore, 'Lotario dei conti di Segni', pp. 255–6.

[23] Appendix I, 5; Alberzoni, 'Gli inizi degli Umiliati', p. 201 gives the corrected text; compare *PL*, 214, cols. 921–2 where the phrase referring to the Brera is missing. On the likelihood of T (mistranscribed as J in *PL*) referring to Trancherius, not Tancred, see Alberzoni, '"Sub eadem clausura sequestrati"', pp. 71, 88, n. 21.

[24] Grundmann, pp. 160–1.

Innocent was a means of organising themselves as one institution, and Innocent's letter makes it clear that this desire came from the Humiliati themselves.

The *arenga* includes word play perhaps reflecting the sense of humour noted by Imkamp as typical of the pope's personal involvement.[25] It opens with a passage on the need for believers to be 'of one body and one soul, just as, according to the Apostle, all the faithful are one body in Christ . . .' It goes on, however, to point out the variety of virtues and works and the diversity of offices and orders in the Church, 'in which that is, the different orders fight in order'. The importance of this diversity is then expounded: 'For indeed, in this way, variety does not lead to discord, but rather generates greater concord of souls, leading not to deformity but to seemliness; nor should it be censured but rather commended.'[26] Innocent acknowledges that in some circumstances it is prudent to advocate unity: 'when such diversity or dissension of orders and offices gives rise to scandal or hinders the progress of religion, it is wise to reduce them to a unity of proposal or rather a uniform proposal'.[27] This recognition of the dangers of diversity, however, is presented as coming from the Humiliati themselves, accounting for their appeal to the Curia: 'lest the diversity of your proposals should provoke scandal in any minds or hinder the progress of religion, they [the Humiliati representatives] humbly came to us, petitioning us to take care to bring you to unity by our letters . . .'[28] In response, Innocent now wrote to the whole body of the Humiliati, requesting that they should come together as one 'both in mind and body' and, with the counsel of the prelates he now appointed to assist them, 'modify their proposals to one honest and regular proposal of life'. The clerics were to live under a different rule and unity of regulation (presumably the existing *ordo canonicus*) and laws or rules were to be prescribed for the laity, be they married or living apart, which were to

---

[25] W. Imkamp, *Das Kirchenbild Innocenz' III* (Stuttgart, 1983), pp. 87–8; an example is the untranslatable alliteration of provosts and *proposita* first identified by Maccarrone, *Studi*, p. 286; see below, n. 27.

[26] Appendix I, 5: 'sane quod hujusmodi varietas [PL = veritas] non parit discordiam, sed concordiam magis generat animorum, non deformitatem sed decorem inducit; nec reprehenditur, sed potius commendatur'; Alberzoni, 'Gli inizi degli Umiliati', p. 204 note 45; on *arengae* and their reading and misreading, see Boyle, 'Innocent III and vernacular versions of scripture', pp. 97–107.

[27] Appendix I, 5: 'si quando talis ordinum et officiorum diversitas vel dissensionis parturit scandalum, vel impedit religionis profectum, ad unitatis propositum vel propositi potius unitatem est provide reducenda'.

[28] Appendix I, 5 (Alberzoni, 'Gli inizi degli Umiliati', p. 206 n. 48): 'ne propter diversitatem propositorum [PL: praepositorum] vestrorum scandalum in aliquorum posset mentibus suscitari vel religionis impediri profectus, nos humiliter adierunt, suppliciter postulantes ut vos ad unitatem per nostras curaremus litteras invitare'.

be sent to the Apostolic see, sealed by the Humiliati and the papal delegates, so that they could be both corrected and approved.[29] Finally, Guy *de Porta Orientale* and other 'discreet and suitable men, supporters of religion and lovers of truth and justice', were to be sent to Innocent with their letters, so that they could explain the mind of the Humiliati fully to the pope and, on their return, account for the pope's corrections or approval to the Humiliati.

This passage provides useful clues to curial understanding of the situation leading the Humiliati to approach them. First, the reference to scandal (*scandalum*) is surely resonant of the context of penance for notorious sin, associated as it was with the rituals for public penance and correction.[30] It certainly fits well with Innocent's earlier instruction that Adelard require the Humiliati of Verona to make a public refutation of their errors, symbolically and pragmatically equating the Humiliati with public penitents. The letter also suggests, however, that it was the *fear* of scandal or hindrance to the progress of religion which had led the Humiliati to the Curia, not any actual scandal, though in so far as the letter reports what the Humiliati allegedly said, both sides appear to agree that this scandal would be quite likely to arise. The text also implies that it was the Humiliati who, when faced with this problem, asked the pope to find a means of producing unity among them and that the pope initially accepted this undertaking rather than proposing it himself. Certainly uniformity and unity were issues which appealed to Innocent. In a letter of 19 April 1201 to missionaries in Livonia he invited them, regardless of their different professions as monks and regular canons, to unite under 'one regular form of life and honest habit' so as to avoid scandal, 'lest such differences in your observances and different habits should cause scandal among those to whom you preach one Gospel'.[31] He showed similar enthusiasm for unity years later in his treatment of the women religious of Rome, whom he sought to bring together under one roof.[32] This initial acceptance of the

---

[29] Appendix I, 5 (Alberzoni, 'Gli inizi degli Umiliati', p. 205 n. 47): 'ut vos, filii clerici [PL: dilecti], sub una de cetero regula et regulari unitate vivatis, tam laicis qui cum uxoribus suis vivunt et mulieribus que vivunt cum viris, quam viris et mulieribus aliis, qui vite prioris formidantes deformia et turpia detestantes seorsum vivere referuntur, certas leges vel regulas potius praescribentes'.

[30] See M. Mansfield, *The Humiliation of Sinners: Public Penance in Thirteenth-Century France* (Ithaca, London, 1995).

[31] Discussed in M. Maccarrone, 'I papi e gli inizi della cristianizzazione della Livonia', *Gli inizi del cristianesimo in Livonia-Lettonia* (Vatican City, 1989), pp. 31–80, 78–80; see also his *Studi*, pp. 334–7 and 'Riforma e sviluppo della vita religiosa con Innocenzo III', p. 41.

[32] See B. M. Bolton, 'Daughters of Rome: all one in Christ Jesus!', *Women in the Church*, ed. W. J. Sheils and D. Wood, SCH, 27 (Oxford, 1990), 101–15.

idea of unity for the Humiliati in 1200, however, need prove only how much the idea appealed to him, not that he first proposed it.

Licet multitudini also incidentally provides further information about the early composition of the Humiliati, who included married couples living together and women and men living in communities, but also involved clerics (mistranscribed in *PL* as *dilecti*).[33] Indeed, the clerics were singled out for special responsibility, prescribing 'laws or rules' for the lay members to be indicated to the pope.

The text of *Licet multitudini* makes no mention of heresy, concentrating instead on the public sin of scandal, and the same emphasis is central to *Diligentiam pii patris*, addressed to the Second order in June 1201, though error plays a more prominent role here. The *arenga* begins with the love of a 'dutiful father and the anxious care of a true shepherd', recalling the parables of the Prodigal son, the Lost sheep and the Lost coin.[34] These are given as models for any prelate or especially the pope, 'to whom the sheep of Christ are principally committed' and who must 'foster pious resolve', not only among Catholics who live in ecclesiastical unity, but also in 'those who are believed by some not to follow the path of truth fully in some matters, having corrected those things in which they seem to deviate' (*exorbitare*) and also 'bringing back those who err, because the Lord says that he called not the just but sinners to repentance'. Those who cause scandal in the Church must be 'cut off with apostolic correction' and that which was seen as superstitious must be 'smoothed with the file of ecclesiastical discipline' (*districtio*), so that 'by cutting away what is unessential, what was concealed might come to light and that which *seemed* doubtful might become certain'. The Humiliati have sent messengers to the Curia 'in order to lay to rest, or rather to bury, the scandal' which had been raised against them by many '*believing* that they were not observing ecclesiastical constitutions'.[35] Here scandal is no longer feared, it has been provoked and is not to be tolerated, yet the ambiguity remains. The use of 'believe' and 'seem' which I have italicised here is deliberate, for it was not true error, but scandal raised by others in the Church which was the problem.

The *arenga* of *Non omni spiritui*, to the First order, at first adopts a more harshly explicit tone, warning that not all spirits are to be believed, but must be tested to establish whether they are spirits from God, 'since the Angel of Satan frequently transfigures itself into the Angel of light and many come to us in sheep's clothing who are really rapacious

---

[33] Above, note 29.   [34] Luke 15.   [35] Appendix I, 8 (my italics).

wolves'.[36] Caution is needed in separating the sheep who should return to the fold from the goats, 'in as much as we are often misled by the appearance of virtue, and evil is often covered in the false cloak of truth'. Each individual case must be carefully evaluated, 'in so far as human judgement allows, scrutinising even hidden things, lest we damn the just or absolve the poisonous, lest the good be called bad or the bad good'. Here is an echo of Innocent's letter to Adelard and the justification for the long-drawn-out process to which the Humiliati were subjected. Yet the implication of the approval is of course that the Humiliati who are now returning to the Church are the sheep, not the heretical goats; they are the good who risked being called bad, not the bad who might have been called good. The condemnation of 1184 had led to misunderstanding (confusing sheep and goats) and to scandal, which had hindered the growth of the movement, and it was this which had led the Humiliati to approach Innocent. The papal letter now set the record straight.

In *Licet multitudini credentium* in 1200, Innocent had identified those who visited him as James of Rondineto, Lanfranc of Lodi 'and others' unnamed. As we have seen, the letter is addressed to two other provosts in person: L[anfranc] of Viboldone and T[rancherius?] of Vialone, but only to the chapters of James' and Lanfranc's own houses of Rondineto and San Cristoforo, Lodi.[37] This has been used convincingly to suggest that the letter was drafted while James and Lanfranc were at the Curia.[38] It is indeed possible that the first stage in negotiations had taken place at the Curia for, although Innocent states that he has written to the three local ecclesiastics involved, it is certain that at least one of the three chosen, Peter, abbot of Lucedio, was present at the Curia late in 1200. This is clear from the text of *Olim causam*, issued that year, settling the dispute over property given to the Humiliati by the bishop of Tortona but contested by the Templars, in which Peter of Lucedio is described explaining the problem to the pope *viva voce*.[39] This was a routine discussion of a complex legal question which did not involve the Humiliati directly; nonetheless, it indicates once more that Innocent's knowledge of the movement was not limited to the representations of their named emissaries.

---

[36] Appendix I, 9.

[37] Appendix I, 5; this also shows that Lanfranc came from San Cristoforo Lodi, and that this house became one of the four to govern the order in 1201, not Ognissanti in Borghetto Lodigiano (Fossadolto), as Zanoni, p. 60, had assumed.

[38] Alberzoni, 'Gli inizi degli Umiliati', p. 203 n. 43.   [39] See p. 86.

THE REPRESENTATIVES OF THE HUMILIATI

James of Rondineto and Lanfranc of Lodi came to the Curia as representatives of the Humiliati to ask to be brought into unity. Their authorisation to do so was not questioned. Innocent also met other unnamed members of the movement at this date and summoned to his presence Guy *de Porta Orientale* and other 'suitable and discreet men, cultivators of religion and lovers of truth and justice'.[40] In *Incumbit nobis*, 7 June 1201, superiors of the Third order were listed by initial, but no names or other information survives about any of them. Slightly more can be gleaned about the provosts of the First order. If the superior of Vialone addressed in 1201 is indeed Trancherius, he may be identified as the Trancherius, son of John *de Braida* who had been a minister of the community in 1183, and was therefore a long-standing member of the movement by the turn of the century, though nothing more is known of his career before or after 1201.[41] By contrast, Lanfranc of San Cristoforo Lodi cannot be documented before 1201, but may have been the Lanfranc responsible for the foundation of the house of Ognissanti at Fossadolto on the road to Rome (*strata romea*) between 1201 and 1203 and, as its first provost, 'sent [a proctor] to Rome' to obtain papal privileges for the community and the nearby chapel of San Giorgio given to it by bishop Arderic of Lodi before 1208.[42] Whether or not he is the same individual, Lanfranc of Ognissanti certainly earned episcopal esteem, for at his death, before 1217, the bishop came to pay his respects.[43]

As Alberzoni has recently demonstrated, there is still more evidence concerning the careers and activities, both before and after 1201, of the two remaining representatives named, James of Rondineto and Guy *de Porta Orientale*. This suggests that neither man was likely to have been a mere cypher moulded by papal policy.

James of Rondineto

James is first documented from 1189, as one of the representatives of the men and women in the 'congregation and fraternity of Rondineto' in Como.[44] He is identified as a member of the Rusca family who belonged to the highest level of social and religious life in Como and

---

[40] Appendix I, 5: 'viros idoneos et discretos, cultores religionis et veritatis ac iustitie amatores'.
[41] Above, p. 53.
[42] *VHM* II, p. 190; and see now also Mercatili Indelicato, 'Per una storia degli Umiliati nella diocesi di Lodi', pp. 343–492.
[43] Below, p. 236.   [44] Above, p. 54.

remained associated with the Rondineto community at least until the 1230s and 1240s.[45]

As we have seen, records from 1198, now lost, describe him as provost and he was certainly a cleric or priest.[46] He may also have had some legal training. Between June and December 1208 he acted as one of the papal judges delegate in a long-running dispute over the exercise of parochial rights between, on the one hand, the bishop of Tortona and the archpriest and chapter of San Lorenzo Voghera and on the other, the abbess of the monastery of Sta Maria del Senatore in Pavia and the priest of Sant'Ilario, a dependent chapel of the monastery in Voghera. Documents concerning the case, including hitherto unpublished papal bulls now in the Archivio di Stato in Milan, have recently been edited by Maria Pia Alberzoni.[47] These show that the case had previously been entrusted to a number of judges, including Albert, bishop of Vercelli and his successor Lothar, neither of whom had been able to conclude matters before promotion to higher office. James was now appointed together with the archdeacon of Como, William *de Quadrio*. James was nominated by the abbess of Sta Maria del Senatore and the records suggest that there was understood to be potential danger to the judges should they go to the region in question. The case was therefore heard in Como. The bishop of Tortona failed to send representations and the case was determined on the evidence presented to the earlier judges. Sentence in favour of the monastery was given in December 1208. A second papal letter, however, sent in April 1209, reveals that the bishop's party used a standard ruse to avoid judgement, rejecting the authority of James of Rondineto, and the case was once again referred to new judges, Aliprand, bishop of Vercelli, and the archdeacons of Milan and Pavia.[48]

Although his authority as a judge was rejected by the losing side, this case shows James acting as an eminent figure in wider ecclesiastical affairs and this prominence is also to be found in his relations with his own order. In April 1211 he was at Trezzo in the retinue of Gerard *de Sesso*, the newly appointed papal legate and cardinal bishop elect, and witnessed, perhaps petitioned, Gerard's letter warning the ecclesiastics of his legation not to prevent the Humiliati holding meetings (*colloquia*

---

[45] 'Le carte di Santa Maria Vecchia di Como', ed. Biondi *et al.*, documents 16, 17, 21; Alberzoni, 'Gli inizi degli Umiliati', p. 210 n. 58; *VHM* II, p. 22; Alberzoni, 'Giacomo di Rondineto', pp. 117–62.

[46] Above, p. 55.

[47] Alberzoni, 'Giacomo di Rondineto', pp. 117–62 and see appendix I, 13 and 15.

[48] *Ibid.*; see also G. G. Merlo, '"Capella cum adiacente parrochia": Sant'Ilario di Voghera tra xii e xiii secolo', *Bollettino storico-bibliografico subalpino*, 85 (1987), 325–86.

sive parlamenta).[49] It is perhaps a sign of James' efficient and prompt diplomacy that the status of Gerard as legate and cardinal bishop elect of Albano is first definitively recorded in this letter, so that responding to the petition of the Humiliati provost may have been one of Gerard's first acts on acquiring the legation.

James is also named first in a list of the witnesses hearing a dispute between Obizo, bishop of Parma, and his chapter brought before Gerard in the bishop's chapel in Parma in June 1211.[50] Although the reason for his presence on this occasion is not otherwise clarified, once more James is revealed moving in circles stretching far beyond the immediate confines of his own city and apparently enjoying the support of a prelate concerned with the Church in the north as a whole. To some extent this reflects status acquired after the approval of 1201, yet there is other evidence that James had also been a good diplomat in the papal Curia in 1200–1. Perhaps it was because he was impressed by James that Innocent III singled out Rondineto to receive the only gift for a northern church recorded in the papal biography, the *Gesta Innocentii*, completed in 1208. Rondineto received a gift of precious vestments suited for a community of canons, including two chasubles (one red and purple, the other black and purple), a red dalmatic with a saffron cross, a red tunic decorated with fine small gold work, an orphrey which was 'decently decorated' and a silk stole with an orphrey.[51]

Such generosity suggests that James had played a major role in negotiations at the Curia at the turn of the century, and his prominence both in the order and on the wider stage remains apparent until 1211. His continuing authority within the wider Church is again documented in November 1218 when he was one of those appointed by cardinal Hugolino, papal legate in the north (later pope Gregory IX), to receive the oath of the citizens of Vercelli to promote peace and concord in preparation for the crusade.[52] In the intervening years, however, James had apparently left Rondineto for an obscure house whose affiliation is not documented: the legate's commission refers to him as 'late provost of Rondineto and now of Dorano'.[53] No reason is given for this transfer from the major house at Como, but the new responsibility he took on

---

[49] Appendix I, *16, 19 April 1211; Cipollone, 'Gerardo da Sesso vescovo eletto', pp. 223–39 and 'Gerardo da Sesso, legato apostolico', p. 362 n. 22.

[50] Affò, *Storia di Parma*, III, appendix, document 30, pp. 326–7, from the chapter archive of Parma: 'In capella Parmensis Episcopi presentibus Domino Jocobo [sic] preposito de Reudenaria [sic] Guarnerio de Carillo Novariensi Canonico Magistro Jacobo Novariensi atque Uberto Monacho sancte Marie Fontis vivi testibus de lite et controversia . . .'.

[51] *Gesta*, col. ccviii.

[52] Alberzoni, 'Giacomo di Rondineto', p. 150.   [53] *Ibid.*

makes it appear unlikely to have been induced by either frailty or dishonour.

Guy de Porta Orientale[54]

The activities of Guy *de Porta Orientale* are, like those of James of Rondineto, well documented, and he has frequently attracted the attention of past historians, especially those keen to demonstrate that there was an important 'noble' element in the new order.[55] Guy came from a family of indubitably high status in Milanese economic and ecclesiastical life. Arnolf III, archbishop of Milan in the late eleventh century (1093—7), may have belonged to the same family and other kin were active in property deals in Milan and beyond throughout the twelfth century.[56] As we have seen, there may also have been some form of link between the family, in the person of Guy's father of the same name (died c. 1172), and St Bernard's visit to Milan in 1135. This has also been associated with evidence that the elder Guy gave generously to Bernard's foundation of Chiaravalle, thereby confirming the close ties between the family and the Milanese church, a tradition continued by his son.[57]

The first indisputable records for the activities of the younger man however, date only from December 1172, when they show him already involved with the Milanese church. Guy, 'son of the late Guy known as *de Porta Orientale*', returned tithes on lands in the area of Varese to archbishop Galdinus della Sala, who then ceded them to Peter *de Bussero*, archpriest of Monte Velate above Varese, for 160 silver lire.[58] Two years later, in June 1174, he and his brother Adderardus invested Conrad Menclozzi with lands in Linate, to the south-east of Milan.[59]

---

[54] I have not been able to consult an article by Maria Pia Alberzoni on Guy *de Porta Orientale* forthcoming in *Il monachesimo italiano nell'età comunale (1088—1250)*. *Atti del convegno del Centro storico benedettino italiano, Pontida 3—6 September 1995*.

[55] *VHM* I, pp. 44—7, 194—6; Zanoni, pp. 272—5; Grundmann, p. 160; Bolton, 'Innocent III's treatment of the Humiliati', p. 79; Tagliabue, 'Gli Umiliati a Viboldone', pp. 11—15; Alberzoni, 'Gli inizi degli Umiliati', pp. 212—17; see also Paolini, 'Le Umiliate al lavoro', p. 234 n. 12.

[56] Fonseca, 'Arnolfo', pp. 284—5; Tagliabue, 'Gli Umiliati a Viboldone', p. 14; A. Lucioni, 'La cella di S. Sepolcro di Ternate e il monastero di Sant'Ambrogio', *Il monastero di Sant'Ambrogio nel medioevo. Convegno di studi nel XII centenario: 784—1984* (Milan, 1988), pp. 395—412, 404 n. 47; cited Alberzoni, 'Gli inizi degli Umiliati', p. 217 n. 78.

[57] Above, p. 10; Giulini, *Memorie spettanti alla storia . . . di Milano*, III, pp. 226—7, refers to 'un vecchio codice', from Chiaravalle seen by Puricelli, recording numerous donations by Guy.

[58] Alberzoni, 'Gli inizi degli Umiliati', p. 215.

[59] *Pergamene milanesi dei secoli xii—xiii*, VI, pp. 25—6; on the Menclozzi family, who had extensive lands in this area eventually acquired by the Humiliati at San Pietro Gessate, see R. Perelli Cippo, 'Sulla linea dei cistercensi. Accordi per la costruzione di una roggia in un documento milanese del 1266', *Nuova rivista storica*, 70 (1986), 159—73, 160—7.

Guy may have been able to win the support of ecclesiastics for the first Humiliati. It has been suggested that his action in backing Viboldone in 1176 broke down the opposition of the provost of the *pieve*, who stood to lose both financially and in reduction of his flock.[60] Certainly the agreement was considered important, as demonstrated by the attendance of several senior churchmen, including the archdeacon Hubert Crivelli, later pope Urban III.[61]

Guy may himself have been a member of the Third order. He was never called either *frater* or *humiliatus*, yet the formula of Innocent III's letter, *Licet multitudini credentium*, addressed to members of the First and Second orders and then to Guy and the brothers 'of his profession with him' (*et omnibus fratribus eius professionis cum ipso*), must surely be interpreted as including Guy among the lay Third order.[62] Tiraboschi, who did not know this letter, assumed that Guy was a Tertiary and it would certainly help to explain the pope's specific invitation to him and other 'suitable and discreet men', to come to the Curia with the letters of the Humiliati, in December 1200.[63] The memory of this visit may have lain behind a description by Galvano Fiamma of Guy dining with the pope and receiving water from him.[64]

It was undoubtedly this activity as a successful advocate for the new movement, duly approved by Innocent in 1201, which won Guy special status in the order. Two late accounts highlight his role. A letter of confirmation issued by pope Benedict XI in 1304 describes Guy's contribution as inspired by pious intentions.[65] Eighteen years later, the compiler of the *Instrumentum transactionis* which includes the 1176 Viboldone agreement, prefaced the text with praises of Guy: describing him as 'a noble and powerful man . . . a great *Capitaneus* and fearing God, who built several houses of religious and especially houses of the Humiliati brethren'.[66] There is as yet no direct evidence for this claim that Guy built religious houses, but as well as links with Viboldone, Fiamma associated him with the house of San Giovanni in the Porta Orientale area of Milan.[67] In the fourteenth century and later, he was

[60] Tagliabue, 'Gli Umiliati a Viboldone', p. 14; above, p. 46.   [61] Above, *ibid.*

[62] Above, p. 69; Alberzoni, 'Gli inizi degli Umiliati', p. 216, argues that Guy was not a member of the Humiliati.

[63] Above, p. 71.

[64] Galvano Fiamma, *Manipulus florum*, col. 632; on Galvano, see above, pp. 8–10.

[65] Benedict XI, *Le registre de Benoît XI*, II, pp. 499–500 no. 817; cited Tagliabue, 'Gli Umiliati a Viboldone', p. 14; *VHM* I, p. 195.

[66] *Instrumentum Transactionis* (above, p. 45): 'Quondam nobilis et potens vir Dominus Guido de Porta Orientali, qui fuit magnus Capitaneus et timens Deum, et qui construxit quamplures domos religiosorum et maxime domos fratrum Humiliatorum'.

[67] For Fiamma's account, above, p. 9.

venerated as blessed and by the sixteenth century was acclaimed as founder of the Third order.[68]

Beyond the documents of 1176 and 1200–1, there is other evidence to suggest that Guy may have been promoting the Humiliati. In June 1193 he was appointed one of four executors in the will of Castella, widow of Spandilatte *de Senedogo*. The executors were instructed to distribute her property to the poor as they saw fit.[69] In view of the fact that, fifteen years later, in 1208, Castella donated her house to the local Humiliati of the *Senedogo*, it has been suggested that the *pauperes* indicated in the document of 1193 might have been *pauperes Christi* or in other words, in this case the Humiliati.[70] Whether or not this had been Castella's intention in 1193, Guy may well have had some role in her later decision to make her bequest to the 'Humiliati women who now live in the house of the Humiliati of the Senedogo and will come to live in this house' (*femine humiliate que modo stant in casa Umiliatorum de Sinedochio et que venient stare in ipsa casa*).[71] We cannot know whether she chose to join the community herself as Alberzoni has also suggested, but Guy's role behind the scenes is certainly plausible.[72]

The last extant record concerning Guy once more implies that he held a prominent position within the movement of the Humiliati. On 3 July 1209, brother Otto *de Casteliono*, minister of the Brera, and brother Turbandus of the *domus sancti Maurilii* in Milan sold a farm (*sedimen*) in Pioltello to eight Humiliati sisters of the *domus braide de Rancate*. The farm had been acquired by a brother Airoldus on behalf of Guy *de Porta Orientale* 'and all the Humiliati and Humiliate of the kingdom of Italy'.[73] This unusual terminology is not repeated in other documents and the precise status of Guy is not made clear, but he was being associated with the Humiliati in what was probably intended as a comprehensive manner. He was also acting in close collaboration with a minister of the Brera, a house of the Second order. Whether or not he

---

[68] *VHM* I, pp. 193–4 citing 1504 missal: 'Beatus Guido de Mediolano, qui hujus Religionis fundator extitit'.

[69] Zanoni, p. 273; Piacitelli, 'La carità negli atti di ultima volontà milanesi del xii secolo', p. 174 and document 17.

[70] Piacitelli, 'La carità negli atti di ultima volontà', p. 174 note 26; Alberzoni, 'Gli inizi degli Umiliati', p. 216 n. 75; the document, now in Halle, is catalogued in 'Documenti relativi a monasteri padani nel fondo "Morbio"', pp. 5*–10*; on the status of the 'domus de Senedogo' as a double house, probably belonging to the Second order, see Alberzoni, *Francescanesimo a Milano nel duecento*, p. 124 n. 33; the term 'Senedogo' used to describe both Spandilatte and the Humiliati house, suggests that this area of Milan was associated with a *xenodochium* or hospital.

[71] Alberzoni, 'Gli inizi degli Umiliati', p. 216 n. 75; Tagliabue, 'Gli Umiliati a Viboldone', p. 31 n. 33.

[72] Alberzoni, 'Gli inizi degli Umiliati', p. 216 n. 75.

[73] Zanoni, pp. 274–5: 'et omnium Humiliatorum et Humiliatarum regni Italie'.

was himself a Tertiary, these ties tend to confirm Guy's determining role in the early years, linked with all three elements of the order in the area of Milan.

Both Guy *de Porta Orientale* and James of Rondineto were active on behalf of the Humiliati as a whole, effective diplomats and well equipped to put the Humiliati's case before the papal delegates.[74] The acceptance of such representatives marks a significant point of arrival in the development of the Humiliati as an order for, although not yet officially recognised, it reveals that the movement had acquired the central organisation necessary to claim such an identity and to appoint proctors. In spite of their diverse proposals, the three strands were demonstrating the ability to take collective action and it was to this body that Innocent addressed himself in *Licet multitudini credentium*, providing a progress report on events at the Curia to be sent to those remaining behind in the north.

This view of the Humiliati as an emerging order contrasts strongly with the impression of diversity and transience apparent in the evidence available for the twelfth-century experience of the Humiliati. It would be unwise in view of this to posit a clearly defined structure, or to date it much before the end of the twelfth century. Indeed, the continued problems after 1201 suggest that widespread acknowledgement of the rule was not achieved until much later.[75] Nonetheless, this contrast between the notarial and papal records highlights the importance of combining the two. While the notarial records show diversity and only intermittent evidence for all but a few key houses, the papal record suggests that a common purpose and a common identity (or at least a need for one) was beginning to be accepted. It is not possible to trace the beginnings of this process, but James of Rondineto and Guy *de Porta Orientale* were surely key agents in its successful promotion.

THE PROCESS OF APPROVAL

The Humiliati proctors certainly could not have anticipated the nature of Innocent III's response. They had asked him for some sort of letter of approval to encourage them to unity, but Innocent had appointed a full enquiry, not necessarily a welcome prospect. There were of course precedents for this recourse to judge-delegates, both in the work of preceding popes and during Innocent's own pontificate. The use of apostolic legates to promote papal decrees and policy in both political

---

[74] See now Alberzoni, 'Giacomo di Rondineto', pp. 152–4 for the suggestion that James Rusca and John of Meda may have been the same man.
[75] Below, chs. 5–7.

and ecclesiastical fields had seen continuous growth since the pontificate of Gregory VII (1073–85), who had first used them as an instrument of reform.[76] The desire to exploit the wisdom of an external authority had increasingly been fulfilled by the use of Cistercians who had given Alexander III support during the schism and crisis of 1159–77. Whilst certainly experts in local affairs, Cistercian abbots were perhaps more likely than bishops to be able to hold aloof from local politics, since they were 'in' but not 'of' the diocese in which their houses were established, and thus might find it easier to impose their authority. Innocent himself had already used Cistercian abbots in cases of doubtful orthodoxy, both to examine a group from Metz accused of heresy and to counter the Albigensians in Languedoc.[77]

The *Gesta* refers to a parallel situation. Innocent appointed 'prudent visitors' to examine carefully the life and customs of the Church and its prelates in various provinces in order to encourage reform and the elimination of abuses.[78] His letters often reveal the names of these appointees. Naturally they were men whose views on Church discipline coincided with his own, and frequently they were personally known to him. They included Gerard *de Sesso*, bishop Lothar of Vercelli (1205) and Siccard, bishop of Cremona (d. 1215).[79] Peter of Lucedio was also often involved and his collaboration with Albert of Vercelli on behalf of Innocent in examination of the Humiliati proposals should probably be seen as an earlier phase in the policy of appointing 'visitors' for the reform of the Church in the north, itself later replaced by the use of apostolic legates.[80]

This use of local expertise is paralleled in Innocent's treatment of the Trinitarians, whose rule he approved in 1198.[81] When John of Matha approached the pope and presented his proposal for a new order to ransom christians captured by the infidel, Innocent referred the question to Odo, bishop of Paris (1197–1208), and Absalom, abbot of the Augustinian house of St Victor (1198–1203).[82] These men examined John's intentions and wrote to Innocent, sending him a copy of the new rule. Innocent then made a few additions and allowed John himself to

[76] Robinson, *The Papacy 1073–1198*, p. 146.
[77] Boyle, 'Innocent III and vernacular versions of scripture', pp. 103–5; Robert of Saint-Marien, *Chronicon*, p. 271; Vicaire, *St Dominic and his Times*, p. 82.
[78] *Gesta*, cols. 172–3.
[79] For example, above, pp. 75–6; on Lothar see now Alberzoni, 'Innocenzo III e la riforma della chiesa in "Lombardia"', pp. 145–50.
[80] *Ibid.*, passim.   [81] Zanoni, p. 92 n. 1.
[82] *Register*, I, 481, p. 704; on Odo, see Robert of St-Marien, *Chronicon*, p. 272 and de Saint-Marthe et al., *Gallia christiana*, VII, cols. 78–86, 672–3.

do so, before approving it in December 1198.[83] The parallels with the case of the Humiliati are instructive: the use of local men, careful perusal of their conclusions, further consultation with the interested party and finally the papal statement. The differences are equally illuminating. Maleczek has recently argued that everything which the pope considered important came before the cardinals as an advisory body.[84] By this standard, the approval of the Trinitarians, which was not referred to the cardinals as a whole, was less 'important', perhaps because less problematic, than that of the Humiliati.

Notwithstanding a certain trepidation, which all petitioners must have felt at the prospect of being examined by eminent and highly trained churchmen, the method chosen by Innocent had some points to recommend it to the Humiliati. Not least was the consideration that the bishop of Vercelli and the two abbots were reasonably accessible in physical terms, perhaps reducing the number of long and expensive journeys to the Curia to present their case. This treatment also appears favourable when compared with Innocent's approach to the canonisation process for Gilbert of Sempringham (d. 1189), finalised in January 1202. This first involved a local enquiry begun in 1200 under the auspices of archbishop Hubert Walter of Canterbury. A dossier of material, including a short life of the saint, reports of his miracles, and letters supporting his cult from the archbishop, King John, numerous bishops and abbots, was then taken to Rome by two Gilbertine canons who, after a difficult journey, arrived in the city in the heat of August 1201. Yet, despite the distances and difficulties involved, Innocent sent them back to obtain more evidence and to bring real witnesses to testify to Gilbert's miracles in his presence and under oath.[85] Gilbert was finally canonised after a second enquiry and further messengers had been sent to Rome, including five canons and several laymen who had witnessed miracles themselves.[86]

Others were perhaps more fortunate and found the route to approval simpler, as the treatment of Francis, aided by bishop Guy of Assisi (1204–28) and Cardinal John of St Paul, was to show.[87] Nor was Francis unique in the support he received from the episcopate: the case of the little-known order established in Val des Choux in the diocese of Langres was entirely managed by a friend of Innocent's, Guy de Poré,

---

[83] *Register*, I, p. 703.   [84] Maleczek, *Kardinalskolleg*, p. 319.

[85] Innocent III, *Selected Letters of Pope Innocent III Concerning England*, pp. 26–32; *The Book of St Gilbert*, pp. lxii–lxiii.

[86] The process is now best summarised in B. Golding, *Gilbert of Sempringham and the Gilbertine Order* (Oxford, 1995), pp. 60–5.

[87] See F. E. Andrews, 'Innocent III and evangelical enthusiasts: the route to approval', *Innocent III and his World*, ed. J. C. Moore (forthcoming, Hofstra, 1999).

cardinal bishop of Palestrina and archbishop of Rheims.[88] Guy had come across the community while travelling through the diocese as bishop elect. Having carefully inquired into their merits, the new bishop wrote to Innocent describing their life and petitioning him for approval on their behalf, which the pope duly gave in February 1205.[89] As with the Trinitarians, however, the regular life which this community of monks adopted (described by Jacques de Vitry as reminiscent of both Cistercian and Carthusian practices) did not raise the same difficulties presented by the Humiliati.[90] They had not been condemned by Lucius III and there was no question of uniting clerics, monastics and married couples in the same structure. It was perhaps these last considerations, as well as the potential or real scandal aroused, which caused Innocent to ensure that in the case of the Humiliati a comprehensive investigation was carried out.

The first delegates

Of the three men chosen by Innocent to conduct the first enquiry into the *proposita* of the Humiliati, the abbot of Cerreto remains the most elusive. He was employed by Innocent to intervene in a dispute concerning the cathedral canons of Milan in February 1199, but there is no trace of his action on the pope's behalf in any other extant letter.[91] His abbey lay within the diocese of Lodi, not far from the important Humiliati community of San Cristoforo which sent Lanfranc to petition Innocent in Rome. This and the abbot's Cistercian credentials may well have recommended him to Innocent. Nonetheless, his contribution cannot have been substantial, since by the time the Humiliati were ready to present their proposals for examination, he had already 'gone the way of all flesh'.[92]

It was usual in letters of delegation to stipulate that if one party could not undertake the task in hand the others, or occasionally one alone, should continue. Certainly in legislative terms Albert of Vercelli and Peter of Lucedio, even without the abbot of Cerreto, were eminently suited to the task. They could bring to bear not only local expertise but monastic, canonical and episcopal understanding of the needs of the Church and the duties and rights of those within it. Moreover Albert and Peter were not strangers to each other. The abbey of Lucedio lay within the diocese of Vercelli and they had acted together as papal

---

[88] On Guy see de Sainte-Marthe *et al.*, *Gallia Christiana*, IX, cols. 101–4; on the Valiscaulians see A. Dimier, 'Val des Choux', *DIP* IX (1997), cols. 1671–2.
[89] *Register*, VII, 218.   [90] Vitry, *HO*, 17, pp. 120–1, appendix, p. 297.
[91] *Register*, I, 563.   [92] Appendix I, 9.

The early Humiliati

delegates on a number of occasions, starting perhaps in January 1196, when pope Celestine III commissioned them to settle a dispute between the canons of Oulx and the monks of San Giusto of Susa.[93]

During the first years of Innocent's pontificate Albert in particular was frequently employed as his representative, reflecting both Innocent's trust and his recognition that Albert enjoyed authority and respect beyond his diocese.[94] In September 1198, for one example among many, Innocent involved Albert in a case concerning the cathedral chapter of Milan, where a falsified bull had been used in the appointment of a canon (the bull had been removed from another letter and re-attached).[95] Various letters and references in the *Gesta* underline the importance that Innocent attached to the issue of forgery.[96] It is indicative of his confidence in Albert that this matter should be delegated to him.

The origins of this cordial relationship with Rome can be traced back over most of Albert's career as a bishop, if not before. He was a regular canon at Sta Croce Mortara in the Lomellina and he became provost there in 1180.[97] Pope Lucius III appointed him, together with Boniface, Superior of the order of Sta Croce Mortara and bishop of Novara, to find a solution for the long-standing dispute between the bishop of Tortona and the monastery of Senatore in Pavia, over the rights of the chapel of Sant'Ilario in Voghera (the case later entrusted briefly to James of Rondineto).[98] Thus his career as an ecclesiastical judge began early. In 1184 he was elected bishop of Bobbio, but he was transferred to Vercelli early in 1185, before his consecration.[99] He was certainly efficient in both sees, obtaining privileges from both Urban and Lucius III which confirmed his episcopal authority.[100] He was also active in Church affairs at both provincial and diocesan level. In August 1198 he was one of the electors who approved the translation to the see of Pavia of Bernard, bishop of Faenza, a distinguished canon lawyer and

---

[93] *Oulx*, 207, pp. 215–17.
[94] On Albert's career see now Mosca, *Alberto Patriarca di Gerusalemme* (Rome, 1996).
[95] *Register*, I, 349; for similar cases see *ibid.*, 37, 53, 187.
[96] *Gesta*, col. 85; Poole, *Lectures on the History of the Papal Chancery*, pp. 143–61.
[97] Pezza, *L'ordine mortariense*, pp. 11, 45; Bull, 'Canonici regolari di Sta Croce di Mortara', cols. 145–7; Mornacchi, 'Aspetti della vita comune presso i canonici regolari mortariensi in Genova', pp. 154–62; 'I necrologi eusebiani', ed. Colombo, pp. 6–8.
[98] F. Dessilani, 'Ricerche su Bonifacio preposito generale dell'ordine mortariense e vescovo di Novara (1159–1194)', *Aevum*, 63 (1989), 225–47; Pezza, *L'ordine mortariense*, p. 53. See above, p. 75.
[99] Minghetti, 'L'episcopato vercellese di Alberto durante i primi anni del xiii secolo', pp. 99–112.
[100] *Italia pontificia*, VI/2, p. 244; *Bobbio*, II, p. 204; *Acta pontificum romanorum inedita*, III, 385, pp. 338–9, 390, pp. 341–2.

decretalist.[101] This must represent the tip of the iceberg in terms of his effective involvement in such issues. In his own diocese he appointed a theologian to teach in the Cathedral chapter, set up an annual diocesan synod and introduced revised statutes for a group of canons in Biella.[102]

In the 1180s, Albert appears to have identified strongly with the imperial party, which makes his later authority under Innocent rather more interesting. As early as January 1185, while Urban was blocked in Verona by imperial forces, Albert, as bishop elect of Bobbio, had witnessed an imperial bull for Sta Giulia, Brescia and in 1187 he witnessed a diploma of Henry [VI]'s at the troubled diet of Borgo San Donnino.[103] In the early 1190s his support for Henry VI, who returned south after a three-year absence early in 1191, became conspicuous. Often together with Boniface of Novara, he was regularly in the imperial entourage. In February 1191 he was at the imperial diet in Lodi, travelled south with Henry in April and in November and December went with him to Genoa, Milan and back to Lodi.[104] He witnessed numerous imperial bulls and was rewarded for his perseverance with imperial confirmation of the property of the cathedral of Sant'Eusebio, Vercelli.[105] In 1194 and 1195 Albert was again with Henry and in the autumn of 1196 was chosen to join Markward of Anweiler and others in a planned embassy to pope Celestine III to improve imperial–papal relations.[106] The sudden change in circumstances caused by the deaths of both Henry VI in September 1197 and Celestine III in January 1198, however, put an end to Albert's close association with the imperial party. He had already returned to his diocese by June 1197 and there was no further contact.[107]

In the light of Albert's imperial associations, in particular those with Markward, whom Innocent was to describe as the new Saladin, he might be considered an unlikely choice as papal representative in the delicate negotiations with the Humiliati.[108] Yet the necrology of his cathedral church of Sant'Eusebio in Vercelli describes him as a most faithful mediator between the Roman Church and the empire, winning

---

[101] *Register*, I, 326; on Bernard, see Pennington, *Pope and Bishops*, pp. 89, 96–100 and below, p. 94.

[102] *Vercelli, Capitolare*, 564, pp. 320–2 (4 April 1194); Savio, *Gli antichi vescovi d'Italia*, II/1, p. 485; see now also, Mosca, *Alberto Patriarca di Gerusalemme*, pp. 271–96 and appendix 5.

[103] Savio, *Gli antichi vescovi d'Italia*, I, p. 484; 'Die Regesten des Kaiserreiches unter Heinrich VI 1165(1190)–1197', ed. Baaken and Baaken, 44.

[104] *Ibid.*, 116, 148, 179–83, 190–1, 193, 195, 197.   [105] *Ibid.*, 191.

[106] *Ibid.*, 334, 353, 355–6, 370–2, 451–2, 535–6, 538–43, 545–6, 551–2, 569, 573; T. C. Van Cleve, *Markward of Anweiler and the Sicilian Regency* (Princeton, 1937), p. 64.

[107] *Vercelli, arcivescovile*, 23 (19 June 1197).

[108] *Register*, II, 212; E. Kennan, 'Innocent III and the first political crusade: a comment on the limitations of papal power', *Traditio*, 27 (1971), 231–49.

the love of both pope and emperor.[109] This optimistic account may well reflect how his pursuit of the imperial party was understood by his contemporaries: not as a rejection of the papal view, but rather as a pragmatic acknowledgement of the dual role of a bishop, tied to both pope and emperor. Precisely because he had travelled widely and was a skilful politician, winning favours from both sides, and always with the advantage of his diocese in mind, Albert could be expected to under-stand the delicate issues of authority as well as of orthodoxy involved. Furthermore, a bishop who had been not only keen to promote episcopal authority but had also succeeded in winning a certain amount of autonomy from imperial rule by the pursuit of imperial privileges would surely have been welcome to Innocent.[110]

As a bishop with established political and pastoral authority, Albert was an excellent choice for Innocent to have made and Peter, abbot of Lucedio from 1184 to 1205, seems to have been an equally active figure.[111] Lucedio was one of the major Cistercian houses of northern Italy and its abbot was a powerful and influential figure in Lombard affairs, a role reflected as we have seen in his involvement in trying to resolve the dispute between the bishop of Tortona and the Templars of *Lombardia* over a house and oratory given to the Humiliati by bishop Hugh (1183–93).[112] The dispute was long winded and complex and was only settled in 1200, after it had been referred by Innocent III to two cardinal auditors, John, cardinal priest of Santo Stefano in Celio-monte, and Hugolino, cardinal deacon of Sant'Eustachio (later pope Gregory IX).[113] The sentence was significant enough to be included in Gregory IX's Decretals. Its importance here, however, is because it provides evidence that Peter was at the Curia late in 1200 and that he was equipped to explain legal decisions to the pope *viva voce*.[114]

In April 1199, Albert and Peter were among ten prelates, including the archbishop of Milan, chosen by Innocent to try and resolve a long-running dispute between Parma and Piacenza over Borgo San Donnino, part of the pope's bid to establish peace in the West in preparation for the crusade. Indeed, the letter was addressed to Peter, who seems thereby to have been accorded particular authority.[115] A

---

[109] 'I necrologi eusebiani', p. 7.

[110] On this see Ambrosioni, 'Monasteri e canoniche', p. 629.

[111] On the problems of identification of Peter, see J. C. Moore, 'Peter of Lucedio (Cistercian Patriarch of Antioch) and pope Innocent III', *Römische Historische Mittelungen*, 29 (1987), 221–49.

[112] Appendix I, 6.   [113] Maleczek, *Kardinalskolleg*, pp. 107–9, 126–33.

[114] Appendix I, 6: 'salva ei quaestione proprietatis, de qua in hoc iudicio nihil est actum, sicut praedictus abbas de Locedio nobis exposuit viva voce'.

[115] *PL*, 214, col. 580; *Register*, II, 39.

month later, on 24 May 1199, they were involved in trying to settle another dispute, that between the monastic and canonical communities of Sant'Ambrogio in Milan.[116] This had lasted intermittently since the late eleventh century and revolved around the exercise of the care of souls, the rights and duties of the two communities in celebrating the liturgy and questions of furnishings and light in the basilica. Innocent had ordered Philip *de Lampugnano*, archbishop of Milan, to resolve the quarrel in March 1198, but Philip had been slow to act, occasioning Innocent's irritation, and events had finally exploded into a riot in the basilica itself in December 1198.[117] The pope turned to Albert and Peter as external judges, whose authority would not be undermined by involvement in the political factions of Milan, in which Philip seems to have been particularly embroiled.

The details of the arbitration process have recently been reconstructed[118] and are of interest here because they may form a partial model for the contemporary treatment of the Humiliati. Both parties in the dispute were required to take an oath submitting themselves to the eventual decisions of the two judges and a preliminary meeting of all parties was convened on 21 May 1200. Bargaining continued with depositions by both sides throughout the following year, leading to a definitive sentence only eighteen months later, in November 1201. Unable to resolve the fundamental question of the care of souls, the judges limited themselves to finding separate solutions for various points in dispute, including chopping down trees which blocked the entry of light into certain windows of the basilica. The effect of their decisions nonetheless left the canons in a strong position, as the monks did not achieve the wider rights they had demanded. Perhaps inevitably after decades of dispute, neither side was satisfied, and they appealed once more to the pope. Innocent, however, taken up with crusade preparations, cut short the appeal and demonstrated his faith in his judges by simply confirming their sentence in September 1202.

Innocent's good relations with Albert and Peter and the reasons behind his choice, may be further illustrated by brief consideration of their careers after 1201. Both men continued to act as auditors in a variety of disputes.[119] In 1203 Albert was appointed as one of the

---

[116] Ambrosioni, 'Controversie tra il monastero e la canonica di Sant'Ambrogio', p. 675; some documents now partially edited in 'Documenti del monastero e della canonica di Sant'Ambrogio', pp. 559–65.

[117] *Register*, I, 315.

[118] Ambrosioni, 'Controversie tra il monastero e la canonica di Sant'Ambrogio', *passim*.

[119] See, for example, M. Pogliani, 'Il dissidio fra nobili e popolari a Milano. La controversia del 1203 tra l'arcidiacono e il primicerio maggiore', *Ricerche storiche della chiesa ambrosiana*, 10 (Milan, 1981), 5–111.

convenors of a chapter at Piacenza, one of six called by Innocent to promote reform in regular houses immediately subject to the Apostolic see.[120] Monastic reform was extremely important to Innocent and elsewhere the reforming chapters were presided over by men such as the archbishop of Bourges and the abbot of Cluny.[121] As convenor, Albert was thus identified closely with reform and placed on a level with some of the foremost leaders of Western christendom. In 1205 this status was confirmed when he was elected patriarch of Jerusalem. Innocent's letter encouraging Albert to accept is particularly revealing.[122] Perhaps because an earlier candidate had refused, Innocent was very keen to convince Albert to go east. He therefore praised his abilities in a manner which might be dismissed as a matter of form, except that he emphasised, in a manner which is far from formulaic, just how much he had relied on his bishop's support in northern Italy, committing to his care even the most arduous negotiations (including of course the Humiliati).[123]

The career after 1201 of Peter of Lucedio is equally revealing of his outlook and relations with Rome. After some years in the east on the fourth crusade,[124] in 1205 or 1206 he was elected abbot of Lucedio's mother house, La Ferté, a position of great influence in the Cistercian order. After less than a year, however, he was chosen as bishop of Ivrea and thus returned to northern Italy, late in 1206.[125] Despite briefly abandoning his see because of his horror at the state in which he found it, in 1208 he was elected bishop of Thessalonica and Innocent wrote encouraging him to accept the office.[126] Peter seems to have hesitated before accepting and perhaps even before he had decided, was chosen for the more prestigious position of patriarch of Antioch, which he accepted and where he was to remain until his death in 1217. Innocent's letter, dated March 1209, to Albert, by now patriarch of Jerusalem,

---

120 See Maccarrone, *Studi*, pp. 226–46, 328–34; see also Minghetti, 'L'episcopato vercellese di Alberto', p. 109.

121 Maccarrone, *Studi*, pp. 229–38.

122 See now B. M. Bolton, '"The serpent in the dust, the sparrow on the house top": attitudes to Jerusalem and the Holy Land in the circle of pope Innocent III', forthcoming in *Christians and the Holy Land*, ed. R. Swanson, SCH 37 (Woodbridge). For the sequence of events concerning the election see *Register*, VI, 129, 130.

123 *Register*, VII, 222, p. 394: 'valde necessarius sis in partibus Lombardiae utpote cui secure in arduis etiam negotiis committimus vices nostras'; *Gesta*, col. cxl, describes Albert: 'virum utique vita et scientia et fama praeclarum'; Innocent refers to his approval of the appointment in a letter to Peter Capuanus, *PL*, 215, cols. 699–702; see also Maleczek, *Kardinalskolleg*, pp. 73–6.

124 See E. A. R. Brown, 'The Cistercians in the Latin empire of Constantinople and Greece 1204–1276', *Traditio*, 14 (1958), 63–120, 77–8.

125 *Ivrea*, II, 3, pp. 217–20; *PL*, 215, cols. 1004–8 (with errors).

126 *Ivrea*, II, 3, pp. 217–19; *PL*, 215, col. 1425.

informing him of the appointment, makes it clear that Albert himself had been active in promoting it.[127] It describes the canons who made the election acting 'through your concern' (*tuo studio mediante*) and expressed the hope that Peter and Albert should be aided by mutual solace. Since Peter and Albert had hardly been in the same land for several years, this rapport must surely date back to the years in which they had dealt with the Milanese cases of Sant'Ambrogio and the Humiliati, if not before. As such it is further evidence, if any were needed, that the combination of Peter and Albert had been a happy one, for the Humiliati, for Innocent and for the local prelates themselves.

Seen in the context of their ecclesiastical careers, Albert and Peter were natural choices for Innocent to have made. They were two men who must have been similar in age, whom he knew could work well together and who could bring monastic, canonical and episcopal experience to bear, as well as local expertise. Innocent knew at least one of them personally and, like Celestine before him, felt able to trust their judgement, despite their imperial connections. He seems to have been justified. Both men were adept politicians, managing to steer a middle course, fulfilling both secular and ecclesiastical commitments and thus ideally suited to the task of finding an acceptable solution to the Humiliati dilemma in the Lombard Church.

The process of the first enquiry

How this first enquiry into the Humiliati *proposita* was actually carried out is undocumented, but during the same period Albert and Peter were working to settle the controversy at Sant'Ambrogio and Peter was involved in the Tortona dispute.[128] It is reasonable to suppose that similar techniques were applied to the Humiliati. As with the depositions made by the monks and canons of Sant'Ambrogio or later in the dispute at the cathedral of Milan, Albert and Peter must have considered the Humiliati's written proposals, perhaps discussing details with them and listening to their views, but in the end their ecclesiastical authority would have been decisive. The proposals as they were sent to the Curia drawn up in written form under their seals, must therefore have contained contributions by both Albert and Peter as well as the Humiliati themselves.

The general lines of the new order originated with the Humiliati, but Albert and Peter made direct contributions which are not difficult to

---

[127] *PL*, 216, cols. 18–19.   [128] Above, p. 86.

identify. The final letters refer directly both to Albert's former community of Sta Croce Mortara and to certain Cistercian practices. In *Non omni spiritui*, members of the First order, living according to the *Ordo canonicus* and the *institutio* of the order, were instructed that they should celebrate Mass 'according to the customs of the Church of Mortara', a provision which must reflect Albert's personal interest.[129] The Mortara communities followed the Rule of St Augustine, practised manual labour and undertook to care for pilgrims on the road.[130] They included young boys (*pueri adolescentes*) in their congregation whom the canons undertook to bring up and educate.[131] They also accepted male and female lay *conversi*, leading to the not infrequent practice of clerics and laity living in the same community. The similarities with the Humiliati do not concern unusual practices, yet the parallels between the activities of the community at Mortara and the development of First order Humiliati communities suggest a close relationship. Viboldone was a 'canonical' community but later accepted lay couples and boys.[132] Moreover, several Humiliati houses were placed on roads and cared for pilgrims.[133] The similarities, existing or potential, surely made it easier for Albert to accept and regulate the new order. Albert's influence may also be detected in the christocentric spirit of the new rule. While patriarch in the Holy Land, he was to confirm the form of life (*vite seu conversationis formula*) for the hermits on Mount Carmel.[134] His work does not survive in the original, but Cicconetti has shown how it may be broadly reconstructed.[135] Although he argues that there are no similarities between the legislation for the Humiliati and the Carmelites, he himself draws comparisons and points out that that they both fit into the evangelical currents of the time.[136] He concludes that Albert, whose role was essentially to give juridical organisation to the order, was working not from one specific rule, but 'from his own knowledge and experience'.[137] By 1206 this undeniably included the Humiliati.

---

[129] Appendix I, 9: 'secundum consuetudinem Mortariensis Ecclesie'; a parallel for this is provided by the Rule of the Trinitarians, who were examined by the bishop of Paris and the abbot of St Victor and who were to observe certain Victorine customs. *Register*, I, 481; see also below, p. 107, n. 36.

[130] Above, n. 97.

[131] Mornacchi, 'Aspetti della vita comune presso i canonici regolari mortariensi', pp. 158–60.

[132] See table 6.2, p. 193.

[133] For example, Ognissanti on the *strata romea* at Fossadolto (Borghetto Lodigiano), appendix I, 39: 'passim pauperes et peregrinos transeuntes recipiunt et eis necessaria subministrant'.

[134] 'Vita S. Alberti', ed. Papenbroek, pp. 769–99; see also A. Jotischky, *The Perfection of Solitude: Hermits and Monks in the Crusader States* (University Park, Penn., 1995), pp. 123–31 and now Mosca, *Alberto Patriarca di Gerusalemme*, pp. 544–5.

[135] Cicconetti, *La regola del Carmelo*, esp. pp. 108–26, 386–423.

[136] *Ibid.*, p. 377.   [137] *Ibid.*, pp. 115, 423.

The areas where Peter of Lucedio may have contributed are also fairly clear cut. The *institutio* of the Humiliati refers to confession to the virgin Mary, which reflects Cistercian practice, and administration of the whole order was to imitate that of the Cistercians. The four senior provosts, of Viboldone, Lodi, Rondineto and Vialone, were to enjoy authority over other houses, 'just as in the Cistercian order, the Father abbots are accustomed to enjoy over the lesser abbots'.[138] They were also to hold General Chapters at least every year. Such modelling on the Cistercians was surely first suggested by Peter of Lucedio, though no doubt also promoted by brother Rainier, one of the curial group to examine the Humiliati, also a Cistercian by profession.[139]

A recent study of the liturgy of the first Humiliati notes the strong dependence on north Italian cathedral traditions, in particular associated with Vercelli and Ivrea.[140] In this the Humiliati were like other new orders, adopting local liturgical traditions, and the connection with Albert and Vercelli is direct. The reasons for a link with Ivrea, however, are less obvious. In 1200–1 Peter was not yet bishop there, yet Wickstrom argues that the early Humiliati traditions may have been so close to those of Ivrea as to be originally identical.[141] There is unlikely to be documentary certainty, but further research may yet show that Peter's active interest in the Humiliati continued when he became bishop of Ivrea.

The corrected proposals as they were sent to the Curia already contained recommendations made by the first delegates which were simply adopted by the second. The problem of the three different strands had been overcome by providing a unitary framework within which they could operate, but the unity and 'single proposal of life' (*unicum propositum*) apparently sought by the Humiliati had proved impossible to achieve.

The *proposita*, corrected and sealed by Albert and Peter as well as by the Humiliati, were to be re-examined once they had arrived in the Curia. The influence of those personally and physically close to the pope deserves to be considered in detail. Yet Innocent's initial reliance on local prelates well versed in Lombard ecclesiastical affairs must have been decisive in the way that the new order was to be received. In an area beyond the immediate influence of Rome, much of the decision making was in the hands of such local abbots and bishops, a process

---

[138] Below, pp. 107–8; appendix I, 9: 'sicut in Cistertiensi Ordine Patres Abbates in minoribus consueverunt Abbatibus obtinere'.

[139] Below, p. 95.

[140] Wickstrom, 'The Humiliati: liturgy and identity', pp. 202–11.

[141] *Ibid.*, p. 205.

formalised later in the pontificate by the use of visitors and then of legates.[142] As long as they followed lines acceptable to Rome, it is unnecessary to assume that decisions inevitably emanated from the Curia.

It is not realistic, however, to assume that the second, curial delegates were no more than a rubber stamp. Such enquiries by members of the Curia had come to encompass Church business at all levels, resulting in a continuous passage of proctors and others through Rome, each bent on achieving victory in some local or not-so-local dispute.[143] The Curia dealt with a great variety of cases. Maleczek, in his study of Peter Capuanus, the most prominent of the curial delegates, concludes that their role in the case of the Humiliati is 'impossible to determine'.[144] Yet, as with the prelates in the north, their interests and activities will help to illustrate the influence they may have exercised on the formation of the new order.

The curial delegates

The three men chosen, Gratian, cardinal deacon of SS Cosma e Damiano (1178–1205), Peter Capuanus, cardinal priest of San Marcello (1200–14), and brother Rainier, were all important in the Curia of Innocent III and enjoyed positions of great authority or responsibility. Gratian was a nephew of pope Eugenius III (1145–53) and after studying law at Bologna had been active in and on behalf of the Curia since 1168.[145] He had been involved in negotiations concerning the reinstatement of Thomas Becket in 1169 and had won the archbishop's admiration. Created a cardinal by Alexander III, he enjoyed a reputation for honesty and incorruptibility and was frequently entrusted with the examination of legal questions.[146] In 1186 he was with Urban III in Verona and was one of the signatories of Urban's privilege for Viboldone.[147] Innocent used his services as an auditor and also sent him with Peter cardinal priest of Sta Cecilia to try and achieve peace between Pisa and Genoa in the second half of 1198 in preparation for the crusade.[148]

In 1200–1, when called upon to consider the Humiliati case, Gratian was already an experienced judge and administrator, perhaps with some

---

[142] See Alberzoni, 'Innocenzo III e la riforma della chiesa in "Lombardia"', *passim*.

[143] R. Brentano, *Two Churches: England and Italy in the Thirteenth Century* (Berkeley, Los Angeles, London, 1968), pp. 35–48.

[144] Maleczek, *Pietro Capuano*, p. 101.   [145] Maleczek, *Kardinalskolleg*, pp. 71–3.

[146] *Ibid.*, p. 72 n. 49.   [147] Appendix I, 3 and above, p. 47.

[148] *Register*, I, 8, 164, 290, 295; *Register*, II, 30; *Gesta*, col. xci.

memory of Viboldone, rather older than the other men chosen and coming towards the end of nearly four decades in the Curia. By contrast, in these early years of Innocent's pontificate, the other two members of the Curia chosen, Peter Capuanus, cardinal priest of San Marcello and brother Rainier of Ponza, were much closer to the young pope.

By 1201 Peter Capuanus had had several years' experience of the Curia and of legatine authority, having first achieved the office of cardinal in 1193, when he was created cardinal deacon of Sta Maria in Vialata by Celestine III. Maleczek has dedicated a major study to his life and in particular to his involvement in the fourth crusade, undoubtedly the most important role in his career.[149]

He had studied at Paris, possibly with Lothar *de Segni*, the future pope Innocent III. Under Celestine he acted as rector of the papal enclave of Benevento and as legate, first to Sicily and later to Bohemia and Poland. While on his way north he dealt with questions of Church discipline in northern Italy (including Verona), and on his return he suffered an undignified attack at the hands of count William Pelavicini and some citizens of Parma and Piacenza, which prevented him from attending the election of the new pope in January 1198.[150] Capuanus must have been only too aware of the parlous state of both ecclesiastical and lay society in northern Italy.

During these early years, Capuanus enjoyed Innocent's favour and in the very first months of his pontificate Innocent appointed him, together with cardinal Soffred of Sta Prassede, as legate to the crusade, one of the new pope's most deeply felt concerns and thus a sure sign of esteem. Yet this meant he was not to spend long at the Curia. By the time of his return in the first months of 1206 he had provoked the condemnation of Innocent who saw him as a major reason for the failure of his crusade. In a blistering letter, Innocent attacked him for deserting the Holy Land, absolving from their crusading vows those who remained to serve the Latin empire in Constantinople and ending all hope of union with the Greek Church by permitting Latin persecution.[151]

After 1206, Capuanus played only a minor role in the Curia, but his writings give some clue to his interests and reputation. He compiled a theological *Summa* and a collection of *distinctiones* or *alphabetum*, neither

---

[149] Maleczek, *Pietro Capuano*, esp. pp. 103–230; he is not to be confused with the younger man of the same name, a theologian created cardinal deacon of San Giorgio in Velabro in 1219 by Honorius III.

[150] *Italia pontificia*, V, pp. 168–9, VII/I, p. 244; *Register*, I, 3; Maleczek, *Pietro Capuano*, p. 68.

[151] *PL,215, cols. 699–702*; English translation in *The Crusades*, ed. Brundage, pp. 208–9.

of which was particularly original. Yet the *distinctiones*, a list of figurative meanings of biblical terms intended for use in sermons, shows his awareness of the need for well-equipped preachers, a theme close to Innocent III's heart and certainly important to the Humiliati. A recently discovered sermon of his against the Cathars confirms this interest.[152]

His work also appealed to an enthusiast on the fringes of the Church, Durand of Huesca, leader of the Catholic Poor, former Waldensians who were reconciled to the Church in 1207.[153] Durand used Capuanus' *distinctiones* as the basis for his own collection, recently identified by Richard and Mary Rouse and probably compiled between 1207 and 1213.[154] The text is dedicated to Bernard, bishop of Pavia who was well aware of the local dangers of heresy, having written a life of his predecessor in Pavia, bishop Lanfranc, which reveals the extent of heresy in the city and Lanfranc's success against the 'garrulity of pseudo-preachers'.[155] Yet Bernard had welcomed Durand to Pavia and his support, when the Catholic Poor's right to preach depended on obtaining permission from a generally wary episcopate, was undoubtedly very welcome.

The verse prologue of Durand's text also includes a eulogy of Capuanus which makes the author's debt clear, describing him as 'The chief of this work . . . a special man . . . Jewel of philosophers, Glory of Christians'.[156] There is no direct link here between Capuanus and Durand.[157] Perhaps we should dismiss the verses as a literary topos. Yet Durand's enthusiasm for Capuanus' work suggests that the cardinal was known as a supporter of the new evangelical enthusiasm, his work a useful tool in the task of preaching. This enthusiasm may also have been prompted by knowledge of Capuanus' role in approving the Humiliati, whose treatment provided a direct precedent for Durand's own reconciliation with the pope. Durand visited Milan in 1209, where he was made welcome by the archbishop, Hubert *de Pirovano* (1206–11), and where he surely heard of, or met, some of the Humiliati himself and perhaps learnt of Capuanus' role in their ratification.

We cannot know precisely what had led Innocent to choose

---

[152] Paris, Bibliothèque nationale, lat. nouvelles acquisitions 991; identified by Dr Nicole Bériou to whom I am grateful for this reference; the manuscript is almost entirely illegible.

[153] See Thouzellier, *Catharisme et valdéisme en Languedoc*, pp. 215–37, 255–62, 303–424; Selge, *Die ersten Waldenser*, I, pp. 193–227.

[154] Rouse and Rouse, 'The schools and the Waldensians', pp. 86–111.

[155] Bernard Balbo, 'Vita de S. Lanfranco', ed. D. Papenbroek, pp. 620–30. Discussed in D. M. Webb, 'The pope and the cities: anticlericalism and heresy in Innocent III's Italy', *The Church and Sovereignty c. 590–1918: Essays in Honour of Michael Wilks*, ed. D. Wood. SCH Subsidia, IX (Oxford, 1991), pp. 135–52.

[156] Rouse and Rouse, 'The schools and the Waldensians', p. 108.

[157] But see *ibid.*, p. 94.

Capuanus to examine the Humiliati or whether it was fortuitous circumstance, owing to his timely presence in the Curia between travels. What we can say is that his interests in countering heresy and improving the tools of the Church to do so by encouraging better preaching undoubtedly coincided with the aims of the Humiliati themselves and perhaps made him better disposed towards them.

Innocent's choice of brother Rainier seems certain to have been based on intrinsic considerations and the important tasks entrusted to him by Innocent mark an early example of what Maleczek identifies as a new departure: the pope's use of curial personnel of lower status, including his chaplains.[158] Rainier had originally been a Cistercian monk at Casamari on the southern border of the papal states, where he was closely associated with Joachim of Fiore (1135–1202), the founder of the order of Florensians, whose disciple and intimate he became.[159] In 1192 both Joachim and Rainier were threatened with condemnation as fugitives by the Cistercian General Chapter should they not present themselves.[160] Nothing is known about Rainier's career in the mid-1190s but the Cistercian threat does not seem to have materialised, for by 1198 he enjoyed authority with the new pope and prestige within the Curia.

Although the origins of this status are impossible to trace, for the years after 1198 the evidence for its existence is clear. In 1198–9, Innocent entrusted him both with numerous delicate missions and with the general promotion of reform and the confutation of heretics, often leaving the final decisions to Rainier's own discretion.[161] The numerous papal letters which refer to Rainier's legations are always full of praise, describing him as a 'man equipped with divine power in words and deeds' and 'of honest life and experience'.[162] While this is comparable to his descriptions of and attitudes towards other delegates, with Rainier Innocent went further.[163] His letter of October 1198, extending his legatine powers, refers to the 'no small honour' accruing to God and the Roman Church because of Rainier's purity and praiseworthy actions, a saint-like description for a man still living.[164]

Rainier moved to Fossanova, a Cistercian house on the Via Appia south of Rome, because of ill health, but continued to enjoy close links

---

[158] Maleczek, *Kardinalskolleg*, p. 331.
[159] Bolton, 'For the see of Simon Peter: the Cistercians at Innocent III's nearest frontier', 150–2.
[160] 'Vita beati Joachimi abbatis', ed. Grundmann, p. 534; *Statuta capitulorum generalium ordinis Cisterciensis*, I, p. 154.
[161] *Register*, I, 92–4, 99, 125, 165, 239, 249, 395, 448–9, 494; *Register*, II, 72, 113–14.
[162] *Register*, I, 165. *Register*, II, 114.   [163] Compare above, p. 88.
[164] *Register*, I, 395.

with the Curia and probably became Innocent's confessor.[165] In 1201
he was involved in the canonisation process of Gilbert of Sempringham,
being called upon by Innocent to interpret a papal dream concerning
the saint and, according to the records of the process, the pope
performed the canonisation partly because of his recommendation.[166]

Rainier undoubtedly enjoyed great prestige with both pope and
cardinals and although he seems to have retired to the island of Ponza
for the last years of his life, he maintained contact. This can be inferred
from the remarkable eulogy written in 1207–9 by cardinal Hugolino of
Ostia to lament the death of Rainier, his friend and spiritual father.[167]
Hugolino was not a Cistercian, yet he wrote of Rainier as an essential
influence on his own formation, sadly incomplete because of the
untimely death of his guide. His reaction is surely a reflection of
Rainier's spiritual presence in the papal Curia.

Examination of the Humiliati case by the two cardinals and brother
Rainier took place sometime between the creation of Capuanus as
cardinal priest of San Marcello (December 1200) and the issuing of the
letters in June 1201. The process used should probably be compared to
that for the canonisation of Gilbert of Sempringham. The *Book of St
Gilbert* reports that 'a careful discussion . . . took place among the
cardinals in the pope's presence, the evidence which the messengers had
brought was inspected and the witnesses who had come were put under
oath and carefully examined'.[168] The image of Innocent listening intently
as the cardinals and, in this case, brother Rainier, discussed the matter
before them, fits well with the text of *Incumbit nobis* to the Third order of
the Humiliati in June 1201, in which he states that he had their *proposita*
carefully examined in his own and his brother cardinals' presence and had
made certain corrections for which he was at pains to win their
approval.[169] In *Diligentiam pii patris* to the Second order, however, he
refers to two separate examinations, his own and that of Rainier and the
cardinal-delegates, so that it is unclear whether these took place together,
or whether Innocent and the cardinals as a body simply cast an eye over
the work of those entrusted with this specific task.[170]

---

[165] *PL*, 214, col. 1053; *Annales Cistercenses*, ed. Manrique, III, p. 369: 'Fratrem Rainerum, qui
Innocentio e sacris confessionibus erat'.

[166] *The Book of St Gilbert*, p. 177.

[167] '"Analecta Heidelbergensia" Varietà', pp. 363–7; cited F. Robb, '"Who hath chosen the
better part?" (Luke 10,42), pope Innocent III and Joachim of Fiore on the diverse forms of
religious life', *Monastic Studies*, 2 (Bangor, 1991), 157–70, 166 n. 75.

[168] *The Book of St Gilbert*, p. 175.

[169] Appendix I, 7; Maleczek, *Kardinalskolleg*, p. 319, concludes that the use of expressions such as
'de fratrum nostrorum consilio' employed here infers a closed meeting of pope and cardinals.

[170] Appendix I, 8.

CONCLUSIONS

Whatever the precise manner in which the consideration of their case was carried out, the process by which the Humiliati were brought back into the Church was by no means entirely the product of papal intervention in the provinces. It was perhaps made possible by the election of a new and more flexible pope, but there had already been some form of reconciliation with the bishop of Verona. Those involved in examining the Humiliati were not all equally suited to the task. No in-depth apportioning of responsibility can be attempted, yet the men involved were not mere rubber stamps for papal decisions. They were accustomed to acting at their own discretion and could bring to bear wide experience both of the secular and regular Churches as well as of the temporal world of politics. They shared many of the concerns and enthusiasms of Innocent himself, but these were not simply adopted in imitation of the pope. Brother Rainier certainly had wide experience of the dangers of heresy acquired during his legation to Languedoc, and those in the north must have had a particular understanding of the need for forces to combat the thriving heresy in the towns. Peter of Lucedio and Gratian had at least administrative knowledge of Humiliati communities. Albert of Vercelli was to show renewed enthusiasm for similar movements later in his career.

Yet the role of the Humiliati themselves should not be under-estimated. Many of the early leaders remain relatively obscure figures, but James of Rondineto and Guy *de Porta Orientale* were men accustomed to authority. Although they were not apparently consulted in the final stages, as the Trinitarian John of Matha had been, the essential character and structure of the new order was already determined before these men returned to the Curia in 1200–1. The tripartite framework may well have originated with them. What they had hoped to obtain was greater unity. The prelates involved established that this was not possible, or perhaps not even necessary. If the new Cistercian-style unitary framework enabled them to achieve a respectability which would overcome the scandal and difficulties which variety might provoke, then there was no need to try and force a single *propositum* on the whole movement. If we also accept that the Humiliati had long had constructive relations with senior churchmen[171] and were now closely involved in and contributing to this process of reconciliation, arguments that Innocent 'sowed the seeds of their destruction as a primitive evangelical movement', by forcing them into 'a diocesan structure

---

[171] Above, ch. 2.

97

which led to the ultimate vitiation of their early form', also fall by the wayside.[172] The structure, or the desire for it, was already there.

The purpose of this chapter has been to analyse the role of the Humiliati themselves and of the pope's delegates, but Innocent's own contribution must be given some consideration. He was enthusiastic from the beginning and set the ball rolling (or at least allowed it to roll), by permitting the Humiliati's petition to be heard, and he bore the final responsibility. He tells us that he corrected texts prepared for him and it seems likely therefore that most of the details of the letters of approval were prepared by his delegates. As Webb has recently pointed out, 'it is as well to remember that he [Innocent] could only act where he had information'.[173] The pope himself frequently complained of lack of time.[174] What the delegates presented to him was therefore crucial. The compromises established on the key issues of lay preaching and oath-taking, however, were perhaps too important to be left to these men. In particular, although he may not have created a 'lay preaching brother-hood in a legal public sense', the decision to allow the laity to hold meetings and exhort one another to a better life was a delicate one.[175] It was likely, as Innocent recognised, to provoke episcopal opposition and he warned bishops not to refuse permission.[176] It was surely too important to be left to his delegates' authority alone.

In light of these characteristics and the evidence for his personal involvement in the case, it would be unwise to argue that Innocent was not personally engaged in the final stages of the process leading to the approval of the Humiliati, as he was in its beginning.[177] Yet it was his delegates and perhaps above all those in the north who, together with the Humiliati themselves, determined in detail the nature of the new order and its rule.

---

[172] Bolton, 'Innocent III's treatment of the Humiliati', p. 82; recent work arguing that spirituality and institutions are not mutually exclusive (as this argument implied) is listed in Brolis, *Gli Umiliati a Bergamo*, p. 124 and n. 115.

[173] Webb, 'The pope and the cities', pp. 135–6.

[174] For examples, see *PL*, 217, cols. 311, 381, 398.

[175] Zerfaß, *Der Streit um die Laienpredigt*, p. 209; see also d'Avray, *The Preaching of the Friars*, p. 27, n. 1.

[176] Appendix I, 7.   [177] See above, pp. 66–9.

Chapter 4

RULES

. . .according to God and your *institutio* approved by the Apostolic See. . .[1]

The key to understanding the daily life of any regular community lies in the rule or rules adopted and the customs evolved to supplement and refine them. Thus the rule of Benedict is the fundamental guide to the monastic life embraced by innumerable religious communities in the medieval Latin West, but the details of daily observance for particular Benedictine houses are to be found in customaries, in the occasional dispensations of papal letters or in the constitutions issued by chapter meetings and other legislative authorities. Similar regulatory texts could be listed for each of the great orders of the middle ages.

By contrast, there seem to be no extant customaries or constitutions for the early thirteenth-century order of the Humiliati and much therefore remains elusive.[2] There is nonetheless a parallel group of linked normative texts: on one hand the papal correspondence of June

---

[1] Appendix I, 9.

[2] Cremascoli, 'La regola', pp. 51–5, published a text of a *propositum* or constitutions which he claimed dated to the early thirteenth century. The manuscript, now Lodi, Biblioteca comunale B 17, dates to the end of the thirteenth or early fourteenth centuries and contains nothing amounting to constitutions; see now Castagnetti, 'La regola del primo e secondo ordine', pp. 163–250, appendix 2. A papal letter of 1246 (appendix I, 58), allows for constitutions and John of Brera, *Excerptum*, ch. 29, p. 342 refers to constitutions drawn up at a chapter held in Milan in 1291, but these do not appear to survive. Tiraboschi published some of the fourteenth-century constitutions in *VHM* III, pp. 99–227. The earliest extant manuscripts of these are both fifteenth century: Brera AG XI 3 and Biblioteca vaticana Reginense latina 2001; a list of books and manuscripts received by the national library of the Brera in 1803 included Brera AG XI 3 and two other copies of constitutions, one of the fourteenth and one of the fifteenth centuries. Both have since gone missing; see S. Castelli, 'Un antico elenco braidense e i codici dei "conventi soppressi" nelle biblioteche milanesi', *Italia Medioevale e Umanistica*, 34 (1991), 199–257; a detailed discussion of Reginense latina 2001, which varies in some points from the text given by Tiraboschi, is in Mercati, 'Due ricerche', pp. 178–81. As Mercati notes, further work is required on two other manuscripts, listed by Zanoni, pp. 252–3, but with very little detail: Ambrosiana H 210 inf. (a fifteenth-century codex) and F 82 sup. (with sixty-nine numbered documents).

1201 and later and on the other a rule of life or *institutio*.[3] The use made of these texts is not, however, clear cut and requires further investigation before we can hope to understand the details of daily observance. In order to simplify this investigation, this chapter concentrates first on the situation prescribed at the beginning of the thirteenth century. In a separate section at the end it then gives brief consideration to the evolution of regulations concerning oath-taking, fasting and diet, three essential elements of observance.

1201

Of the documentation produced in 1201, the letter to the Tertiaries, *Incumbit nobis*, is the most straightforward. After a brief account of the need for the pope to favour religion and a short description of the process of approval, it provides a unique guide to their regime, inserted in this letter '. . . for greater precaution, word for word'.[4] The first section is an account of the virtues to which they should aspire, constructed around Gospel quotations. Thus they are to keep humility in their hearts and gentleness in their ways, just as Christ said 'learn from me because I am meek and lowly in heart' (Matthew 11:29). Humility is then linked to obedience, due to the prelates of the church both because of the usual link with Paul's injunction, 'Obey them that have the rule over you and submit yourselves, for they watch for your souls as they that must give account' (Hebrews 13:17) and because 'there is no true humbleness if it forsakes its companion obedience.'[5] The need for patience in adversity and turning the other cheek and the importance of the love of God and their fellowmen are then expounded in the same way.[6]

These first virtues are followed by a long passage justifying oath-taking, a subject considered worthy of lengthy and identical treatment in all three papal letters, which here make no distinction between the expectations for the three orders.[7] As the anonymous chronicler of Laon makes clear, the early Humiliati rejected oaths.[8] This was perhaps both because several gospel passages prohibited swearing and because,

---

[3] See Dubois, 'Les ordres religieux', on the meaning of these terms.
[4] Appendix I, 7; for parallels with the *Memoriale propositi* approved by Honorius III in 1221, see Stewart, *'De illis qui faciunt penitentiam': The Rule of the Secular Franciscan Order*, pp. 188–99.
[5] Appendix I, 7: 'Non est enim vera humilitas, quam comes obedientia deserit.'
[6] Using Hebrews 10:34, Matthew 5:39–41, Romans 12:19, 1 Corinthians 6:7, Luke 21:19, 6:37, 10:27, Matthew 5:44–5 and Romans 12:20.
[7] Appendix I, 7–9.
[8] See above, p. 39.

through long tradition, monks did not swear oaths.[9] It was thus capable of interpretation as a desirable and observable element of a purer life. The swearing of oaths was, however, an essential part of the structure of medieval civil and ecclesiastical life. Oaths bound individuals to one another and to their communities, they allowed the fluid process of commerce and justice. In particular, purgation by oath was used in ecclesiastical courts when there was a lack of witnesses or written instruments as proof.[10] Although probably not intended, the refusal to swear oaths and to engage in the legal process adopted by the early Humiliati was in effect a rejection of these structures and a threat to the very foundations of authority. Objection to oaths had become a hallmark of heresy, identified with the Waldensians and was to bring automatic condemnation in canon three of the Fourth Lateran Council in 1215.[11]

It is not surprising, therefore, that the longest section in each of the letters is that dedicated to the justification of oath-taking in certain circumstances. The arguments adopted belong to a long tradition of thought about oaths stretching back to Augustine and developed through monastic commentaries on the rule of Benedict intended to show why monks should not swear. Since the purpose here was the opposite, it is likely that the ideas are mediated through the standard canonist's textbook of the twelfth century, Gratian's *Decretum* (*causa* 22) and late twelfth-century apologia for catholic practice written by men such as the ex-heretic Bonacursus or the Paris master and monk, Alan of Lille (d. 1202–3), who based his work on his experience opposing heretics in Languedoc.[12] Such works used a selection of standard biblical and patristic passages to make their case, providing point by point analysis of those which appeared to prohibit all oath-taking, in order to show how it was legitimate in certain circumstances. The arguments were undoubtedly familiar to Innocent III who may well have had a hand in composing this section, since a letter to the Benedictines of Châtillon in 1206 later included in the Decretals develops many of the same points at a date when the men Innocent had delegated to the Humiliati case in 1201 had either passed away or

[9] For example, Smaragdus, 'Expositio in regulam sancti benedicti', book 2, ch. 4, §27, pp. 108–10.
[10] See Baldwin, 'The intellectual preparation for the canon of 1215 against ordeals', p. 617.
[11] Constitutiones concilium Lateranense IV, 3, in *Conciliorum oecumenicorum decreta*, p. 235: 'si qui vero ex eis [the accused] iuramenti religionem obstinatione damnabili respuentes, iurare forte noluerint, ex hoc ipso tamquam haeretici reputentur'; on the Waldensians, see for example, Alan of Lille, 'De fide catholica', 2, 18–19; *PL*, 210, col. 390–4.
[12] Gratian, 'Decretum', 22.1; Bonacursus, 'Vita haereticorum', 10, *PL*, 204, cols. 783–4; Alan of Lille, 'De fide catholica', 2, 18–19, *PL*, 210, cols. 392–4; see Evans, *Alan of Lille*. I am grateful to Peter Biller for first drawing my attention to such parallels.

moved to tasks away from the Curia.[13] Neither the choice of texts nor the analysis of them in the papal letters, drawing out the meaning and implications for the Humiliati, is essentially new. The authorities chosen are almost all to be found in Gratian. However, the deployment of quotations and argument does not appear to be identical with any one earlier text. Certainly the patristic passages used by Alan and others are not present and many of the implications of the argument drawn out by such authors (concerning, for example, the alternative of the ordeal as a temptation of God) are not ventured here.[14] The concentration on New Testament quotations reflects the need to convince Humiliati doubters on their own terms. In what follows, parallels with Alan of Lille's work (written c. 1185–1200) will be noted simply to show the relationship of our text with a representative example of the intellectual context in which it was written.

The exposition begins with a problematic biblical passage: 'But above all things, my brethren, swear not, neither by heaven, neither by the earth, neither by any other oath: but let your yea be yea and your nay, nay; lest ye fall into condemnation' (James 5:12).[15] This is then glossed: 'As regards oath-taking, unwise or spontaneous desire of the will shall not induce you, but [rather] when there is something to be done which compels you through urgent and pressing need.'[16] This assertion is then treated in two parts, dealing first with the problem of unwise or spontaneous swearing. The discussion begins with a quotation from Christ in the Beatitudes:

It hath been said by them of old time, 'Thou shalt not forswear thyself, but shalt perform unto the Lord thine oaths:' But I say unto you, Swear not at all; neither by heaven; for it is God's throne: Nor by the earth; for it is his footstool; neither by Jerusalem; for it is the city of the great King. Neither shalt thou swear by thy head, because thou canst not make one hair white or black.

(Matthew 5: 33–6)[17]

The first passage from James is then repeated: 'Above all things my brethren swear not, neither by heaven, neither by the earth, neither by any other oath' and the key phrases are glossed to show that the prohibitions are not comprehensive:

---

[13] *PL*, 215, cols. 825–7; X. 2.24.26.
[14] See for example, Alan of Lille, 'De fide catholica', 2, 19, cols. 393–4.
[15] *Ibid.*, 2, 18, col. 392.
[16] 'Ceterum ad praestandum juramentum non vos indiscretus vel spontaneus voluntatis affectus inducat; sed si quando fuerit faciendum ingens et urgens necessitatis articulus vos compellat.'
[17] Compare Alan of Lille, 'De fide catholica', 2, 18, cols. 392–3.

When he says 'swear not', he prohibits a spontaneous oath, that is because oath-taking is to be done of necessity, not of the will.[18] When he adds 'neither by heaven nor by the earth', he prohibits a random oath; that is because swearing is not to be by a creature but rather by the Creator.[19] 'But let your yea be yea and your nay nay', that is because in affirming or denying, you reveal through your mouth what you bear in the heart.[20]

Having established the first part of the proposition, that random and spontaneous oaths are to be avoided, the letter then sets out to demonstrate that oaths sworn in cases of necessity are legitimate. The words of Christ himself are used to argue that he was in a sense swearing an oath when he spoke of the truth: 'Indeed, it does not apply to a simple affirmation or denial but rather to the truth, as Christ frequently says in the Gospel according to John: "Verily, verily I say unto you."'[21] This is followed by a passage suggesting that the greater guilt lies with those who demand the oath, rather than the one giving it: 'For what is greater than these arises from evil, involving not guilt so much as punishment, nor so much swearing the oath as demanding it. This certainly proceeds from a certain weakness of unbelief, which always concerns punishment, although not always guilt.'[22] Finally, the letter cites five biblical passages shown to favour oath-taking when necessity demands. The first passage is a line from Hebrews which was widely used to justify taking an oath as evidence in court, particularly in cases involving the clergy: 'For men verily swear by the greater: and an oath for confirmation is to them an end of all strife' (Hebrews 6:16).[23] The second comes from the Apocalypse: 'The Angel also, which John saw in the Apocalypse, "standing upon the sea and upon the earth, lifted up his hand to heaven and sware by him that liveth for ever and ever"'

---

[18] *Ibid.*, 2, 18, col. 392: 'Sponte enim et sine necessitate jurare, vel falsum jurare, grande peccatum est; ex necessitate autem jurare scilicet ad asserendam innocentiam, vel ad foedera pacis confirmanda, vel ad persuadendum auditoribus quod eis utile est, malum non est, est enim necessarium.'

[19] 'Cum addit neque per coelum neque per terram, jurationem prohibet indiscretam, quia videlicet non est jurandum per creaturam, sed magis per creatorem'; this had long been prohibited, *Sacrorum conciliorum nova et amplissima collectio*, I, col 679 (Pius I, 142–50); cited in Crosara, '"Jurata voce". Saggi sul giuramento', p. 290 n. 40. X.2.24.26 explains the prohibition: 'lest the honour due to the Creator be transferred to a creature'; see also Alan of Lille, 'De fide catholica', 2, 18, col. 393.

[20] 'Sit autem sermo vester: est est, non non, idest quod affirmando vel negando profertis ex ore, geratis in corde.'

[21] John 14:12 (for example).

[22] 'Quod autem his abundantius est, a malo est, non tam culpe quam pene, nec tam juramentum prestantis quam exigentis; quod utique de quadam incredulitatis infirmitate procedit quod semper spectat ad penam etsi non semper ad culpam.'

[23] See Baldwin, 'The intellectual preparation for the canon of 1215 against ordeals', p. 617; Alan of Lille, 'De fide catholica', 2, 19, col. 393.

(Apocalypse 10:5–6).[24] The third is from Jeremiah, prophesying about the future times of grace: 'And thou shalt swear, the Lord liveth, in truth, in judgement and in righteousness; and the nations shall bless themselves in him and in him shall they glory' (Jeremiah 4:2) and in conclusion there are two passages from Paul to show that he frequently swore: 'For God is my witness' (Romans 1:9) and 'By your rejoicing brethren, which I have in Christ Jesus' (1 Corinthians 15:31).[25]

After this careful explanation of the need for oaths, the letter continues with a list of other necessary virtues based on biblical precedent: treat others as you wish them to treat you, strive to enter through the narrow gate (Matthew 7:12–15), do penance, do not sin (1 Corinthians 15:34) and live peaceably with all men (Romans 12:18). The second section of the letter then becomes more specific. Usurous and ill-gotten gains must be returned and injury done to others rectified (Matthew 5:24).[26] Nor may they possess tithes for, as Gregory VII had decreed, the laity are prohibited from holding tithes which canonical authority demonstrates to have been given for pious purposes.[27] Rather tithes and first fruits must be paid to the clergy to whom they belong for distribution according to the will of the diocesan bishop. Any profits and produce which remain are to be distributed as alms and all that is superfluous to the just needs of their communities is to be given to the poor, but not in such a way that 'other men be eased and ye burdened' (2 Corinthians 8:13). They are not to lay up treasures on this earth, but rather lay them up in heaven (Matthew 6:19–20), nor should they love the world (1 John 2:15–17). Any who are married, however, may not leave their wives unless on account of fornication or 'except it be by consent for a time' (1 Corinthians 7:3–5).

Gospel injunction remains the essential source throughout the text, but the last section includes further pragmatic requirements and is less closely based on the Bible. The brethren are to fast on the fourth and sixth day of each week (Wednesdays and Fridays) except during Pentecost and from Christmas to Epiphany, unless illness, weakness or work should prevent them. When they are not fasting they will have just two meals, lunch and dinner, and the food is to be frugal. They are to say the Lord's prayer before and after eating and are to observe the seven canonical hours: matins, prime, terce, sext, nones, vespers and compline. The Lord's prayer is to be said seven times at each hour 'because of the seven gifts of the Holy Spirit' and at prime they are to add the 'symbol' of the Creed. Their clothing is to be neither too grand

---

[24] Compare *Ibid.*, cols. 393–4.   [25] Compare *Ibid.*, col. 394.
[26] Meersseman, *Dossier*, p. 279 n. 4 notes parallel with Gratian II, 14.6.1.
[27] Meersseman, *Ibid.*, n. 5 notes parallel with Gratian II, 16.7.1.

nor too abject, but such that it does not appear irreligious, because neither pretended filth nor exquisite elegance are appropriate for a christian. They are to assist any in their society who lack temporal things or are hindered by illness, as is already their custom. Should one of them die, the brethren are to be informed and come to the funeral and shall say the Lord's prayer and the *Miserere* twelve times for his or her soul, as long as they intend to stay in their order and keep to their way of life (*propositum*).[28] They are also to say the Lord's prayer three times each day for the living and three times for the dead of the fraternity and once for the peace of the Church and the whole christian people.

It is to be their custom to come together each Sunday in an appropriate place to hear the word of God and for one or more of the brethren of tried faith and expert in religion who are 'mighty in deed and word' (Luke 24:19), with the permission of the bishop of the diocese to propose words of exhortation to the assembled group. They should encourage them to honest customs and pious works but are not to speak about the articles of faith or the sacraments of the Church. No bishop is to obstruct these meetings, for the spirit is not to be quenched (1 Thessalonians 5:19). Finally, they are to follow this form of life, which the pope has carefully examined, wisely corrected and wholesomely approved, 'out of a pure heart and of a good conscience and faith unfeigned' (1 Timothy 1:5), so that they may 'deserve to receive eternal reward from him who is the rewarder of merit and searcher of hearts'.[29] The letter closes with the usual *sanctio*.

Incumbit nobis stands alone as a guide to the life of the Tertiaries. It makes clear the daily and weekly routine of the members, their aspirations and obligations and the mutual support they provide. It also regulates their relationship with external authority (bishops are not to hinder their exhortations) and clarifies the position on oath-taking. As we have seen, this last issue is dealt with in the same manner in the letters sent to all three orders, but the remaining letters are otherwise much less straightforward as sources for the regimes of the First and Second orders. *Non omni spiritui* and *Diligentiam pii patris*, issued respectively for the First and Second orders, are records of events to confirm the respectability of the communities and a guide to their general ethos, rather than practical regulations for daily life. *Diligentiam*

---

[28] '[Q]uatenus in ordine et proposito permanere et perseverare intenditis et disponitis Domino adjuvante . . .'.

[29] '[V]ivendi formam, quam nos diligenter examinare, prudenter corrigere ac salubriter approbare curavimus, de corde puro et conscientia bona et fide non ficta servetis, ut ab eo, qui meritorum est retributor et cordium perscrutator, mercedem mereamini recipere sempiternam . . .'.

pii patris for the Second order is the shortest of the three letters. The *arenga* furnishes a brief account of the process of enquiry and justifies the intervention of the 'father' (the pope) to foster catholic resolve.[30] The *dispositio* then stipulates four basic instructions, all of which concern the externals of the Second order's existence. It is taken into the protection of the see of Peter and its property, present and future, is to be safeguarded. In their houses, in which they live in common 'for the praise of God, the regular *institutio* according to the approval of the apostolic see is to be observed inviolably'.[31] They are to pay tithes on their property to the churches to which they belong but, perhaps consciously echoing Cistercian practice, are exempted from payment on the products of their handicrafts, the fruits of their gardens and the feed for their animals, immunities justified because they give 'greater offerings to the Church and more fruitful alms to the indigent'.[32] The fourth requirement and final section of the letter is identical to *Incumbit nobis*: they are to swear oaths in cases of compelling need and to observe their papally corrected and approved form of life with pure hearts, good consciences and unfeigned faith, so that they may 'deserve to receive eternal reward from him who is the rewarder of merit and searcher of hearts'. This is followed by the usual *sanctio*.

Such precepts give only a vague idea of the intended regime. The communities were evidently expected to support themselves by handicrafts and perhaps animal husbandry and were to be particularly concerned with charitable works and aiding the destitute. This is clearly insufficient as a norm by which to regulate the everyday life of a number of people living in common and the text does indeed refer to a papally approved 'regular form of life' (*institutio regularis*) which is not to be contravened. The nature of this form of life is not, however, specified.

A similar relationship between papal enactment and *institutio* pertains for the First order: *Non omni spiritui* is a far more extensive document than *Diligentiam pii patris*, but again it is not a guide to everyday existence. It is concerned with the external life of the community: its legal rights, duties, administration and issues which might provoke episcopal opposition or dispute. Thus it begins with an *arenga* on the reasons for papal intervention and a description of the process by which

[30] See p. 72.

[31] '[I]n locis vestris, in quibus ad obsequium Dei communiter vivitis, institutio regularis secundum approbationem apostolice sedis inviolabiliter observetur . . .'.

[32] Appendix I, 8: 'de artificiis autem, que propriis manibus exercetis, ortorum fructibus, et vestrorum animalium nutrimentis, nullus a vobis decimas exigere, vel extorquere presumat, ut ex iis largiores oblationes Ecclesiis, et uberiores elemosinas [sic in Brera AD XVI, 3] indigentibus impendatis'; on Cistercian tithes see Constable, *Monastic Tithes*, pp. 190–7, 251–4.

the order was given approval.[33] *Non omni spiritui*, however, has much longer and more detailed instructions and concessions than those indicated in *Diligentiam pii patris*. As before, the protection of the see of Peter is extended to their churches and persons and their possessions, present and future, are safeguarded in generic terms, but in this case the letter details property of the houses of Viboldone and Rondineto, including Ronco Martano, which had been donated to the community of Rondineto in 1189.[34] The peace and calm of their communities is also protected, with apostolic prohibitions against any theft from their houses or granges or anyone daring to set fire, spill blood, or otherwise do violence. The *ordo canonicus*, 'according to God and their *institutio* approved by the Apostolic see', is to be observed inviolably in their churches. They are not to pay tithes, but rather may receive them, with episcopal consent. Their provosts, if priests, may confer the tonsure of clerics on literate laymen (*laici litterati*) who take the regular habit among them. They may receive both clerics and lay members as long as they are free and absolved. There is to be no transfer by either brothers or sisters without the permission of the provost, unless to a stricter discipline (*arctioris religionis*), but those who depart with written authority are not to be restrained.[35] They may receive churches wishing to adopt their form of *religio* (unless from a stricter discipline) and may also build new churches on their property, provided that the rights of other churches are not thereby prejudiced and they have the diocesan bishop's consent. Business agreements (sales, exchanges, investitures and pledges of property) made by the chapters of the order are to be strictly observed. Their priests, deacons and subdeacons may celebrate solemn mass according to the customs of Mortara and may do so during interdicts and with the brethren of the Second order present, provided that they remain behind closed doors and celebrate in low voices without ringing bells.[36] They are to receive the chrism, holy oil, consecration of altars or basilicas and ordinations to holy orders from the diocesan bishop, though should he not be a catholic, or prove unwilling, they may choose another bishop, as long as he has the grace and communion of the Apostolic see.

The privilege then outlines the administrative structure for the new order which is to centre on four men, the provosts of Viboldone, San

---

[33] See pp. 72–3. [34] See p. 54.

[35] On the development of attitudes towards *transitus* see Picasso, 'San Bernardo e il "transitus" dei monaci', pp. 181–200.

[36] The customs of Mortara, discussed by R. Crotti Pasi, 'Il codice II-12 della biblioteca civica di Pavia, le "consuetudines Mortarienses"', *Bollettino della società pavese di storia patria*, new series 31 (1979), 23–62, are now printed in full together with the rule in Mosca, *Alberto Patriarca di Gerusalemme*, pp. 561–617.

Cristoforo Lodi, Vialone and Rondineto. These are to take it in turn to carry out the annual visitation of all houses and exercise authority over the lesser provosts according to the Cistercian model.[37] There is to be an annual General Chapter, called by the four main provosts, with four prelates of the Second order and four ministers from the Third, but lay members are to be excluded from discussion of spiritual concerns.[38] If any one of the four principal provosts should prove unworthy he is to be removed from office by the other three. The election of provosts is to be carried out through the offices of an arbiter who will nominate three brothers as electors (two clerics and one lay) who will then fast for three days, together with the whole community. After this they are to enquire about the wishes of all the community and the election shall be by unanimous vote or by the majority (or the Benedictine *sanior pars*).[39] Those to be consulted include both the brothers and sisters: women were expected to have a voice in houses of the First order. Finally, the new provost must be a *clericus* at least and shall receive the cure of souls from the diocesan bishop, who may not deny confirmation to any provost elected and approved in this way. The privilege ends with the passage on the need for oaths, the injunctions against those doing violence against their houses or persons mentioned above and the usual *sanctio*.

This privilege immediately raises questions about the nature of the *institutio* and *ordo canonicus* prescribed. No copy of an *ordo canonicus* or rule of St Augustine for the early Humiliati survives. Moreover, where the formula *ordo canonicus* is used for other houses, it is usually followed, as Zanoni noted, by phrases specifying which *ordo* is to be adopted: 'the *ordo canonicus* according to God and the rule of the blessed Augustine and the rule and *institutio* of the Premonstratensians'.[40] A similar situation pertained for the *ordo monasticus*, which was usually specifically associated with the rule of Benedict.[41] By contrast, in the privilege for the First order of the Humiliati, *Non omni spiritui*, this formula is simply 'the *ordo canonicus* according to God and your *institutio* approved by the Apostolic see'.[42] Reference to Augustine is omitted, leaving simply their own, papally approved *institutio*.

---

[37] See p. 91.
[38] The text does not give a name to describe the superiors of the Third order, but the ministers of *Incumbit nobis* are certainly intended; on the use of these titles in practice, however, see below, pp. 148–9.
[39] *RSB*, 64, pp. 144–8.
[40] Cited in Zanoni, p. 94; see Dubois, 'Ordo', *DIP*, VI (1980), cols. 806–20.
[41] *Ibid.*; for contemporary examples (monastic and canonical), among many others, see: *Register*, I, 174, pp. 252–61, p. 254 (1198); 284, pp. 394–5, p. 394 (1198).
[42] Appendix I, 9: 'ordo canonicus secundum Deum et institutionem vestram per Sedem Apostolicam approbatam'.

The only extant candidate for identification with such a papally endorsed *institutio* is the text of the rule known by its incipit, *Omnis boni principium*. This survives in its earliest form in two manuscripts: a fourteenth-century authenticated copy of a papal privilege issued by pope Gregory IX in June 1227, *Cum felicis memorie*, and a mid- or late thirteenth-century codex which also refers to the 1227 bull.[43] *Cum felicis memorie* contained, as Gregory himself tells us, the rule carefully corrected by Innocent III and retained at the Curia, which Gregory had had copied and secured with his own seal for greater safety, so that the text could not be corrupted.[44] Zanoni published an abbreviated transcript of the version in the archive of the Curia Arcivescovile, Milan, omitting prayers, liturgical details and reference to *Cum felicis memorie*, but including the chapter rubrics from unspecified codices of the rule.[45] Since there is as yet no edition of the rule, his transcript and chapter divisions will be used in what follows, except where the early manuscripts differ notably.

Two questions are raised by this body of evidence. First, if the rule were compiled and approved by 1201, why do the earliest surviving texts of *Omnis boni principium* both refer only to 1227? Second, was this the text referred to in both papal bulls and intended as a rule of life for the First and Second orders?

In answer to the first point, a simple solution would be to argue that *Omnis boni principium* was only issued to the order in 1227. This hypothesis certainly matches evidence concerning professions of faith which become more rule-conscious after this date (see below, chapter 6). A later date might also resolve contradictions between the letters of 1201 and *Omnis boni principium* on the election of the superior and, most notably, on the important issue of tithes.[46] In chapter 39 of *Omnis boni*

---

[43] ACA Milan, A/2 (fourteenth-century authenticated copy); Ambrosiana D 58 inf. (codex, second half of thirteenth century); Zanoni discusses the manuscripts, pp. 252, 257, but see now Castagnetti, 'La regola del primo e secondo ordine', appendix 1, who also lists a fragment in Ambrosiana Trotti 263 fol. 1r–v, which once belonged to the Gambara house in Brescia. I have had access only to microfilms of most Ambrosiana manuscripts and have therefore been unable to give folio numbers here.

[44] Appendix 1, 28: ACA Milan A/2, *arenga*: 'Cum felicis memorie Innocentius papa predecessor noster regulam vestram studiose correctam apud apostolicam sedem curaverit reservare nos eam sicut correcta extitit in eodem presenti pagina adnotari fecimus ad cautelam et bulle nostre appensione muniri. Quatinus nulli de cetero sit facultas eandem alicuius amistione fermenti regulam depravare.' Innocent did indeed refer to his intention of keeping a copy in the curia in his letters to both the First and Second orders: for example, Appendix 1, 9: 'cujus exemplar ad majorem cautelam apud sedem apostolicam reservamus'.

[45] *Omnis boni principium*, transcribed Zanoni, pp. 352–70 on the basis of ACA Milan, A/2; discussed pp. 94–112; recently reprinted with line numbering in Mosca, *Alberto Patriarca di Gerusalemme*, pp. 665–84.

[46] On elections, see pp. 108, 114, 129.

principium the brethren are ordered to pay tithes 'on farms and possessions to those to whom they belong'.[47] This was standard practice for a lay community. As we have seen, however, in *Diligentiam pii patris* and *Non omni spiritui*, Innocent III gave both orders some form of exemption from tithe payment and allowed members of the First order to receive tithes, as long as they had the consent of the diocesan bishop. Such contradictions might be thought to reflect two different periods of writing, or at least that the text of the rule was not examined so carefully in 1201 because it was not to be issued. Yet we are told by Gregory that Innocent did indeed correct the text of *Omnis boni principium* and Innocent himself refers to an exemplar held at the Curia. The disagreement cannot therefore be explained by proposing a date in the 1220s for the composition of this rule. Rather, the conflict between the instructions in the two texts may be resolved if we consider the exemptions in *Diligentiam pii patris* and *Non omni spiritui* as the 'final correction' which Innocent himself claimed to have made.[48] The tithe exemptions are the pope's last, personal concessions, overriding the rule and designed to mark his particular favour for the new communities. The contradictions therefore need not prompt us to seek a late date for the composition of *Omnis boni principium*.

If we accept that the rule could have been written in 1201, we are nonetheless left with explaining why the earliest surviving copies of the rule are linked to the 1227 bull. It does not seem probable that a newly established order should be expected to survive for twenty-six years without a rule of life, particularly when the letters of 1201 make explicit reference to the observance of a papally approved *institutio* and there were accusations of heresy to be quelled. Moreover, in 1226 Honorius III wrote to the Brera community instructing them to observe Innocent III's rule.[49] It is surely more likely that while a copy of *Omnis boni principium* was held at the Curia for safekeeping, another was indeed brought back north by the delegates of the Humiliati in 1201, Lanfranc of Lodi and James of Rondineto. It may not, however, have been widely accepted at this date and was therefore reissued in 1227 inserted in a papal bull which gave it renewed authority.[50] This hypothesis also fits well with evidence for the difficulties in establishing uniform observance in the early order.[51] Lanfranc and James may not have found it easy to get the rule accepted. Gregory IX therefore took the sensible step of reissuing an authoritative version of the rule. This

---

[47] *OBP*, 39, p. 366: 'de prediis autem et possessionibus decimas persolveritis ad quas pertinent'.
[48] See p. 96.
[49] Appendix I, 21.
[50] See now Castagnetti, 'La regola del primo e secondo ordine', p. 211.   [51] See p. 203.

was backed by further measures, including the introduction of papal visitation, designed to bring the order into line.[52] It was therefore the 1227 version which circulated most effectively and was most likely to be copied by later scribes. The renewed emphasis on the rule means that it is finally widely adopted and indeed, as we shall see below, its use begins to be reflected in notarial sources such as professions of faith.[53]

The second and still more important question of whether *Omnis boni principium* can be identified as the apostolically approved *institutio* referred to in the correspondence for both the First and Second orders can perhaps best be approached once more details about the text and its sources have been established.

OMNIS BONI PRINCIPIUM

Use of other texts

Omnis boni principium is not a rule written *ex novo* and, as was common, the organisation is not entirely systematic, often based on simple associations of ideas.[54] It resembles the *regulae mixtae* of the seventh and eighth centuries in its inclusion of passages from different earlier rules.[55] The rule of St Benedict is used extensively, even though the result is not perhaps 'substantially Benedictine' in its effect.[56] Zanoni identified fifteen sections based on Benedict when he published his transcript in 1911.[57] To these may be added a further seven which borrow directly from the Benedictine rule and still further passages which were inspired by it.[58] Zanoni also noted that significant sections were taken from rules and texts of quite different genesis. These he identified as Isidore's *De summo bono*, Gregory I's *Regula pastoralis* and the *Regula canonicorum* of Chrodegang, as transmitted through the Aachen decrees of 816–17, the *Institutio Canonicorum Aquisgranensis*.[59] The passage from Isidore, on the need for the prelate to act like a doctor, had also been used by Chrodegang and was to be found in the Aachen decrees, as were parts, though not all, of the passages taken from Gregory. Direct copying from the Aachen document can be discounted, however, since the discrepancies are substantial. A different source was almost certainly

---

[52] See p. 204. [53] See p. 180. [54] See *La règle du Maître*, I, p. 7.
[55] See M. Dunn, 'Mastering Benedict: monastic rules and their authors in the early medieval west', *English Historical Review*, 105 (1990), 567–94, 569.
[56] Zerbi, 'La rinascita', 56 quotes Zanoni, pp. 93–100, to suggest that the rule is not Benedictine 'in sostanza'.
[57] See n. 63 below. [58] *Ibid.* and n. 117.
[59] Zanoni, p. 98; Gregory the Great, *Regula pastoralis*, part 2, 'De vita pastoris', chs. 1–6, pp. 174–218; *Institutio canonicorum aquisgranensis*, pp. 308–421.

used for Gregory's *Regula pastoralis*, either in the form of a full text, or an abbreviated version, such as might be found in a *Florilegia* collection. Moreover, the Aachen *institutio* and Chrodegang were also used in the rule of the order of Sta Croce Mortara to which belonged Albert, bishop of Vercelli, one of those charged by Innocent with examining the Humiliati.[60] It seems extremely likely that the main source for the elements identified by Zanoni as Chrodegang or Aachen was in fact the rule of Mortara familiar to Albert. The selections from Benedict may equally reflect the experience of the other prelate involved at this stage, the Cistercian Peter of Lucedio. The text we have therefore reflects the expertise of those engaged in approving the Humiliati, and indeed there is little in *Omnis boni principium* which is totally new. Out of a total of forty-five chapters, however, twenty-four contain elements which in this particular form have as yet no identified source and the chosen combination of diverse material was certainly novel.[61]

The relationship between the source texts and *Omnis boni principium* is well illustrated by the use made of Gregory I's writings in chapter 1, on the sort of man the prelate ought to be. The main argument of the second section of Gregory's *Regula pastoralis* is summarised, eliminating many of his details and examples. The enumeration of the basic qualities is taken from the list in Gregory's first chapter and then each is expanded upon, using only the opening paragraphs from his chapters 2 to 6.[62]

The use of the rule of Benedict is similarly selective. Benedictine practice is identifiable in chapters on the cellarer, the porter, the property of the community, guests, meetings, prayer, sleep, lateness, obedience, receiving and giving gifts and private property, care of the sick, bedding, travel, on those required to do burdensome tasks, on recalcitrant sinners, on punishments being adapted to match the crime, on not associating with the excommunicate, on novices, manual labour and on the desirable qualities to be cultivated by the brethren. In all, passages from twenty-seven of Benedict's chapters were used here.[63] Many were copied almost verbatim, with only a straightforward exchange of terminology to fit the Humiliati.[64] Other chapters were more fundamentally paraphrased or adapted, or passages were inserted. An important example is to be found in the adaptation of the

---

[60] See pp. 84, 90; for transcripts of the rule and customs of Mortara, see now Mosca, *Alberto Patriarca di Gerusalemme*, pp. 561–617.

[61] The as yet unsourced passages include brief sections or single sentences in the prologue and chapters 1, 2, 4, 7, 9, 10, 12, 14, 16, 19, 20, 21, 25–6, 29–31, 34, 37–40, 43–5.

[62] Gregory the Great, *Regula pastoralis*, pp. 174–218.

[63] *RSB*, 3, 4, 5, 16, 22, 24, 26–8, 31–4, 36, 41, 43, 48, 51, 53, 55, 58, 63, 66, 68, 71 and 72.

[64] For example *prelatus* replaces *abbas*.

Benedictine rule in chapter 45. Here, when discussing the desirable qualities that the brethren should cultivate, the original had read: 'do not give false peace, do not relinquish love, do not swear lest you perjure yourself, offer truth from the heart and mouth'.[65] *Omnis boni principium* reads only 'do not give false peace, do not relinquish love, offer truth from the heart and mouth'.[66] The prohibition on swearing has been neatly removed, reflecting the concern of Innocent and his delegates that the Humiliati should swear 'in cases of compelling need', and not continue the heretically tinged practice of rejecting oath-taking.[67]

The use made of the rule of Chrodegang, mediated through the rule of Mortara, is not as extensive as that of Benedict, being limited almost exclusively to the canonical hours.[68] Thus Chrodegang/Mortara is the main source for passages in chapters 9 on nocturns, 15 on prime, 18 on terce, sext and nones and chapters 11, 13 and 20, respectively justifying the practice of the night office, matins and vespers.[69] Finally, chapter 17 is very close to Mortara chapter 34 (and also reminiscent of the rule of the Master), in its instruction to the brethren to drop everything when the sign is given and hurry to the office, unless they are working too far away, in which case they must celebrate where they find themselves 'in fear of the Lord'.[70]

The regime

The forty-five chapters of the rule cover in some detail most aspects of the daily life of a community. The prologue sets out the basic ethos of the order, underlining the importance of Christ, without whom nothing can be achieved. The christocentric emphasis is repeated later, where Christ is mentioned as a model eight times. Particularly note-worthy is a passage in chapter 37 on obedience where, to Benedict's instruction that the brothers shall obey one another 'knowing that by this road of obedience will they go to God', *Omnis boni principium* adds 'just as for us Christ was obedient to the Father even unto death'.[71]

---

[65] *RSB*, 4, pp. 26–7.   [66] *OBP*, 45, p. 369.   [67] See pp. 100–4.

[68] For the exception, see below n. 85; Zanoni noted the main parallels with Chrodegang and Aachen in his transcript. Therefore only parallels with the rule of Sta Croce Mortara are given, unless he omits the reference.

[69] *OBP*, 15, pp. 359–60 compare RCM, 28, p. 579; *OBP*, 18, p. 360 compare RCM, 30, p. 580; *OBP*, 11, pp. 358–9 compare RCM, 26, p. 578; *OBP*, 13, p 359 compare RCM, 27, p. 578; *OBP*, 20, p. 361 compare RCM, 31, p. 580.

[70] '[c]um timore divino'; see also *La règle du Maître*, 55, pp. 258–9.

[71] *RSB*, 71, pp. 158–9; *OBP*, 37, p. 366: 'nam et Christus factus est obediens Patri usque ad mortem'; this is close to Philippians 2:8.

The prologue is followed by a detailed description of the ideal prelate which uses Isidore (perhaps via Chrodegang), but is essentially based on Gregory I and is mirrored at the end of the rule by a portrait of the ordinary brother. Starting with the superior is justified by comparison with a painter who begins from the head and later paints the limbs.[72] The prelate is then likened to a medical doctor, caring for the brethren with discretion, so that each receives the 'remedy according to the wound'.[73] He must be 'pure in thought, first in works, discreet in silence, profitable in speech, a neighbour to everyone by sympathy, absorbed in contemplation above all men, a companion of well-doers through humility and prompt in the zeal of justice against the vices of transgressors'.[74] The meaning and practice of each of these virtues is then discussed, again following Gregory, before going on to deal with the manner of his election.

The election of the prelate is to take place each year at Septuagesima, when 'religious friends and helpers of Christ's family' are to come together to choose three of the brothers to act as electors. These religious friends and helpers are defined as those who 'are still living justly in the world, in fear of the Lord and, as far as in their power, giving up unjust customs; who visit the sick, distribute anything super-fluous to the poor, loving God and their neighbours'.[75] By contrast to the process for the election of the provosts in *Non omni spiritui*, outsiders are given a remarkably fundamental role in the life of the community, only one step removed from the choice of the prelate whose personality was key to the well-being of the house, as underlined by the emphasis on his authority throughout the rule.

The end of chapter 1 and chapters 2 to 8 of the rule discuss, in essentially Benedictine terms, the installation and first duties of the prelate and other officers of the house, the holding of chapter meetings and the care to be taken of the house's property and guests. There are, however, also one or two points where material has been inserted which may tell us more about the particular concerns of the rule's

---

[72] For similar examples, see Guidoni, *La città dal medioevo al rinascimento*, pp. 170–1.

[73] *OBP*, 1, p. 353: 'hoc summopere perpendens ut iuxta qualitatem vulnerum exhibeat fomenta curationum . . .'.

[74] *OBP*, 1, p. 353: 'ut cogitatione sit mundus, operatione precipuus, discretus in silentio, utilis in verbo, singulis compassione proximus, precunctis contemplatione suspensus, bene agentibus per humilitatem socius, contra delinquentium vitia per zelum iustitie erectus', based on Gregory I, see above, n. 62.

[75] *OBP*, 1, p. 354, with corrections from Ambrosiana D 58 inf.: 'religiose amici et adiutores Christi familie in unum conveniant qui adhuc in mundo iuste conversantes in timore Domino serviunt ac pro posse suo iniuste habita reddentes, qui infirmos visitant, superflua etiam pauperibus distribuunt Deum diligentes et proximum'.

compilers.[76] The most substantial insertion is chapter 7 on the cook, which ordains that a brother shall be chosen who can fulfil the office well and without complaint. Chapter 4 on the porter adds to Benedict's text instructions from the rule of Mortara that all visitors are to be taken straight to the prelate or his deputy, emphasises control on entry and exit at the gate and concludes by warning that any holding this office who are disobedient or impudent will be punished in the same way as other negligent ministers.[77] Finally, in chapter 8 on the holding of chapter, the manner of punishment for those presuming to follow their own will or daring to oppose the prelate differs from that advocated by the Benedictine rule. Whereas Benedict specifies graduated penalties, from secret warning to excommunication, *Omnis boni principium*, here as elsewhere, advocates separation from the brethren at the table and oratory similar to that frequently recommended by Chrodegang and in the rule of Mortara.[78] The guilty shall be subject to separation 'until he or she shall come to their senses and satisfy both God and the prelate'.[79]

The following section of the rule, chapters 9 to 22, which, as we have seen, relies heavily on the rule of Mortara, outlines the routine for the daily round. This begins at dawn with lauds and then prime, at which the brethren make confession to each other.[80] After prime they all go to work in silence, interrupted only by the hours of terce, sext, nones and vespers.[81]

Silence while at work is strongly emphasised in chapter 16. The brethren are warned 'to hide forever, as if they had sworn, anything that they hear or observe in the community, not saying or implying it in any way, unless to the prelate or his deputy so that he or she may take the appropriate action'.[82] After vespers they are to go back to their work or to dinner and after dinner they shall either work or, if they know letters, may read until sunset, if the prelate allows.[83] At sunset the brethren come together for a communal drink before going to the oratory to say the Lord's prayer followed by compline.[84] After this they rest in their beds in silence until the sign for nocturns or, again if the prelate allows, they may keep vigil or work for a while before sleep. As in the rules of

[76] As Tiraboschi suggested, *VHM* I, p. 83.   [77] *OBP*, 4, pp. 355–6; RCM, 22, pp. 575–6.
[78] For example, Chrodegang, 52, col. 1080; RCM, 38, p. 583, *RSB*, 23.
[79] *OBP*, 8, p. 357: 'donec resipiscat et deo ac prelato satisfaciat'.
[80] *OBP*, 12, 13, 15, pp. 359–60.   [81] *OBP*, 16, 17 and 18, p. 360.
[82] *OBP*, 16, p. 360: 'quicquid audiunt aut sentiunt in societate nulli aliquo modo dicant vel innuant, sed quasi iurassent illud perpetuo celent, nisi prelato vel ei qui loco eius erit, ut quid sit agendum provideat . . .'.
[83] *OBP*, 19 and 20, pp. 360–1: '. . . et post cenam cum silentio usque ad occasum soli vel operentur vel legant qui litteras sciunt, prelato concedente'; the meal-times vary according to the fasts, see below, p. 118.
[84] *OBP*, 21, p. 361.

Benedict and Mortara/Chrodegang, they must each sleep in a separate bed and, if possible, all in one dormitory with a light burning.[85] Nocturns is celebrated at midnight after which those who do not wish to work may either pray or rest in their beds.[86] Into this work-centred routine the prelate may insert a chapter of faults which is to be held 'when it pleases him', though the fact that this chapter of the rule is inserted between sections on lauds and confession at prime suggests that it was intended to be held in the early morning.[87]

In this second section, the insertions of new material are more extensive than those in chapters 2 to 8. Chapter 9, on the hours of prayer, uses both Benedict and Chrodegang, but still adds a long section describing the prayers and responses for the night office.[88] Most notably, this insertion instructs them to say the Lord's prayer five times for the dead, five times for their dependants (*familiares*) and five times for benefactors, each to be followed by the kyrie and the relevant *capitula* which are given.[89]

Chapter 10 is one brief sentence, offering the brethren the alternatives of prayer, sleep or work after the night office. The emphasis on labour, as we have seen, is repeated throughout the day, when they are expected to work continuously, but here it is also proposed at night. The brethren are given the choice between reading or working both after vespers and dinner and even after compline, when they may either sleep, pray or work.[90] The balanced structure of life in the Benedictine rule would be lost to any member of the order choosing to work such long hours. Indeed, it has been estimated that in summer the Humiliati (men and women) may have worked as many as twelve hours a day.[91] Only the office, chapter, meals and the evening drink need interrupt the work routine, if the prelate or brethren so desired.

Other insertions in this second section concern lauds and confession to God, the virgin Mary, the saints and the brethren (where Chrodegang/Mortara had advocated only confession to God and the brethren).[92] The inclusion of specific reference to Mary may reflect Cistercian practice, perhaps introduced here by Peter of Lucedio.[93] The manner in which the brethren are to say vespers and compline is also

[85] Chrodegang, 13, col. 1065, 49, cols. 1078–9 based on *RSB*, 22, pp. 70–1; RCM, 32, p. 580.
[86] *OBP*, 9 and 22, pp. 357–8, 361.   [87] *OBP*, 14, p. 359.
[88] *RSB*, 16, pp. 60–1; Chrodegang, 14, col. 1065.   [89] *OBP*, 9, pp. 357–8.
[90] *OBP*, 19 and 21, pp. 360, 361.   [91] Paolini, 'Le Umiliate al lavoro', pp. 262–3.
[92] Lauds: *OBP*, 12, p. 359; Confession: *OBP*, 15, pp. 359–60; RCM, 28, p. 579; Chrodegang, 18, col. 1067, much abbreviated.
[93] See, for example, *Les 'ecclesiastica officia' cisterciens du xiie siècle*, ed. Choisselet and Vernet, p. 455 n. 199, I am grateful to Dr Peter King for drawing my attention to this reference.

slightly modified and distinctions are made between feast and ordinary days, as they are in the chapter on the night office.[94]

The second half of the rule is less systematic. Chapters 23 and 24 deal with discipline, but the subject is not treated in full until chapters 33 to 37. The intervening chapters deal with a variety of subjects, from silence, property, the sick, eating and fasting, to clothing, bedding and journeys.

The observance of silence, already treated in chapter 16 on work, is once more stressed in chapters 25 and 26. It is acknowledged that silence is not always appropriate, since it may 'abandon in error those who could be educated'.[95] Nonetheless, silence is here praised as a virtue in itself. The brethren are enjoined to curb their tongues as a general rule 'lest our religion be useless or in vain'.[96] Silence is, however, specifically to be observed from the time of the evening drink until after prime, during the Office and meals, in the church, dormitory, refectory, warming room, kitchen, mill and work room (*operatorium*), in the knowledge that in this observance, their prayers will penetrate the skies.[97] In particular they are not to talk while at work, unless absolute necessity requires it, although the only reason that the over-night silence may be broken is to speak of something pertaining to the work in hand.[98]

The second half of chapter 25 warns the brethren of the dangers of certain types of speech: as well as lies, they are admonished to avoid disparagement, or even listening to it, since by doing so, both the speaker and listener are guilty of the same crime.[99] To these are added disputation which begets fights, judgement and condemnation, jeering or words which lead to laughter, vain speech, complaining, adulation, laughter itself and cursing. They are instead to speak only of what is good for the strengthening of the faith so that it gives grace to those hearing.[100]

Chapters 27 on common property and 28 on the care of the sick are

[94] *OBP*, 21, p. 361.

[95] *OBP*, 25, p. 362: 'cultus iustitie est silentium, nec tamen semper est silendum sicut neque semper loquendum; est tempus tacendi et tempus loquendi, nam sicut incauta locutio in errorem protrahit, ita indiscretum silentium eos qui erudiri poterant in errore derelinquit'.

[96] *OBP*, 25, p 362: 'a quibus igitur refrenare linguam semper debeatis, ne nostra religio sit inutilis vel vana'.

[97] *OBP*, 26, p. 363: 'scientes procul dubio quod hec custodientes suis orationibus celum perforabunt'.

[98] *OBP*, 26, p. 363; RCM, 29, p. 580.

[99] *OBP*, 25, p. 362, with corrections from Ambrosiana D 58 inf.: 'set nec detrahentes audias. Vtrisque enim simile crimen imputatur'.

[100] *OBP*, 25, p. 362: '. . . omnis sermo malus ex ore uestro non procedat, sed si quis bonus est ad edificationem fidei ut det gratiam audientibus'.

very Benedictine. Chapters 33, 34 and 36 of the rule of Benedict are used, with only one noteworthy adaptation. This was the perhaps significant omission of the Benedictine prohibition on the possession of books and pens (*graphia*), suggesting that some of the Humiliati were expected to have their own pens and books rather than just those held in common, and confirming therefore that their members included the literate.[101]

Chapter 29 outlines the times of eating and fasting as they are to be observed during the day and at different times of the year.[102] On ordinary days the brethren are to eat after sext and after vespers. The second of these meals had been fitted into the routine outlined in chapters 9 to 21, but the first, that after sext, is not mentioned there and indeed the number of fast days is so high that a midday meal would be the exception rather than the rule. When fasting, they are to eat after nones, except during Lent, when they are to wait until after vespers.

There are two periods of continuous fasting during the year, Lent and Advent, as well as the three days imposed at Septuagesima for the election of the new prelate. Otherwise fasting is to be observed for three days a week except from Easter to Pentecost, when it is restricted to the Friday after the octave of the Resurrection, the eve of the feasts of St Philip and St James, the three Rogation days and the eve of Pentecost. The prelate is allowed some discretion to decide whether the community should fast on the second of the three days allocated in each week, except at Christmas, in Lent and on the major feasts. Brethren on journeys may also disregard the fasts, if they have permission.[103] If the full regime were respected, however, the community would be fasting for a total of approximately two hundred days in the year.

When they do eat, the meal is to include one or two suitable cooked dishes, with an optional extra dish at dinner if the prelate gives licence. Eggs, cheese and fish are normally permitted (meat is not), but when fasting, eggs, cheese, and milk are to be avoided, so the staple diet would appear to be fish, bread, vegetables and wine.[104]

The next two chapters of the rule concern the clothing of the brothers and their bedding, though no mention is made of the sisters' clothing. Benedict had allowed for diversity according to climate, as well as for spare tunics for the night and to facilitate washing.[105] Here,

---

[101] On Humiliati literacy see for example, p. 125; on the membership of notaries, who would need pens and other equipment, see p. 191.
[102] *OBP*, 29, pp. 363–4.   [103] *OBP*, 32, p. 364.
[104] Withdrawal of the portion of wine is a punishment for those coming late to table: *OBP*, 24, p. 362.
[105] *RSB*, 55, pp. 124–7.

the brothers are to have a shirt, breeches, a fur, a long robe, a cloak, a lambskin, various types of footwear (sandals, socks and clogs) and night-shoes.[106] The lambskin or fur was traditional monastic garb and perhaps particularly welcome in the bitter winters of northern Italy.[107]

The same provision for cold weather is allowed in bedding: as well as a mattress, pillow and two woollen blankets, the brethren are again allowed to have a sheepskin. In addition, the sick may have a feather mattress and sheets of tow or linen. As in the rule of Benedict, all the beds are to be regularly inspected by the prelate and if any private property (*opus peculiare*) is found the owner is to be severely punished.

The five chapters dealing with discipline in the community are Benedictine in derivation. Chapters 33 (on those ordered to do burdensome tasks), 36 (on not associating with excommunicate brethren) and 37 (on obedience) are almost identical to the rule of Benedict. Chapters 34 and 35, however, include important insertions. Chapter 34, on recalcitrant brethren, first uses Benedict chapter 28 but modifies it. Where Benedict advocated excommunication, *Omnis boni principium* is closer to Chrodegang and Mortara, imposing only exclusion from the table or oratory. Then, after the end of Benedict's text, *Omnis boni principium* adds a section ordaining that recalcitrant sinners shall be made to sleep outside the dormitory, hear the hours outside the oratory and speak to no one except the prelate or one of the brethren sent to make him or her see sense. If they wish to withdraw they are to be given simple clothes and necessary covering and food for one day.[108] If any who have withdrawn without permission wish to return, they are first to return any stolen property and will then be interrogated by the prelate in chapter, will take the last place and have silence imposed on them, for as long as the prelate chooses. Chapter 35 adds to this a note on matching the punishment to fit the crime and on the correction of less serious faults, once more replacing Benedict's penalty of excommunication with exclusion from the table.

In the final eight chapters of the rule the vast majority of the material is neither directly Benedictine, nor taken from Chrodegang/Mortara, but much of it is clearly derived from practices found in monastic customaries. Chapter 38 makes provisions for personal hygiene. The brethren may choose to be bled three times a year, in April or May, September and February, more often if the prelate allows.[109] This is linked with the eating of meat, prohibited in the following sentence,

---

[106] *OBP*, 30, p. 364.   [107] See, for example, 'Capitulare monasticum 817', p. 345.
[108] *OBP*, 34, p. 365 with correction from Ambrosiana D 58 inf.: 'detur eis a prelato tegumentum necessarium et unius diei uictum'.
[109] *OBP*, 38, p. 366.

unless when ill or weak. Shaving or trimming of beards and hair-cutting are optional and are to be allowed only once a month unlike, for example, the Aachen monastic capitularies which had allowed shaving once every fifteen days.[110] For these tasks each of the brethren is to have his or her own comb, knife and needle, so that 'all can be done in peace and silence.'[111] Finally, washing of heads is allowed every fifteen days, while the brethren are to wash each other's feet three times a year, at Christmas, on Maundy Thursday and on the Eve of Pentecost. Those doing the washing are to be chosen by the prelate or his deputy.

Chapter 39 deals with the attitude to be taken to any land owned by the house. Farms are to be worked with the brethren's own hands, or at their own expense, and they are not to accept rents for them, unless with the licence of the common chapter, for some just cause. They are forbidden to possess honours or estates and are instructed to pay tithes, a requirement perhaps overruled by Innocent III.[112] This passage then rather unexpectedly goes on to discuss the ceremony for entry into the order of married couples. The link may be the expected donations of property that such couples might make, although this aspect is not discussed here. In a manner similar to emerging marriage customs, the couple are to swear perpetual chastity in front of the church and are then to be received into the order, the man going among the brothers and the woman among the sisters according to the rule.[113]

The way such new members are to be received is then considered, although no further mention is made of the sisters. Chapters 40 and 41 deal with the testing of vocation, the vows to be taken and the treatment of novices. In a manner not unlike the reading of the rule to Benedictine postulants, those wishing to enter the order are to be informed about the details of the rule and the 'proposal of poverty' (*propositum paupertatis*) by the prelate, who must emphasise that postulants will have to give up self-will and dismiss all secular things. If they persist they are then to go away and return anything held unjustly, pay any debts, give satisfaction as far as possible to others and provide for any children or dependants (*familie*). If postulants have small, weak or sick children, however, for whom they alone can provide, they are not to be accepted into the order. Any property is to be disposed of, though some may be used to buy suitable clothing as allowed by the rule and the rest may be given to the prelate if he wishes to accept it. The novice then undergoes a probationary year during which, in imitation of the Benedictine practice, a 'wise and discreet master' is to be appointed to

---

[110] 'Capitula monachorum', pp. 200–4, 201, para. 5.
[111] *OBP*, 38, p. 366: 'ut in pace et silentio cuncta peragantur'. [112] See above, pp. 109–10.
[113] On the acceptance of couples and of children, see below, pp. 192–8.

look after the novices and to warn them of the difficulties and trials ahead. At the end of the year they may choose to withdraw or, if the prelate and brethren approve, may be received into the order. The ceremony of profession is then described in detail, after which the rule ordains that the prelate shall allocate them a stall (*stalio*) in the choir and a place in the refectory and dormitory.[114]

The last chapters of the rule deal once more with work, with the sisters and finally with the desirable qualities which the brethren should cultivate. Chapter 42 reiterates that the community are to live by the labour of their own hands, both to acquire food and clothing because this will itself bring blessing and because it is more blessed to give than to receive (Acts 20:35), another reminder of the importance of charity. Perhaps because it follows the chapter on the reception of novices, this section directs that the community is not to accept gifts or donations from anyone who has not returned ill-gotten gains, or at least promised to do so, unless they should be in need or out on a journey, when they may accept the necessities of life from anyone.

Chapters 43 and 44, on the treatment of the sisters, insist throughout on the need to keep them apart and to preserve their chastity. They are to be loved as spiritual sisters and cared for as though they were the brides of Christ. The community is to have a separate cloister for them, to which access by the brothers is extremely restricted. Anyone writing or receiving letters from them, or sending anything else, is to be subject to severe penalties, if not expulsion from the congregation. Even the prelate is not to speak alone with the sisters, unless he can be seen by several people. Nor is he to give anyone else permission to speak to them, unless in his presence or that of his deputy. The only exception is to be when the sisters make confession to a priest and this is always to be in a place where both can be seen. Should any of the sisters fall sick, the prelate, accompanied by another 'most honest brother' is to visit them, but only to discuss the health of body and soul. No one is to enter the cloister of the sisters before dawn or after sunset, unless through unavoidable necessity. Finally, the prelate and some of the honest brethren are to attend the chapter of the sisters twice, or at least once a month. This is to be done so that something of the rule under which they must live may be read to them and they may hear words 'concerning the heavenly kingdom and the lives of the saints'.[115] This, incidentally, is the only reference to the possible contents of Humiliati

---

[114] On professions, see ch. 6 below.

[115] *OBP*, 44 p. 369: 'bis vel semel ad minus in mense sit prelatus ipse cum aliquibus honestis fratribus in capitulo sororum, ut eis aliquid legatur de regula vel legi faciat, sub qua vivere debent ac sermonem habeat vel haberi faciat de celesti regno et vita beatorum'.

exhortations or sermons in thirteenth-century sources potentially written or vetted by the Humiliati themselves.

The rule ends with a long discourse on the virtues of the ordinary brethren, deliberately placed to match the opening chapter on those of the prelate.[116] As we have seen, much of this is based on the rule of Benedict.[117] What is added is a development of the same themes close to the rule of Mortara: that the brethren must offer a good example and avoid judging their seniors.[118] This they must do if they wish to progress in religion.

Authorship

The parallels between sections of *Omnis boni principium* and the Mortara rule make it extremely likely that Albert of Vercelli was closely involved in compiling the new *institutio*, choosing (and omitting) practices which were familiar in order to construct an appropriate model of life for the Humiliati. The Cistercian Peter of Lucedio may equally prove to have been responsible for the selections from the rule of Benedict and perhaps for introducing the Cistercian practice of confession to the virgin Mary. The extant rule should thus be seen as the result of collaborative effort between these prelates and the Humiliati leaders, a view supported by two internal factors: the authoritative style of the language used and, at one point at least, the contradictory use of source texts.

The language strongly suggests that much of the text was prepared by a superior or external legislative authority. On the whole the construction of sentences avoids the use of personal pronouns: 'the brethren shall come together . . . each shall sleep in their own beds'. However, the authority behind these instructions is revealed in occasional passages using the first person plural: 'we freely grant' (*libere concedimus*).[119] There are other variations: in the prologue the writer or compiler uses the first person singular, describing himself with a rhetorical flourish as 'I, unwise and ignorant writer' (*ego imprudens et inscius scriptor*) and on occasion the use of the first person plural is fairly neutral, as in chapter 1: 'we took care to portray what kind [of man] the prelate ought to be' (*curavimus depingere qualis prelatus esse debeat*).[120] In some cases the tone

---

116 *OBP*, 45, p. 369: 'sicut superius in primo huius regule capitulo depinximus prelatum, ita in hoc inferiori et ultimo capitulo qualis esse debeat subiectus curavimus ostendere'.

117 The source was not identified by Zanoni, but is based on ideas in chapter 4 of Benedict with additions from 5, 63 and 72 (pp. 26–7, 32–5, 142–5, 158–61).

118 *OBP*, 45, pp. 369–70; RCM, 11–12, pp. 567–8.   119 *OBP*, 44, p. 369.

120 *OBP*, prologue and 1, p. 353; 25, p. 362.

even suggests an author identifying with the group, as in a reference in chapter 25 to 'our religion'.[121] Nonetheless, the dominant tone is one of legislative authority, establishing the rules for a new order: that authority was surely the prelates Albert and Peter, together with the Humiliati representatives themselves.

In chapters 2 and 3 there is some evidence of internal contradiction which may confirm this multiple authorship of the text. In the first of these chapters, the newly elected prelate is instructed to call together two or three brethren, with whose help he is to appoint the cellarer, porter and cook.[122] The following chapter states, however, that the cellarer is to be elected by the whole congregation of the brethren.[123] Unless we are to assume that the copying of texts was indiscriminate, whoever assembled chapter 2 (for which as yet I have found no direct source) was probably not the same as the compiler of chapter 3, which is based very closely on chapter 31 of the rule of Benedict.

We may therefore conclude that *Omnis boni principium* was produced by a group of individuals and that this group probably included Peter of Lucedio and certainly included Albert of Vercelli. It must also, however, have included the Humiliati leaders, James of Rondineto and Lanfranc of Lodi.[124] As Grundmann argued, the original statutes presented by the Humiliati served as a foundation on which the new rule was established.[125] The contribution of Innocent III himself is less easy to identify. Although there are some medical metaphors of the sort he particularly enjoyed using, there are also, as we have seen, points which contradict the letters.[126] It may well be that Innocent's corrections are to be found in the correspondence of 1201 rather than in *Omnis boni principium*.

Intended recipients

As we have seen, the rule assembled by this group combines canonical and monastic elements, for example in the observance of the office or

---

[121] *OBP*, 25, p. 362. The transcript in Zanoni repeats this use of 'our' in the following line, but this is not found in Ambrosiana D 58 inf.: 'a quibus igitur refrenare linguam semper debeatis, ne nostra religio sit inutilis uel uana et a quibus non semper set pro tempore cessare, ut ex uestris [sic] uerbis non condempnemini'.

[122] *OBP*, 2, p. 355.   [123] *OBP*, 3, p. 355.

[124] For the suggestion that James of Rondineto may have played an important role, see now Alberzoni, 'Giacomo di Rondineto', p. 133.

[125] Grundmann, p. 76.

[126] See for example Innocent III, *Selected Letters . . .Concerning England*, pp. 117–20, p. 118 (1209): 'like a skilled doctor varying the resources of his medical art, applying the knife when fomentations are of no use and with a draught of warm water curing ailments which have not responded to drastic medicine'.

the discipline required. Some key elements of both forms of life are, however, missing. For example, the care of souls, central to the rule of Mortara, is not found here. Can it have been intended for houses of both the First and Second orders?

It will have become apparent above that there are numerous parallels between the two types of regular Humiliati community. According to the papal correspondence of 1201 both will include women as well as men and both will include laymen (a layman is mentioned as an arbiter in the election of the provost of a First order house).[127] It might be objected that if it were intended for both types of house, it is strange that the title of the superior used in *Omnis boni principium* is prelate, as used in the papal correspondence for the Second order. It should, however, be noted that the extant bull *Cum felicis memorie* issued with the text in 1227 is addressed in generic fashion to the 'Ministers and brothers and sisters of the order' and that the use of distinct titles is not in fact standardised in papal correspondence with the order until mid-century.[128] In the absence of an alternative rule or *institutio* at this date and in view of the combination of monastic and canonical elements, which would not have been necessary had there been no intention to combine the two groups, it seems most likely that *Omnis boni principium* should indeed be identified as the *institutio* approved by the Apostolic see for both orders. It may be what survived of initial attempts to build one single *propositum* out of the various *proposita* of the Humiliati. Which begs the question of what kind of religious were thereby created.

Maccarrone argues that Innocent III did not intend to create monks or canons. *Licet multitudini*, sent to the Humiliati in 1200, emphasises 'not so much the place as the vow, not so much the habit as the disposition', which Maccarrone interprets as meaning that the discipline to be imposed would not involve the cloister and the habit, the duties characteristic of the monastic life.[129] He goes on to argue that the Second order was the 'most original branch of the order', because the pope gave the juridical status of religious to the unmarried laity, without making them 'true monks under a monastic rule, nor religious of the type of the hospital and military orders'.[130] This view has been widely accepted. In a study of north Italian monasticism, Zerbi excludes the Humiliati,

---

[127] See p. 108.   [128] Zanoni, p. 132.

[129] Appendix I, 5: 'non tam locum quam votum, non tam habitum quam affectum'. Maccarrone, *Studi*, p. 286. Tiraboschi had earlier argued that the First order were not canons until the fifteenth century. *VHM* I, p. 87.

[130] Maccarrone, *Studi*, p. 288; see also his 'Riforma e sviluppo della vita religiosa con Innocenzo III', p. 49.

because this type of life lies outside the monastic environment and belongs rather to the flourishing of new models of 'evangelical life' . . . which reach their highest expression in Francis of Assisi. [131]

Maccarrone did not use *Omnis boni principium*. Zanoni, who did, argued that the lay Second order prayed 'according to the manner of the laity', by which he meant that they did not use the Psalter and that the text was simplified, removing biblical verses and prayers or references to the Psalms.[132] Zanoni's view reflects a passage in a mid-thirteenth-century sermon describing the Humiliati by the Dominican Humbert of Romans: 'the lay men and women have certain other prayers which they say according to the lay manner'.[133] There are indeed cases in *Omnis boni principium* where the Lord's prayer was laid down as an alternative to the Psalms.[134] Jacques de Vitry's account in the *Historia Occidentalis* also confirms that those who did not know the canonical hours said the Lord's prayer (*oratio dominicam*). Yet Chrodegang's rule has similar arrangements without impugning the canonical status of the community and Vitry also states that both laity and clerics said the hours, day and night, and that most were literate, presumably in Latin.[135] Those unable to learn the prayers would surely have been very few. Moreover, Zanoni excluded the liturgical elements from his edition of *Omnis boni principium*, but the full text includes Psalms and references to the usual daily round of offices expected of 'true monks'.[136] The text also refers both to the habit and to the cloister. There are some unmonastic elements, such as the insistence on oaths, which were normally prohibited for monks.[137] However, reference to *Omnis boni principium* seems to confirm the regular flavour of elements in the new order. Whether or not members of the Second order were true *religiosi*, the aim was to establish uniform regular observance. This was achieved by combining elements of the Benedictine rule familiar to the Cistercian Peter of Lucedio with the canonical routine of Albert's original community at Sta Croce Mortara. Key passages were adapted or omitted to suit the new order. The combination of monastic and canonical elements and the absence of any other early rule make the conclusion that the *institutio* referred to in the letters to both the First

---

[131] Zerbi, 'La rinascita monastica nella bassa milanese dopo l'anno 1000', 56.

[132] Zanoni, p. 99.

[133] Humbert of Romans, *Sermones ad Humiliatos*, comp. Zanoni, pp. 261–3: 'Laici autem et laicae habent certas aliquas orationes, quas dicunt secundum modum laicalem'. A sermon on the Humiliati was included in his 'De eruditione praedicatorum', part II: 'De modo prompte cudendi sermones', ch. 38.

[134] For example, *OBP*, 9, p. 357.   [135] Vitry, *HO*, 28, p. 144.

[136] They are not in the manuscript on which he based his transcription, ACA Milan, A/2.

[137] See above, pp. 100–4.

and Second orders was *Omnis boni principium* inescapable. This was to be observed together with the instructions in the papal letters which distinguished certain practices for members of the two orders, in particular adding the customs of Mortara for the First order and establishing their status as belonging to the *ordo canonicus*.

1201: A SUMMARY

A history of Humiliati spirituality cannot be written on the basis of the letters of Innocent III in 1201 and the text of *Omnis boni principium*. Nonetheless these do serve as a guide to the ideas behind the new order. *Incumbit nobis* lays out a plan of life for married lay people, dedicated to work and prayer and providing mutual support in a fraternity brought together each week to hear exhortations to a pious life. They will also provide alms for the needy.[138] *Omnis boni principium* is traditional in outlook, emphasising monastic virtues such as obedience and advocating common property rather than poverty, as revealed in passages such as those on the acceptance of rents and the prayers for benefactors, whose donations were evidently to be encouraged.[139] It is also highly pragmatic, setting regulations such as those concerning the acceptance of the proceeds from ill-gotten gains, which could be overridden by the prelate in case of need. No Humiliati brethren were to die of starvation.

The text of *Omnis boni principium* is closely based on earlier rules, yet certain omissions and choices of emphasis reveal what is special about the new communities, or 'congregations', as they are sometimes called in the text. There was no lector or group reading, but unlike Benedict's rule, there was no explicit prohibition on personal books or pens and some brethren may have been reading after vespers. The sisters were not expected to read, but were to have the rule read to them and to hear exhortations. While the papal privilege for the First order *Non omni spiritui* refers to their participation in the election of provosts, the sisters are much less noticeable here. Indeed, while *Omnis boni principium* was undoubtedly intended for both sexes (and the term *fratres* can often conveniently be rendered as 'brethren' to encompass them both), the paucity of references to the women is indicative of the marginal role assigned to them. There is, for example, no provision for the women in the section on clothing.

Incumbit nobis lists humility as the first virtue for Tertiaries, but despite

---

[138] I have found no evidence for the assertion that the Humiliati gave special attention to lepers; Little, *Religious Poverty and the Profit Economy*, p. 118.
[139] On this, see also Bolton, 'The poverty of the Humiliati', p. 54.

the name acquired by the movement, it is not otherwise stressed. Rather, manual labour is strongly emphasised, providing a reason not to fast for the Third order and filling all gaps in the daily round of prayers for the regulars. In the regular houses, it is to be undertaken without interruptions in a specially allocated work room. As in the rule of Mortara, work is to be allotted as reason dictates, carried out in silence, with no speaking unless of the work in hand and then only when necessary. Unlike in the Mortara and earlier rules, however, this labour is not based on the need to avoid idleness as 'the enemy of the soul'.[140] In *Omnis boni principium*, the driving force is a slightly adapted version of the biblical injunction: 'if any would not work, neither should he eat' (2 Thess. 3:10), which has become the more direct 'he who does not work will not eat'.[141] This is neither traditional monastic manual labour, nor is it simply intended to support the brethren. It is work both to give sustenance and blessing to the worker (the next sentence cites psalm 127 on the blessings of work), and to provide charity. The importance of this charity was recognised by Innocent, who released the Second order from the payment of tithes on the products of their handicrafts because they would give greater gifts to churches and more fruitful alms to the indigent.[142] Both First and Second orders are to hold land, but it is envisaged that their own labour will sustain their communities and provide the means to give alms.[143]

Perhaps the most remarkable aspect of this regime is the combination of canonical and monastic elements, allowing both the First and Second orders to use the same rule. It has been argued that the twelfth century saw a breakdown of the distinctions between the two orders of monks and clerics and that Innocent III 'certainly equated the two tonsures'.[144] Others have shown how difficult it often was (and remains) to distinguish between medieval monks and regular canons, who were not automatically involved in the care of souls.[145] The use of *Omnis boni principium* with canonical and monastic elements by both the First and Second orders would certainly have narrowed the distinction between the two types of religious. The presence of women envisaged in communities belonging to all three orders of the Humiliati confirms this impression.

The idea established in 1201 was the product of a combination

---

[140] A traditional Benedictine idea: *RSB*, 48, p. 110.
[141] *OBP*, 16, p. 360; RCM, 29, pp. 579–80.   [142] Appendix I, 8.
[143] See also Paolini, 'Gli eretici e il lavoro', p. 158.
[144] See Constable, *Monastic Tithes*, pp. 147–8.
[145] For example, Brooke, 'Monk and canon: some patterns in the religious life of the twelfth century', pp. 110–12.

between the expertise of the papally delegated churchmen and twenty-five years of experience from the Humiliati themselves. Yet a rule only comes to life in the observance. It is not easy to ascertain the extent to which the idea of the order embodied in Innocent III's letters and in *Omnis boni principium* was observed in practice in the early years of the order, in particular as there are no extant early constitutions.[146] Indeed, notarial evidence and papal letters suggest that in some areas the rule was not observed until the 1220s and later.[147] Nonetheless the surviving papal privileges reveal that as the order developed, adaptation and mitigation proved necessary, or at least desirable, in several areas. The idea set out in 1201 and the reality of observance soon diverged.

REGULATION AND PRACTICE

The need for change

The regulations laid down in 1201 were intended to be observed inviolably; however, clarification and modification were soon felt to be necessary. As we might expect, there are signs of doubt about this process, but it was neither as profound nor as controversial as the changes witnessed by the Friars Minor.[148] At least for the First and Second orders, the gap between the idea of the rule and the reality of everyday life was not so difficult to bridge. There had never been a charismatic leader whose embrace with Lady Poverty made institutional development so difficult for many Franciscans to accept. Indeed, there had never been a single individual whose life formed an automatic and immutable model. Many of the changes made were simply the result of the need for tighter regulation and seem to have been achieved without serious conflict.

Nonetheless, the papal letters do show an awareness of the difficulties inherent in changing something which had been intended as an inviolable rule. This is fleetingly revealed later in the century, in the *arengae* of three of Innocent IV's letters concerning minor clarifications and modifications, issued on 30 October 1246.[149] None of the changes were as fundamental as, for example, that introduced in another letter earlier in the same month concerning the new office of Master General, but it is only in these letters that arguments in defence of change were laid out.[150] The adaptations, it was argued, were justifiable because they were intended (in their case as in others), not to diminish, but rather to

---

[146] See above, p. 99 n. 2. [147] See below chs. 6 and 7.
[148] See M. D. Lambert, *Franciscan Poverty* (London, 1961). [149] Appendix I, 58, 60, 61.
[150] Appendix I, 55.

increase their *religio* and were necessary for two reasons. First, because both people and times had changed and second, because the lack of expertise of the 'first few, rough brothers of the order' concerning the 'condition, difficulties, burdens of the order and strength of the brethren' meant their rule contained both difficult and confused duties which the brethren now knew from experience could only be tolerated with serious discomfort.[151] This argument is not entirely plausible, since it disregards the fact that senior churchmen had been involved both in the laying down of the original framework in 1200–1 and in overseeing its development during the first forty-five years of the order's history. As well as the men appointed by Innocent III to investigate and eventually approve the Humiliati rule, ecclesiastics of all levels, from Dominican priors to the papal legates, Gerard *de Sesso* and Goffredus, cardinal priest of San Marco, were involved in promoting and regulating the Humiliati.[152] To some extent the passage is an opportune rhetorical device, designed to justify novelty, about which anxiety was common-place. Yet, since it also introduces a bull which includes clarification of the process of elections which had certainly been confused in 1201, it is also at least in part a fair account of events.[153]

The papal letters 1201–c. 1250

In addition to the usual confirmations of apostolic protection, the papal letters to the Humiliati in the first half of the thirteenth century cover a recurrent range of subjects concerning both the internal observance of a religious community and its relations with the outside world. These include, among others, the observance of silence, fasting, diet, attending the office during interdicts, oath-taking and taxation.[154] It would not be practical here, nor even realistic, given the incomplete nature of the evidence, to attempt to cover all aspects of their observance. Brief consideration of three particularly fruitful areas, oath-taking, fasting and diet, will serve to represent the general lines of change and underline some key aspects of their regime.

---

[151] Appendix I, 60.
[152] See for example, appendix I, *16, 32, *36, *37.
[153] Each year, the chapter is to elect one man to choose three brothers of the convent to enquire into everyone's preferences and then elect as prelate the brother whom the majority or wiser part of the chapter shall consider suitable. The involvement of religious friends, envisaged in *Omnis boni principium* has been replaced by the choice of an individual, perhaps like the arbiter mentioned in *Non omni spiritui* for the First order. See above, pp. 108, 114.
[154] See appendix I.

Oath-taking

The danger of rejecting oaths was very apparent to those investigating the Humiliati at the turn of the century, and the letters produced reveal their concern to make it clear that swearing oaths was not in itself anathema and indeed was necessary in certain circumstances. As we have seen, the letters established that the Humiliati were not to indulge in unnecessary swearing but were to give oaths in cases of compelling need. This definition allowed them to insist on avoiding swearing in daily conversation, something long considered desirable for good christians, but reintegrated them into the normal workings of social relationships.[155] It left room for generous interpretation, giving no indication of what might amount to compelling need. This very generosity made further clarification more or less inevitable, however, and some traces of this process survive in papal letters from the late 1220s and beyond.

In 1227 Gregory IX wrote to Henry *de Settala*, archbishop of Milan, concerning the fact that unspecified secular authorities, presumably the *podestà* and/or commune of Milan, had often forced the Humiliati to take oaths, even over very minor matters.[156] Gregory ordered the archbishop to ensure that oaths were no longer required, unless when acting as witnesses, to give a calumny oath, for peace or faith, or for 'urgent need and evident utility'.[157] The need for witnesses to give oaths or for oath-taking to ratify peace or as a test of faith was well established.[158] The calumny oath required a plaintiff to call upon God 'to witness that he had not brought his action simply to harass the defendant and that he intended to prove his claims honestly', while the defendant 'swore that he would offer an honest defence to the plaintiff's claims and that he was not doing so out of malice'.[159] The same conditions, allowing oaths in cases of peace, faith, calumny and testimony, had been made in the *Memoriale propositi* of 1221, so the Humiliati were here drawing closer in their practices to the order of penance then established.[160] These were very specific categories for

---

[155] On the desirability of avoiding unnecessary swearing, see for example, Peter the Chanter, 'Verbum abbreviatum', 127, *PL*, 205, cols. 23–370, 322–3.

[156] Appendix I, 31.

[157] *Ibid.*, 'testimonii, calumpnie, pacis et fidei . . . urgens necessitas et evidens utilitas'.

[158] Gratian 22.1.1: Iuramentum pro federe pacis est faciendum (Council of Toledo); for an example of an oath for peace at which a Humiliati superior was present see *Il 'registrum magnum' del comune di Piacenza*, 468, 499, 605, 704 and below, p. 240.

[159] Brundage, *Medieval Canon Law*, p. 131.

[160] See Stewart, '*De illis qui faciunt penitentiam*', p. 193; see also Nicholas IV's bull for penitents in Brescia, *Supra montem* (1289): penitents were to avoid swearing in common speech (*communi loquela*), but should swear 'videlicet pro pace, calumpnia et testimonio perhibendo ac etiam in

legitimate oaths; however, the generalised provision of 'urgent necessity and evident utility' remained. The vagueness persisted in the next letter concerning oath-taking, issued in July 1232, which also saw an extension of the practice: the Humiliati of *Lombardia* and the March were not only to swear oaths themselves in cases of need or acceptable utility (*utilitas probabilis*), but might also require them, presumably in the same cases.[161] The distinction implied in 1201 between the greater guilt of those who extracted oaths compared to those who swore them was no longer heeded.[162]

These letters show that the Humiliati still attached importance to the question of oath-taking and perhaps felt the need for papal support to introduce changes, but the way in which the rule was interpreted in practice still remains unclear. Only in 1238 is there finally a more tangible clue. Gregory's letter to the community of Rondineto in Como in October of that year suggests that the rule had been interpreted as excluding oaths for temporal matters.[163] This, it was claimed, had often caused unspecified damage to the house, presumably in judicial and financial matters, hindering their activities in the courts and the marketplace.[164] Therefore Gregory, quoting the standard passage on the oath as the end of all controversy, now allowed them to take oaths freely 'as reason required' and notwithstanding the contrary provisions of their rule.[165] Thus we may assume that at least at Rondineto, the phrase *urgens et evidens utilitas* had until then been interpreted as limiting the use of oaths to spiritual or perhaps ecclesiastical affairs.

This 'liberalisation' of oath-taking was addressed only to the provost and brethren of Rondineto. Perhaps they in turn allowed their daughter houses to benefit from the privilege, but there is no surviving evidence to suggest that it was ever applied to the whole order. That the objection to oaths was a live issue is revealed in charters allowing the exemption of individuals from oath-swearing, because they were Humiliati. In a transaction between residents of Vaiano and the church of Sta Maria Beltrade and others, for example, the Humiliatus Ucellus *de loco Maconago* was declared exempt from the oath on these grounds.[166] That in the case of Tertiaries at least this objection was

---

contractu emptionis venditionis et donationis ubi videbitur expedire'. Meersseman, 'Ordo
  fraternitatis', I, p. 440.
[161] Appendix I, 41.   [162] Above, p. 103.
[163] Appendix I, 52: 'secundum regulam vestram vobis pro temporalibus iurare non licet'.
[164] *Ibid.*: 'sepe detrimentum incurrere vos contigat'.
[165] *Ibid.*: 'ut cum ratio postulaverit libere iurare possitis predicta regula non obstante', see above,
  p. 103.
[166] *Gli atti del comune di Milano*, I, 61 (24 May 1220): '[com]missum fuit iuramentum quia

opposed by some secular authorities is further revealed in two letters from Innocent IV in 1251 to the Master and brothers of the Third order in Milan and to the archbishop of Milan and the bishop of Pavia.[167] Among other prohibitions concerning military service and the keeping of horses, the *podestà* and commune were ordered to refrain from forcing the Tertiaries to swear oaths and the two bishops were charged with ensuring that the exemption was observed. This is of little help, however, when considering the situation in the houses of the First and Second orders. This issue was undoubtedly crucial to lay men and women living in their own homes and as an integral part of the local community. It must have lost much of its significance for the members of regular communities, where only the superiors and occasional obedientiaries might expect to be directly involved in temporal affairs.

The house of Rondineto and perhaps its daughter houses had obtained the right to swear oaths freely in temporal as well as spiritual matters, but for the rest of the order, the provisions made in 1227 and 1232 seem to have remained the only guide: they might both require and swear oaths in legal disputes, to ensure peace or prove faith and in cases of need or evident or acceptable utility. There continue to be examples of members of the order avoiding oaths. Yet, if as appears to be the case, these changes were driven by petitions from among the Humiliati themselves, they suggest a dramatic shift in attitudes towards oaths in the decades after approval of the order in 1201.

Fasting and diet

The adaptation of provisions concerning the fasts and diet of the regular Humiliati shows a similar desire for clarification and a tendency towards relaxation of the provisions of *Omnis boni principium*. These had undoubtedly been harsh: if all the possible fasts were observed then the community would have been fasting for as many as two hundred days in the year. Some discretion had been left to the prelate, who could decide whether the community should fast on the second of the three days allocated in each week, except during the major feasts. Brethren undertaking journeys were also allowed to disregard the fasts, if they had permission.[168]

This regime was the subject of the first surviving dispensation issued

Humiliatus'. For other earlier and later examples, see Crotti Pasi, 'Gli Umiliati a Pavia nei secoli xii e xiii', and now Brolis, '"Quibus fuit remissum sacramentum." Il rifiuto di giurare presso gli Umiliati', pp. 251–65.
[167] Appendix I, 88, 89. [168] See above p. 118.

to the order, that given to the Brera in 1226.[169] The superior of the house was to be allowed to dispense with the rules of fasting (and silence) in times of work. As *Omnis boni principium* strongly emphasised the importance of work and gave it a prominent place in the daily round at all times, this privilege gave the superior of the community very wide discretionary powers. This was further extended in a vague letter to the ministers of the whole order issued at the end of May 1227. Once more the association was made with manual work. It was asserted that both brothers and sisters supported themselves 'for the most part' by the 'labour of their hands', a phrase reminiscent of the earlier accounts of Jacques de Vitry who wrote of Humiliati work in both his accounts of the order, noting in his letter of 1216 that they lived by the labour of their hands, a statement which he slightly modified by the time he wrote the *Historia occidentalis*, recording only that they did so 'for the most part' (*ex magna parte*).[170] This, according to the papal letter, made it very difficult for the brethren to observe the rule. So, when necessity dictated and especially in the summer, they could now be released from the duty of silence and fasting, although solemn fasts were to be observed.[171]

Just as the regulations concerning fasting were being relaxed, the Humiliati were also allowed some dispensation in the rules concerning the contents of their meals.[172] The rule prohibited the use of meat unless for the weak and ill, but Gregory gave the brethren licence to use fat or lard on days when others used meat. His reason was linked to the topographical position of the order: 'chiefly because in many of the places in which you live, oil is not abundant'.[173] Some sort of fat was necessary to alleviate the diet and as olive or other oil was not easily available, meat fat had to be used.

A letter of 1246 gives some idea of what this provision concerning fat actually meant. Innocent IV wrote to the whole order, allowing them licence to use fat from the feast of the Holy Cross in mid-September to All Saints (1 November), 'just as they had been allowed to do from Easter to the feast of the Holy Cross' and permitting them to disregard any customs to the contrary.[174] We must assume therefore that between 1227 and 1246 the order was legitimately using fat between Easter and mid-September and that after 1246 this was extended to include most of

---

[169] Appendix I, 20.   [170] Jacques de Vitry, *Lettres*, p. 73; Vitry, *HO*, 28, p. 144.
[171] Appendix I, 25. This letter also allowed them to use sheets and mattresses, thereby confirming the practice established in *Omnis boni principium*.
[172] Appendix I, 23.
[173] *Ibid.*: 'praesertim cum pleraque locorum in quibus consistitis, oleo [sic] non abundent [sic]'.
[174] Appendix I, 56.

the autumn. It is typical that Gregory's vagueness should be tidied up and regulated by Innocent IV.

An indication that fat was being used by the order is again given in a letter sent four years later, in August 1250, to the Master (the superior for the whole order introduced in 1246).[175] Some brethren, having transferred to the Humiliati (the text does not tell us where they came from), were still bound by previous vows not to use fat. Innocent therefore allowed the Master to release newly professed members from this promise and permit them to eat fat according to the institutions of the order.

Innocent IV, whose generosity towards, or at least intervention in, the affairs of the order seems to have been far-reaching, also addressed the problem of fasting. *Unigenitus dei filius* sent to the Second order (October 1246) clarified and modified the times of fasting once more.[176] From Pentecost (fifty days after Easter) to the feast of St Michael (29 September), except on Fridays and the fasts established by the Church, they were not required to fast. From St Michael to Advent (October and November) and from the eighth of Christmas to Septuagesima (January) they were to fast on the second, fourth and sixth days (Monday, Wednesday and Friday). The periods of continuous fasting laid down in *Omnis boni principium* thus presumably remained: Lent, Advent, and the three days at Septuagesima for the election of the new prelate. But the restriction of fasting to only one day a week, which *Omnis boni principium* had ordained only from Easter to Pentecost, was now extended to cover the whole summer, up to the end of September. Thus the provision made by Gregory allowing for dispensation at the discretion of the prelate in summer was enlarged upon and defined.[177] The discretionary powers of the prelate were reduced and uniformity of practice, a recurring theme, was perhaps enhanced.

The last surviving thirteenth-century papal letter concerning the food of the Humiliati also dates from the pontificate of Innocent IV.[178] In November 1253 he wrote to his nephew William dei Fieschi, cardinal deacon of Sant'Eustachio (1244–56), instructing him to investigate and settle as he saw fit a request made by the Second order of the Humiliati.[179] William had also been one of the signatories of an important privilege reforming the constitution of the order in October

---

[175] Appendix I, 85.
[176] Appendix I, 60; fifty privileges or letters concerning the Humiliati survive from his pontificate.
[177] On the same day a similar but more generous privilege was issued for the Third Order, Appendix I, 61.
[178] Appendix I, 101.   [179] *Ibid.*

1246, *Ex ore domini*, and by 1253 he had already been their cardinal protector for two years, and in February 1254 Beltramus, the first Master General of the order, calls him this when recording a letter he had received from him.[180] The Humiliati had claimed that they could not observe the provision made in the rule that during times of fasting they must abstain from eggs, milk and cheese. They had therefore asked Innocent to allow them to use these foods on days when no fast was imposed by the church. Unfortunately William's decision, which might help to clarify more precisely what the Humiliati were eating, does not survive.

CONCLUSIONS

The papal letters show the gradual relaxation of some of the more difficult aspects of observance. The members of the order were to some extent assimilated to the society which surrounded them. As far as oath-taking was concerned, a compromise was established which enabled the regular Humiliati to maintain their adherence to biblical prohibition, while participating in the essential business of supporting large numbers of members, buying, selling and exchanging property and protecting their rights in court. At the same time the Tertiaries were to be protected from undue pressure to swear oaths. The same pragmatism lay behind adjustments in the rule concerning fasting and their diet, introducing a regime which would enable the brethren to maintain a heavy work routine without excessive difficulty. The contradictions in the early legislation concerning the election of superiors were also removed.

The regime established in 1201 and some of the changes introduced in the following decades have been outlined here on the basis of papal regulation, using letters and privileges produced at both a physical and an administrative distance from the houses of the order of the Humiliati. It is now time to focus on the notarially produced sources, to seek an impression of the order 'on the ground' which both demanded and sustained these modifications. These sources and the occasional insights of contemporary observers will enable us to ascertain the extent to which the form of life envisaged here was in practice adopted in the houses of the Humiliati in northern Italy. The remainder of this book will combine the evidence of papal letters and of notarial records, in a first attempt to piece together the observance and practices of the Humiliati order in the early decades of its development within the Church.

---

[180] Appendix I, 59, *104, *104b.

Chapter 5

IN SEARCH OF COMMUNITIES

Now this *religio* has so multiplied in the diocese of Milan that they have
constituted one hundred and fifty conventual congregations, men on
one side, women on the other, not counting those who remain in their
own homes.

Jacques de Vitry[1]

The Humiliati brethren who both sought and sustained the rules and
their modifications described in earlier chapters are not easy to document in the early thirteenth century. Nothing which they wrote
survives from this period and the archives of their houses have been
dispersed. Yet the fragmentary survival of material produced by notaries,
the 'sales, exchanges, investitures and pledges of property' envisaged in
the papal privilege for the First order in 1201, do allow us to find traces
of their activities.[2] Together with professions of faith and the occasional
insights from contemporary narrative sources we can begin to explore
the features of this new order: the buildings, the brethren who lived in
them and the ties which bound them together. These sources are not
without their problems and these will be discussed in the course of what
follows. Nor can we expect instant uniformity and unity in a movement
born out of diverse groups spread across the landscape of northern Italy,
an area where strong forces militated against uniformity for any religious
order and political divisions tended to isolate cities and communities
from one another. The next three chapters will nonetheless sketch in
what can be seen of the development of an *ordo Humiliatorum*, defined
in organisational terms as a network of houses bound by observance of a
common rule and centralised administration.[3]

In most of what follows the focus will be on the houses of the First
and Second orders. Such an emphasis is easily justified. Undoubtedly

---

[1] Jacques de Vitry, *Lettres*, p. 73. [2] See above, p. 107.
[3] See Dubois, 'Ordo', *DIP*, VI (1980), cols. 806–20.

the emergence of the Third order and its acceptance by Innocent III marked a key stage in the evolution of the Church's response to lay religious enthusiasm. However, these issues have been considered in depth by historians in the past such as Herbert Grundmann and Rolf Zerfaß.[4] Moreover, beyond the basic text of Innocent's letter *Incumbit nobis*, we have relatively little information to enable us to reconstruct the daily routine and practical experience of the members of the Third order. Certainly the novelty of this new movement attracted more attention in the accounts of contemporary observers than did the more traditional aspects of the order. Often indeed, their very existence in the thirteenth century is only revealed by these narrative sources, already familiar to students of the field, or by sporadic references in charters, for example to the exemption of an individual from swearing an oath, because they were Humiliati.[5] By contrast, the impact of the regular communities has frequently been overlooked by historians. Yet for these regular communities we have a great deal more information in the notarial records which will enable us to trace the outline of the *ordo Humiliatorum*.

The present chapter provides some of the nuts and bolts for this undertaking, starting with the terminology used to describe their communities, their buildings and churches. It then turns to the Humiliati themselves: their superiors, terms of office and duties, the size of their communities and the participation of women, before closing with the evidence for ties between houses, using a case study of the area of Verona to illustrate the possibilities.

DOMUS HUMILIATORUM. A QUESTION OF TERMINOLOGY

The excerpt from a letter which Jacques de Vitry sent home in 1216 given at the opening of this chapter is commonly cited to illustrate the extraordinary growth of the Humiliati in the first decades of the thirteenth century. The medieval passion for impressing with numbers should certainly make us wary of expecting numerical precision. Vitry was an enthusiast for new forms of the religious life and does not claim any source for his statistic. His figures cannot be tested against contemporary documentation. Yet in view of the inadequacies of extant sources and of the number of communities undocumented in the twelfth century, but recorded in the papal letters of 1200–1, his account

---

[4] See above, pp. 27, 28, 30.
[5] The accounts of the Anonymous of Laon, Jacques de Vitry, Burchard of Ursberg and Humbert of Romans were given extensive and repeated consideration throughout Zanoni's work; see also Grundmann, pp. 90, 126, 160 and Bolton, 'Sources', pp.128–132; on oaths, see pp. 100–4, 130–2.

The early Humiliati

of astounding growth is not unconvincing. Although an outsider in the
Milanese world, he was reporting personal observations and perhaps
information obtained from conversations with members of the order
whom he had observed preaching in the squares of the city.[6] There is
no reason to doubt the substance of his claim that the Milanese
Humiliati were enjoying enormous success and had founded any
number of communities by the time he travelled through the diocese in
1216, just fifteen years after their approval. His observation is also
confirmed by recent studies of other areas which have traced remarkably
high numbers of communities in cities such as Bergamo and its district.[7]
However, the nature of the 'conventual' communities Vitry describes
requires further investigation. Were these well endowed and substantial,
quasi-monastic establishments or ephemeral, *ad hoc* gatherings destined
to a glorious but brief notoriety?

An obvious starting point for an appraisal of Vitry's conventual
congregations (*congregationes conventuales*) is the terminology of the
notarial sources, but this is not unequivocal. In the twelfth-century
documentation *congregatio fratrum*, *congregatio et fraternitas*, *mansio*, *casa
commune* and *canonica* had all been used, as well as the vague form *illi de
. . .* which raises more questions than it resolves.[8] After 1200 this range
expanded to include among others *collegium*, *communitas*, *conventus*,
domus, *societas*, *universitas* and in mid-century, *monasterium*. Some of
these terms were commonly used for a wide variety of corporate
entities, but most were also frequently applied to groups of monastic or
canonical religious. Beyond confirming the obvious point that the
Humiliati were recognised as 'groups' of religious, they are not helpful
in furthering an understanding of the distinctive nature of their communities. In the case of *fraternitas*, Chenu argued that as well as carrying
technical weight as a term to describe monks and canons, it might also
imply more anarchic values of fraternity and protest.[9] Yet, if the use of
fraternitas by or for the Humiliati was in any way anarchic, it seems to
have provoked no response from contemporaries. Moreover, the most
common form used by notaries is neither *fraternitas*, nor Vitry's
congregatio, but *domus*, linked either with a place name, as in *domus de
Rondenario*, or with the name of an individual, as in *domus fratris
Guilelmi*, and in either case with the identifier *humiliatorum* or, when
women alone were intended, *humiliatarum*.

Domus is not simple to interpret since it carries potential for a double
meaning, in the spatial sense of a physical structure and that of a group

---

[6] Vitry, *HO*, p. 145.   [7] See for example, Brolis, *Gli Umiliati a Bergamo*, pp. 27–8.
[8] Above, ch. 2.
[9] Chenu, '"Fraternitas." Evangile et condition socio-culturelle', pp. 385–400.

138

of people, the household living there.[10] Work on the depositions made
by heretics in Bologna has also shown that *domus* was sometimes used
without any implication of communal residence: it referred simply to a
meeting place and assumed the role for the Cathars that a church
building held for catholics.[11] The use of *domus* in a Humiliati context
might thus be thought to describe a meeting place, perhaps used for the
weekly assemblies of Tertiaries, but not necessarily anything more
conventual in Vitry's sense. Yet the notarial sources yield several clues
which suggest that this was not the case.

In the first place, the frequent use of *domus* when indicating the place
where a contract was agreed, shows that it was commonly understood
to indicate a building as well as a community and further details of the
location occasionally give some sense of the structures involved. Thus
'courtyards' (*curia, cortivo, curte*), or porches (*porticus, porticalia*), were not
uncommon features and in 1251 a new Humiliati community in Milan
next to the Dominican church of Sant'Eustorgio had a building with
windows overlooking the friars' garden.[12] Other terms suggest a still
more substantial complex of buildings, closer to the group of buildings
envisaged in *Omnis boni principium*. As we have seen, two early
communities were perhaps associated with hospitals, at Bardonezza on
the river Po and *Calventia* in the diocese of Tortona.[13] Humiliati
ownership of neither building is, however, certain and much of the
reliable evidence here is very late. In 1249 a community in Zevio near
Verona had an oratory, dormitory and refectory.[14] In 1256, San Pietro
Viboldone had a 'palace' substantial enough to house the General
Chapter.[15] In 1260 the Humiliati of the *domus magna* in Ranchate in the
Porta Nova of Milan had a *hospitio* and in 1270 acquired another; in
1268 the Humiliati sisters of the *domus* Sant'Agnese in the parish of San
Martino al Corpo in Milan exchanged a group of buildings for a house
or *hospicium*; while at Borgovico in Como in 1272 the Humiliati of the
domus of brother William *de Canova*, led by a provost and apparently
belonging to the First order, had a former dyeshop (*tinctoria*) and a
hospicium large enough to house a meeting called to settle a dispute with
a neighbouring house.[16]

The fact that in some cases a *domus* originated quite literally as the
house of an individual who donated or willed it to the Humiliati,

---

[10] Paolini, 'Domus e zona degli eretici', 380–1 and n. 40.   [11] *Ibid.*, p. 380.
[12] Appendix I, 87 and below, p. 243.   [13] Above, pp. 50–1, 53–4.
[14] ASVer, Ghiara 218.   [15] Appendix I, *110d.
[16] Ranchate: ASMi, 385 Sta Caterina, 1260 and 1270; Sant'Agnese, Milan: *Gli atti del comune di Milano*, II/1, 532 (1268); Borgovico: Morelli, 'La casa di Rondineto', 8 (1272); Arizza and Longatti, 'Gli Umiliati in diocesi di Como', 140. Below, pp. 218–19.

whether or not that person entered the religious life, is perhaps the strongest evidence to support the case for seeing these *domus* as residential buildings. Thus in 1229 a benefactor in Lodi, Bregundius Denarii, bequeathed his house for the foundation of a community.[17] In a similar way the prominent *domus de Gambara* in Brescia was founded by Albricus *de Gambara* and continued to attract members of this family as brethren throughout the century.[18] It would not be difficult to extend such a list substantially.[19] Innumerable documents also refer explicitly to brethren residing in a *domus*, and in a few the phrase *in domo habitationis* underlines this purpose.[20] Of course, such careful specification could mean that in other contexts *domus* indicated a meeting place, while the occasional equation of *domus* with *mansio*, carrying implications of a stopping place on a journey, may mean that in some cases even a residential building may have been little more than a hostel.[21] Perhaps such arguments can never be conclusive. Certainly some houses did act as foci for meetings. The Dominicans of Sant'Eustorgio in Milan were very keen to prevent their new Humiliati neighbours holding preaching meetings at their new building.[22] There is, however, no explicit suggestion in the extant notarial sources that *domus* was used to indicate a group of people or a meeting place to the exclusion of a residential purpose. On balance, it seems likely that *domus* was used by notaries to indicate a building with a residential community. It is not possible on the basis of this evidence to establish whether such a *domus* was what Vitry describes as a 'conventual congregation', or to verify the affiliation within the order of any community so described, but its use may suggest a spatial fixity or stability absent in the use of terms such as *locus* frequently applied to mendicant settlements, but only rarely found in Humiliati records.[23]

The sporadic use of monastery (*monasterium*) later in the century is

---

[17] Appendix III, 8.

[18] See the Necrology of this house, *VHM* III, pp. 287–98, 290.

[19] For other examples, see pp. 79, 199–200.

[20] For examples, appendix II; appendix I, 87: 'Fratrem Arnoldum de Vedano ministrum humiliatorum medii ordinis qui habitare consueverunt Modoetiae in domo quae dicitur communis fratrum humiliatorum'.

[21] See, for example, Lodi: *VHM* II, pp. 7, 14, 22; Vercelli: *S. Solutore* 21: (1244) 'ecclesia et mansio' of San Cristoforo; Cremona: (1244) 'domus mansionis Iohannis de Celso Cremone site super Rodanum', *Le pergamene degli Umiliati di Cremona*, I; Asti: (1281): 'conventus, domus, sive mansionis', *Documenti intorno alle relazioni fra Genova e Alba*, II, *1270–1321*, 471; see also Crotti Pasi, 'Gli Umiliati a Pavia', 319–24, 326–8, 332; G. Forzatti Golia, 'Gli ordini religiosi della diocesi di Pavia nel medioevo', *Bollettino della società pavese di storia patria*, new series 41 (1989), 3–27, 8 and Du Cange, *Glossarium*, s.v. 'mansio'.

[22] Below, p. 243.

[23] Pellegrini, 'Gli insediamenti degli ordini mendicanti e la loro tipologia', p. 565; for rare Humiliati examples, below, p. 141 and for the 'locus fratrum humiliatorum', at Rovigo in 1255,

similarly inconclusive. The *monasterium humilatorum de subtus* documented at Vicenza in 1261 suggests an acknowledged monastic community and the house of the Humiliati *de medio* in the city was also called a monastery.[24] In neither of these cases, however, is there any consistency in usage; monastery never replaced the alternatives in Vicenza, *domus et monasterium* is a frequent combination, even the mouthful *monasterium loci domus* is to be found, while in other documents of the same period referring to the same communities, monastery was not used at all – *conuentus dicte domus et sui colege* [sic] and *loci et collegi et conuentus* are among the alternatives.[25] Nor does the term seem to have been used elsewhere at this date, even for larger Second order houses including the Ghiara in Verona or the Brera in Milan; but such absence of titles is by no means a clear guide to status. Already in the 1190s San Cristoforo Lodi was called a *canonica* and the same title was used for Viboldone at least by the 1250s and for Ognissanti in Borghetto Lodigiano by the 1270s, if not earlier.[26] These all accommodated First order communities which were charged with responsibility for the order as a whole in 1201. Yet Rondineto in Como, also undoubtedly a house with a First order community and enjoying the same administrative status in the order as Viboldone and Lodi, remained a 'congregation and fraternity'. It is not called a *canonica* in extant records from the thirteenth century.

ECCLESIE DE HUMILIATIS

A better guide to the nature of these houses, their institutional security and permanence is the appearance of direct references to Humiliati churches and places of worship. From the beginning many Humiliati were linked with church buildings. The very first record is of the group at Viboldone building its own church, while other early communities were apparently entrusted with the care of new or existing churches, as at Bardonezza (1180), Sta Maria in Piacenza (1180), Sta Maria Maddalena near Pavia (1182) and Sta Maria di Ronco Martano *de valbixaria*

which by 1288 was listed as a *domus* of the Second order, Adami, 'La "domus sancti Bartholomei de Rodigio"', pp. 15, 17 and *VHM* III, p. 266.

[24] ASVic Ognissanti 2, 17 July 1261; 14 February 1262; 30 August 1267; 14 October 1265, 3 March 1266, 15 May 1267 and 1 April 1269; the documents from the 1260s in the Ognissanti archive (busta 2), were transcribed by Dr Lisa Bolcati in preparation for her *Tesi di laurea* presented at the Università degli Studi di Verona, supervised by Professor De Sandre Gasparini who kindly allowed me to consult the draft transcripts; see now Bolcati and Lomastro Tognato, 'Una *religio nova* nel duecento vicentino'.

[25] ASVic Ognissanti, 2, 28 May 1262, 19 October 1263; see also *ibid.*, 11 March 1267, 9 October 1267, 11 March 1269.

[26] Ognissanti: *CDL*, II/II 378 (1274): 'domino Stephano de Mellegnano preposito canonice omnium sanctorum'.

near Como (1189).[27] The *canonica* of San Cristoforo Lodi also had its own church by 1195 and an oratory attached to a hospital entrusted to Humiliati in the diocese of Tortona was the subject of a claim by the Templars in 1200.[28] As has been argued, the existence of these places of worship and of the clergy to minister to them suggests a more integrated ecclesiastical experience than is usually associated with the early Humiliati. Innocent III confirmed the legitimacy of their actions in 1201 when he authorised the First order both to receive churches should they wish to adopt the Humiliati way of life and to build them *ex novo* on their own land as long as they did not jeopardise other churches and the diocesan bishop gave permission.[29] Evidence from the first decades of the new century shows that they acted on this in several cases. The community of Ognissanti at Fossadolto on the road to Rome (*strata romea*) near Lodi started building their own church c. 1201–3 and were still building it in 1236, the delay apparently having been caused by the opposition of bishop Arderic of Lodi who had wished the church to be under his *providencia et forcia*, while the community claimed the right to build without episcopal authorisation.[30] In the meantime they had nonetheless obtained a nearby chapel of San Giorgio from Arderic, possession of which was confirmed by Innocent III in 1208.[31] At Rondineto in Como, a church is first mentioned in 1198 and again in 1211, after which the reference is not repeated until the late thirteenth century, when there are also references to a court and cloister.[32] In the 1230s, however, a priest, Giroldus of Rondineto, a long-standing member of the community, was elected superior of the church of Sta Maria di Ronco Martano which had been entrusted to Rondineto in 1189, almost a decade before a church is documented at Rondineto itself.[33] In view of this additional responsibility, it seems very likely that Rondineto already had a church of its own in the 1180s.

In the area of Milan early Humiliati churches include Oriano (near Cassago Brianza, north of the city), where a letter taking them into papal protection issued in 1208 refers to their church 'built with the licence of Philip, archbishop of Milan of happy memory'.[34] At the turn

---

[27] Above, ch. 2.   [28] Above, p. 53.   [29] Appendix I, 9.

[30] See now Mercatili Indelicato, 'Per una storia degli Umiliati nella diocesi di Lodi', pp. 364–71, 483; *VHM* II, pp. 185, 189 (incorrect date); *CDL*, I/I, 322.

[31] Appendix I, 12; Mercatili Indelicato, 'Per una storia degli Umiliati nella diocesi di Lodi', p. 484.

[32] Above, p. 55; *VHM* II, pp. 22, 156; Morelli, 'La casa di Rondineto', 9 (1273), 18 (1294), 22 (1296), 23 (1296).

[33] Above, p. 54; *VHM* II, p. 22, III, pp. 303–5; 'dominus Giroldus prepositus de Rondenario' documented from 1217 is almost certainly the same man; 'Le carte di Sta Maria Vecchia di Como', nos. 16 and 17; Morelli, 'La casa di Rondineto', 1 (1235).

[34] Appendix I, 14.

of the century (c. 1201) Philip also gave the Milanese Brera community permission to build an oratory, but either nothing was done immediately or, as at Ognissanti near Lodi, the building took a long time to complete.[35] John of Brera, the fifteenth-century chronicler of the order, implies a date of 1208 for the building of the 'old church' of the Brera, when he states that it was constructed sixty-seven years before the third Master General, Lodorengus, laid the first stone of the church for the *domus de Marliano* in Porta Ticinese in 1275.[36] A document of 1230, however, refers to the newly built church and on the verso a contemporary hand notes that the church was built on 1 June 1229, indicating either the beginning, completion or consecration of the new building on that day.[37] Another early example was the church of Sta Maria e Ognissanti *de Galgari* in Bergamo, almost certainly consecrated in August 1221 by bishop John Tornielli (1211–30).[38] In May 1228 the Humiliati church of San Michele in Alessandria, represented by a provost Amicus, requested permission from the monastery of San Siro Genoa to build an oratory with cemetery in the parish of the monastery next to their house in Genoa in the Pratum area, near the church of Sant'Agnese.[39] In the early 1230s the archpriest of Monza allowed the Humiliati of Sant'Agata to have an oratory and cemetery for their own use, a concession extended to the house of Mediovico in 1250 (where a church had been built by 1255).[40] Meanwhile, in September 1239, the Humiliati of Florence received the ancient but dilapidated church of San Donato alla torre from bishop Ardingus (1231–49), in order that they might 'bring religion back to a better and greater state'.[41] Finally, a reference from Vercelli in 1242 to the church of San Cristoforo provides no clues to when it was built and it may have been an earlier structure.[42]

The size and precise function of these churches is not immediately apparent. *Oratorium*, used to describe the disputed property in the diocese of Tortona in 1200, was the word used in the rule of Benedict to indicate the place of prayer for the community and in these early Humiliati examples may often have indicated a small chapel or room set

[35] Appendix I,★10.
[36] John of Brera, *Chronicon*, ch. 25, p. 250; Lodorengus was elected at the General Chapter held at Viboldone in 1273 after the resignation of Peter; Alberzoni, '"Sub eadem clausura sequestrati"', n. 108.
[37] Appendix I, ★38.
[38] On the basis of new documentation Brolis, *Gli Umiliati a Bergamo*, pp. 41–2, corrects the date of 1211 given by Tiraboschi and others (*VHM* II, p. 66).
[39] M. Calleri, 'Su alcuni "libri iurium" deperditi del monastero di San Siro di Genova', *Atti della società ligure di storia patria*, new series, 34 (1994), 157–84, 180; on Amicus, see below, p. 214.
[40] Appendix I, ★43,★86; Longoni, 'Origini degli Umiliati a Monza', 11 (1255).
[41] Appendix I, ★54.   [42] *S. Solutore*, 21 (1244).

aside for worship, rather than a separate building, particularly when more than one oratory is recorded. In his history written in the 1220s, Jacques de Vitry was careful to point out that the brothers and sisters in Humiliati houses lived separately:

so that neither in church nor in other places can they speak or see one another unless rarely. Even when they come together for the preaching of the divine word, there is a wall placed between so that usually they are separated from each other.[43]

Vitry's account may be somewhat idealised, but it is likely that he was describing communities seen during his travels in 1216 and his version matches a relatively early record of separate places of worship in Verona. On the same day in 1224 the professions of faith of male and female brethren in the double community of the Ghiara took place independently in the 'oratory of the humiliati sisters' and in the 'oratory of the brothers of the said humiliati'.[44] Such oratories cannot have been very large and there may well have been little more than the wall Vitry describes separating them. No other early records specifically refer to separate places of worship for women and men. Other double houses, however, had oratories described as 'of the sisters': from the 1220s in Zevio near Verona, from 1232 in San Paolo Verona, in 1244 in Porto and by 1259 in Monza at the *domus de Carrobiolo* (Sant'Agata).[45] Male brethren occasionally used these oratories too, which suggests that the label may refer to ownership or intention rather than everyday use.[46] In the case of Sant'Agata *de Carrobiolo* in Monza, however, permission to build a church had been granted as early as the 1230s, so the oratory of the sisters recorded in 1259 may have been a more enclosed space within a larger construction.[47]

Whether or not men and women worshipped apart in these houses, in others the lack of a place of worship forced brethren to attend churches outside their communities. This practice is not frequently documented in notarial sources, but according to a will from the 1280s, in Vicenza in the 1220s the brethren of the community *de subtus* had attended the church of San Lorenzo, later changing to San Silvestro, a

---

[43] Vitry, *HO*, 28, p. 145: 'quod neque in ecclesia neque in alio loco sese mutuo nisi raro possunt alloqui uel uidere. Quando etiam ad predicationem diuini uerbi conueniunt, muro interposito, a se inuicem plerumque separantur.'
[44] Appendix II, 9–10.
[45] De Sandre Gasparini, 'Aspetti di vita religiosa, sociale ed economica di chiese e monasteri nei secoli xiii–xv', p. 136; below, appendix II, 11 (1230), 12 (1232); ASVer, Ghiara 193 (1244), *VHM* II, pp. 296–7 (1259); Longoni identifies Sant'Agata with the domus Carrobiolo, 'Origini degli Umiliati at Monza', p. 24.
[46] Below, p. 183.   [47] Appendix I, *43.

church belonging to the monastery of Nonantola.[48] It was in part concern about such outings which led to a letter from Innocent IV in 1246, almost certainly petitioned by the order.[49] The *narratio* commented on the enormous expansion of the order and recalled the example of Old Testament figures such as Noah who, on leaving the ark and receiving the blessing of God to grow and multiply, built an altar as a mark of devotion. The pope noted that although some Humiliati communities were large they were not yet honoured with a titular church, while others had a church but lacked priests, so that the brothers and sisters were obliged either to do without the office or to go out in public, 'mingling in the turbulence of the world, not without great danger to their souls'. He therefore decreed that, while taking into account the capability of the houses and the quality of persons, churches were to be built in Second order communities which did not already possess one and priests were to be found to minister to them. As we have seen, several early communities already had their own churches or places of worship and this was not restricted to houses of the First order. Priests are also documented and in 1201 the provosts and brethren of the First order were specifically authorised to celebrate the office during interdicts with members of the Second order present. Nonetheless, the letter indicates that the numbers of brethren had so multiplied that more were now needed.

There is, however, some evidence that action may not have followed promptly. A decade later Alexander IV responded to a complaint from the proctor of the order by repeating his predecessor's instructions and threatening the Master General with ecclesiastical censure should he fail to have churches built in Second order houses which did not yet have one and ensure that suitable brothers of the Second order were promoted as clerics, subdeacons, deacons and priests, so that they might celebrate the office.[50] Perhaps it was difficult to keep pace with the rate of growth: the 150 houses in the area of Milan numbered by Jacques de Vitry were to become 220 convents of the Second order and seven *canoniche* of the First by the 1280s, according to the Milanese writer (and Humiliati) Bonvesin da la Riva.[51] Yet there is a cluster of new references to Humiliati churches from across northern Italy and as far afield as Siena in the mid- and later thirteenth century revealing an increase which was surely in part a response to the demands expressed in the papal letter.[52]

---

[48] Bolcati and Lomastro Tognato, 'Una *religio nova* nel duecento vicentino', p. 152.
[49] Appendix I, 63.   [50] Appendix I, 109.
[51] Bonvesin da la Riva, *De magnalibus mediolani. Meraviglie di Milano*, pp. 82–3.
[52] For example, churches are documented at Florence from 1250 (appendix I, *80); the Gambara,

The proliferation of references to churches also confirms the premise of Innocent IV's letter that by this period many more houses in the order were sufficiently established to undertake extensive building works. Unfortunately it is not possible to draw general conclusions on the type of work undertaken or to illustrate it in any detail. Two well-documented extant buildings provide some idea of the difficulties. At Viboldone, the present structure, completed in the fourteenth century, encloses the original twelfth- and thirteenth-century buildings. These have recently been shown to have borne similarities with the model used in the neighbouring Cistercian abbeys of Chiaravalle, Cerreto and Morimondo and to have consisted in an original small chapel, equivalent in size to the choir of the present church, which was extended westward, perhaps in the 1230s, to reach as far as the first bay of the present fourteenth-century building.[53] By contrast, Ognissanti in Florence, begun in the 1250s and completed before 1300, used a typical Mendicant plan.[54] On this basis, it might seem reasonable to argue that the Humiliati simply adopted dominant contemporary models, Cistercian in the twelfth century, Mendicant in the thirteenth. Yet, as with so much of the early Humiliati's experience, generalisation is unwise. Other surviving buildings are mostly fourteenth-century constructions and can provide no clues to the earlier picture.[55]

This survey of the notarial terminology allows us to construct some hypotheses about the physical structure of Humiliati communities in the first decades of their orthodox existence. The use of *domus* may reflect a stability of purpose absent in the use of *locus* applied to early Mendicant communities. The varied terminology used by notaries to describe communities and their buildings, and occasionally the surviving buildings themselves, provide a few further clues to their residential nature. *Canonica* is used for some but not all communities belonging to the First order, but is not used for Second order houses. As we saw in chapter 4, however, houses of the First and Second orders both used the same

Brescia (consecrated 1251, Guerrini, 'Gli Umiliati a Brescia', p. 199); Monza: at the 'domus de Mediovico', 1255 (Longoni, 'Origini degli Umiliati a Monza', 11); SS Maria e Bartolomeo at Rovigo, 1255 (Adami, 'La "domus sancti Bartholomei de Rodigio"', p. 15 and n. 73); Sta Caterina in Rancate (a house of women), 1257 (AsMi, 385 Sta Caterina); San Tommaso, Siena 1262 (Angelucci, 'Gli Umiliati a Siena', p. 266); San Marco, Chivasso, 1265 (*Casale* 13, 7 March 1265); Sta Maria Nova at the Ghiara, Verona 1265 (ASVic Ognissanti 2, 9 March 1265, ASVer, Ghiara 302); San Giovanni, Zevio 1265 (ASVer, Ghiara 303); Monlué near Milan 1267 (Zanoni, p. 192; John of Brera, *Chronicon*, ch. 25, p. 250).

53 See Marrucci, 'Il territorio e il complesso di Viboldone', pp. 78–81.
54 Appendix 1, *80; for the plan see Hueck, 'Le opere di Giotto per la chiesa di Ognissanti', pp. 37–50, fig. 2.
55 For example, San Michele, Paganico near Siena, begun 1297; Angelucci, 'Gli Umiliati a Siena', pp. 274, 279–80 (where she also discusses the style of other Humiliati churches).

regulatory text, *Omnis boni principium*, which suggests that the differences between them were not as great as might be expected. The blurring of boundaries often makes it difficult to distinguish between communities of the different orders.[56] Lists of houses categorised by order and in territorial divisions recorded by John of Brera in the fifteenth century date only from the late thirteenth century (1288 and 1298) and are only partially complete, while notarial records very rarely note the order to which a house belonged.[57] Such hazy distinctions may also have lain behind Vitry's description of 'conventual congregations', where men lived apart from women. Although he demarcates the Tertiaries who 'remain in their own homes', he does not discriminate between types of regular community, giving no hint of the differentiation between First and Second order houses outlined in the papal correspondence.

The most reliable indicator of the status of these communities and one which suggests that they were expected to endure is the increasing use of churches belonging to the order from mid-century, a trend paralleling the experience of the Franciscans in the same decades.[58] It cannot be said that this evidence provides an adequate guide to the built environment or physical security of the order as a whole in the early and mid-thirteenth century. Rather, the sources allow us to draw traces in the sand, suggesting that the order of the Humiliati had a substantial number of residential, 'conventual' houses, not infrequently with their own churches. Frustrating though it remains, little more can be said. It is now time to turn to the residents of these houses themselves.

THE HUMILIATI

Superiors

The papal letters of 1201 drew a neat distinction between types of superior for the Humiliati, naming provosts in the First order, prelates in the Second and ministers in the Third. As Zanoni noted, however,

---

[56] See Alberzoni, 'Gli inizi degli Umiliati', p. 229.

[57] The lists included by John of Brera are in *VHM* III, pp. 265–7 (1288), 270–85 (1298); see now Broggi, 'Il catalogo del 1298', pp. 3–44, and for a rare notarial exception, the reference in the profession of faith made by members of the house of Zevio to the 'regulam huius congregationis *secundi* ordinis', in 1230, Appendix II, 11; other notarial references are much later, for example: the 'domus secundi ordinis' in Modena in 1264, Romagnoli, 'Gli Umiliati a Modena', p. 490, and the 'domus humiliatorum sancte Marie primi ordinis qui appellatur domus fratris Ottatii porte Vercellina', in Milan in 1287, ASMi, 526 Pta Vercellina. (I am grateful to Dr Daniela Castagnetti for referring me to this busta.)

[58] See Moorman, *A History of the Franciscan Order*, pp. 155–60.

this pattern is not repeated in the papal correspondence until mid-century and nor is it always immediately clear in the language of notarial sources.[59] Provost does seem to be used for superiors of the First order: documents from Rondineto, Viboldone, Ognissanti in Borghetto Lodigiano, Oltreticino in Pavia, San Cristoforo in Vercelli and later from Novara, among others, all use the title.[60] As we might expect, there are some oddities: in 1245 two documents drawn up by the same notary concerning a transaction at which the ministers of the Ghiara and Zevio houses were present describe the superior of the double house of the Beverara in Verona as brother John *minister proposto* [sic = *propositus*], whereas in 1240 it had been simply minister.[61] The variation, however, simply confirms the need to allow for notarial preference or error and is in any case unusual. Whether alone or in combination with other titles, the use of provost to designate a superior is at least a strong indicator that a community was thought to belong to the First order.

Distinctions between Second and Third order communities on the basis of titles are more difficult to establish. Prelate, the papal title for the superiors of the Second order, does not seem to have been used in the Veronese documents in the thirteenth century, nor in Pavia, but in other communities, prelate and minister were often interchangeable and elder (*ancianus*) and rector are also found.[62] The superior of the Brera in 1198 was a prelate and in documents throughout the century is alternately described as 'prelate and minister', or just one of the two.[63] Such combined titles were often used for the same man. There was a 'rector and minister' at the house of Sta Maria in Pertica, Pavia in 1221, which appears to have accepted Tertiaries.[64] Again, at the Ghiara in Verona (certainly a Second order house) in 1240 there was a 'rector and

---

59 Zanoni, p. 132.
60 Morelli, 'La casa di Rondineto', table 9 (1249, 1264, 1272, etc.); Tagliabue, 'Gli Umiliati a Viboldone', p. 17 (from 1214); on Ognissanti in Borghetto Lodigiano (1236), see *VHM* II, pp. 183–9 and now Mercatili Indelicato, 'Per una storia degli Umiliati nella diocesi di Lodi', *Sulle tracce*, pp. 365–440; on Oltreticino, see *Documenti degli archivi di Pavia relativi alla storia di Voghera*, 140 (1259); on San Cristoforo Vercelli, see *S. Solutore*, 21 (1244); on Novara see, for example, *L'ospedale della carità di Novara*, 100 (1288), 135 (1288).
61 See ASVer, Beverara 5 (1239–40), 6 (1245), 9 (1249), 11 (1251), 12 (1261) and appendix 1, (1245); for a late example, see ASVer, Ghiara 296 (1263); the status of the Beverara as a double house is confirmed by several references to brothers and sisters (for example, ASVer, Beverara 6 (1245), 7a (1245), 11 (1251), 12 (1261)); this corrects Barbieri, 'Un insediamento dell'ordine degli Umiliati', p. 197.
62 Crotti Pasi, 'Gli Umiliati a Pavia', p. 333; *ancianus* was widely used by the Cathars, see for example, Anselm of Alessandria, 'Tractatus de hereticis', ed. A. Dondaine, 'La hiérarchie cathare en Italie', *Archivum fratrum praedicatorum*, 20 (1950), 234–324, 315–16.
63 Milan, Trivulziana, fondo belgioioso cartella 291, no. 2; see Alberzoni, '"Sub eadem clausura sequestrati"', appendices 1 and 2.
64 Crotti Pasi, 'Gli Umiliati a Pavia', p. 326; on the entry of Petracius Calciatus, perhaps a Tertiary and his wife, below, p. 198.

minister', though in another document of 1240 and in 1241 the same man was simply minister, in 1242 he was rector and in other documents between 1242 and 1245, simply a proctor, or 'minister and proctor'.[65] In Como in 1249, one man was identified as prelate or minister of a hospital linked to the Humiliati.[66] Unlike the Franciscan order, where early imprecision in the use of titles such as minister, custodian and guardian was replaced by greater precision after the death of Francis, the variety of names used by the Humiliati becomes more extensive as the century progresses and the number of surviving documents increases.[67] In the 1260s there was a prelate at the *domus nova* in Cremona and at the houses of San Tommaso and Sta Maria Nova in Mantua, while elsewhere minister continued to be preferred.[68] There was a rector at Casale in 1243 and at Oggiono, north of Milan, in 1264, a 'minister and prior' in Modena from 1264, a 'minister and rector' at Ronco near Verona in 1266, a prior at SS Filippo e Giacomo in borgo Lame, Bologna in 1272, a 'prior and rector' at Bologna in 1275, a 'prior, rector and administrator' at San Giovanni *de Porris* in Novara in 1277.[69] The use of prior, alone or together with other terms, appears late in the century, and as we might expect, indicates either a deputy to the superior of the same house, as used at San Giovanni *de Porris* in Novara and in Pavia, or the superior of a dependent house, as used in Bologna in the borgo Lame house subject to Pontevico in Brescia, or in the house of San Marco in Tortona, founded by San Michele in Alessandria.[70] These documents hint at the demarcation of hierarchies and separate duties, a tendency also implicit in the appearance from mid-century of the term *canevarius* in communities such as the Brera, Rondineto and Viboldone to indicate a brother with special responsibilities, usually involving the administration of land and in the case of Viboldone, including the acceptance of new brethren.[71] Although this evidence is late and a poor guide to institu-

---

[65] ASVer, Ghiara 171 (1240), 173 (1240), 176 (1241), 178 (1242), 180 (1242), 182 (1242), 190 (1243), 192 (1243), 194 (1244), 200 (1245).

[66] ASCo, Ospedale di Sant'Anna, ospedaletti antichi 5, 4, transcribed in Arizza, 'L'ospedale di San Vitale', 10 (1249): 'prelato seu ministro'.

[67] Iriarte, *Storia del francescanesimo*, p. 147.

[68] ASVic Ognissanti 2, 9 March 1265, 30 August 1267.

[69] *Casale* 202 (1243); Oggiono: Longoni, 'Gli Umiliati in Brianza', 13; Modena: Romagnoli, 'Gli Umiliati a Modena', appendix 1.2 where she gives a list of titles at the 'domus S. Luca' 1264–1389; Ronco: ASVer, Beverara, 24; Bologna: Spinelli, 'Gli Umiliati in Emilia-Romagna', p. 140; Novara: *L'ospedale della carità di Novara*, 129 (1277).

[70] *L'ospedale della carità di Novara*, 102 (1288), 129 (1277); Crotti Pasi, 'Gli Umiliati a Pavia', p. 333; for Bologna and Tortona see below, p. 171.

[71] Brera: ASMi, 470 Brera, 4 December 1251, 15 October 1255, 22 February 1256, 12 March 1271, 28 October 1271; *Gli atti del comune di Milano*, II/1, 627 (1271); Rondineto: Morelli, 'La casa di Rondineto', table 9 (1279); Viboldone: *Gli atti del comune di Milano*, II/2, 738 (1276).

tional developments early in the century, it does suggest increasing need for, and perhaps interest in, organisational structures.

Women as superiors

The Humiliati movement is often assumed by historians to have been particularly attractive to women, a response to what used to be termed the *Frauenfrage*, providing them with an opportunity to pursue the religious life not easily available in the established orders and allowing them an active role. Jacques de Vitry certainly writes of the conversion of 'matrons and virgins' alongside the 'noble and powerful citizens' convinced by their preaching.[72] Both he and Humbert of Romans, the Dominican Master General (died 1277) who wrote two sermons addressed to the Humiliati towards the end of his life, highlight the proximity of men and women in their communities. Both authors also, however, emphasise the strict separation between them.[73] Humbert wrote a sermon addressed to the sisters in which he contrasted their virtue with the vices of other religious women. While some women live enclosed but alone, a state which he sees as potentially a great danger, not only are the Humiliati sisters enclosed, but they also live together, providing fraternal love to each other and the brothers, 'as women did in the primitive church'. Moreover, he continues, they do not live under the rule of women but of a provost who rules over both men and women in the same house, 'for rule by a man is better, in whom wisdom and virility are greater than in a woman'. Humbert also compares them favourably with communities which accept only virgins, 'who are consecrated and solemnly make the divine office'. By contrast, the Humiliati receive all types of women, they are not consecrated and, as members of the laity, hear the office from clerics, having their prayers according to the lay manner. They are close to clerics 'who can minister to them at all times'. Finally, he describes their dedication to work, contrasted with sisters who either work little or are meddlesome.[74]

---

[72] Vitry, *HO*, 28, p. 145.

[73] For Jacques de Vitry, see above, p. 144; Humbert of Romans, 'Sermo ad sorores de ordine humiliatorum', comp. Zanoni, p. 262: 'In Italia sunt quaedam mulieres religiosae quae morantur cum Humiliatis sequestratim ab eis'; see also Brett, *Humbert of Romans*, pp. 151–66.

[74] Humbert, 'Sermo ad sorores', comp. Zanoni, pp. 262–3: 'Item sunt quaedam inclusae solitariae, quod est interdum occasio magni periculi; hae autem sunt insimul viventes et charitatem fraternam invicem et in fratres exercentes, sicut in primitiva Ecclesia fiebat a mulieribus . . . Item sunt quaedam religiosae, quae subsunt regimini muliebri, hae autem subsunt alicui praeposito, qui praeest tam viris quam mulieribus in eadem domo. Constat autem quod melius est regi a viro in quo praesumitur maior esse prudentia et virilitas quam a foemina . . . Item sunt quaedam monasteria in quibus non recipiuntur nisi virgines, quae consecrantur et faciunt solemniter officium divinum; hae autem recipiunt omne genus mulierum, nec consecrantur et

Humbert's account of the hard work of the sisters gives a positive view of their endeavours and they are at least portrayed as a support, not a distraction for their male brethren. He also implies that the order had large numbers of clergy available to assist the sisters 'at all times', but particularly emphasises the idea that they were subject to male governance. Humbert may have had personal knowledge of their activities during his time as Master General of the Dominicans (1254–63)[75] – certainly other members of his order had close ties with the Humiliati by mid-century. Nonetheless, placed as it is in a sermon, this picture reflects above all Humbert's version of the virtuous life. His idealised picture needs to be tested against the notarial records, which allow both a wider sample and a longer chronological view.[76]

There are certainly large numbers of women recorded in many Humiliati houses and they are frequently found living alongside men. Notwithstanding Humbert's view, however, there are numerous examples of female superiors. There was a *prelata* at the Brera in 1227, a *magistra* at Ognissanti in Borghetto Lodigiano in 1236, a *ministra et antiana* in Busto Arsizio in 1243, a *ministra seu prelata* at Sta Caterina in Milan in 1257 and a sister Asperina was *ministra* at Ronco near Milan in December 1261, though a woman called Aspera had been a simple sister of the house in February of the same year, perhaps indicating that she was newly elected.[77] The Necrology of the Humiliati of the Gambara house in Brescia, which seems to have been begun in the thirteenth century, refers to the death of the sister of the founder, brother Albricus, in 1249, describing her as lady Armelina, 'builder (*hedificatrix*) and mother of this house in both temporal and spiritual affairs'. The same necrology refers to the death of sister Beatrix, *domina et ministra* of the

---

sicut laici audiunt divinum officium a clericis, suas orationes more laicorum habentes . . . Item sunt multae quae vix habent copiam ministrorum providentium eis de confessione et sacramentis, unde sequuntur pericula interdum; hae autem sunt iuxta clericos qui haec omnia tempore omni possunt eis ministrare . . . Item sunt multae quae partum aut curiosa operantur; hae autem . . . de lana et lino operantur assidue et fusum manibus apprehendunt'. On Humiliati sisters and work, see Paolini, 'Le Umiliate al lavoro', pp. 229–65.

75 See Brett, *Humbert of Romans*, pp. 65–79.

76 On the Dominicans and the Humiliati, see below, pp. 242–6, 252.

77 Brera: Alberzoni, ' "Sub eadem clausura sequestrati"', p. 104; Ognissanti: *VHM* II, p. 189; Busto Arsizio: Bondioli, *Storia di Busto Arsizio*, I, p. 74 and document 9: 'ministra et anciana'; Sta Caterina: *Gli atti del comune di Milano*, II/1, 191; Ronco: ASMi, 470 Brera, 21 February 1261, 14 December 1261: two brothers are also listed with the sisters: in February: 'fratres Jacobus Fichus et Guidotus Malevestitus . . . et sorores Belaestas et Adraxia et Varentia et Asperina et Margarita et Rica et Bonnasia et Pax et Adraxia de Vicomercato et Julliana et Contessa et Paribella omnes sorores predicte domus'. In December the list includes some different individuals (and different spellings), 'frater Martinus et frater Iacobus fratres et humiliati ipsius domus et Aspera ministra ipsius domus et Bellastate de Roncho, Addelaxia de Roncho, Martina de Roncho, Malgarita [sic] de Roncho et Contisia de Merate et Martina de Verderio sorores et humiliate ipsius domus'.

house of Pontevico in May 1259 and of Concordia, 'who was mother and lady of this house [the Gambara] in both temporal and spiritual affairs' in 1289.[78] There are other examples from the second half of the century, including a *priora* in Bologna in 1276 and in Rancate in 1283.[79] The clearest and most extensive evidence for the presence of *ministre*, however, comes from Veronese documents recording the profession of new members.[80] The relative scarcity of such records for other areas covered by the order may explain the apparent lack of early representation of women elsewhere. A *ministra* is named at the Ghiara in 1209 and 1224, at one house in Zevio from 1218 and at another in 1223, 1230, 1245–6, 1248–9, 1253 and 1255, at the San Paolo house in 1232 and 1235 and at Porto in 1244.[81] Women clearly enjoyed some authority in these houses; however, as Humbert indicated, they were not often independent of the authority of a male superior, a question to which we will return below.[82]

Terms of office

Many superiors remained in office over long periods, perhaps confirmed each year in elections as laid down in *Omnis boni principium*, though there are very few records of elections held.[83] There seems to be no thirteenth-century evidence to either confirm or gainsay the distinction posited by Tagliabue between the terms of office of provosts appointed for life and prelates (and presumably ministers, *prelata* and *ministre*), appointed for one or two years.[84] Certainly provosts, where documented, seem to have held office for long periods. James of Rondineto was provost for at least thirteen years (1198–1211) and perhaps longer,

---

78 *VHM* III, pp. 287–98, 291, 295, 296; Guerrini, 'Gli Umiliati a Brescia', p. 196.
79 Bologna: Spinelli, 'Gli Umiliati in Emilia-Romagna', p. 141; Rancate: ASMi, 385 Sta Caterina, 10 June 1260, 12 May 1269, 11 February 1272, ASMi, 1899 Sta Margherita, 1 April 1283, T. Martellini, 'Le pergamene delle abbazie e commende, dei conventi e dei monasteri di Milano conservate presso l'Archivio di stato di Milano (fondo di religione, parte antica)', *Studi di storia medioevale e di diplomatica*, 11 (1990), 7–77, no. 189; see also Longoni, 'Origini degli Umiliati a Monza', document 19 (1263); ASVic Ognissanti 2, 30 August 1267; *Le pergamene degli Umiliati di Cremona*, 18 (1279).
80 See appendix II.
81 Ghiara: appendix II, 2 (1209), 9–10 (1224); Zevio: appendix II, 8 (1224), 11(1230), ASVer, 172 (1245), 206 (1246), 213 (1248), 215 (1248), 218 (1249), 242 (1253), 258 (1255); San Paolo: appendix II, 12 (1232), ASVer, Ghiara 149 (1235); Porto: ASVer, Ghiara 193 (1244); for the *ministra* at Zevio in 1218, see p. 178.
82 The *ministre* received new brethren with the kiss of fraternity at the orders of the male ministers; see appendix II.
83 For isolated exceptions, below, pp. 178, 205.
84 Tagliabue, 'Gli Umiliati a Viboldone', p. 17; but see Marco Bossi, 'Chronicon sui Humiliatorum ordinis', Zanoni, pp. 350, 352.

while in mid-century a brother Stephen was provost of the same house for at least fifteen years (1249–64).[85] At Ognissanti in Borghetto Lodigiano in 1236 (by which date the community was at least thirty years old), Hubert, the provost, had been preceded by only two men, Lanfranc and Hugh. Of these two, Lanfranc had certainly died, since reference is made to his funeral, but Hugh was still alive during Hubert's tenure of office, though he may have been removed following a dispute.[86] James of Rondineto also left office before he died, while in Pavia in the 1250s and 1260s, brothers Guy and Michael, both members of the Piscariis family, were each provosts of the Oltreticino house over several years.[87] By contrast, it has been shown that in the 1260s in the double house of SS. Maria e Bartolomeo in Rovigo (listed as belonging to the Second order in 1288) the ministers changed each year and at San Luca in Modena, again a Second order house, there was a continuous alternation of personnel.[88] In many earlier cases, however, references to an individual as minister of a particular house are repeated over several years, as they are for provosts, without reference to others in between: in the Ghiara in Verona, Pantanus is recorded as minister in documents from 1222 to 1226 and brother Saladin was minister (or on occasion rector) from 1233 to 1245 and again in 1253.[89] If there were indeed yearly elections to the office of minister, they must often have been little more than rubber-stamping of the status quo. In other cases, the occasional use of the title *ancianus*, always found in combination with another title, may perhaps indicate that the choice of superior was based on seniority of profession or age and this is made explicit in documents from Verona which refer to the *minister maior professus*.[90] Such practices must encourage longer tenure of office by all types of superior.

Like the men, some women held office or returned to office repeatedly over several years. In the 1240s sister Iema is recorded as

---

85 On James, above, pp. 74–7; on Stephen, Morelli 'La casa di Rondineto', 5 (1264) and p. 22*, table 9.

86 *VHM* II, p. 184; on Hugh, see *Il 'registrum magnum' del comune di Piacenza*, 468, 499, 605, 704 (all 1217); gaps in notarial copies of witness lists led the editors to think that a monk, Obizo Mancasole, was provost of Ognissanti at this date, but Hugh's name is clearly included in document 468; on these superiors, see now Mercatili Indelicato, 'Per una storia degli Umiliati nella diocesi di Lodi', p. 471.

87 Alberzoni, 'Giacomo di Rondineto', pp. 149–50; Crotti Pasi, 'Gli Umiliati a Pavia', p. 333.

88 Adami, 'La "domus sancti Bartolomei de Rodigio"', p. 28 n. 124; Romagnoli, 'Gli Umiliati a Modena', appendix 1.2.

89 Pantanus: appendix II, 9–10 (1224), ASVer, Ghiara 79 (1222), 105 (1225), 108 (1225), 110 (1226); Saladin (for example): ASVer, Ghiara 143 (1233), 151 (1237), 152 (1237), 157/158 (1238), 162 (1238), 164 (1239), 168/169 (1240), 171 (1240), 173 (1240), 174 (1241), 176 (1241), 178 (1242), 180 (1242), 192 (1243), 194 (1244), 200 (1245), 242 (1253), 248 (1253), 249 (1253).

90 For example: *minister et ancianus* at Contegnaga (Brescia) in 1245, Guerrini, 'Gli Umiliati a Brescia', p. 205; for *minister maior professus*, see appendix II.

ministra at Zevio in November 1245, November 1246, April and June 1248 and January 1249.[91] A sister Iema had joined the community as long before as August 1205 so, if this is the same woman, she may well have been chosen because of her age and experience.[92] No other women superiors are documented at the house between 1245 and 1249, but it nonetheless remains unclear whether Iema was *ministra* for over three years or whether another woman held the office in 1247. Other examples reflect links between houses. A sister Bonafemina was *ministra* at Zevio in 1230 and at the house of San Paolo in Verona in 1232.[93] A sister Biata was *ministra* at San Paolo in 1235 and a sister Bia, who may be the same woman, was *ministra* at Zevio in the 1250s.[94] As Baldi Cammarota has shown, the Zevio community founded San Paolo and the possibility that a single *ministra* was moving between the two houses may show both that the links remained strong between these two communities and that there was at least some mobility between houses for women, as there was for men.[95]

Duties

Whereas the rule and letters of 1201 give extensive discussion of the necessary qualities and duties of prelates and provosts, the notarial archives provide only sketchy indications of the role of superiors, male or female. As we might expect, men often acted on behalf of their communities in the business of sales, exchanges, purchases and other transactions. In most cases this authority seems to have been held *ex officio*, but in some the male superior was specifically appointed as proctor by the chapter of a community, and in others proctors who were not the superior were chosen.[96] An example from mid-century is informative about the workings of such chapters, though it does not refer specifically to proctors. In the house of the Humiliati of San Giacomo *de Mediovico* in Monza in 1255, an initial group, who met *in capitulo ecclesie* and included the minister, brother Iunius and three brethren, made an agreement with eight men representing the canons of San Giovanni, concerning the use and letting of a mill and other

---

[91] ASVer, Ghiara 172 (1245), 206 (1246), 213 (1248), 218 (1249), 215 (1248).
[92] Appendix II, 1.   [93] Appendix II, 11–12.
[94] ASVer, Ghiara 149 (1235), 258 (1255).
[95] Baldi Cammarota, 'Origine della "domus" degli Umiliati di San Cristoforo in Verona', p. 9; on the mobility of male brethren see below, pp. 170, 182.
[96] See for example, the election of Miranus, minister of the Brera as proctor to act in disputes 'que vertantur seu verti possent' between his house and two brothers, William and Albert 'qui dicuntur Saporiti'. ASMi, 470 Brera, 21 October 1251; for a non-ministerial proctor in Baldaria: ASVat, Baldaria 5374, 25 July 1242.

property.[97] Later on the same day the agreement was read and approved by seven other brothers 'in the public chapter of the house'.[98] The document refers to the brothers and sisters of the *congregatio*, but the sisters were not apparently involved in the decision-making process. Indeed, as we might expect, male brethren often acted as syndics or proctors in the pursuance of legal disputes or commercial transactions for female houses. Once more the evidence is late but interesting: in 1268 Poma, daughter of the late Mascharius *de Balsemo* and widow of Cominus *de Contissa*, entered the Humiliati house of the Senedogo in the Porta Nova in Milan. The contract was stipulated in the presence of the second Master General, Peter *de Brissia* (Brescia), in itself a remarkable event since this is the only such reference to the physical presence of the Master General at the entry of a new member in the thirteenth century. One of the other witnesses was brother Peter *de Misenti* of the *domus nova*, outside the Porta Nova, who is described as 'rector and provider and having care of' the Humiliati women of the Senedogo.[99] The need for a male representative may sometimes explain cases where a man acted for the women but is not identified as a brother, or those where there were clearly a vast majority of women with only one or two men in a community. In 1212, Guidottus and Lanfranc *qui dicitur de Orliano* (Oriano near Cassago Brianza) were invested with a farm to administer (*sedimen ad massaricium*) on behalf of the Humiliati sisters of Oriano, who included Berta, sister of Lanfranc.[100] In Garbagnate Rotta in 1218, Vassallus Ferrarius was invested with an entire holding (*massaricium*) by the archpriest of Monza on behalf of five Humiliati sisters.[101] In Pavia in 1242, the one brother and nine sisters of the house *que . . . fuit porcorum* in Porta Palazzo appointed brother Nicholas *de Aveto*, perhaps a member of the house, as their 'nuncio, syndic, proctor and agent' in a dispute with the monastery of San Pietro in Ciel d'Oro.[102] Again in Pavia, in 1253 Thomas *de Çacono*, acting as minister of the female contingent of the Humiliati *de Cadrona*, purchased four

---

[97] Longoni, 'Origini degli Umiliati a Monza', 11.

[98] *Ibid.*, 'in publico capitulo eiusdem domus'.

[99] Zanoni, pp. 322–4: 'presente fratre Petro de Misenti . . . rectore et provisore et curam habente Humiliatarum dicte domus'; Peter may be a brother or other relative of a brother Stephen 'de Misenti' named as a representative of the Brera in ASMi, 470 Brera, 28 June 1264.

[100] Longoni, 'Gli Umiliati in Brianza', 2 (1212); the farm lay 'a mane ipsarum mulierum'.

[101] *Ibid.*, 3 (1218): 'omiliatorum [sic] sororum domus de Garbaniate Rupte'; the term 'massaricium' was used to describe a collection of lands administered on behalf of a community by one or more individuals; see for example, *I registri del monastero di s. Abbondio in Como: secolo xiii*, *passim*.

[102] Crotti Pasi, 'Gli Umiliati a Pavia', p. 330 and appendix 3, pp. 341–2: 'nuncium, syndicum et procuratorem et actorem'.

perches of vineyard.[103] Another example records the attendance at a council meeting in Vercelli in November 1257 of Martin, provost of the Humiliati of San Martino *de la Catesso* in Vercelli, on behalf of the 'whole order of the Humiliati, or of the Humiliati brethren', to receive a donation from John *de Panclerio*, destined to the Humiliati sisters of Sant'Agata in Vercelli.[104] The sisters presumably could not attend themselves. Finally, in 1261, male brethren from Rondineto in Como were present in the house of the Humiliati sisters of San Vitale in Como, at a sale made by the Humiliati of *Colliate* to the Hospital of San Vitale.[105]

Unlike members of other major orders, there is no evidence that these men resented or resisted their responsibilities towards their Humiliati sisters. The women, however, did sometimes take a more prominent role. In 1267, the chapter of the *domus de medio* in Vicenza, which included the minister brother Semprebene and the *ministra*, sister Armerina, together with three brothers and four sisters met, 'in general chapter . . . at the ringing of the bell in the usual way', to agree a sale of property to the *domus nova* in Cremona.[106] Other records show that on occasion, at least in the second half of the century, the women acted autonomously and had distinct property. In 1252 the male and female sections of the Humiliati *de Cadrona* in Pavia owed rents separately to the monastery of San Pietro in Ciel d'Oro for vineyards and land.[107] In 1272 the sisters of the house of brother William *de Canova* in Borgovico in Como had their own vines and garden, separated by a wall from those of their brothers.[108] In 1260, at the house in Porta Palazzo Pavia (*que domus fuit porcorum*) the *ministra* acted in her own right in the sale of a plot of land, as did Bonita, *ministra* of the 'humiliati ladies called *de Capuziis*' in the contrata of San Salvatore in Monza in the purchase of two dilapidated houses in 1263.[109] References to a *ministra* in a house with several sisters and only one or two brothers may suggest that the female superior enjoyed some authority over brethren of both sexes.[110] While there is no record of Humiliati women teaching or preaching, some clearly did enjoy a degree of independence in managing their

---

[103] *Ibid.*, p. 328.

[104] *VHM* II, p. 48, now also in Valentini, 'Gli Umiliati a Vercelli nel 1271', p. 38.

[105] Arizza, 'L'ospedale di San Vitale in Como', 14 (1261).

[106] ASVic Ognissanti 2, 30 August 1267: 'in generali capitulo . . . ad sonum campanum more solito congregato'.

[107] Crotti Pasi, 'Gli Umiliati a Pavia', p. 329.   [108] Morelli, 'La casa di Rondineto', 8.

[109] Crotti Pasi, 'Gli Umiliati a Pavia', p. 331; 'duabus domibus dirupatis', Longoni, 'Origini degli Umiliati a Monza', 19 (1263); but see also *ibid.*, 29 (1291), when a contract agreed by two women who had transferred to the community was subject to the consent of the archpriest of Monza, without which it would be 'cassa et irrita et nullius valoris'.

[110] For example, at Ronco in the 1260s, above, n. 77.

temporal affairs, not unlike the status of wealthy widows in the world outside the cloister.

Size

There is no evidence that a standard size, such as the number twelve associated with traditional monasteries, or laid down by Bonaventure as the minimum for the Franciscan *conventus*, was adopted by the Humiliati in the thirteenth century.[111] By the early fourteenth century, the convents of Franciscans in Italy seem to have had an average of about seventeen friars.[112] Humiliati houses may often have been smaller, but there were many more communities in any one city or region. Records of the chapters of houses coming together to make decisions or of those on whose behalf an agreement was made give some indication of their size. Thus at Oriano in 1212 there were ten sisters in a single house, while at Garbagnate Rotta in 1218 there were just five.[113] The documents only rarely state, however, whether those listed include the whole community and often we must assume that they do not. Moreover, much of the evidence is late and may not in this case reflect earlier experience. In 1227 the Brera had thirty brothers and twenty-two sisters, but in 1230 there seem to be only twenty-one brothers, while a damaged document of 1251, which has lost a large area from the top left corner, lists twenty-eight brothers (including the minister) in what survives and the missing space may have included anywhere between five and nine others.[114] Even where the record is unequivocal, the size of a community probably varied greatly over the years. In December 1228, the *domus de Biolzago*, north of Milan, numbered three brothers and thirteen sisters, but in June 1229 only one man and ten women were named.[115] In February 1261 two brothers and twelve sisters were listed at the house in Ronco near Milan, but in December of the same year there were only seven sisters and the names are not all the same.[116] In other examples, numbers may appear reasonably constant: in 1260 the *domus magna de Ranchate* numbered sixteen sisters and still had the

---

[111] Deroux, 'Les origines de l'oblature bénédictine', p. 16; Iriarte, *Storia del francescanesimo*, p. 152; this changed in the fourteenth century when the constitutions laid down the numbers of clergy to be received by each *canonica*: *VHM* III, pp. 102–4.

[112] See Moorman, *A History of the Franciscan Order*, p. 351.

[113] Longoni, 'Gli Umiliati in Brianza', pp. 806–7.

[114] Appendix I, *38; ASMi, 470 Brera, 21 October 1251; Alberzoni '"Sub eadem clausura sequestrati"', appendix 1 (1227).

[115] Longoni, 'Gli Umiliati in Brianza', 7, 8. [116] See n. 77 above.

same number in 1269, but by 1272 this had risen to nineteen, and there may well have been other fluctuations in intervening years.[117] Some communities recorded as few as five sisters or brothers, while others later in the century numbered nearly sixty.[118] Crotti Pasi lists examples from Pavia which date from 1219 to mid-century and range from seven brothers at Sta Maria in Pertica in 1219 to nineteen at the Oltreticino house in 1256.[119] A Cremonese record lists nine sisters in 1244 at the *domus mansionis Iohannis de Celso*, while a papal letter of 1231 refers, perhaps optimistically, to eighty brethren, including both men and women, at Ognissanti in Borghetto Lodigiano.[120] The reason for these variations is not easy to ascertain. Certainly there was some mobility among the brethren. In a deposition made by brother Vitale of Ognissanti in Borghetto Lodigiano in 1236 he explains his ignorance concerning certain episodes in the community by arguing that 'he spent many years between Bergamo and Bologna, at his houses which are in those cities'.[121] The vows of new brethren also allow for some mobility between houses, perhaps for work, which might account for some fluctuations.[122] New recruits and the death of older brethren, or the sporadic presence of Tertiaries to boost numbers, may account for others. Thus Vitry's 150 'conventual congregations' in the Milanese diocese may have housed anywhere between 750 and 5,000 or more brethren. While the higher figure is improbable, the lower is certainly too small.

Catchment areas

Although inconclusive about size, these same records do provide clues to the geographical catchment area for some Humiliati houses, as place names occasionally occur in the second names of members. This is a problematic area since some geographical names became the surname of prominent families (*de Porta Orientale, de Porta Romana, de Casteliono*) while in others, place names may indicate the birthplace of forebears,

---

[117] ASMi, 385 Sta Caterina, 10 June 1260, 12 May 1269, 11 February 1272; a later document, *ibid.*, 4 March 1292, lists only six sisters but describes them as acting on behalf of the rest of the community: 'nomine et vice totius capituli et conventus illarum sororum'.

[118] Five sisters at Garbagnate Rotta, 1218, Longoni, 'Gli Umiliati in Brianza', 3; fourteen men and forty-four women at the Ghiara in Verona in 1272. Archivio capitolare di Verona I, 21 fo. 2v; I am grateful to Professor G. De Sandre Gasparini for this reference.

[119] Crotti Pasi, 'Gli Umiliati a Pavia', p. 332.

[120] *Le pergamene degli Umiliati di Cremona*, I (1244); appendix I, 39.

[121] *VHM* II, p. 187: 'per plures annos stetit inter bergamum et bononiam ad suas domos que sunt in illis civitatibus'; see now also Mercatili Indelicato, 'Per una storia degli Umiliati nella diocesi di Lodi'; see also brother James of Vicenza and Cremona, below p. 170.

[122] See below, p. 182.

even if recent, rather than that of the brethren themselves.[123] Yet even this may help to show the extent to which the order appealed to new arrivals in towns rather than older established families. Once more the documents from the area of Verona are particularly informative. Over half of the sixty-eight new members recorded entering these houses between 1209 and 1250 are named as coming from families linked in some manner to identifiable towns in the area: two were from Verona itself (one from the Campo Marzio area of the city, who entered the Ghiara and one *de Verone* who went to Zevio), four were from Zevio and the vast majority of the rest were from locations within about 20 kilometres of Verona.[124] Five were perhaps from greater distances: Bolzano, Mantua and Cremona, though in the case of those from Cremona and Mantua the names are adjectival, using the form *Mantuana* not *de Mantua*, perhaps indicating that the moment of transition dates further back.

Elsewhere the records are generally less complete. At Ognissanti in Borghetto Lodigiano, depositions made in the 1230s give a place of origin only for two brothers: John, 'formerly of Verona', who declared that he had been in the house for twenty-four years and James 'formerly of Milan' who had been in the house about fifteen years.[125] Similarly, in Cremona, lists of members from the *domus super Rodanum* in 1244 (nine sisters), the *domus nova* in 1283 (eleven brothers) and the *domus S. Gulielmus* in 1295 (eighteen brothers), include only one double name: Albert *de Virola* in 1295.[126] An Albert *de Cerexia* also appears as a minister in a document of 1250, but such references are hardly a sufficient basis from which to draw any conclusions.[127]

A similar lack of evidence is apparent for the other houses of the order, though some are better documented than others. In the 1270s and 1280s the house of San Giovanni *de Porris* in Novara attracted recruits from Gallarate, Pagliate, Suno, Cara, Novara itself, Legnano, Monferrato, Monticello and Milan.[128] Not all of these are readily identifiable: Monticello may refer to Monticello d'Alba, 95 kilometres to the south-west, Monticello Brianza, 60 kilometres east, or to one of

[123] See *Genèse médiévale de l'anthroponymie moderne: l'espace italien. Mélanges de l'école française de Rome. Moyen âge*, 106 (1994).

[124] See appendix II and ASVer, Ghiara 149, 161, 165, 193, 196, 172, 206, 213, 218, 242, 249, 258, 296, 303, 353; locations around Verona: Cologna Veneta, Caldiero, Illasi, Mozzecane, Trevenzuola, Tomba di Sotto, Roverchiara, Porto, Lonigo, Nogara and Legnago.

[125] *VHM* II, p. 188; see now Mercatili Indelicato, 'Per una storia degli Umiliati nella diocesi di Lodi', pp. 480, 482.

[126] *Le pergamene degli Umiliati di Cremona*, 1 (1244), 30 (1283), 35 (1295).   [127] *Ibid.*, 3

[128] This list is based on *L'ospedale della carità di Novara*, 129 (1277), 130 (1277), 132 (1280), 131 (1283), 100 (1288).

several other small locations. Monferrato may refer either to Casale Monferrato or to the Monferrato area south-west of Novara. The others range between 20 and 45 kilometres from Novara. Earlier evidence is available for the Brera in Milan, where in 1230, brethren are listed from Albiate, Desio, Monza, Piacenza and Trezzo, a list which extends in later documents to include Cantù, Cremona, Gallarate, Garbagnate, Masnago, Parabiago, Robbiate, Sabbione, Vanzago and Varese, as well as several from Milan itself.[129] Again not all the locations are easily identifiable, but the majority lie within 15 and 50 kilometres as the crow flies from Milan.

Although incomplete and generally late, these documents do suggest that the appeal of the Humiliati was generally limited to an area with a radius of less than 50 kilometres and more often still to individuals already resident in the area where the house was placed, though perhaps newly arrived. The house of the Brera attracted a very few recruits from slightly further away (Cremona and Piacenza), as did the Ghiara in Verona or San Giovanni *de Porris* in Novara. There were Humiliati houses in many of the locations named as places of origin for brethren in these communities, which suggests either that some recruits preferred to enter a house at some distance from home or that their names do indeed indicate the origins of forebears, while they had already been residing in the area of the house they entered. In none of these cases would it be possible to use this evidence to argue that the appeal or prestige of such key houses was greater, since we cannot distinguish between the two relative centripetal forces, of the houses and of the cities themselves.

Sisters in First order Houses

The early presence of women in communities of the First order indicated in Innocent III's letter *Non omni spiritui* is confirmed by notarial evidence from three or four houses after 1201.[130] At the First order house of Ognissanti in Borghetto Lodigiano there were sisters from the start: in 1236 sister Flora, the *magistra*, described herself as one of the first sisters 'who were there from the beginning at the building of the said church', referring to a period some thirty-three years earlier.[131]

---

[129] Appendix I, *38 (1230) ASMi, 470 Brera, 21 October 1251, 471 12 July 1276, 15 November 1281, 26 April 1284, 31 May 1284, 1 July 1284, 31 August 1284, 21 August 1284, 11 November 1291, 28 September 1293, 18 October 1296; on the difficulties of identifying these, see now, Alberzoni, '"Sub eadem clausura sequestrati"', 82–4.

[130] Appendix I, 9.

[131] *VHM* II, p. 189; see now Mercatili Indelicato, 'Per una storia degli Umiliati nella diocesi di Lodi', p. 483.

Women are also documented from the very beginning of the community at Rondineto in Como. In 1189 the superiors were described as acting on behalf of the 'men and women who are or have been in the congregation and fraternity of Rondineto'.[132] In 1232, sisters Victoria and Guglielma Rusca were named as recipients of a yearly gift of oil for as long as they should live from Guglielma's sister and Victoria's niece, Agnexia Rusca, a nun in the monastery of Sta Maria in Como, who had received an inheritance from her father Arderic Rusca.[133] Later in the century the women in the community seem to have been far outnumbered by the men, but the archives refer to sisters again anonymously in 1264 and by name in 1279 when a Jacoba *de Sancto Benedicto*, is described as professed and dedicated to God in the house.[134] Finally, a document from February 1344 shows that women had been long-term members of the community until that date. Only then did the last sisters leave and this was because 'the number of their sisters was reduced to so few that of the sisters in the said church none remain except Marchesina alone and sister Johanina'. As a result, they could no longer live there conveniently and now moved to join the sisters or nuns of the order of the Humiliati *de Pontexelo* in Como, of whom they had 'heard and understood that . . . both by fame and deeds they have a good reputation and lead an honest life'.[135] They were prompted by the consideration that it would be 'more profitable to them, both for the utility of their souls and comfort of their bodies if they transferred from that place to another with sisters or nuns in which they could lead their lives more comfortably and end their days in thought for their souls'.[136] The transfer was approved by the chapter

---

[132] *VHM* III, p. 304: 'virorum et mulierum qui et que sunt et erant [sic] in congregatione et fraternitate de Rondenario'.

[133] 'Le carte di Sta Maria Vecchia di Como', 21 (1232).

[134] '[D]omina Iacoba', daughter of dominus Antonius de Sancto Benedicto de Cumis, 'sorore professa dicte domus de Rondenario et Deo dicata [sic] ipsi domui'; Morelli, 'La casa di Rondineto', 11, 12 (June 1279) and table 9.

[135] First documented in 1295–8, the Pontexelo house stood at the beginning of Borgovico, near the Cosia torrent; Arizza and Longatti, 'Gli Umiliati in diocesi di Como', p. 139.

[136] '[N]umerus ipsarum sororum ad tantum esset reductus quod ex sororibus in dicta ecclesia non supersint nixi [sic] solum Marchexina . . . et soror Iohanina . . . considerantes etiam predicte Marchexina et Iohanina quod utilius esset eis tam in utilitate anime quam corporis recreacionem de dicto loco se transfere [sic] ad alium locum aliarum monialium seu sororum in quo posent [sic] suam vitam comodius deducere et in pensiero sue anime vitam finire . . . audito et intellecto quod . . . tam ex fama quam ex operibus bonam famam et honestam vitam deducant'; this document was known to Tiraboschi, who mentioned it in passing, *VHM* II, p. 22, but is now missing from the archive. After completing her study of the house of Rondineto, however, Dr Morelli was shown it by a dealer in Como and was able to make a transcription, which she kindly showed to me.

of Rondineto and James *de Lomeno* of Bergamo, the tenth Master General of the order, who was present.[137] Thus ended over one hundred and fifty years of coexistence.

Like Rondineto, Viboldone is generally poorly documented for the thirteenth century, but a late record reveals that the community accepted a husband and wife with seven children in 1276 and the adults promised to live 'as brothers and sisters of the house'.[138] There is no implication that this was a new departure, but nor is it possible to ascertain when women first joined the brothers there. The house of William *de Canova* in Borgovico in Como, which was led by a provost and seems to have belonged to the First order, also certainly had women in the community in 1272, but their presence cannot as yet be projected back earlier.[139]

The status of these women in First order houses is not immediately clear. Although Innocent's letter to the First order recognised the rights of sisters in the election of the superior, it otherwise refers to them only in restrictions on *transitus* to other orders.[140] There are no records of canonesses in any extant documentation.[141] Were they perhaps professed in the Second, monastic order, or were the distinctions meaningless when clerical status was not at issue? In 1232, sisters Victoria and Guglielma at Rondineto in Como are described as *consorores*, which might imply a separate status; however, in 1279 sister Jacoba was named as *soror professa* while *confrater* is often used in Como documentation, apparently to indicate all the brethren of the congregation.[142] It is not used entirely consistently or in ways which seem to imply lower status and may simply be a local notarial style.[143] Nonetheless, it may eventually be possible to establish that members nominally belonging to different 'orders' of the Humiliati were living in the same community, under authority to the same superiors. If so this might explain the rarity of indications of the precise order to which a house belonged. Houses of the First order may have accommodated brethren of the Second and perhaps of the Third order alongside their clerical members.

---

[137] James was the second Master General bearing this name: *VHM* I, pp. 118–22.
[138] See table 6.2, p. 193.   [139] Morelli, 'La casa di Rondineto', 8 (1272).
[140] Appendix I, 9.
[141] Nor can I find evidence that this is what Innocent intended to create, as Little argues, *Religious Poverty and the Profit Economy*, p. 116.
[142] On sister Jacoba, above, p. 161; Morelli 'La casa di Rondineto', 11 (1279).
[143] Morelli, 'La casa di Rondineto', 5 (1264), 8 (1272), 9 (1273), 11 (1279), 12 (1279), 16 (1292), 17 (1293), 19 (1295), 22 (1296), 23 (1296), 24 (1297), 25 (1297); for its use in other Como houses, see, for example ASCo, OSA ospedaletti antichi cartella 8, 5 (1290).

THE DEVELOPMENT OF AN *ORDO*

Links between communities

The development of a wider feeling of belonging to an order, in the sense of a congregation with a collective identity, essential to the development of any corporate body, is not easy to assess. The Cistercians had adopted the term *ordo* in this sense of a 'constituted religious order' early on in their history and by the pontificate of Gregory IX (1227–41), the same term was commonly used in papal correspondence for the Cluniacs.[144] It is used in a similar way in the address clauses of the papal letters for the Humiliati in 1201 and the bull for the First order, *Non omni spiritui*, explicitly refers to the presence of members of the 'Second order' at masses celebrated during interdicts.[145] They are first specifically identified as a *religio* and named as Humiliati in official documentation in the letter of Gerard *de Sesso* of 1211.[146] From 1220 *ordo Humiliatorum* is commonly, but not exclusively, found in papal correspondence.[147] *Ordo* is not, however, widespread in notarial records. In Verona it is first found in 1230, but is not found again until 1240 and is never used regularly in the thirteenth century.[148] In Turin it is found in a document of 1244, in Bergamo in 1255 and in Vicenza in 1267.[149] Other examples could be illustrated, but *ordo* is not a standard notarial formula for the Humiliati and its occasional use would provide few clues to the acknowledgement of ties beyond the single *domus* and therefore of a common sense of identity and participation in a wider *ordo Humiliatorum*.

Evidence concerning links between houses and between different 'types' of Humiliati does, however, seem to suggest participation in a wider institution. For example, an agreement of February 1230 was designed to protect the rights of all those who might be affected by the building of the new church of the Brera in Milan. This included not only parishioners, but also the Humiliati living in the neighbourhood, who might perhaps expect to be buried there and whose rights were explicitly protected.[150] Some sort of link is implied between the regular

---

144 See Dubois, 'Ordo', *DIP*, VI, cols. 812–14.
145 Appendix I, 9.   146 Appendix I, *16.   147 Appendix I, 19.
148 See below, appendix II, 11 (1230), ASVer, Ghiara 166 (1240), 171 (1240), 296 (1263), 353 (1281).
149 Turin: S. *Solutore* 21 (1244); Bergamo: Brolis, *Gli Umiliati a Bergamo*, Appendix 2, 6 from ASBg, Archivio Notarile, cartella 1, 1, p. 169, *imbreviature* of the notary Bartolomeo Carbonari; Vicenza: ASVic Ognissanti 2, 30 August 1267.
150 Appendix I, *38: 'pro aliis vicinis qui essent de ordine Humiliatorum salvum sit jus ipsis Humiliatis de Braida seu ecclesie sue'; on this agreement, see below, pp. 226–7.

community and Tertiaries in the vicinity, who looked to the Brera as their meeting place and church.

This implication of close ties between the Brera and Tertiaries in the surrounding area is not clarified in the documentation after this date, but there is some evidence from Como which may indicate similar links, this time involving a First order house. In 1235 the priest Giroldus, acting on behalf of the Rondineto community, paid off debts of 34 lire of the new money owed by brother Otto *de Brezia* and his 'congregation and fraternity' in Como.[151] The loan had been obtained to pay for the cost of wool (a rare, early and indirect link with wool-working perhaps?), using the house of the community as equity, but Otto had died before repayment had been made in full. By paying off the creditor Giroldus acquired the house in which Otto and his fraternity had lived in Borgovico, Como. No mention is made of the purpose of this payment, nor of surviving members of the fraternity; indeed the document makes no reference to the Humiliati in relation to either community. It seems quite possible, however, that as well as increasing the patrimony of Rondineto itself, Giroldus was supporting a fraternity of Tertiary Humiliati who had run into difficulties. Certainly, a First order Humiliati community was to be documented in Borgovico in 1272.[152]

The documents frequently refer to the intervention of brethren from one house in the activities of another. As we have seen, male brethren often acted on behalf of female communities, but this was not the only sort of tie between houses. In 1235 Salander, minister of the *domus humiliatorum de Florenti[ol]a*, was present at Piacenza, when Hubert provost of Ognissanti in Borghetto Lodigiano delivered a papal letter concerning a dispute in which Ognissanti was involved to the provost of the *domus duodecim apostolorum* in Piacenza.[153]

An alternative and perhaps more reliable indicator of the development of links, and therefore of conscious participation in the wider order, may, however, be found in evidence that some larger communities enjoyed influence beyond the confines of the individual house. A clear early example of such prominence is provided by the Ghiara, in Verona. Already in 1204 the Humiliati of this house had established a daughter-house in Zevio, which in turn founded the house of San Paolo in the *ora sancti paoli*.[154] Professions of faith might be made in the

---

[151] Morelli, 'La casa di Rondineto', 1 (1235).   [152] See p. 139.

[153] *CDL*, II/1, 315 (1235); Salander may be from Florence or nearby Fiorenzuola, see now Mercatili Indelicato, 'Per una storia degli Umiliati nella diocesi di Lodi', p. 390, n. 158.

[154] Baldi Cammarota, 'Origine della "domus" degli Umiliati di San Cristoforo in Verona', pp. 8–9.

Ghiara although the postulant was destined to live in a house in Zevio or Porto.[155] A will drawn up in September 1226 further reflects the importance of the Ghiara, which received 10 lire, while the other houses in the area received only 40 shillings each.[156]

Such dominance by one house is also at least hinted at in other cities: the Necrology of the Humiliati of the Gambara house in Brescia describes the minister of that house, Albricus *de Gambara* (d. 1252), as 'Father and greatest benefactor of all the Humiliati houses of this territory and also of the whole order' and the death of the minister, brother John, in 1299 is occasion to record the house as the greatest of all the houses of the Humiliati in that region.[157] The description may of course be a late addition to the Necrology, but suggests that the superior of this house, and by association the house itself, enjoyed a position of influence in the area. This is not decisive evidence, but elsewhere the picture is more concrete. In Como, as we have seen, the provost of Rondineto exercised authority over other houses and not always Humiliati ones, in the area. As well as taking responsibility for Sta Maria di Ronco Martano and assisting the fraternity at Borgovico, he presided at the profession of a new brother for the Hospital of San Vitale in 1249, though the Humiliati were only given express responsibility for the hospital in the fourteenth century.[158] In Milan there is evidence that by mid-century the *domus nova* was particularly prominent. In 1251 the prelate, brother Guy *Vicecomes*, is described as visitor of the Gessate house and sent two brothers as nuncios to assist at the stipulation of a contract there and to confirm it.[159] As we have seen, in 1268 a brother from the same house seems to have enjoyed similar responsibilities at the Humiliati house of the Senedogo in Porta Nova.[160]

Local or regional hierarchies: the evidence for networks

In some areas these ties became part of formal city or district-wide hierarchies, with superiors identified as ministers of the city, or city and district (*districtus*) and not always associated with a particular dominant 'mother' house. In June 1201, Innocent III's letter *Incumbit nobis* to the

---

[155] See appendix II, 5, 7.   [156] Appendix III, 6 (1226).

[157] *VHM* III, pp. 290, 293: 'Pater et Benefactor maximus omnium domorum Humiliatorum huius terre et etiam totius Ordinis'; 'Minister hujus Domus maximus omnium Domorum Humiliatorum hujus Terrae'.

[158] ASCo, Ospedale di Sant'Anna, ospedaletti antichi 5, 4, transcribed in Arizza, 'L'ospedale di San Vitale', 10 (1249).

[159] Alberzoni, 'Il monastero di Sant'Ambrogio e i movimenti religiosi del xiii secolo', pp. 186–7 and nn. 59–60.

[160] See above, p. 155.

Third order listed the ministers of various cities, from which it may be inferred that for the Tertiaries at least some form of city-based identity was envisaged.[161] The evidence for the regular houses comes from the notarial archives and is later, dating mostly from the third and fourth decades of the century. In Vicenza in 1225, brother Taurellus received a donation on behalf of his own community and that of another neighbouring house and in May 1227 he acted on behalf of 'the fraternity and community of the Humiliati of the city of Vicenza', indicating a wider responsibility.[162] In Seveso, north of Milan, a link seems to have existed at the level of the *pieve*: in 1230 a brother and Humiliati sisters of the *domus de supra Humiliatarum de loco Cixano* stipulated a contract with the consent of a brother Cotius and brother James, described as ministers of the *domus societatis Humiliatorum plebis de Seviso*, who may have been either regular or Tertiary Humiliati.[163] In Pavia there was a similar situation. In 1219 a house is described as being newly founded as part of the congregation of the Humiliati of Pavia: 'the house of the fraternity of the Humiliati newly constituted under the congregation and in the congregation of the Humiliati of Pavia'.[164] Again, in 1226, Lanfranc *de Veglevano*, described as 'minister of the humiliati of the city', gave his assent to the renting out of a house and other property to a creditor by the minister and brothers of the *mansio* of Sta Maria in Pertica.[165] Finally, in just one much later example, the 'membership' of both Second and Third order houses in a single area-wide community is made clear. In 1259, Redulfus Riboldus, Hubert Buzella and brother Tuttobellus bought land in Vedano on behalf of the 'Second and Third orders of the Humiliati of Monza'.[166]

These documents imply a sense of 'city identity' and it has been suggested that the term *minister . . . de civitate* in Pavia may reflect a differentiation between the Humiliati of the city and those of the surrounding contado.[167] Whether or not this distinction was significant in Pavia, it does not seem to have been important in other areas, where an identity of interests between city and diocese emerged. In 1217 a donation was received by Castellus a tailor, Martin *de Sesto* and William *de Brembio*, who were described as 'ministers of the *mansio* of the

---

[161] Appendix I, 7.
[162] ASVic Ognissanti 1, 3 August 1225, 16 May 1227: 'in loco et vissu [sic] fraternitatis et communitatis humiliatorum de civitate Vicencie'.
[163] Zanoni, p. 133 n. 2.
[164] Crotti Pasi, 'Gli Umiliati a Pavia', appendix 1 (1219), p. 338: 'domus fraternitatis humiliatorum de novo constitute sub congregatione et in congregatione humiliatorum de Papia'.
[165] *Ibid.*, 2 (1226), pp. 339–41: 'minister humiliatorum de civitate'.
[166] Longoni, 'Origini degli Umiliati a Monza', 17 (1259).
[167] Crotti Pasi, 'Gli Umiliati a Pavia', p. 333.

Humiliati of the diocese of Lodi', acting on behalf of the *societas humiliatorum*.[168] Eight years later, in 1225, two of the men, William and Martin, were further described as 'Ministers of the Humiliati of Lodi and diocese'.[169] There was no separation between city and contado here. A similar association, though between city and district (*districtus*) not diocese, is found in a later document from Bergamo. In 1255 in the house of Torre Boldone brother John *bonelli de Viana* and the Humiliati of the house presided at the entry of a new brother on behalf of the house and 'all the order of the Humiliati of the city and district of Bergamo'.[170]

These documents do not amount to a complete record. Yet they are important indicators of a wider sense of identity at least at a local level. There is no clear provincial structure in the order equivalent to that developed in the Dominican or Franciscan orders. The *fagie* or districts used in catalogues of houses drawn up in 1298 and 1344 followed the dioceses and may have had some administrative purpose, but cannot be traced earlier than the end of the thirteenth century.[171] Moreover, as Besozzi has shown, in the *fagia* of Seprio, north-west of Milan, the list of houses given in 1298 follows their topographical spread through the area, not a discernible administrative pattern.[172] Nonetheless sources from two areas show some sort of active regional association before the 1290s. One is rather late. In 1268 a dispute in Modena was subjected to brother Roland 'minister of the order of the brothers of the Humiliati of Parma, Reggio, Modena, Bologna and Borgo San Donnino', all cities along the via Emilia.[173] The Humiliati did not, however, spread widely in Emilia until the mid-thirteenth century and beyond. They are recorded early on in Piacenza and diocese (1180), Parma (perhaps in 1211, certainly by 1246) and Bologna (1218), but in Modena only by 1264–5 and for Reggio Emilia this reference to brother Roland in 1268 is the first to a house there (and may indicate intent rather than achieved settlement, since the Humiliati are otherwise only documented in 1288).[174] Recorded communities in other cities in the region are also

---

[168] *VHM* II, p. 7.   [169] *Ibid.*, p. 18.

[170] '[T]ocius ordinis humiliatorum civitatis et districtus Pergami', below, p. 174.

[171] *VHM* III, pp. 265–7, 270–85; the origins of this use of *fagia* are obscure (Du Cange, *Glossarium*, s.v. 'Fagia' lists nothing similar to its use here), but the territorial meaning is clear; see *VHM* I, 324–5 and now Broggi, 'Il catalogo del 1298', p. 7 n. 13.

[172] Besozzi, 'L'ultimo preposito degli Umiliati di Cannobio', pp. 415–16.

[173] Romagnoli, 'Gli Umiliati a Modena', p. 495 and n. 31 and appendix 2: 'minister ordinis fratrum domorum Humiliatorum de Parma, Regio, Mutina, Bononia et Borgo Sancti Donini'; she notes the prominence of Parma.

[174] For Piacenza, above, p. 51; the Parma community was perhaps the group which Salimbene de Adam was to portray in typically lively terms in the 1280s: 'magister Rolandus, episcopus Spoletinus . . . voluit emere locum eorum [of the Humiliati] cum toto territorio quod ibi

later and in several cases the first reference is a catalogue of First order houses which John of Brera dates to 1288: Dozza, Faenza, Borgo San Donnino and Fiorenzuola.[175] The regional structure implied in the title of brother Roland may therefore reflect innovations in the second half of the century.

Verona: a case study of local hierarchies

Verona is undoubtedly the best documented of the Veneto towns and indeed among the best recorded of all areas occupied by the Humiliati. Here the sources give the impression of a gradual progression towards a wider sense of common identity and community, first in the city and district of Verona itself and then between Verona, Vicenza and Mantua. In 1212, one of the earliest surviving Veronese documents records the existence of ministers with some sort of authority over the whole city and diocese: 'ministers of the *universitas* and community of the Humiliati of Verona and diocese'.[176] This position is perhaps similar to that of Lanfranc, 'minister of the city' in Pavia, but the precise nature of their authority is not clear. In Veronese documents from the 1220s (and there are very few documents for the intervening years) these senior ministers were usually called minister *maior* or *anterior*, though Pantanus is occasionally described as 'minister of the humiliati brethren of Verona and its diocese and district (*districtus*) who congregate at the Humiliati house of the Ghiara in Verona'.[177] These records illustrate the particular prominence of both Pantanus and his house, but there was usually more than one senior minister at any one time: in 1224 Pantanus and Bartholomew Laurudus were together described as 'senior ministers . . . of the fraternity of the Humiliati', while in 1230 brother Taurellus, senior minister, was acting 'on behalf and in the name of his associates, the senior professed ministers'.[178]

The vast majority of commercial transactions, in which the single ministers of individual houses acted alone with the consent of their own

habebant, ut dixit michi, et dare eis mille libras imperialium, ut habitaret ibi estivo tempore vel quandocumque sibi placeret. Sed quia ducentas libras imperialium volebant adhuc plus quam ille dare vellet, dimissa est venditio et emptio supradicta.' Salimbene de Adam, *Chronicon*, ed. Scalia, pp. 865–6.

175 See Spinelli, 'Gli Umiliati in Emilia-Romagna', pp. 139, 144, 149–51, 155, 161 and corrections in Romagnoli, 'Gli Umiliati a Modena', p. 489; on the catalogue see John of Brera, *Chronicon*, ch. 34, pp. 264–7.

176 Appendix II, 7: 'm[inistri] uniuersitatis et communitatis humiliatorum Verone et episcopatus'.

177 For example: appendix II, 9 (1224); ASVer, Ghiara 108 (1225), 110 (1226), 123 (1228): 'minister fratrum humiliatorum Verone et eius episcopatus et districtus qui congregantur ad domum humiliatorum a Glara de Verone'.

178 Appendix II, 8 (1224), 11 (1230).

communities, do not refer to a senior minister, but such superiors sometimes seem to have been involved in agreements which concerned the passage of property to the order. Brother Gerard, 'formerly of Vicenza, senior minister of the community and *universitas* of the Humiliati of Verona and district', was present when a donation was made to the Ghiara in 1228, while in 1237, Ubicinus, son of the late Gerard *de Tugrario*, left land for the poor to be distributed by the 'communal ministers of the houses and colleges of the Humiliati of Verona'.[179] The variation of terminology in this text may not of course refer to senior ministers, but to all the ministers of the separate houses as a group, but the sense of a city community was clearly apparent to the testator, his notary, or the named Humiliati executors who may have been present.

The clearest idea of the higher authority of the senior ministers is given in the records of the entry of new brethren.[180] In the context of Milan, Alberzoni has suggested that the older houses in the city held certain spiritual responsibilities towards those in the immediate suburbs of Milan and that because of these relations, they were involved in the administration of property.[181] There is as yet little direct evidence for this spiritual involvement in Milan itself, but these Veronese documents perhaps illustrate the possibilities. The senior ministers personally accepted the promise of the postulants, allocated them to the different houses of the city and its district and ordered the ministers of those houses, both men and women, to receive them with the kiss of fraternity.[182] A clue to the grounds for their authority is perhaps to be found in the occasional use of the expression *minister maior professus* suggesting that they were the longest-professed or most long-standing ministers of the community, comparable perhaps to the use of *ancianus*.[183]

The area for which these Veronese ministers were responsible is usually termed city and district, but the occasional use of diocese may indicate that the two were more or less equivalent.[184] Such usage, which continues at least until the 1250s, once more confirms that any

---

[179] ASVer, Ghiara 123 (1228): 'qui fuit de Vicencia, minister maior et anterior communitatis et uniuersitatis humiliatorum Verone et districtus'. Appendix III, 10 (1237): 'ministri communalibus domuum et collegiorum humiliatorum Verone'.

[180] See for example appendix II, 8 (1224), 9 (1224), 11 (1230), 12 (1232).

[181] Alberzoni, 'Il monastero di Sant'Ambrogio e i movimenti religiosi', pp. 198–9; a brother of the *domus nova* was *visitor* to a suburban house, see above, p. 165.

[182] '[I]n osculo fraternitatis', see appendix II. [183] See above, pp. 148, 153.

[184] ASVer, Ghiara 35 (1212), 110 (1226); a fourteenth-century document uses both, perhaps to ensure comprehensiveness: 'omnium monasteriorum et aliarum domorum dicti ordinis humiliatorum existencium in ciuitate suburbiis districtus et diocesis Veronensis'. *Ibid.*, bolle papali 5 (1322).

separation between city and contado was not of great significance in the order.

From 1228 until mid-century there seems to have been some sort of formal link between the *universitates* of the Humiliati of the cities of Verona, Vicenza and Mantua, without this being either a formal province or a mother–daughter house network. The first document to mention a link beyond the confines of the city and its district comes from Vicenza. In October 1228, just a year after the first reference to the 'fraternity and community of the Humiliati of the city of Vicenza', Bartholomew, minister of the *domus de medio humiliatorum de Berica* with brother Tedald, minister of the *domus humiliatorum inferiorum de Berica ubi stat dominus Bellotus* and brother Oliverius, minister of the *domus humiliatorum de sancto Salvario*, bought land on behalf of 'all the Vicentine and Veronese Humiliati and their districts'.[185]

Such references are explicit in the Vicentine documents only until 1235, but other evidence confirms the continuity of contacts.[186] Veronese material from 1230 to 1249 frequently links the cities of Verona, Vicenza and also includes Mantua. In 1230 a profession of new recruits was made to the 'congregation of the Humiliati of Verona and its district, Mantua and its district, Vicenza and its district' and this formula continued regularly, though not exclusively, in documents of profession until 1249, after which it does not seem to occur.[187] After this date, professions record commitment to the congregation of Verona and district alone, but the links continued in other ways.[188] In 1265 a sale of land by the Humiliati of the *domus nova* in Cremona to the *domus de medio* in Vicenza was stipulated in the Ghiara in Verona, in the presence of brethren from the houses of Zevio, Porto and the *domus nova* of Sta Maria in Mantua.[189] In 1267, another agreement in the *domus de medio* in Vicenza, concerning money owed to a brother James who had been at the house but had moved to Cremona, for cloth and rent on a plot of land and to cover his travelling expenses, was witnessed by the minister of the Pontevico house in Brescia and the prelates of the

---

[185] ASVic Ognissanti 1, 23 October 1228: 'omnibus humiliatis Vicentine et Veronense et eorum destrictus [sic] in integrum intus et de foris'; see also 16 May 1227; the 'domus de medio' is called the 'domus maioris', 4 December 1228 (*ibid.*).

[186] ASVic Ognissanti 1, 4 December 1228, 19 November 1229, October 1235, 26 September 1235.

[187] Appendix II, 11 (1230); for the exceptions, both by the same notary, see ASVer, Ghiara 206 (1246), 213 (1248); they offer themselves only to the 'congregacio humiliatorum Verone et eius districtus'; see also appendix II, 12 (1232), ASVer, Ghiara 149 (1235), 161 (1238), 165 (1239), 193 (1244), 196 (1245), 172 (1245), 218 (1249).

[188] *Ibid.*, 242 (1253), 249 (1253), 258 (1255), 303 (1265).

[189] ASVic Ognissanti 2, 9 March 1265.

houses of San Tommaso and Sta Maria in Mantua.[190] In the second case, the presence of a minister from Brescia, but not Verona, may indicate that by this date links between the cities were contingent and had lost any ties to a particular regional structure, perhaps reflecting new emphasis on the wider order.

The dangers of placing too much weight on such sources are self-evident. The surviving notarial records are a haphazard collection of documents with a very uneven survival rate: after all, almost nothing survives from Mantua. Nonetheless, whether there is really an element of progression towards unity or not, the sense of a wider regional identity, centred on Verona, is undoubtedly present from the 1220s to the 1240s. This has no real parallels elsewhere at this date. There are some well-documented mother–daughter networks, but the records are mostly late. Both Viboldone and Rondineto (among others) founded daughter-houses in Milan, perhaps as commercial outlets or places for their brethren to stop over while in the city.[191] Sometime before 1251 the *domus communis* of Monza founded a new house near Sant'Eustorgio in Milan, though not without opposition from its neighbours.[192] The house of San Michele in Alessandria had daughter-houses led by priors in Tortona (San Marco), Asti (Sta Trinità), Florence (San Donato, later Ognissanti) and Genoa (Sta Marta).[193] Rondineto was the mother-house of San Luca in Brescia, while as we have seen, from the 1270s at least, San Paolo di Pontevico, also in Brescia, had a daughter-house in Bologna, SS Filippo e Giacomo, led by brother Martin 'prior and rector' and subject to brother Gabriel, 'prelate of the house of the Humiliati brothers of the church of San Paolo of the Humiliati of Pontevico in the city of Brescia'.[194] The Humiliati of Parma were almost certainly involved in founding the house of San Luca in Modena, first documented in 1264, and they continued to enjoy authority over it.[195] Similarly, a hospital founded in Turin in 1244 was very probably subject to the Humiliati church of San Cristoforo in Vercelli, to whose superior the founding donor made his commitment.[196]

The existence of networks may substantially pre-date the first mention in the records, but, at the present state of research, can be documented only in the 1240s and beyond. Nonetheless, by the second

---

[190] *Ibid.*, 30 August 1267: 'frater Iacobo de domo noua de Cremona . . . olim frater dicte domus de medio . . . pro expensis factis eundo et ueniendo omne dicte debite et pecie recuperando'.
[191] Zanoni, p. 197.
[192] Appendix I, 87; on the ensuing dispute, below, pp. 242–4.   [193] Below, pp. 213–16.
[194] The link between San Luca and Rondineto is not apparent in the extant archives of Rondineto but see appendix I, *110 and VHM II, p. 283. Spinelli, 'Gli Umiliati in Emilia-Romagna', pp. 140–1.
[195] Romagnoli, 'Gli Umiliati a Modena', pp. 492, 496.   [196] *S. Solutore*, 21.

and third decades of the thirteenth century there are signs of common identity and active association between different houses and members of the Humiliati order in some areas. These are based on the cities and their surrounding districts or dioceses, occasionally reaching further afield in networks linking different cities, as occurred around Verona. The movement of individuals between houses, sometimes at substantial distances apart, can also be documented, though most of the evidence is late. This goes some way towards establishing that a wider sense of belonging to an order with distinct administrative responsibilities existed at local or regional level. One particular type of evidence, however, the professions of new members, will allow us to clarify the particulars of this picture and reveal the extent of uniform observance.

Chapter 6

NEW MEMBERS AND PROFESSION
OF VOWS

. . . et in osculo fraternitatis eam osculauit . . .[1]

The kiss of fraternity marking the reception of a new member into a community is both a public, ritualised act and a very private, even intimate moment and the sources which record it carry this same dual value for the historian. On the one hand records of entry allow a brief insight into the personal life of a community, divulging names and relationships, the networks to which individuals and communities belonged and the aspirations of new members. On the other, by recording the words and rites used, they reveal the variations in practice and evolution of uniform observances which mark the emergence of an identity as an *ordo Humiliatorum*. This chapter uses the records of entry into houses of the First and Second orders of the Humiliati to explore these two issues. It looks first at the evidence for vows and rituals of profession as they moved towards uniform, regular, observance and second at the more personal questions of motivation and the networks of friends and family to which the postulants belonged.

Uneven document survival makes it impossible to draw a picture applicable throughout northern Italy. A context can be established by reference to a small sample of sources from quite a wide area, but the focus is inevitably on the district of Verona, where an unusually large number of records for the entry of new recruits survive.[2] This emphasis may disguise other local variations, but it is nonetheless an appropriate study, both because of the lack of general awareness of such records in past writing and because it will provide a framework against which any future discoveries of documentation may be assessed.[3]

Two key types of document record entry. The first details the vows

---

[1] Appendix II, 6.   [2] See appendix II and below, n. 8.
[3] See appendix II, preface.

and ritual involved, with only non-specific references to property. The second registers the transfer of property 'between the living' and many have survived as records of ownership, to which the entry of individuals into the community appears almost incidental.[4] An example of the second type records the entry of John *Zamboni de Strethella de Nembro* into the house of Torre Boldone in Bergamo in 1255 and his donation of 12 lire to pay for food, clothing and other necessities, 'as the other brothers have and is their custom'.[5] Spiritual concerns are mentioned: John is committed to stay as a brother and *socius* for as long as he shall live and 'in service to God in the usual manner'.[6] The main thrust, however, is the legal contract, drawn up before witnesses and defining the rights of each party, which include the renunciation of claims by John's family and an undertaking from the Humiliati to pay any outstanding communal taxes. It has been suggested that such documents mark a preliminary stage, followed at a later date by full religious profession.[7] This would explain the distinction between the two types of record: those which simply record the transfer of property and the acceptance of an individual or the agreement of terms and those which record the personal commitment of individuals to a *religio*. At present, however, we have no record of any individual undergoing the two separate ceremonies. It may be that the two categories of document should rather be accepted at face value as reflecting two different types of entrant within single communities, a point to which we shall return.

The Veronese documents, which form a remarkable series dated between 1205 and 1281, record the entry of twenty men and forty-eight women into the houses of the Ghiara and San Paolo in Verona itself, to a house in Porto, and to three different houses in Zevio: an early original community, a new foundation led by a husband and wife, Marchesius and Merida, and a later house called *de Broilo*.[8] Of these records, a remarkably high number (twenty-seven) belong to the first category of document, detailing the ceremony and vows taken by new entrants. It is tempting to suggest that in Verona the Humiliati community adopted earlier than elsewhere the Benedictine practice of

---

4 See for example, appendix II, 1 (1205) and the much later record of the entry of Azzo 'de Bussero' into the house of the Brera in 1289, Zanoni, pp. 191–2, Alberzoni, 'L'esperienza caritativa presso gli Umiliati', pp. 212–14.
5 ASBg Archivio notarile, Cartella 1,1: Imbreviature of Bartolomeo Carbonari, p. 169: 'sicut alii fratres habent et est mox eorum'; summary in Brolis, *Gli Umiliati a Bergamo*, appendix 2, 6.
6 *Ibid.*, 'ad seruicium dey more solito'.   7 Brolis, *Gli Umiliati a Bergamo*, p. 115.
8 See appendix II and ASVer, Ghiara 149 (1235), 161 (1238), 165 (1239), 172 (1240), 193 (1244), 196 (1245), 206 (1246), 213 (1248), 218 (1249), 242 (1253), 249 (1253), 258 (1255), 296 (1263), 303 (1265), 353 (1281); on the houses see De Sandre Gasparini, 'Aspetti di vita religiosa, sociale ed economica di chiese e monasteri nei secoli xiii–xv', pp. 134–42.

keeping a record of the brethren's vows in the monastery as a written reminder of the commitment made.[9] Such written copies of vows survive in some numbers from the fifteenth century, after the order had adopted the Benedictine rule.[10] The retrospective language of the documents here, however, shows they were drawn up by notaries after the event and cannot be the written copies of vows prepared by postulants and placed on the altar as part of the ceremony. Nonetheless, they served the Benedictine purpose since they record the names of the postulants and at least an abbreviated form of their vows. This purpose is confirmed by dorsal annotations which appear from 1212, often in the same hand as the document itself and describe them simply as the records of profession: 'charter of profession of sister N' or, more vaguely, 'of the sisters of Zevio'.[11]

The formulaic language in which all such documents were couched poses some difficulties of interpretation. In some cases, scribal copying from one document to the next may disguise a gap between ritual practised and that recorded, for when the outcome is the same, nuances may not interest the scribe. Yet, while mindful of the difficulties of copying, there is no need to doubt the concrete nature of the processes described. Since the notaries who drew up the record often had intimate links with the houses concerned, they may be relied upon to indicate at least what was understood to have happened.[12] Nonetheless, it must be borne in mind that the documents give only a partial picture and that some practices may either have been common long before they were recorded, or may never have been recorded at all. Even when the notary himself was certainly a member of the community, which may be the case for several of the early professions recorded here, the temptation to take short cuts, saving both time and materials, is apparent.[13] The abbreviated form of some of the documents, which simply record that the postulants did the same as their predecessors, serves as a constant reminder that what we have is an incomplete account.[14]

---

[9] *RSB*, 58, p. 132.

[10] *VHM* I, pp. 87, 96; four parchment copies of vows painstakingly written out by sisters joining the order in the 1560s are bound into Puricelli's *Historia Ordinis Humiliatorum*, ed. P. P. Bosca (1677), following fo. 624. Ambrosiana C 74 inf.

[11] Appendix II, 7 (1212), 8 (1224), 11 (1230), 12 (1232); ASVer, Ghiara 149, 165, 172, 193, 242, 249; ASVer, Sto Spirito App. pergamena 98 verso, 7 February 1218: 'jebeti [=Zevio] profesione marchisius et eius uxor etc'.

[12] See table 6.1, p. 191.   [13] See table 6.1, brother Enricus and appendix II, 7 (1212).

[14] Appendix II, 6, 10; appendix II, 3 is a list of names included on a parchment between two records of professions and may also have been intended as some sort of record of their commitment.

THE VOW

In their only substantial divergence, the two early manuscripts of *Omnis boni principium*, dating from the second half of the thirteenth and the early fourteenth centuries, provide different texts for the vow of professands.[15] Zanoni published the version from the archive of the Curia Arcivescovile in Milan, which includes only a promise of obedience to the prelate and his successors, according to the rule of the congregation:

I brother ★★★ promise obedience, according to the rule of this congregation, to the prelate and his successors. By the grace of God, amen.[16]

The unpublished codex now in the Ambrosiana has a fuller formula, including the four elements of poverty, chastity, stability and obedience to the prelate and his successors, again according to the rule of the congregation:

I brother N promise for the remainder, to live without anything of my own, in chastity, stability and obedience, according to the rule of this congregation, to prelate N and his successors. By the grace of God, amen.[17]

It is not possible to ascertain the expectations of the papal representatives and the first Humiliati legislators on the basis of these documents, since one or other rendering must be an adaptation and without a third no preference can seriously be established. Yet the reference in both formulae to obedience according to the rule largely circumvents the problem, since the rule itself ordained the poverty, chastity and stability included in the Ambrosiana version. The first vow thus implicitly included the same elements as the second. Of greater interest here, however, is the gradual development of practice revealed in the notarial records.

The earliest document to record some sort of oral commitment, rather than simply the transfer of property and entry, is that of Albert *de Scanna uaca* of Porto in May 1211. The same manuscript records three separate ceremonies, all of which took place in the house of the Ghiara, but which record the entry of individuals at different dates and into different houses. In May 1211 Albert entered the house of Porto near

---

[15] Above, p. 109 n. 43.

[16] ACA Milan, A/2: (*OBP*, 40, p. 367) 'Ego frater ★★★ promitto obedientiam secundum regulam huius congregationis, prelato et successoribus eius. Deo gratias, amen'. The asterisks are in the manuscript.

[17] Ambrosiana D 58 inf.: 'Ego frater talis promitto de cetero vivere sine proprio, castitatem, stabilitatem, obedientiam, secundum regulam huius congregationis, prelato illi et successoribus eius. Deo gracias, amen.'

Legnago. In May or June of the same year a female relative, Maça *de Scanna uaca*, entered the Ghiara. In January 1212, Laçarinus and Luchesa, the daughter of a notary, Carlaxarius *qui dicitur bixolus*, entered the Ghiara and in the same ceremony Ota joined the house of Zevio.[18] Although the document is much worn and full of holes, the text is sufficiently complete to enable us to establish the essentials of their undertaking.

Albert entered the community of Porto stating that he wished to stay there or elsewhere for the rest of his life, in obedience, according to the will of the ministers and their successors and of God.[19] Maça probably used the same formula: the notary recorded that she did everything in the same manner as Albert and would obey the ministers in all things 'as though her father'.[20] The extant formula for Laçarinus, Luchesa and Ota is slightly more complete: each vowed, speaking for themselves (*suo proprio ore*), that they wished to stay and to obey the ministers and their successors acting on behalf of the chapter of all the Humiliati and to live for the rest of their lives 'according to the way of the Humiliati' (*secundum modum humiliatorum*).[21]

All three records were drawn up on the same parchment by the same notary but there does not seem to have been a standard formula such as might have been provided by use of the rule. Unlike Albert, Laçarinus, Luchesa and Ota made no explicit commitment to God. The basic undertaking was, however, very similar. They all expressed their desire to stay in obedience for the rest of their lives in the house which they now entered or, in Albert's case, in any other, presumably chosen by the ministers. This is not unlike provisions in *Omnis boni principium* that the postulant shall promise to stay with the brethren and shall later, after the year-long novitiate, declare whether he or she still wishes to stay.[22] In the rule, however, these elements do not form part of the vow and in this version there is only an oblique allusion, in the promise of obedience and the subjection to the ministers, to the formula of the promise given in the rule. The postulants committed themselves to stay for the rest of their lives, which suggests that *stabilitas* was expected and perhaps that poverty and chastity were assumed. Yet this is not stated and there is little here to indicate that the traditional monastic or canonical promises of regular observance, advocated in *Omnis boni principium*, had yet been adopted. The words of the postulants make no overt reference to the observance of the rule, using only the generic

---

[18] Through donation or purchase the house later acquired property from Carlaxarius' widow, perhaps Luchesa's mother, ASVer, Ghiara 164 (1239).

[19] Appendix II, 5 (1211). [20] Appendix II, 6 (1211). [21] Appendix II, 7 (1212).

[22] *OBP*, 40, p. 367.

phrase 'according to the way of the Humiliati', in the last of these cases. This might perhaps stand in place of the traditional, explicit, Benedictine commitment to the rule, equally common in the new orders such as the Dominicans, whose early vows, referring to both the rule and *institutio*, were probably formulated some years later, in the General Chapter of 1220.[23] It might equally, however, recall the contractual formula found, as we have seen, in the entry of John *Zamboni de Strethella* as late as 1255 (*sicut alii fratres*) or that of Albert, Manfredinus and Garscenda, their sister, in the Ghiara in 1209, who made no vow, but were received 'according to the condition of the other brothers and sisters'.[24] On one side the postulants accepted that they would live like the other brethren, neither better nor worse, on the other the community offered membership with neither preference nor prejudice.

The idea that the Humiliati had a particular way of doing things and that all were to share in it, but not yet a widely recognised rule, is reiterated in the foundation record of a second community in Zevio, led by Marchesius and his wife Merida, in 1218.[25] Earlier historians assumed that this recorded the formation of a house by the members of one family, including the parents and seven daughters; however, it has recently been noted that no family connection is documented.[26] The ceremony included a series of vows. First Marchesius and Merida swore to observe perpetual chastity, as required in *Omnis boni principium*, but equally typical of public penitents and confraternities.[27] Next, the whole community undertook to place all their property in common and promised to care for each other and to observe mutual fraternity. The sisters then elected Marchesius and Merida as minister and *ministra* of the community, 'according to the manner of the Humiliati who congregate at the Ghiara house'. Finally, they made their vows to their minister, Marchesius and to his successors, promising obedience, chastity, reverence and renouncing personal property and their own will (*voluntas*).

There is a clear departure here from the practice recorded in the documents of 1211–12, which may partially reflect the change of notary, but also certainly reflects the particular solemnity attending the foundation of a new house. The sisters took much fuller vows and for

---

23 Thomas, 'La profession religieuse des dominicains', pp. 9, 23.
24 Appendix II, 2.
25 ASVer, Sto Spirito App. pergamena 98; Biancolini, *Notizie storiche delle chiese di Verona*, IV, pp. 807–8, now in De Sandre Gasparini, *La Vita religiosa nella marca Veronese-Trevigiana*, pp. 152–3.
26 De Sandre Gasparini, 'Aspetti di vita religiosa, sociale ed economica di chiese e monasteri nei secoli xiii–xv', p. 136; Zanoni, pp. 56–7 and n. 2; Meersseman, 'Ordo fraternitatis', I, pp. 325–6.
27 *OBP*, 39, p. 366; see, for example Meersseman, 'Ordo fraternitatis', I, pp. 283–304.

the first time a priest was present, Gualimbertus of San Vitale in Verona.[28] The sisters, like their superiors, made the first explicit reference to a promise of chastity. They also promised obedience, subjecting their wills to the minister and undertaking to hold everything in common and to live without personal property. Here finally, are the three basic elements of the regular life explicitly stated. There is still, however, no reference to a rule and the commitment to *stabilitas* is less clear. The election of Marchesius and his wife as their ministers (perhaps a foregone conclusion since the community were to live in the house of Marchesius), took place in a way acknowledged as that used at the Ghiara, perhaps under instruction from the members of that house who were present as witnesses.[29] The sisters were not committed to staying in Zevio and might choose to go to the Ghiara if the majority agreed. If any of them wished to leave, however, but yet not go to the Ghiara, they were not to be allowed to have any of the goods or property belonging to the fraternity. In other words, they were strongly discouraged from leaving and any departure was not to be allowed to damage the well-being of those remaining. Nonetheless, they were not committed for the rest of their lives, as Albert and the earlier postulants had been.

The community of Marchesius and Merida lived in a house belonging to the couple and their initial promises of mutual assistance and fraternity bear strong resemblance to those of a confraternity rather than a monastic community. The second vows, however, made by the sisters to their newly elected superiors, while omitting any reference to *stabilitas* do include the three traditional elements of poverty, chastity and obedience. Documents recording entries made in June 1224 to the original house in Zevio and to the Ghiara in Verona itself, point to a similarly traditional, monastic emphasis in the communities. On 9 June Avenante, daughter of Richelda formerly *de Nogara* and Ota, daughter of Rizardus a shoe maker, entered the house of Zevio. They made their promise to God and the ministers, vowing to remain chaste and to live without possessions, to show obedience and reverence to the senior professed ministers, present and future and in particular to the minister and *ministra* of the house in which they lived, subject to the will of the

---

[28] On Gualimbertus, who had extensive contacts with the Humiliati, see De Sandre Gasparini, 'L'assistenza ai lebbrosi', pp. 44–9.

[29] These were Pantanus and Bonaçonta 'humiliatorum', both of whom were later ministers and 'senior ministers'; Riprandus *de fossato*, who was the third witness present, also enjoyed long association with the Humiliati and had previously acted as a witness: appendix II, 2 (1209), 7 (1212).

ministers and according to what they now held or should in future hold to observe, 'God giving'.[30]

On 11 June in the same year, a remarkably large group of seventeen women and two men entered the Ghiara, making a very similar vow, promising to live in perpetual chastity and poverty and in obedience to the senior professed ministers and the minister of the Ghiara.[31] The three elements of the vow, chastity, poverty and obedience, are once more made explicit and linked to a form of *stabilitas* which may be that intended in the incomplete formula of Albert *de Scanna uaca* in 1211 discussed above: the new brethren put themselves at the disposal of the ministers and would remain in whichever house the superiors wished them to be placed.

The Humiliati vows recorded in these documents still make no mention of observance of a regulatory text such as the rule or *institutio*, by this date an integral part of both the Dominican and Franciscan profession formulae.[32] Even the generic reference to the 'way of the Humiliati' is lost by the 1220s. In 1230 this situation changes, however, when the text of the vow taken by five postulants is first given verbatim and includes the name of the pope responsible for approving it (Innocent III), a practice found in other formulae, such as that of the later Franciscans, laid down in the Constitutions of Narbonne in 1260.[33] Given the gap in the series of documents between 1224 and 1230, we cannot be certain about the exact timing of this development and the notaries recording earlier ceremonies may simply have chosen to set down a shortened version excluding the full vow. Entries into the order in the years between 1224 and 1230, for which no records survive, may have included the full text of the vow and reference to the rule. Nonetheless, it is worthy of note that the first reference to a vow made according to the papally approved rule of the second order should date to 1230. Just three years earlier, in June 1227, Gregory IX had reissued the rule approved by Innocent III and admonished the order to observe it.[34] He had followed this with the inclusion of the Humiliati among those to be subject to papal visitation.[35] In 1230, for the first time, postulants entering the Humiliati community in Verona made explicit reference to Innocent's rule. *Post hoc* does not mean *propter hoc* and it would be impossible to prove beyond doubt that the Veronese were acting in direct response to the papal exhortation and visitation or

---

[30] Appendix II, 8.   [31] Appendix II, 9 (1224).

[32] Thomas, 'La profession religieuse des Dominicains', p. 5; Rocca, 'La triade di obbedienza, povertà e castità', col. 940.

[33] Gribomont, 'Le formule di professione in occidente', col. 940.

[34] Appendix I, 28, and above, p. 110.   [35] See below, p. 204.

to moves from within the order which may have prompted the pope's letter. There is evidence, however, that the Veronese Humiliati were aware of papal decisions, since another letter issued in that year survives in the archive of the Ghiara in Verona in a copy drawn up by Milanese notaries.[36] For the first time since 1201 there is clear evidence for contacts between Milan and Verona. Reference to the papally approved text in this profession of faith may well reflect these renewed ties, marking an important stage in the acknowledgement of a uniform rule and acceptance of a wider identity as an order.

The formula of the promise made by the five postulants in 1230 is lengthy:

I give and offer myself and my belongings to God and the congregation of the Humiliati of Verona and its district (*districtus*), Mantua and its district, Vicenza and its district and I promise obedience to brother Taurellus, senior professed minister, receiving for himself and in the name of his associate senior professed ministers, who are now or in time will be ministers of the aforementioned congregation and in particular to the minister of the house in which I now live, or in time shall live, according to the will of the senior professed ministers and according to the rule of this congregation of the Second order, given and approved by the lord pope Innocent, by the grace of God, Amen.[37]

This text raises numerous questions. It is much longer than the formula of the promise in the surviving *Omnis boni principium* texts, though much of the length is taken up with the details of the congregation and the ministers. The essential elements are the oblation of self and property to the congregation, the promise of obedience to present and future ministers and the commitment to the rule of the Second order as approved by Innocent III (by which we must understand *Omnis boni principium* combined with the provisions of the papal letter, *Diligentiam pii patris*). It once more omits however, any explicit promise of either poverty or chastity, two of the three traditional vows. This is not unlike the early Dominican formula, which included only obedience to the superior and the rule, or that of the early Franciscans whose vows were not clearly articulated.[38] The earliest Dominican formula included the all-embracing phrase 'I make profession' (*facio professionem*), but otherwise promised only obedience, to God, the saints and the Master according to the rule and *institutio* of the order, until death. The earliest Franciscan promise similarly included reference to 'making profession' (*professionem faciendo*), and the postulant who undertook to observe the rule and life of the Friars Minor simply gave himself to the order (*et sic*

---

[36] Appendix I, 24.   [37] Appendix II, 11.
[38] De Sandre Gasparini, 'Il francescanesimo a Verona', p. 121.

tradam me praesenti ordini ipsorum).[39] In all three cases, the acceptance of the rule made acceptance of the other elements implicit. The specific oblation of self, rather than merely the monastic offering of property (suggested but not formally required by Benedict) recalls canonical formulae which had developed during the eleventh and twelfth centuries.[40] They were used by contemporary orders such as the Hospitals of Sto Spirito: 'I offer and deliver myself to God . . .' (*offero et trado meipsum Deo . . .*), where *stabilitas* was not consonant with the aims of the order.[41] It is certainly significant that in the first instance the new members joined the congregation of the area and only secondarily made a commitment to a particular house. Indeed, the commitment was essentially to the will of the ministers who had authority over the place of residence of each postulant. Although not specified in this document, already in 1211 Albert *de Scanna uaca* seems to have left the precise location open and in 1223 the postulants had promised to stay wherever the ministers wished to place them: *ubicumque eas ponere uoluerint*. Use of this phrase was to become more or less standard practice in the following decades.[42] It is not unlike the Mendicant custom of making profession to the 'Master' or 'Father', rather than in an individual place. Yet, where the Mendicant formulae were designed to fit the universal mission of orders where *stabilitas* had no place, this argument cannot hold for an order in which mendicancy and itinerancy were not part of the original idea. At most, its use here may indicate that members might be moved from one house to another according to need.[43]

The Veronese documents after 1230 do not always give identical wording for the vow. Such standardisation in documents drawn up by different notaries and in varying circumstances would be highly suspect. Nonetheless, 1230 marks a watershed in the formulation of the profession and hence perhaps in the regular identity of the new order. The reference to the rule of the Second order is specifically repeated in 1232 and then omitted until 1253 when it appears in a document from Lodi, but the formula of the vow remains very similar, varying only in details such as the ministers to whom the promise was made until 1281.[44] Only then do new elements appear, including the prostration of the postulant and the explicit promise of stability of customs (*stabilitatem morum*

---

39 The development of these formulae is discussed in detail in Thomas, 'La profession religieuse des Dominicains'; see also Rocca, 'La triade di obbedienza, povertà e castità', col. 940.

40 Thomas, 'La profession religieuse des Dominicains', p. 12.

41 See Brune, *Histoire de l'ordre hospitalier du Saint-Esprit*, pp. 87–8.

42 Appendix II, 8 (1224), 9 (1224), 10 (1224), 12 (1232); ASVer, Ghiara 193 (1244), 196 (1245) 172 (1245) but in the last two examples has become: 'ubicumque ministri eum mittere uoluerint', while 213 (1248) has the alternatives 'mittere uel ponere'.

43 For evidence of mobility, above pp. 154, 170.   44 Appendix II, 12; *VHM* II, p. 13.

meorum).[45] Such modifications may reflect increasing detail in notarial recording or changed circumstances in the order, or both.[46]

RITUAL

As the formula of the profession was changing during these years, so too was the ritual accompanying the vows. *Omnis boni principium* laid down a mixed ritual, combining the practice of *professio in manibus* used by canonical groups with elements of the monastic ceremony *super altare*. After making known their intentions in chapter, the postulant was to be led to the church or oratory. Following the petition and prayers he or she offered self and possessions in the hands of the prelate (*in manibus prelati*), holding a lighted candle and a document with the words of the promise. After the profession, these were to be placed on the altar (*super altare*), or before the cross and the postulant received with the kiss of peace and fraternity by the whole community and given a place in the choir, refectory and dormitory.

As with the formulation of the vow itself, the Veronese documents reveal that the ritual recorded by notaries bore only slight resemblance to the provisions of *Omnis boni principium*, at least in the early years. Indeed, until the 1230s there is even less to suggest that the text of a particular rule was known to the participants. Even in the 1230s, the canonically inspired *inmixtio manuum* of the rule is not mentioned, though a similar practice developed which may have been in imitation of this.

The early ceremonies took place simply *in domo* or in the *curia* or *curte domus*.[47] There is no reference to an oratory until 1224 when, as we have seen, the Ghiara appears to have had separate oratories for the brothers and sisters, though the distinction in use is not yet clear, since one of the sisters to profess in that year did so in the oratory of the brothers and later there are professions of brothers in the oratory of the sisters at Zevio and at San Paolo in Verona.[48] Reference to the ceremony taking place before the cross only appears in 1230, in the same document which saw the first recorded full formula of vows and reference to the rule.[49] The presence of a priest among the witnesses is

---

[45] ASVer, Ghiara 353 (1281).

[46] See now Castagnetti, 'La regola del primo e secondo ordine', on the introduction of an adapted form of the rule of Benedict for the Humiliati in the late thirteenth century which might account for such new practices.

[47] Appendix II, 1 (1205), 2 (1209), 5 (1211), 6 (1211).

[48] Above, p. 144 and appendix II, 9 (1224), 10 (1224), 11 (1230); ASVer, Ghiara 149 (1235).

[49] Appendix II, 11.

mentioned first in 1218 and again in 1224.[50] The presiding role of a priest, deacon or *clericus*, usually a secular cleric from the area, sometimes from the local *pieve* or baptismal church, only becomes common practice, however, after 1230, when the vows were usually made standing both before the cross and before a priest.[51] The acceptance of the postulant into the community with a kiss, traditionally associated with the *inmixtio manuum*, is to be found as early as 1211, but reference to a lighted candle and the written profession of vows held by the postulant is first made only in 1230. In that document, the five postulants are described standing with a candle and the text of their profession in their hands. They read out the vow, which committed them to the observance of Innocent's rule and then gave the candle and parchment to the minister. He returned them, after which the postulants placed them before the cross 'with respect and reverence'. The minister and *ministra* and all the brethren then received the new members with the kiss of peace and in sign of fraternity and submission (*subiectio*). Finally the minister imposed the same form of *stabilitas* found in the previous documents, ordering them to stay in the house of Zevio at the will of the senior professed ministers. This practice, which was to become routine, of handing the candle and written vow to the minister before placing them before the cross, followed by the kiss, is probably as close to a formal *inmixtio manuum* as these early thirteenth-century Humiliati ever came.

Once more the year 1230 marks a *terminus ante quem*, by which date at least some aspects of the observance of the papally approved rule had reached the Veronese community, directly or indirectly. The early years had seen a fluidity of practice which was not lost after this date. There continue to be records which do not refer to a full ceremony in this manner and as late as 1255 a profession seems to have taken place with no priest present.[52] Yet a new formality and official quality is undoubtedly present, particularly in the direct appeal to the authority of the papal rule and in the profession before the cross, strongly evocative of the *super altare* profession of traditional monastic communities. Later documents reveal the development, or at least the recording, of increasingly formal practices.

In June 1248 a document recording an exchange of property between the Humiliati of Zevio and Aldevrandinus, son of the late Peter *de Madio*, lists thirty-seven members of the community in Zevio, sixteen

---

50 Appendix II, 9; ASVer, Sto Spirito App. 98 (1218), De Sandre Gasparini, *La Vita religiosa nella marca Veronese-Trevigiana*, pp. 152–3.

51 The priest of San Pietro in Zevio, the *pieve* church, was present at professions in 1248 and 1253; see ASVer, Ghiara 213 and 242.

52 ASVer, Ghiara 258.

of whom appear to be those mentioned in earlier records of profession.[53] The list includes thirteen men and twenty-four women of whom four men and twelve women have the same names as those of earlier documents of profession. Even allowing for the use of the same names by different individuals, there are too many which match the earlier documents for this to be coincidental. This nonetheless leaves a significant margin for whom no record of entry survives, a reminder of the incomplete nature of these sources. The witness list of the 1248 document, however, also includes a rare reference to a novice, perhaps one of several, since he is described as 'brother Pense of the novices living in the said house'.[54] Some form of noviciate had thus been adopted. Moreover, the use of the title brother or sister to describe the postulants before profession, first recorded in 1235, may indicate that a noviciate had been in use for some time, the name reflecting that the individual had been in the house for a probationary period and was therefore already known as brother or sister before making their final vows.[55] A rather later document from Vicenza confirms that a probationary period was imposed. In 1268, *Domina* Richa, widow of Bartholomew *Pixole*, made a donation of fifty gold coins (*aurei*) and several fields to the *domus de subtus* or lower house in Vicenza for her niece or grand-daughter, Bartholamea, daughter of the late Albert, formerly *de Cantobello*, who was a novice in the house (*que est in probatone* [sic] *in dicto monastero*).[56] Yet the first mention of a novice in a record of profession dates only to 1281. In March of that year a brother Daniel from *ualle pulixella*, made his profession in the house of Zevio after completing a year-long probation. As required in *Omnis boni principium*, he had been offered but had rejected licence to leave if he so wished.[57] This undoubted delay between practice and record in profession serves as a final reminder of the dangers of seeking too definitive an account on the basis of the extant documentation.

The addition of some details to the records appears arbitrary: in 1263 a single record notes the time of day of a profession in the *Broilo* house in Zevio, made after terce and lunch.[58] Nonetheless, the gradual addition of some details seems to reflect increasing institutional security from mid century. In 1249 sister Vivendera made profession in a house in Zevio and was allocated a place in the oratory, refectory and

---

[53] ASVer, Ghiara, 215 (1248).
[54] *Ibid.*, 'frater Pense nouiciorum qui morantur in predicta domo'.
[55] ASVer, Ghiara 149. See also appendix 1, ★104b for novices at San Marco, Tortona in 1253–4.
[56] ASVic, Ognissanti 2, 25 October 1268.   [57] ASVer, Ghiara 353 (1281).
[58] ASVer, Ghiara 296.

dormitory of the house.[59] In 1259, a new entrant to the *domus de Carrobiolo* in Monza made vows including obedience to the senior master (*magister maiore*) or Master General of the whole order, an office created in 1246.[60] In 1268 the second Master General, Peter *de Brissia*, was himself present at the entry of Poma, widow of Cominus *de Contissa*, to the house of the Humiliati *de Senedogo* in Milan.[61] The record of 1259 is also the first to mention that the ceremony took place before an altar rather than simply before the cross. A subsequent document from Zevio, dated 1265, is the first to refer to the ceremony taking place in a church belonging to the same community, the *ecclesia sancti Iohanni wagleliffe* [sic] *umiliatorum*.[62] Once more, these may reflect nothing more than a change in notarial practice, yet they could also indicate that a more permanent structure than the oratory mentioned in earlier documents had recently been built or acquired and the timing coincides with references to Humiliati churches elsewhere.[63] The general impression of an increasingly secure presence is inescapable.

The reference to the Master General in three of the documents here marks a clear sense of a shared identity and of participating in a centrally administered order. The similarity between the texts of the Veronese professions and those produced in Lodi in 1253 and Monza in 1259 points in a similar direction. Certainly there are differences, though these may be exaggerated by the summary form in which the notaries chose to record the vows. Sister Jacoba made her profession in the house of the Humiliati sisters *de Paulo* in Lodi in September 1253 in the presence of four male brethren from other houses, including the provost of San Cristoforo in Lodi.[64] Sister Benuenuta *de Monte* entered the house of the Humiliati *de Carrobiolo* in Monza in July 1259 without apparently making an explicit oblation of self and promised obedience to the prelate of the community and, as we have seen, to the 'senior master' of the whole order, not to the senior professed ministers of the area.[65] Both Jacoba and Benuenuta held a lighted candle and written

---

59 ASVer, Ghiara 218: 'det ei sorori locum in oratorio et refectorio et dormitorio'.

60 *VHM* II, pp. 296–7.

61 *Gli atti del comune di Milano*, II/1, 534; see now Mercatili Indelicato, 'Per una storia degli Umiliati della diocesi di Lodi', pp. 490–2 for the case of Dorata, wife of Ricardus Culdebos who joined the Humiliati sisters of Paulo in Lodi in 1273 as a *conventualis* but without taking the habit as a sister, witnessed by the provost and two brothers of San Cristoforo Lodi and with the consent of the prelates of the houses of San Calimala and Gessate in Milan, 'visitatorum dicte domus et aliarum domorum Humiliatorum et Humiliatarum de Laude'. Her husband had chosen to join the Cistercians at Cerreto.

62 ASVer, Ghiara 303. 63 Above, p. 146 n. 52.

64 *VHM* II, p. 13; Humiliati from San Cristoforo and Milan also attended at the entry of Dorata as a *conventualis* in the same house, above, n. 61.

65 *VHM* II, pp. 296–7.

vows in their hands but neither record describes the ceremony of
placing these before the altar, the kiss of fraternity or the directive to
stay in the house. These later omissions are, however, almost certainly a
result of notarial choice (or, in the case of the document concerning
Jacoba, perhaps the desire of the editor, Tiraboschi, to be brief). The
documents record nothing after summarising the vow, yet the women
had to do something with the candle. The differences lie mostly in the
recording. What stands out are the similarities in both the vow (made to
the rule approved by Innocent) and the ritual, suggesting that by this
date there was general recognition of standard practices in the order.

This may not have been a new development. Certainly the proximity
of Lodi and Monza to Milan and to the base of the Master General
might be used to argue that standard practices were acknowledged there
from an earlier date and reflect the influence of the new superior. Such
arguments are, however, impossible to evaluate unless and until further
and earlier examples of such documents come to light for other areas
outside Verona. All that can be stated with certainty is that there is a
terminus ante quem of the 1250s, by which date Humiliati practice was
broadly similar in three different areas which stand some 130 kilometres
apart.

The second category of documents, which do not record the details
of a religious ceremony or a vow, make varying degrees of commitment. Perhaps still more than the full records of profession, they are
informative about the individuals who entered the order and occasionally about elements of practice not mentioned in the documents
discussed so far. For example, they provide details concerning clothing.
Omnis boni principium remarks that, before entry, postulants might use
some of their money to buy suitable clothing if they wished, but the
documents discussed above make no mention of a formal vestiture.[66]
The first recorded blessing of a habit is in fourteenth-century constitutions for the order.[67] Nor is there any indication that novices wore
distinctive dress, as ordained for all religious by Gregory IX.[68] Nonetheless, three documents, from Verona, Milan and Bergamo, suggest at
least that separate provision for clothing was made. In 1251, Grosius,
son of the late Ubicinus *Zorzi* gave brother Taurellus, minister of the
Ghiara, a piece of land in Cerea, because of his sister Bonasia's
dedication in the house. He specified that one field was to be used to
provide for her clothing and that part was a legacy from their father.[69]

---

[66] *OBP*, 40, p. 367.   [67] *VHM* III, p. 113.
[68] x.3.31.23; Doran, 'Oblation or obligation? A canonical ambiguity', p. 139.
[69] ASVer, Ghiara 230 (1251): 'occasionem sue sororis Bonasie que est edidicata [sic] in dicta domo
scilicet unum campum pro uestimentis ipsius et . . . pro legato condam sui patris'.

In 1268 Poma joined the Humiliati *de Senedogo* in Porta Nova, Milan with her servant Irvita. She donated 170 lire terzoli, some of which had already been spent on preparations for entry, including doing up the house in which she was to live and in particular, 10 lire for clothing for Irvita.[70] Similarly, when he entered Torre Boldone in 1255, John *Zamboni* was to receive food, other necessities and clothing, though this time apparently provided by the Humiliati themselves.[71]

While Bonasia was probably a fully professed sister in the Ghiara, the cases of Poma, who was to live in a separate house with her servant, and of John *Zamboni*, do not seem to fit this model. Before considering their status in more detail however, let us turn to the personal side of the evidence about profession and the motivation behind the decisions of new recruits.

POSTULANTS AND RECRUITMENT: METHODS, MOTIVATION AND CHOICE

In the *Historia Occidentalis*, Jacques de Vitry wrote a revealing description of Humiliati preaching which indicates that the Mendicants were not alone in their ability to sway a crowd. The Humiliati were particularly good, he writes, at opposing heretics, even converting them to their own religion:

For now the formidable heretics who are called Patarines are overcome and, thus powerfully and openly exposing their deceits, they [the Humiliati] wisely convince the impious and incredulous using divine scripture and publicly confound them, so that now they [the patarines] do not dare to appear before them and many of them, recognising their errors, having returned to the faith of Christ, have joined themselves to these brothers. Thus those who were masters of error have been made disciples of truth . . .[72]

He also implies, however, that some rather dubious methods of recruitment were in use, catching people while still under the influence of their sermons:

For at the end of their preaching, while by virtue of the warmth of the divine words, the hearts of their listeners are still more inclined to contempt of the world and service of their Creator, they are accustomed to ask those standing around if there are any who, divinely inspired, wish to transfer to their *religio*.

---

[70] *Gli atti del comune di Milano*, II/1, 534.   [71] Above, p. 174.

[72] Vitry, *HO*, 28, p. 146: 'Adeo autem formidabiles hereticis quos paterinos appellant, effecti sunt, et, ita potenter et aperte fraudes eorum detegendo, impios et incredulos ex diuinis scripturis prudenter conuincunt et publice confundunt, quod iam coram ipsis non audent comparere, multique ex ipsis, errorem suum cognoscentes, ad Christi fidem reuersi, ipsis fratribus coniuncti sunt, et ita facti sunt discipulis ueritatis qui fuerant magistri erroris'.

And many passing to them in that drunkenness and fervour of spirit, in a short time they have greatly multiplied . . .[73]

Vitry wished to portray the effectiveness of the preaching of the Humiliati and their success against heretics which went hand in hand with the great growth of the order in a short time. He was not concerned to give a detailed account of recruitment methods used. Nor is there sufficient evidence for the entry of postulants in the early decades of the thirteenth century for a critical assessment of his account. Certainly, such revivalist methods do not fit well with the serious evaluation and commitment to the religious life pictured in *Omnis boni principium* and there are cases which suggest that the Humiliati did not always enquire too closely into the vocation of postulants. In 1264, for example, Guiduccius Beccarius (a butcher) entered the Humiliati house of Modena with his wife and a niece or grandchild because, as he later claimed, he had feared that he might be killed or lose his property in the latest round of factional violence, caused when the Guelf leader invited Obizo d'Este and others to expel the Grasulfi from the city:

because of the fear of death and bodily suffering . . . on account of the faction of the Grasulfi expelled from the city, to whom he was thought to belong by the commune of Modena and by the Aygonus faction and fearful of losing all his property . . .[74]

Once peace returned, Guiduccius demanded that his vows should be annulled and his property returned to him. The ensuing dispute was typically long winded. In 1268 both sides agreed that the original oblation and giving of property had been 'simulated and accomplished not to bind the said Guiduccius but to avoid the dues of the commune of Modena', but a financial settlement was only achieved in 1284.[75]

This case cannot be called typical. Disputes over taxation and evasion do show that communal governments were suspicious of the motives of

---

[73] *Ibid.*, pp. 145–6: 'Ipsi enim, in fine predicationis sue, dum adhuc audientium corda, uirtute diuini sermonis feruentia, proniora sunt ad mundi contemptum et ad creatoris sui seruitium, solent a circumstantibus querere, si qui sunt qui ad eorum religionem, diuinitus inspirati, uelint transire. Multis autem in illa ebrietate et spiritus feruore ad ipsos transeuntibus, paruo tempore multiplicati sunt ualde'. See d'Avray, *The Preaching of the Friars*, pp. 26–8.

[74] G. Tiraboschi, *Memorie storiche modenesi col codice diplomatico illustrato*, 4 vols. (Modena, 1793–5), II, p. 81; now discussed in detail in Romagnoli, 'Gli Umiliati a Modena', pp. 489–91, 523–4 (from which this passage comes).

[75] Romagnoli, 'Gli Umiliati a Modena', pp. 491, 523–4: 'oblatio et datio bonorum . . . simulata et confecta non ad obligationem dicti domini Guiducii, sed ad evitandum Comunis Mutine honera'.

many recruits in joining the Humiliati, as they were of other religious.[76] It has been argued that the decision of Azzo *de Bussero* to enter the Brera house in 1289 'for the love and honour of God and for the benefit of his soul' (*remedio et mercede anime*), wishing 'to assume and be subject to the habit and order and rule', may also have been prompted by a financial crisis.[77] Azzo had long had connections with the house, however, and other evidence suggests that entry was generally a much slower and more serious matter than Vitry's account might be thought to imply. The record of the entry of Adelaxia and her daughters to the house of the domine albe next to Sant'Eustorgio Milan in 1233, records that she made her decision after careful thought, *habita . . . super hac diligenti deliberatione.*[78] This followed standard enquiries by a *missus regis* to ensure there had been no malpractice and that she had not been forced, but it cannot therefore be dismissed as meaningless. Similarly, while the practice of probation cannot be documented with certainty until 1248 and then only in Verona, the same Veronese documents illustrate that, for some of the new recruits at least, the decision to join came after years of association with the order, suggesting a well-thought-out resolution.

Such familiarity with the order before entry is particularly easy to trace using the evidence for notaries. While most records, naturally enough, identify the brethren simply in religious terms, as brothers and sisters or perhaps with a title of office, notaries retained their professional title while in the order. Their careers are therefore rather easier to trace (see table 6.1).

Brother Enricus is described as notary and minister of the Humiliati of the Zevio in 1212 when he received a new postulant, sister Ota, into the community. It is likely that he is the same notary Enricus who drew up other professions for the Humiliati from 1205 to 1235, though he is never again given the double title of minister and notary.[79] On a similar pattern, in June 1224 Taurellus, notary of the sacred palace, drew up a document recording the entry of new members to the Ghiara house.[80] Six years later a brother Taurellus was acting as a senior professed minister in the order, while in 1232 a brother Taurellus, notary, is named as a witness in a document of profession.[81] Again in 1246 there is a brother Taurellus or Torellus named as senior minister.[82] These may not all be the same man, but it is at least possible that these records

---

[76] Zanoni, p. 213.
[77] Alberzoni, 'L'esperienza caritativa presso gli Umiliati', pp. 212–13; Zanoni, pp. 191–2; his wife Castellana joined the nuns of Sant'Apollinare.
[78] See table 6.2, document 1.   [79] See appendix II and ASVer, Ghiara 149.
[80] Appendix II, 9, 10.   [81] Appendix II, 11 (1230), 12 (1232).
[82] ASVer, Ghiara 206.

Table 6.1. *Notaries in Humiliati houses in the area of Verona*[a]

Dates	Name	House	First source (all ASVer)
1210–15	brother Finetus	Ghiara	Ghiara 29
1212	brother Enricus	Zevio	Ghiara 35
1232	brother Taurellus	San Paolo	Ghiara 139
1232	brother Ferrarius	Ghiara?	Ghiara 139
1237–41	brother Rodulfinus	Ghiara	Ghiara 151
1246	brother Amadeus	Zevio	Ghiara 206

[a] A brother Anthony Çignognis, notary, drew up two contracts in Lodi on the same parchment dated 1243 and at San Cristoforo Lodi in 1248; he may have been a Humiliatus, but the parchment is badly damaged. ASMi 187 Lodi, San Domenico, 107. See also appendix I, 59, for a Humiliati notary in Milan.

reflect the career of a notary who first came across the Humiliati during the course of his work, went on to join and had a responsible career in the order. A later, better-documented example, confirms the possibility. In February 1230 a donation 'between the living' made to the order was written up by Rodulfinus son of the late Enrigetus of Legnago, notary of the sacred palace, who is surely the 'brother Rodulfinus formerly of Legnago, notary' documented between 1237 and 1241.[83] Brother Rodulfinus acted both as a witness and as a representative for the house of the Ghiara in these years and in 1238–9 was also drawing up documents for the community. He perhaps ceased to write documents himself, however, sometime before November 1240, when he is described as 'brother lord (*dominus*) Rodulfinus once a notary, formerly of Legnago'. The last reference to him dates from the following year and calls him a notary, but he was acting as a representative for the house and did not write the document himself.[84]

The careers of Taurellus and Rodulfinus suggest that it was long familiarity with local communities of the Humiliati which led to recruitment. Family ties between the recruits confirm the same point.[85] Whether or not Marchesius and Merida's foundation at Zevio in 1218 was one family, other evidence shows that family ties influenced decisions. In 1210 Albert joined his son, brother Wido, who was already in the Ghiara house.[86] In 1211, two members of the *Scanna uaca* family joined separate houses of the order and in 1224, Veronella, daughter of

---

[83] ASVer, Ghiara 134 (1230).
[84] ASVer, Ghiara 151 (1237), 161 (1238), 165 (1239), 173 (1240), 175 (1241).
[85] The importance of family bonds with particular religious houses has been underlined by Bull, *Knightly Piety and the Lay Response to the First Crusade*, esp. pp. 153–4.
[86] Appendix II, 4.

The early Humiliati

brother Bonaçonta, followed her father into the Ghiara.[87] In Brescia, the important Gambara house which was founded by Albricus *de Gambara* continued to attract members of this family as brethren throughout the thirteenth century and beyond, while members of the Rusca family remained linked with the Rondineto community in Como from the 1180s to the 1230s, if not longer.[88] There are at least two ways of looking at this. Perhaps the dedication of the first entrant to the religious life left the relative without visible means of support, so that entry into the order might be an economically motivated decision for other members of the family. These documents suggest, however, that family ties and concern were not necessarily severed after the entry of one individual, a view confirmed by the evidence of family members maintaining contacts. Gerard *de Milio*, whose daughter Iema entered the Ghiara in 1205, acted as a witness at professions in 1210 and 1211.[89] The numerous donations and bequests made because a relative was living in a community confirm the same point.[90] The increased familiarity with Humiliati ideals engendered by having one of the family already in the order meant that other members of the family were more likely to join. Entry into a house certainly did not mean complete removal from family networks.

Family groups

Family groups also entered the houses of the Humiliati *en masse*. As well as the ambiguous example of Marchesius and Merida in Zevio, a series of documents from the area of Milan record the entry of families. Five separate contracts stipulate the conditions for the entry of six adults and seventeen children into Humiliati communities. In the first four cases, one or two adults chose the religious life, giving themselves and all their property to the community and taking their under-age children with them. In the fifth, a grandfather made provision for two under-age granddaughters, but apparently did not himself join the Humiliati. These are summarised in table 6.2.[91]

Zanoni published these documents as unquestioned sources for the Humiliati, but the status of some of these houses is not clear. The Brera and Viboldone communities were indeed two of the most important in the movement both before and after 1201. The *domus Humiliatarum albarum* (no. 1) was however next to the church of Sant'Eustorgio,

[87] Appendix II, 5, (1211), 6 (1211), 9 (1224).
[88] See the Necrology of the Gambara house, *VHM* III, pp. 287–98, 290 and above, pp. 152, 161.
[89] Appendix II, 1 (1205), 3 (1210), 5 (1211).   [90] For examples, see pp. 185, 187.
[91] Brolis, *Gli Umiliati a Bergamo*, p. 114, discusses some fourteenth-century examples.

Table 6.2. The early Humiliati and provision for children: the documents[a]

Date	House	Adults	Children (ages)	Donation	Conditions for children
1. 1233	*Domus . . . Humilitarum albarum . . . apud ecclesiam beati Eustorgii* (Milan)	Domina Adelaxia daughter of the late Hubert Perenzoni and wife of the late Guidotus, son of the late Arguinus *de Osenago* (Milan)	Their daughters: Stada (10) and Madia (5)	*Se cum omnibus iuribus bonis et rebus* (esp. 50 lire terzoli from her dowry and a *sedimen sive cassina* with buildings)	To stay till 14, supported by *fructus* on the donation. May leave to marry between 14 and 18 with a share of the donation but not the *fructus*. After 18 must stay
2. 1255	*Domus Humiliatorum de Sollario in Senago*	Marchisius Burri and Leo Borrinus *de Senago*	Daughters of Leonus: Isabellina, Varenza and Petra (*minoris etatis*)	*Se et sua . . . omnibus suis bonis*	May leave when reach 'legitimate age' taking up to 36 lire each (from property given by Leonus)
3. 1266	Brera (Milan)	Tomardus *de Tomardis*	His children: Guardianus, Filipina and his grand-daughter, Martinela	*Omnibus suis bonis* (including very extensive properties)	May leave *ante tempus professionis* taking 200 lire or equivalent property (Guardianus) or 50 lire (the two girls)
4. 1276	Viboldone (*ecclesia seu canonica seu domus*)	Ambrose Polvale and his wife Contisa	Their sons: Paxinus, Petrinus, Miranetus and their nephews, Martin, Albertinus, Zaninus and Ambrosinus (all under 16)	*Omnibus . . . bonis . . . et in universo orbe nichil in se penito reservato* (extensive properties)	May leave before 16 taking their 'legitimate portion'; after that age, community not bound to continue supporting them unless they make profession

(cont'd)

193

Table 6.2 (*cont'd*)

Date	House	Adults	Children (ages)	Donation	Conditions for children
5. 1277	*Domus fratrum de ordine Sancti Augustini . . . . inferioris Senago . . . domus quondam Fratris Leonis Burri*	(Ottobonus *de Lazate*)	Dolzebellina and Zanebellina, granddaughters of donor (*minoris etatis*)	*Omnia bona*	May leave *quando ad etatem pervenerint*, taking 36 lire each

a Zanoni, pp. 311–18; now re-edited in *Gli atti del commune di Milano*, I, 303 (1233); II/1, 132 (1255); II/1, 132 (1255); II/2, 457 (1266), 738 (1276), III/1, 3 (1277).

which had been in the hands of the Dominicans since 1220. As Zanoni himself pointed out, use of the Humiliati name for this community continued until the 1450s, although the house was certainly Dominican from the mid-thirteenth century.[92] Similar ambiguity surrounds the status of the house in Senago mentioned in documents two and five. In 1255 Marchisius Burri and Leo Borrinus, perhaps relatives, entered the house with the three small daughters of Leo, Isabellina, Varenza and Petra. At this date the community was clearly named as a *domus Humiliatorum*, but in 1277, when Dolzebellina and Zanebellina were placed there by their grandfather, Ottobonus *de Lazzate*, the community is described as 'of the order of Saint Augustine'. This is certainly the same community, since it is identified as the 'house of the late brother Leo Burri [sic]'.[93] Identification with the *ordo canonicus* of the First order of the Humiliati might have inspired the adoption of Augustinian terminology for this house, but its association with the order cannot otherwise be documented.

The association with the 'official' Humiliati in some of these records is therefore tenuous. Yet these groups were surely inspired by similar desires for *umiliatismo* and, given the general invisibility of children in the notarial archives, they are invaluable. In Verona, where there are over 400 thirteenth-century records from the Ghiara archive, no references to children have so far been identified. By contrast, these five documents give details of the names, ages and even the plans for seventeen children and are therefore precious despite the small size of the sample, spread over a relatively long chronological span.

Zanoni used these documents to illustrate his model of the Humiliati as fulfilling what he termed an 'eminently social role'. He described the contracts as primarily the stipulation of corrodies for the adults, with the extra advantage of providing a safe haven for the children of older parents.[94] He also suggested that the children were taught a craft, understood to be wool-working.[95] This idea of children learning a skill, along the lines of an apprenticeship, to equip them to cope with the world as adults, fitted well with his interpretation of the Humiliati as a product of the class struggle and a means of escape from the unbearable hardship of the life of the urban 'proletariat'.[96]

Zanoni's approach has since been extensively modified, but his views cannot (and should not) be dismissed outright. Some of the adults surely

---

[92] Above, p. 57; Zanoni, p. 63 n. 1.

[93] This use of the name Burri confirms the likelihood of kinship between Marchisius and Leo.

[94] On corrodies, see B. Harvey, *Living and Dying in England 1100–1450: the Monastic Experience* (Oxford, 1993), pp. 179–209.

[95] Zanoni, pp. 192–4. [96] Above, p. 29.

were thinking of these Humiliati or quasi-Humiliati communities partly as safe havens for themselves or their children. This is well illustrated by the contract of 1277 in which Ottobonus *de Lazate* made provision for his under-age granddaughters but did not himself enter the community. The case for seeing such agreements as apprenticeships is, however, less strong: they provide remarkably little information about what was expected of, or for, the children during their stay with the Humiliati. Of the five documents, three say nothing whatever and in the remaining two, no mention is made of learning a craft. Stada and Madia, aged ten and five, who entered the *domus Humiliatarum albarum* with their mother in 1233, were to be brought up (*alere et conducere*) by the sisters, supported by the interest on the donation made on their behalf. Between the ages of fourteen and eighteen they might choose to leave in order to marry (but not apparently for any other reason). Similarly, the seven Polvale boys who entered Viboldone in 1276 were to be fed and clothed by the community. They were to live under obedience to the provost and might not ask for any further expenses or interest (*fructus*), but there is no reference to any specific training or apprenticeship to prepare them for adult life.

This acceptance of children could be explained simply as a continuation of a long monastic tradition which, despite objections, continued well into the late middle ages.[97] There is no indication, however, that the Humiliati were involved in the education of children usually undertaken by such traditional communities. Nor is this child oblation. Although there is evidence that in two cases the children (both at Viboldone) chose to remain in the house, the contracts all in fact allowed some freedom of choice, permitting them to leave at a future date, either when they reached a particular age, or before making their profession.[98] This age is not specified in all the documents, but Stada and Madia were free to marry from the age of fourteen, yet had to decide before the end of their eighteenth year. Similarly, the seven Polvale boys entering Viboldone had to make the decision to stay or go before the age of sixteen.

The reception of children could also be explained in purely financial terms. The Humiliati acquired the donations of property which came with the children and which were occasionally substantial. Tomardus *de Tomardis* donated a large property, including extensive vineyards, three farms (*sedimina*) and a house with other buildings and *curte* in the city of Milan, which was to revert to the Humiliati after the death of his

---

[97] Doran, 'Oblation or obligation?', pp. 140–1.
[98] Ambrosinus and Paxinus Polvale both remained at Viboldone, Paxinus apparently as a lay professed brother; Tagliabue, 'Gli Umiliati a Viboldone', pp. 20–1.

daughter Tutabella and her son. Even if the children eventually chose to leave the Humiliati, taking their 'legitimate portion' or a fixed sum, the community would retain something. The financial considerations are, however, only half the story at best. *Omnis boni principium* provides another possible way of viewing such contracts. The rule ordained that adult postulants were not to be accepted if they were responsible for weak, small or sick children.[99] In other words, small children were not to be abandoned and individuals with responsibility for them would be unable to lead a full religious life. By accepting the children, even temporarily, the Humiliati would enable the adults to fulfil their religious vocation, surely an important consideration. The only document in this group which records a reason for choosing to enter the order gives a religious and family one. Tomardus *de Tomardis* entered the Brera with his children Guardianus and Filipina and his granddaughter Martinela because he wished to do penance *together with* his children.[100] These contracts undoubtedly made financial provision for the adults and their offspring, but they also enabled them actively to pursue a full religious life while keeping their children with them. The opportunity they allow for adults to fulfil a religious or penitential vocation without having to abandon their children or wait for them to be old enough may perhaps have contributed to the success of the Humiliati, not just as Tertiaries, but also in their regular houses.

The entry of married couples

In 1277, Ambrose and Contisia Polvale entered Viboldone with their family, undertaking to live 'like the brothers and sisters of the house of Viboldone'. Joint entry was catered for in *Omnis boni principium* where each partner was ordered to promise perpetual chastity, as Marchesius and Merida had done at the foundation of their community in Zevio in 1218.[101] This practice can also be documented in Pavia and there is some evidence to suggest that, as we might expect, a distinction was made between such couples and fully professed brethren.[102] In 1248, on the same day as the profession of Irigetus and Riprandina, two postulants in the house of Zevio, who made the vows which were by that stage customary, Vivian *de Regalo* and lady Altessenda his wife publicly agreed before a priest, to join the order and to observe perpetual chastity:

[99] Above, p. 120.
[100] Table 2, 3: 'quia vult agere penitentiam simul cum Guardiano et cum Filipina'.
[101] Above, p. 178.   [102] Below, n. 107.

they were in agreement to pass to the religion of the order of the Humiliati and
. . . they promised, by mutual stipulation each of the other to observe perpetual
chastity and they requested that a public instrument be made of this . . . [103]

The public instrument was drawn up by the same notary and on the
same parchment as that recording the entry of Irigetus and Riprandina,
but there is no record of this couple taking the same full vows. Nor are
they described as entering the house. Was this the commitment of two
Tertiaries who saw the local Second order community as the focus of
their religious life and therefore made their undertaking there? Or
perhaps they were a different category of member, often called *conversi*
in other communities, lay people associated in some way with a
religious community. The precise status of Vivian and Altessenda may
never be clear, but the entry of Ambrose and Contisia into the *canonica*
of Viboldone can leave us in no doubt that individuals belonging to
different orders of the Humiliati lived in the same communities.[104] This
is confirmed by a much later reference to one of the Polvale boys who
remained at Viboldone as a lay professed brother at least until the
1320s.[105]

This differentiation between the status of different members of the
same community is perhaps how we should see the cases of John
Zamboni and Poma discussed above. They were corrodians or lay *conversi*
associating themselves with a religious community later in life. Albert
who joined the Ghiara in Verona, where his son was already a brother,
also cannot have been a young man.[106] Similarly the notaries who
joined the Humiliati after some years of professional practice were
perhaps older men. Petracius Calciatus, who entered the house of Sta
Maria in Pertica in Pavia with his wife Bellabona in 1219, made his will
in the following year and had died before 1226, when the community
rented out the house 'which belonged to the late Petracius Calciatus'.[107]
It is unlikely that he entered because of ill health, since he acted as a
representative for the community during the summer of 1219.[108] He
entered both 'wishing to provide for himself' (*volens sibi providere*) and
because he wished 'to deliver himself to the honour of God and the
blessed Virgin and all the Saints'. This was not unlike Tomardus *de
Tomardis* who, already a grandfather, entered the Brera in 1266 to do
penance. However formulaic such expressions, it does seem that the
Humiliati were providing a way by which their members might come
to terms with God, as well as corrodies for the older generation.

[103] ASVer, Ghiara 213 (1248).   [104] See also the case of domina Dorata, above, n. 61.
[105] Tagliabue, 'Gli Umiliati a Viboldone', pp. 20–1.   [106] Appendix II, 4 (1210).
[107] Crotti Pasi, 'Gli Umiliati a Pavia', appendix 1–2, pp. 338–41.   [108] *Ibid.*, p. 326.

The donation of property

The documents which record the acceptance of children also record the donation of specific property by adults either on their behalf or because they themselves were entering the order. This distinguishes them from records giving details of the vows discussed at the beginning of this chapter, which never give specific information about the property donated by the postulants. The earliest example, that of Iema, is typical. In August 1205, in the presence of numerous witnesses, she made a donation 'between the living' of all her property present and future and was elected and received as a sister by brothers Boccadeadam and Natale on behalf of the chapter of the Ghiara. There is no reference to a religious ceremony, nor is the nature of the possessions Iema donated specified. What mattered was, first, the record that Iema entered the order on that day and was received in the presence of numerous named witnesses and second, that the donation was comprehensive, no property was withheld for her own use.[109]

In some cases vast properties were donated, but the lack of information in most records may reflect the small size of the donations made, or indeed the lack of any significant donation at all. Nor can we be certain that all new brethren did in fact renounce all their property and rights. From the 1220s the majority of the documents presented here do include a promise to live without property. Earlier on, however this was not always the case. When Albert, Manfredinus and their sister Garscenda entered the Ghiara in Verona in 1209 they donated all their property, but excluded a plot of land in Roverchiara.[110] Similarly, when Petracius Calciatus entered Sta Maria in Pertica in Pavia in 1219 with his wife, he gave himself and his property (*reddidit se et sua*), but in the following year made a will leaving a further 200 Pavian lire to the community.

The donation of a house, in which the donor or his or her family continued to reside, but which became the property of the order, was common. In 1255 Marchisius Burri and Leo Borrinus from Senago, who had dedicated themselves and their dependants (*familiis*) to the Humiliati of Sollario, gave their house to the community and, as Zanoni demonstrated, it was there that the community then lived.[111] The house which Poma had refurbished before joining the Humiliati *de Senedogo* in Milan in 1268 may have been her own:[112] it seems highly likely that Poma continued to live there, although she was to have the

---

[109] Appendix II, 1.   [110] Appendix II, 2.   [111] Zanoni, p. 59.
[112] *Gli atti del comune di Milano*, II/1, 534: 'in redificando domum unam in qua ipsa domina Poma habitat, que domus est in sedimine illius domus Humiliatarum'.

same provisions as the other sisters, both in sickness and in health, and her servant Irvita was to assist the other sisters as well as her mistress. While not often specified, the frequent recurrence of Humiliati houses named after individuals may often derive from donations of houses made on entry by early members of the order, whose homes provided better accommodation for the whole community than previously available. Thus for example, the community of the Gambara in Brescia began in a house donated by that family.[113] Similarly, the *mansio fratris Ardenghi* in Pavia may have started as a house belonging to Ardengus himself.[114] The evidence of names should, however, be treated with caution, since it may on occasion refer to a later superior of the community. The *domus Ferabovis* in Zevio was originally that of Marchesius and Merida and acquired the name of the new minister, brother *Ferabovus*, only after their deaths.[115] The title used may be informative about the superior, not the original donors of the building.

CONCLUSIONS

The evidence so far available concerning professions of faith and the entry of recruits allows us to draw several provisional conclusions about the nature of Humiliati communities and the development of practice in the first half of the thirteenth century.

While some postulants may have been hasty, the choice of the Humiliati was more often the result of long familiarity, through either professional or family ties. Entry often followed careful thought and while it had obvious economic implications, might well be deeply religious. It would not be reasonable to suppose that all recruits were in the same state of religious fervour described by Vitry. Nonetheless, the absence of references to such fervour in the documents should not be interpreted as signifying a lack of genuine piety.[116] Not all the Humiliati were looking only for economic security or protection.

At the same time, it is not possible on the basis of these documents to affirm that membership of the Humiliati inevitably had to be purchased. Examples from innumerable Benedictine communities are very clear about the undertaking expected. In April 1248, for example, Ysabella, wife of Donadeus *de Olcellis*, sold nine perches of land to the monastery of Sta Maria in Biolo beyond the river Adda (*de ultra adua*) near Lodi to enable her daughter to be accepted as a sister there and so that she should be provided for in both clothing and food for the remainder of

---

113 Above, p. 140. 114 Crotti Pasi, 'Gli Umiliati a Pavia', p. 329.
115 Appendix I, *53.
116 See Bull, *Knightly Piety and the Lay Response to the First Crusade*, pp. 153–4.

her life, 'for the price of the said lands'.[117] Membership of this, as of other houses, clearly entailed substantial expense.[118] By contrast, it is not impossible that beyond the symbolic donation of self and possessions, no substantial gift was required to enter a house of the Humiliati. If we accept that some sort of donation was, however, probably usual, it is less easy to establish how much was appropriate. Those who had the means gave generously to the houses they joined, but many donations suggest that a house, the odd field, or small amounts of capital were the main property of the postulants: the majority were 'owner-occupiers', but by no means wealthy individuals – neither Zanoni's 'proletariat' nor patrician.[119]

The two categories of document recording entry throughout the period under consideration perhaps reflect two different levels of membership within the regular communities. In particular, couples making vows of chastity may not have been considered full members of the Second order. The entry of such couples into houses identified with the First order also once more underlines the lack of clear divisions in practice between houses of the different orders. The reception of children, enabling their adult relatives to pursue their religious vocation and removing the need to choose between religion and family, may help to explain the popularity not just of the lay Third order, but also of the regular communities.

Even allowing for the vagaries of notarial records, the evidence suggests that standard procedures in the treatment of postulants developed slowly. The fluidity of practice contrasts with the fixed ideals of the rule set out in 1201. The Veronese sources also imply, however, that the years around 1230 marked a turning point in recognition of the rule and the development of uniform customs. After that date there is an ever-increasing, regular flavour to the records. Although there continue to be variations in practice, the similarity between the Veronese documents and records from Lodi and Monza in the 1250s suggest that by this date if not before, uniformity was also acknowledged outside the area of Verona. This issue and the question of leadership will be discussed in more detail in the following chapter.

[117] ASMi, 191 Lodi, Sta Maria in Biolo, 1 (1248).
[118] On changing views of such gifts, see J. H. Lynch, *Simoniacal Entry into Religious Life from 1000 to 1260* (Columbus, 1976).
[119] For a similar analysis of German Mendicants, see Freed, *The Friars and German Society*, pp. 109–34.

Chapter 7

UNITY AND UNIFORMITY: THE
DEVELOPMENT OF A CENTRALISED
ORDER

Ut quasi unum corpum unum capud habentes . . .[1]

This chapter takes a final look at the questions of unity and uniformity among the early Humiliati, using the extant papal letters to explore the attitudes of central authority. A key requirement for uniformity is united and acknowledged leadership and as we have seen, some local leaders, notably the 'senior professed ministers' of Verona, acquired prominence in the first half of the thirteenth century, which allowed them to impose their customs on houses in the area. Yet the early representatives who travelled to the Curia on behalf of all the Humiliati do not seem to have been replaced. Nor is there early evidence for meetings of the General Chapter as required in the papal legislation of 1201. These omissions perhaps contributed to the continued problems with divergent observance, confirmed as much in papal correspondence as in the notarial documentation discussed in earlier chapters. In 1226 controversy over old and new customs at the Brera in Milan prompted a petition to Honorius III.[2] Partly as a response to such difficulties, in 1227 *Omnis boni principium* was reissued and papal visitations were introduced, apparently for the first time.[3] As we have seen, these actions seem to have produced changes in the practice and recording of professions in the area of Verona.[4] It will be argued here that visitation also contributed to more fundamental constitutional changes which introduced rule by a Master General in 1246 and the complete restructuring of the lines of authority in the order. The second half of this chapter will then consider the activities of the first of these new superiors, as revealed in evidence concerning disputes referred to him, a

---

[1] Appendix I, 55; see also n. 23 below.   [2] Appendix I, 21.
[3] Appendix I, 28, 32–3.   [4] Above, pp. 180, 184.

key source for tracing the process of negotiation necessary to establish uniform observance and united rule.

In December 1226 Honorius III wrote to the community of the Brera admonishing them to observe the rule approved by Innocent III. The letter recalled Innocent's decision to have the diverse observances and various formulae of life which they had unwisely adopted examined and corrected in order to encourage honesty and to recall them to one rule of life. Certain members of the Brera had visited Honorius, however, to inform him that some of their brethren still felt bound by vows made in regard to regulations conceived from the very beginning of the house's institution. Such local customs clearly enjoyed the prestige of greater age than any centrally imposed rule introduced in 1201 and it is perhaps significant that no member of the Brera house appears to have been directly involved in the negotiations at that date. For obvious reasons, no details of the aberrant customs are given in Honorius' letter, but it is alleged that they not only contradicted provisions in Innocent's rule, but even had a less than catholic flavour (*minus catholicum sapiebat*).[5] Thus for twenty-five years not even the most important Second order house in Milan had been following a clearly defined and uniform observance. Nor, it seems, did Honorius succeed in resolving the matter. He released the Brera brethren from their vows concerning these early formulae and exhorted them to observe the papally approved rule, but within a year further papal intervention shows that problems with observance remained.

In March 1227 Honorius III died and it was left to his successor Gregory IX to pursue the question of Humiliati observance. In June he sent them a copy of *Omnis boni principium* as approved by Innocent III, so as to ensure that it was observed.[6] In December of the same year he wrote again and in characteristically strong terms, this time to the archbishop of Milan, Henry *de Settala* (1213–30).[7] His letter was prompted by a petition from the provosts and ministers of the Humiliati of *Lombardia* concerning the archbishop's failure to carry out an earlier papal mandate. This had enjoined Henry to warn and induce all those 'in *Lombardia* and of the March who call themselves Humiliati', either to observe the rule or form of life approved by Innocent III, or 'having

---

[5] Appendix I, 21. [6] See above, p. 109.
[7] Appendix I, 34; on Henry see Alberzoni, 'Nel conflitto tra papato e impero', pp. 227–57, 239–44.

abandoned the name, habit, place and possessions of the Humiliati, to move to another approved order'.[8] Gregory now instructed Henry to ensure that this was done before the following Easter (March 1228) and informed him that he had appointed two Dominicans and a Milanese canon to assist him in the task.[9] No clues are given as to which houses were involved, and no extant sources reveal whether anyone was forced to give up the name *Humiliatus* at this point. Nonetheless, the letter confirms that observance of one uniform rule had not yet been achieved and suggests that the order still had a problem of copyright on the name Humiliati. A finite identity of the official Humiliati was proving difficult to impose.

In a separate action, in September 1227, Gregory IX had ordered the visitation of exempt houses of the order of St Benedict, Regular Canons, the Humiliati and Hospitals in the dioceses of Cremona, Brescia, Bergamo, Padua, Venice and Treviso.[10] Other areas were surely included, but these are the only letters which survive. The mandate excluded the Cistercians and 'poor enclosed sisters', who enjoyed special dispensations, yet it included the houses of the Humiliati, which should equally have been self-regulating through General Chapters.[11] Articles drawn up in 1285, summarising the history and rights of visitation in the order which were then in dispute, suggest that the two processes of visitation, internal and papal, had been enforced simultaneously since 1201 and had both been considered normal.[12] There is, however, no evidence for a General Chapter being held until 1246 and the only early evidence for visitation concerns the papal appointees.[13] One of those named in 1227, John *de Gambara*, a priest, may have belonged to a Brescia family, who enjoyed close associations with the order.[14] He may even have been a member of the order himself. The vast majority of visitors, however, were Dominicans. In Cremona, Brescia and Bergamo, together with John the pope appointed brother Roger, sub-prior of the Dominicans in Bologna and brother

---

[8] The March is either the 'Marca veronese-trevigiana', or the 'Marca anconitana' listed, for example, in appendix I, 51, 64; see A. Castagnetti, *La marca veronese–trevigiana* (Turin, 1986).

[9] 'Al. prior of the Friars preacher of Milan, Al. of Parma of the same Order and Master Oldericus, canon of Sto Stefano in Broilo, Milan'.

[10] Appendix I, 32, 33.

[11] On the 'moniales pauperes incluse', see Iriarte, *Storia del francescanesimo*, pp. 515–17; on General Chapters, see p. 108.

[12] *Petitio dilectorum filiorum*, 8 January 1285, ASVat, Registro vaticano 41 fos. 215v–19v no. 61; summarised transcript in Martin IV, *Les registres de Martin IV (1281–85)*, 553.

[13] The first clear evidence of internal visitation is appendix I, 93 (1251) when the first Master, Beltramus was complaining about the refusal of certain communities to admit him; see above p. 186, n. 61 for internal visitors in the 1270s.

[14] See pp. 140, 151.

Melioratus, another Dominican. In Padua, Venice and Treviso, the visitors were all Dominicans: two priors, Joachim of Sta Maria and Jordan and a brother Gandulf of Padua.

The only direct evidence for the activities of these papal visitors among the Humiliati concerns a further Dominican, perhaps responsible for Como, brother Stephen, provincial prior of *Lombardia*, who was described in July 1236 as 'visitor of the lord pope over exempt places and over the order of the Humiliati'.[15] In the cloister of Sant'Eustorgio, the Dominican church in Milan and in the presence of three Dominican friars, Stephen entrusted the priest Giroldus of Rondineto in Como with the administration and prelacy of the house of Sta Maria di Ronco Martano *de Valbixaria*.[16] This confirmed the election made by three women of the house (Herena, Prudentia and Riccha), of Giroldus as 'pastor, rector and provost of the whole congregation of the house'. Brother Stephen also instructed the sisters to obey Giroldus according to God and the rule of the house. The document then records what appears to be a punitive sanction against two brothers. Stephen ordered brother Ambrose *de Vicomercato* and brother Lazarinus *de Medda* to remain in obedience to Giroldus at Sta Maria di Ronco Martano in remission of their sins, for as long as he (Stephen) should wish.[17] The houses of these men are not given (unless they were in Vimercate and Meda), but the context suggests that they were Humiliati and that they had been guilty of offences against the order not unlike those experienced in other regular communities.[18] It is not impossible that their sin had been to resist the imposition of uniform observance of the papally sanctioned rule.

The process of papal visitation continued throughout the 1230s. In May 1237 the appointment of visitors was renewed in a letter addressed to the Dominican provincial prior of *Lombardia*, perhaps the same brother Stephen active in 1236 and later a chaplain and penitentiary of Innocent IV's, to whom the office of visitation was also delegated in 1246.[19] The letter of 1237 is modelled closely on those of a decade earlier, using the same *arenga* and many of the same formulae. There are, however, some important innovations. The area specified was substantially larger: the visitation was to cover the provinces of *Lombardia* and Romagna (*romaniole*), the Marches of Treviso and Ancona and the cities

---

[15] *VHM* III, pp. 303–5: 'visitator Domini pape super locis exemptis et super ordine humiliatorum', discussed in Morelli, 'La casa di Rondineto', p. 43*.

[16] Above, pp. 54, 107, 142, 165.

[17] *VHM* III, p. 305: 'ut ipsi sint sub obedientia prefati presbiteri Giroldi in eodem loco in remissionem peccatorum eorum usque ad voluntatem suprascripti prioris provincialis'.

[18] See, for example, the rebellious Premonstratensian brethren in 1198, *PL*, 214, cols. 172–7.

[19] Appendix I, 51, 64.

and dioceses of Venice and Genoa. The canons of the order of San Marco were now included, as were churches and places in possession of liberty or not subject to diocesan correction. The powers and duties of the visitor were clarified and appear stricter. As before, they were to correct both the head and members of houses 'effectively and without fear' (*intrepide et efficaciter*), punishing resistance with excommunication. If any place were found to be corrupt (*deformata*), however, and did not wish to reform in its own order, a member of one of the approved orders as was most suitable was to be introduced there. Further opposition was to be countered with the help of the secular arm. The letter is not directed only at the Humiliati, so the provisions are not simply a reflection on the state of this order. It is clear, however, that internal visitation of the Humiliati, as of other orders, had been deemed insufficient. Nor did this situation change after 1246, when fundamental reforms were introduced. A letter issued in November of that year still included the Humiliati among the houses subject to papal visitation.[20]

THE CONSTITUTIONAL CHANGES OF 1246

In the autumn of 1246 Innocent IV issued a series of eleven letters concerning the Humiliati.[21] This probably reflects the activities of a proctor in the Curia who was involved in negotiating two fundamental changes in the structure of the order. The first letter, issued in response to a petition by the Humiliati, records that Innocent had appointed Otto *de Tonengo*, cardinal bishop of Porto (1244–51) (first cardinal protector of the order), to help them elect a single provost or Master General. This had been done through a meeting of the General Chapter and Innocent now confirmed their choice of brother Beltramus, formerly provost of San Luca in Brescia, who was to hold office for life. The pope exhorted the Humiliati to receive Beltramus as *pater et pastor*, with care for their souls and authority over them in both spiritual and temporal affairs. Naturally enough, the letter cites the dangers of division as a reason for the election of one man to rule over the order, comparing their religion to a rudderless ship on the waves of the sea.[22] By comparison, 'like one body, with one head', they will now be able to serve one God and Lord together and more perfectly.[23] This move suggests that the alternating, Cistercian style of government, based on

---

[20] Appendix I, 64.   [21] Appendix I, 55–65.

[22] Appendix I, 55: 'ac religioni uestre uelut nauiculum absque prora projecta in maris fluctibus constitute'.

[23] *Ibid.*: 'ut quasi unum corpus unum capud [sic] habentes, uni Deo et Domino possitis eo perfectius quo communius deseruire'.

the four senior provosts of Rondineto, Viboldone, Vialone and Lodi, had been unable to keep the order united. It might equally indicate that the Dominican visitors had been unable to resolve the problems. It can hardly be a coincidence, however, that the visitors were mainly Dominicans and that the obvious model for the introduction of a Master General was the Dominican order itself.[24] Even the choice of the title, *magister generalis*, reflects Dominican practice.[25] We may never know the extent of their involvement behind the scenes, but it seems very likely that the Dominicans involved in visiting the Humiliati had advocated or inspired changes designed to bring them closer to their own model of government and intended to strengthen the central administration of the order. Certainly this close association with the Dominicans was to remain important in the view of later writers.[26]

The second stage of reform is recorded in the privilege *Ex ore domini*, issued in late October or early November 1246, three or four weeks after the letter confirming Beltramus in office. It amounts almost to a new constitution for the order.[27] Much of the material in the first part of this privilege, which was addressed to the First and Second orders (thereby partially confirming the identity between these two), was a re-confirmation of long-standing duties, rights and privileges. The protection of St Peter and guarantees for their property were renewed.[28] The *ordo canonicus* and the papally approved rule of the First and Second orders were to be observed as before. Their exemptions from tithe payment and licence to receive tithes were reaffirmed. Their superiors, if priests, might tonsure as clerics literate laymen who took the regular habit with them (*qui apud vos habitum receperint regularem*). They might also accept clerics into the order. Transfer to another order after profession was not allowed unless with permission. They might receive and build churches as long as they had the permission of the diocesan and did not prejudice other churches. Burial was to be open (*liberam*), but with the usual restrictions concerning the rights of other churches, the exclusion of excommunicates and public usurers and the consent of the bishop.[29] Their provosts and priests together with deacons and subdeacons might celebrate solemn mass and, as before, during interdicts

---

[24] Similar Dominican influence has been traced in the 'Memoriale' for penitents drawn up in the 1220s; see Meersseman, '*Ordo fraternitatis*', I, pp. 365–70.

[25] See Hinnebusch, *The History of the Dominican Order*, I, pp. 169–250.

[26] Below, p. 252.

[27] Appendix I, 59; variations between Tiraboschi's edition and the original will be noted where necessary.

[28] Including churches and houses in Pavia, Lodi, Piacenza, Parma, Cremona, Brescia, Milan, Vercelli, Alessandria and Verona (in that order).

[29] See also below, pp. 225–9.

must do so behind closed doors and without ringing bells.[30] A new clause specifies that no house of the order is to be allowed to transfer to any other profession, prompted perhaps by the loss of the house of Marchesius and Merida in Zevio to the order of the canons of San Marco in 1239.[31] It is the second half of the document, however, which is of most interest here: the government of the order is placed on a new footing and the duties of the new superior, the Master General, are outlined.

The ultimate authority within the order for visitation and correction in both spiritual and temporal matters now lay entirely with the Master. He was to carry out the visitation of the three orders either himself, or through the office of suitable persons (*diffinitores*), elected at the General Chapter. These officers were to ordain or correct the life of the houses according to the *institutio* of the order as approved by the Apostolic see and were to be elected or deposed according to the constitutions.

As in the Dominican order, the Master was by no means all powerful. Although excluded from the election of the superiors of the order and forbidden to exact taxes, the diocesan bishop, as long as he were 'catholic', was still to provide the Chrism, holy oil, the consecration of altars or basilicas and the ordination of clerics to priesthood. Within the order itself, it was the Master and the General Chapter together which formed the supreme authority. A General Chapter was to be held at least once a year and during it the Master and *diffinitores* were to deal with any matters which might require reform or concern the state or progress of the order. Resolutions agreed in the General Chapter were to remain valid unless or until overruled in a subsequent General Chapter. To favour peace in the order, no one was to be allowed to contradict or appeal against anything concerning discipline or the *institutio*. Any who did so were to be punished. Finally, business arrangements agreed by the Master and chapter of any house were to be honoured unchanged.[32]

In theory at least, a centralised administration was thereby created at a stroke. A clear structure of authority focused on the Master General would replace the rotating system of the first forty-five years. The problems of unity and uniformity apparent in the first half of the

---

[30] The manuscript refers to priests, not prelates as given in Tiraboschi.

[31] This clause is in Brera AD XVII/17a, used by Biancolini for his edition of the letter, but missed by Tiraboschi; on the house of Marchesius and Merida, see above, pp. 178–9 and appendix I, *53.

[32] Tiraboschi's transcript here omits 'of any house', thereby incorrectly implying that only the General Chapter was intended: *VHM* II, p. 203. Challenges may not have been uncommon; the thirteenth-century city statutes of Brescia include a clause confirming that all sales agreed by a majority in any convent of the First or Second orders were to be definitive, 'Statuti di Brescia', p. 139.

century did not, however, disappear, as the experiences of the first
Master General demonstrate.

BELTRAMUS (MASTER GENERAL 1246−57)

Very little is known about the life of Beltramus or of any of the other
thirteenth-century Masters.[33] He had been provost of San Luca in
Brescia and may have used the second name Gochore, applied to him in
a papal letter of 1251.[34] According to this letter he had been chosen
because of witnesses to the honesty of his life and knowledge, but this
did not prevent opponents to his authority expressing their views in the
following years.

Beltramus was confirmed in office as Master General by Innocent IV
on 13 October 1246, but later in the same month Innocent sent three
letters which were addressed to different sections of the order (two to
the Third order and one to the Second), without mention of the
Master.[35] Presumably the proctor had not yet left the Curia with the
letter of confirmation. Certainly after this date nearly all papal correspondence with the order was sent to the Master or the Master and
brethren, as was that of papal legates, unless it concerned the affairs of a
particular house alone. As before, a large number of letters was also sent
to the archbishop of Milan, other bishops and ecclesiastics concerning
matters touching upon the affairs of the order; some of these help to
throw light on the duties (and failings) of the new Master.

According to Galvano Fiamma, in 1256 a 'Bertramus Zothori' was
chosen together with the Cistercian abbot of Chiaravalle, the Guardian
of the Friars Minor and the Dominican prior of Sant'Eustorgio in Milan
to resolve a crisis in the city by choosing a new *podestà* to replace the
competing claimants elected by the *popolo* and the archbishop and
nobles.[36] If this is indeed the same man, it suggests that Beltramus was
acknowledged as the representative of the Humiliati by the citizens of
Milan and that this conferred prominence equal to that of major
ecclesiastical figures associated with the other new orders. The series of
papal letters issued during his generalate show, however, that relations

---

[33] See *VHM* I, pp. 99−112; Mario da Bergamo, 'Beltramo da Brescia', *DBI*, VIII (Rome, 1966), pp. 78−9.

[34] Appendix I, 87; this corrects da Bergamo, 'Beltramo da Brescia', p. 78; see below, p. 212. Tiraboschi notes that John of Brera had identified Beltramus as the founder of the house of San Luca but that there had in fact been a previous provost, Lanfranc, documented in 1236, *VHM* I, p. 101; da Bergamo suggests he had been among the founding group, but does not give his evidence.

[35] Appendix I, 57, 60, 61.

[36] Galvano Fiamma, *Manipulus florum*, col. 686; cited in da Bergamo, 'Beltramo da Brescia', p. 79.

with city governments were not always so cordial. Recurring themes, both before and after 1246, were illicit or excessive taxation (communal and ecclesiastical), forced loans and compulsory involvement in secular duties and offices.[37] Most of these were listed and discussed by Zanoni and, though he incorrectly implied that all concerned defence of the Humiliati's exemption from taxes, there is no need to review them in detail here.[38] They hint at both the financial expertise and wealth of the order by this date and some of the tensions and difficulties the Humiliati met outside the walls of their own houses. They also show that during these years the order acquired renewed privileges extending their right to exercise the care of souls and to preach, which suggest that Beltramus was an effective advocate. For the government and structure of the order itself, however, these letters provide little information, except perhaps to suggest that its leaders and their representatives were successful in their petitioning of the pope, both in Lyons (1246–50) and as he travelled back to Rome (which he reached before November 1253).[39] Eight letters were issued in one month when the pope was in Milan itself, which compares favourably with the twenty-nine letters issued over four years from Lyons, and was only matched by the burst of activity when the order was reorganised in the autumn of 1246.[40] Only once do we have the name of a proctor, when a letter from Alexander IV in 1256 to the Master mentions 'brother Egidius your proctor and [proctor] of the whole order of the Humiliati'.[41] The issuing of letters in groups, however, as in the autumn of 1246 or summer 1249, suggests that a proctor had also been making extended visits to the Curia in those years.[42]

Many of the proctors made their way to Rome to seek the resolution of disputes either with other orders or among the Humiliati themselves, and it is in the letters recording their activities that the structure and reality of authority within the order is revealed most clearly.

---

[37] Appendix I, *40, 66–7, 69, 70, 74, 76–7, 79, 88–91, 95, 97a–c, 98, 102–3

[38] Zanoni, p. 210; he did not discuss appendix I, 88–91; see also G. Biscaro, 'Gli estimi del comune di Milano nel secolo xiii', *ASL*, 55 (1928), pp. 343–495.

[39] His route, which included Genoa, Milan, Brescia and Perugia, can be traced in part using appendix I, 87, 88–93, 95, 96, 97a, 97c.

[40] Milan: appendix I, 88–93, 97a, 97c, Lyons: appendix I, 55–79, 82–5. Autumn 1246: appendix I, 55–65.

[41] Appendix I, 109; perhaps the same brother Egidius *canevarius* at the Brera Milan in 1255: ASMi, 470 Brera, 15 October 1255.

[42] Proctors also probably petitioned some or all of the groups of letters issued by Gregory IX in 1227 (appendix I, 22–35) and 1236 (appendix I, 45–49).

Beltramus and the settlement of disputes

The first dispute with which Beltramus was faced concerned the issue of clerical precedence and arose before February 1248. In that month, Innocent IV wrote to the order confirming the settlement which had recently been achieved.[43] The *narratio* of his letter records that, although there was a long-observed statute in the order that clerics should precede the laity in the church, refectory and elsewhere, this had been the subject of a drawn-out dispute between the lay and clerical members of the community of San Michele in Alessandria. The lay party had appealed to the pope and Innocent had appointed the Cistercian abbots of Tiglieto and Sant'Andrea in the dioceses of Acqui and Genoa to put an end to the controversy. The abbots had determined that the brethren, lay or clerical, should enjoy precedence according to the date of their entry into the order.[44] It was a typically monastic solution to the problem. Beltramus and the four senior provosts of the order (all of whom must have been clerics or priests by virtue of their office) had not accepted defeat, however, and had appealed to Innocent. The pope now overruled this 'iniquitous sentence', which was causing 'serious scandal in the order', ordering the Humiliati to ensure that the original statute was observed both in San Michele and in all houses of the order.

Although there had always been clerics in the order and this letter refers to an earlier statute establishing their precedence, no such statute survives. Whether or not such a decree had been widely adopted in the order before this date, it seems likely that the dispute reflects awareness of contemporary controversies among the Franciscans.[45] Like the Franciscans, the clerical Humiliati wished to emphasise their special status while the lay members wished to maintain the prominence awarded them in 1201 (when a lay member of First order houses had been included as one of those involved in the choice of a new superior). The manner of the appeal by Beltramus and the four provosts also reveals that despite the changes of 1246 the four senior provosts remained actively involved in the consideration of such sensitive issues.

Three years later, Beltramus was involved in a local dispute between the Humiliati and an outside body, the Dominicans of Sant'Eustorgio in Milan in 1251. The dispute had arisen because of the close proximity of

---

[43] Appendix I, 68.

[44] *Ibid.*: 'clerici vel laici qui prius ordinem intraverunt precedant alios'.

[45] See for example, R. Manselli, 'La clericalizzazione dei minori e san Bonaventura', *S. Bonaventura francescano. Convegni del Centro di studi sulla spiritualità medievale*, 14 (Todi, 1974), pp. 181–208; see also John of Brera, *Excerptum*, 21, p. 341.

the Dominicans and a Humiliati house of the Second order newly founded on land next to Sant'Eustorgio by a group from the *domus communis* in Monza.[46] The settlement strongly favoured the Dominicans, who had petitioned the papal letter. The speed with which this papal confirmation was achieved speaks volumes about the Dominicans' ability to reach the papal ear: the settlement was agreed in Milan on 18 May and Innocent IV's letter, sent from Genoa, was issued on 25 June, just five and a half weeks later. The Humiliati, led by their minister, brother Arnold *de Vedano*,[47] had come to an amicable agreement (which amounted to a capitulation) on the instructions of the Master and two ministers:

by the mandate and will and authority and consent of brother Beltramus Gochore, Master of the whole order of the Humiliati and by the mandate and will and consent of brother Miranus, Minister of the Brera and Brother Tuttobellus, Minister of Sant'Agata of Monza and of the other prelates and elders of the Humiliati brothers.[48]

Several copies of the settlement had then been drawn up at the instructions of both sides and of 'brother Beltramus, Master of the whole order of the Humiliati'. The direct intervention by the Master in the affairs of an individual house reflects the seriousness of the problem. The Dominicans were the papal visitors of the order and were also responsible for the inquisition in the region. They had also been there longer. In terms of the internal workings of the Humiliati order it is perhaps still more important that in place of the four senior provosts, Beltramus was aided by two ministers of the Second order, one from Milan where the dispute took place and one from Monza, whence the Humiliati involved originally came and where the agreement had initially been reached. A problem involving the Second order was being kept 'in house'.

A dispute settled in 1253–4 shows the provosts of the four main

---

[46] Appendix I, 87; see also below, pp. 242–4.

[47] Perhaps the same Arnold *de Vedano* documented in the *casa comune* in Monza 1232, Longoni, 'Origini degli Umiliati a Monza', 3.

[48] Appendix I, 87, 'de mandate et voluntate et auctoritate et consensu Fratris Beltrami Gochore, Magistri totius Ordinis Humiliatorum, et de mandato et voluntate et consensu Fratrum Mirani Ministri de Brayda [sic] et Tucebelli Ministri de Sancta Agatha de Modoetia, Prelatorum et Anzianorum aliorum Fratrum Humiliatorum'; Miranus may be one of the brothers of that name documented at the Brera with a variety of second names from 1230: 'de la Cruce' 1230 (appendix I, *38), 1234 (ASMi, 470 Brera, 27 March 1234); 'de Casate' 1236, 1238, 1245 (ASMi, 470 Brera, 14 April 1236, 24 October 1238 16 March 1245); 'de Casale' (ASMi, 470 Brera, 5 January 1240); 'Casalem' (ASMi, 470 Brera, 13 December 1244); he is named as minister from 1234; Tuttobellus may be the man documented as minister of Sant'Agata in Monza in 1232–4, *confrater* in 1255 and *frater* in 1259, Longoni, 'Origini degli Umiliati a Monza', 4 (1232–4), 12 (1255), 17 (1259); below, appendix I, *43.

houses once again acting alongside the Master in a manner reminiscent of the dispute over clerical precedence and also hints at some of the shortcomings of magisterial rule. Once more the dispute involved the house of San Michele in Alessandria. The prior and brothers of the Humiliati of San Marco in Tortona had complained to the Master because the provost and brothers of San Michele claimed that San Marco was subject to them and that they had various other rights. The case had apparently proved difficult to settle, leading the community of San Marco to petition the pope. In December 1253 Innocent IV wrote to Beltramus, pointing out that his apparent failure to resolve the dispute had caused the prior and his brothers serious damage.[49] He therefore instructed the Master, if this were the case, to take care to reach a settlement, according to the statutes and regular observance of the order. At much the same time (letter undated) William, cardinal deacon of Sant'Eustachio, papal legate and second protector of the order (1251–72), had also written to Beltramus. His letter is slightly more detailed: the grounds for dispute were the election of the prior of San Marco, the profession of novices, revenues and other monies due to San Marco and, remarkably, the acceptance of sick brethren *ad conversionem*.[50] William did not wish the case to go before the Curia or elsewhere, 'lest through disputing this they should in a short time consume the substance of their churches which had been acquired by extended toil'. He therefore ordered Beltramus to examine and settle the matter together with the provosts of Rondineto and Viboldone, brother Tuttobellus of Monza, brother Miranus of the Brera and, more surprisingly, the minister of the Milanese province of the Friars Minor. Unlike in the dispute with the Dominicans at Sant'Eustorgio, the Humiliati superiors cannot this time have been appointed as local experts and we must assume that they enjoyed some sort of prestige in the wider order, either because they had been elected as *diffinitores*, a reflection of their personal skill, or because of the age, wealth and size of their houses. Certainly Tuttobellus enjoyed authority in Monza where, in 1255, he was associated with the archpriest Raymond della Torre and the *podestà*, Magatus Marcellinum, in dealing with revenue from tithes in the borgo and territory of Monza.[51]

The projected involvement of a senior Franciscan echoes the visitation of houses by Dominicans; however, it did not materialise. In the settlement drawn up in February 1254 (which includes the texts of Innocent's and William's letters), Beltramus states that he had carefully

[49] Appendix I, 104a.   [50] Appendix I, *104b.
[51] Frisi, *Memorie storiche di Monza*, II, p. 126.

discussed the matter with the Humiliati superiors named, but had been unable to do so with the Franciscan, 'because he was not in these parts'.[52] The final settlement was to apply not just to relations between San Michele and San Marco, but also between San Michele and its daughter-houses in Genoa and Asti, in the hope of removing cause for future controversy.

The solution was agreed in the house of the Brera in the week of Septuagesima and in the presence of the provost of the Humiliati of San Giovanni in Porta Orientale, the prelate and a brother of the *domus nova* in Milan, a brother from Sant'Agata in Monza and 'many others'. The recurrence of the name of the provost of Viboldone and of ministers from the Milan area in these documents, confirms that the government of the order was centred on Milan and its diocese and that within this area the superiors of certain houses (in particular the Brera and Sant'Agata in Monza) enjoyed prominence alongside the original four senior provosts, or on occasion Viboldone alone.

The Humiliati of San Michele were either particularly litigious or good at keeping records, or local autonomy was strong enough to make long-distance congregations especially difficult to hold together, for the last major recorded dispute which Beltramus was called upon to resolve once more concerned rights of the house of San Michele in Alessandria over its daughters.[53] This time the problems lay with the house of Ognissanti in Florence which, like San Marco in Tortona, wished to escape the jurisdiction of the Alessandria house.[54]

The controversy is of particular interest here because it provides the first explicit reference to the activities of *diffinitores* and details of a General Chapter meeting. The documents concerning the dispute record that the house in Florence had been founded, built and ruled as a First order house by brother Amicus, provost of the Humiliati of Alessandria, on land which he had purchased. The bishop of Florence, had at his request laid the first stone of their church.[55] Brother Amicus had ruled the house as a daughter of San Michele in Alessandria in both spiritual and temporal matters, appointing a prior, cellarers and other office-holders as he pleased and exercising the care of souls in the church of Ognissanti. Amicus had resigned, however, leaving all the houses subject to San Michele temporarily without a superior. When the new provost, brother Roland, was elected (presumably by the

---

[52] Appendix I, *104.   [53] Appendix I, *110.

[54] Ognissanti was originally in San Donato, later moved to Sta Lucia; the Humiliati then built their own church of Ognissanti, see appendix I, *54 and *94 and Benvenuti Papi, 'Vangelo e tiratoi. Gli Umiliati ed il loro insediamento fiorentino', pp. 75–84.

[55] Appendix I, *110, *VHM* II, p. 279.

community of San Michele) and approved by the Master, the brothers of Ognissanti elected their own superior, brother Bellingerius and refused to admit brother Roland, denying him obedience and reverence. Both sides had then appealed to the General Chapter, held at Viboldone in April 1256. In the 'palace of the church of San Pietro', Beltramus and the General Chapter had appointed Conrad, provost of Viboldone, brother Gabriel of Brescia (or, if he were unable or unwilling, the provost of Sta Croce Novara) and, once more, brothers Miranus of the Brera and Tuttobellus of Sant'Agata to investigate and settle the dispute. At the wish of the eight *diffinitores*, Beltramus also ordered the two sides, on pain of excommunication, to appear before the said brethren appointed to hear them (or at least before two of them), in the city of Milan and within just fifteen days.[56] He forbade either side to use any document given after that day and particularly ordered them not to send any appeal to the pope.

On 1 May 1256 Beltramus made some modification of the terms, at the wish of the *diffinitores*, perhaps because the original deadline had not been met.[57] Should the two sides appear before only two of the judges, one of these must be a provost (Conrad, Gabriel or perhaps the provost of Sta Croce Novara) and the other must be either Miranus or Tuttobellus. If there were only two judges present, however, they might receive only the *iura partium* and were not to proceed to consideration of the case unless all four were present. He also once more ordered the two sides not to go to any other judge, unless nominated as a higher court by those named here.

The process for settling the dispute thus seems to have been well in motion by May 1256; however, no further progress was made until October, as Alexander IV's letter to the order in that month shows. This reveals that the dispute had spread to the other houses subject to San Michele and that the Master and General Chapter had themselves decided to call on papal authority to settle the case and to strengthen their mandate.[58] The implications were no doubt felt to be important for the whole order.

Alexander wrote as requested, instructing the provost of Viboldone and Miranus of the Brera to call the two sides together, hear the case and settle it, ensuring that their decision was observed by threatening the sanction of excommunication. Again, however, nothing was apparently done until July 1257, when San Michele appointed its proctors for the case. Finally, in August 1257 the case was heard in the *domus nova* Milan, in the presence of Beltramus and other witnesses.

---

[56] Appendix I, *110d.   [57] Appendix I, *110e.   [58] Appendix I, 110c.

Conrad and Miranus took depositions from both sides, consulted with their 'counsellors and associates', Tuttobellus and Gabriel of Brescia, and with two legal experts, James *de Lurago* and Roger Liprandus (*utriusque juris peritorum*) and at last gave sentence. In view of the version of events so far recorded it will be no surprise to learn that they found in favour of San Michele. No trace of a case made by its daughter-houses remains in the sources. Ognissanti was to be perpetually subject to San Michele, which would enjoy 'paternity and power and visitation and correction and institution and destitution' and 'complete rights as a mother must have over a daughter'.[59] Finally, Beltramus ratified and approved the judgement and a copy of it and all related documents was drawn up by Milanese notaries.

The differences between this procedure and the earlier dispute concerning San Michele are particularly revealing. It is clear that a great deal was at stake, yet the cardinal protector does not seem to have been involved. Nor did Beltramus himself judge the case and one of the judges was in fact not even a *diffinitor* of the order. It is surely significant that throughout the procedure those deputed to deal with the dispute included superiors from both First and Second order communities and that when introducing modifications, Beltramus insisted that the judges must include both a provost and one of the two superiors of a Second order house. Including members of both the regular orders of the Humiliati, might improve the chance of the decision being accepted by all concerned. This and the appeal to the advice of legal experts gave the decision greater authority than Beltramus alone could have provided. Such provisions reveal tension over the authority of the Master, whose position could, like that of other superiors, be overruled by appeal to the higher authority of the papacy.

In this case Beltramus seems to have prevented appeal by his subordinates to a higher authority, but his rule did not always go undisputed. In August 1251 Innocent IV had responded to a petition from Beltramus concerning certain provosts, prelates and brethren of the order who, after making their profession, honoured his habit and observed the rule, yet refused to obey him or to admit him for visitation or correction. Innocent thus instructed all members of the order to obey and admit him on pain of excommunication.[60] The issue here, as in the disputes between San Michele and its daughter-houses, was one of jurisdiction, not observance, but implies strong local autonomies, perhaps hostile to innovations such as the office of a Master General.

---

[59] Appendix I. *110, 'paternitatem et potestatem et visitationem et correctionem et institutionem et destitutionem . . . jura in solidum que matris domus in filiam habere debet'.
[60] Appendix I, 93.

Despite prohibitions on appeals to a higher court in the Ognissanti dispute, Beltramus did face independent action at the Curia from members of the order. In 1256 the proctor of the order, brother Egidius, successfully complained to Alexander IV about the failings of the Master General. Alexander's letter dealing with the complaint records that in 1246 Innocent IV had ordered the newly appointed Master to ensure that churches were built (with the necessary consent and support of the diocesan bishop) in houses of the Second order which did not yet have one and that priests were to be found to help the brethren say the office in these and in other churches of the order.[61] Beltramus had been allowed some leeway since he was to act 'as seemed suitable to him, having thought to the faculty and quality of persons in the houses'. Yet, according to the new letter, although ten years had passed and Beltramus had had churches built in some houses, he had omitted to do so in many others and had had no priests ordained for them. The pope therefore ordered Beltramus to have suitable brothers of the Second order promoted as clerics, subdeacons, deacons and priests and, if he should fail, threatened to turn to the provost of Viboldone to force him to do so using ecclesiastical censure.[62]

Although the letter highlights the role of the provost of Viboldone, it suggests that there may have been some tension between Beltramus, also originally a member of the First order, and those wishing to improve the condition and eventually the status of members of the Second order. It also shows that the introduction of a Master General had by no means overcome the forces for division and conflict present among the Humiliati in the first forty-five years of their official history.

CONCLUSIONS

The disputes discussed in this chapter provide a rather different perspective on the history of the Humiliati as an order when compared to the notarial records discussed in chapters 5 and 6. There is some continuity in the account: the slow acknowledgement of the rule suggested in the professions of faith discussed in chapter 6 is also confirmed here. In the late 1220s there were problems over observance at the Brera and it was found necessary to appeal to the pope to resolve both this issue and the problem of those illegitimately claiming Humiliati identity (perhaps the *umiliatismo* proposed in chapter 2 above). The same tendencies towards localism apparent in the develop-ment of regional identities such as that centred on Verona may also be

---

[61] Appendix I, 63; above p. 145.   [62] Appendix I, 109.

detected in the disputes between San Michele of Alessandria and its daughter-houses, reluctant to subject themselves to its distant authority.

In other ways, however, the perspective of these records suggests a better-defined identity as an order. This is partly the effect of curial terminology, which is not always a reliable guide to matters 'on the ground', but in some cases probably does reflect a new reality. In 1227 papal visitors were appointed to the Humiliati as an order. The effectiveness of the Dominicans then chosen and their successors is demonstrated by the reforms of 1246 which brought the administration of the Humiliati up to date, introducing a style of government closely based on that of the order of Preachers. It was perhaps this relationship with the Dominicans which Beltramus wished to safeguard when he instructed the Humiliati next to the Dominican house of Sant'Eustorgio in Milan to come to an amicable agreement, even if this were to amount to a capitulation by the Humiliati.[63]

After 1246, the evidence of disputes, a revealing guide to the realities of power and to the issues which mattered to members of the order, show a powerful central organisation revolving around Milan. This is underlined by the first full record of a General Chapter, held in 1256 at Viboldone, just south of the city and still very much in Milanese territory. Within the order, Beltramus now held ultimate authority, but he did not (perhaps could not) act independently. On occasion Beltramus responded to instructions from the elected *diffinitores* and his position did not make him immune to criticism or disputes about his authority. Indeed, the tension between internal authority and that of the ultimate appeal court, the papal Curia, may have been exacerbated by the introduction of a Master whose intervention was sometimes slow. As well as the four senior provosts, certain superiors of Second order houses, in particular the ministers of the Brera, Milan and Sant'Agata in Monza, seem to have enjoyed wide authority. Nor did this prominence disappear later. The status of the Brera is confirmed when, in 1273, brother Bovus of the Brera was described as one of two vicars general of the whole order during a magisterial vacancy prompted by the resignation of Beltramus' successor, Peter *de Brissia*, in 1272.[64] Sant'Agata in Monza also remained important: in 1272, the provost and convent of the Humiliati house of brother William *de Canova* at Borgovico in Como intended to build a wall next to a stream which ran between

---

[63] See also below, pp. 242–4.
[64] Bovus was Vicar General in 1273 and 1279. The second Vicar General in 1273 was brother James of the *canonica* of Porta Orientale in Milan, perhaps the same man as the provost of that house described as the second vicar in 1279; Alberzoni, '"Sub eadem clausura sequestrati"', n. 108, and 'Il monastero di Sant'Ambrogio e i movimenti religiosi', n. 71.

their own vineyard and the vineyard of the neighbouring Humiliati of brother Atto *de Vico*. There was already a wall with holes in it through which the water flowed and although the new wall would be on their own land, their right to build was disputed by the brethren of the second house who argued that it would diminish the flow of water and prevent them from cleaning or working on the streambed. As the two sides were unable to resolve the dispute, each voluntarily submitted on pain of a 50 lire fine to the judgement of brother Redulfus, provost of the local First order house of Rondineto and brother Roger, the prelate of Sant'Agata in Monza, who in turn took the advice of a judge, Bertramus *de Falchis* of Como.[65] They determined that the existing wall should remain and others might be built as long as they left a fixed opening for the width of the streambed and did not restrict or obstruct it in any way. The choice of the superior of Sant'Agata as one of the judges suggests his status was still widely acknowledged in the order.

These changes show the Humiliati behaving increasingly like contemporary regular orders. The dispute over clerical precedence in particular bears comparison with contemporary conflict over the clericalisation of the Friars Minor. The large number of papal letters issued certainly reflects the better survival rate for documents from the mid-thirteenth century, but it also shows that the Humiliati now sent regular petitions to Rome and had both a proctor for the whole order and a cardinal protector. The relationship between this new order and the Church in the localities, of which they formed a part, will be the focus of the final chapter.

---

[65] Morelli, 'La casa di Rondineto', p. 23* and doc 8 (1272).

Chapter 8

THE HUMILIATI AND THE CHURCH IN
THE LOCALITIES

The relationship between the Humiliati and the Church in the localities, both secular and regular, is fundamental to understanding their identity as a religious order. Some recent studies have considered the situation in individual towns, but no attempt has yet been made to present a broader perspective.[1] New sources are continually appearing and will in future modify details of the account which follows. Nonetheless, it is worth constructing a framework, both as a counterweight to the view of the Humiliati as more or less exclusively a society of manufacturing and commercial experts, administrators and opportunists and to illustrate the nature of the order as an important, if localised, part of the Church.

As has already been argued, the evidence for the Humiliati in the twelfth century shows that they were closer to the establishment of the Church than hitherto recognised.[2] Indeed, after 1201, it was arguably their status as *religiosi*, as trustworthy members of the ecclesiastical establishment, which led to their appointment to communal offices and underlay their relationship with the laity studied by Zanoni. A first step, therefore, towards understanding their impact on the ordinary people of the towns of northern Italy is to establish the contours of their relationship with the institution inside which they operated: that is, within the Church.

It is not easy to isolate this relationship with the local Church, since neither institution was in any sense a homogeneous unit. Even the policies and actions of the papacy, which were in theory centrally directed, so that a single strategy may be identified during a particular pontificate, undoubtedly suffered the impact of inertia. The difficulties

---

[1] For example, Crotti Pasi, 'Gli Umiliati a Pavia', p. 336, see now also Mercatili Indelicato, 'Per una storia degli Umiliati nella diocesi di Lodi'; G. Archetti, 'Gli Umiliati e i vescovi alla fine del duecento. Il caso Bresciano', *Sulle tracce*, pp. 267–314.

[2] Above, pp. 59–63.

of coordinating activities are confirmed by the frequent repetition of the phrase 'if it be so' (*si est ita*) in papal letters, reflecting the dependency of the Curia on the version of events furnished by proctors, so that it was at best able to provide arm's length government. The Church in the localities, represented by the bishops, the secular clergy and the houses of the regular orders, was an even more composite organisation, about which generalisations can hardly be made. At the same time, the order of the Humiliati was extremely localised, so that the reality of one area or town, or even of one house, may often have been quite different to that in another. This variety itself is highly instructive, throwing light as it does both on the nature of the order itself and on the different responses it might elicit in the ecclesiastical hierarchy.

The relations of the Humiliati with the Church centred on their development of a quasi-pastoral role. This was the key element in conditioning relations with local ecclesiastics and an important channel for their relations with the laity. The first section of this chapter will therefore outline the development of this pastoral structure in some detail. The remainder of the chapter will then use a variety of approaches to examine the situation in practice, starting with the evidence of wills to show Humiliati involvement in the burial of the faithful and then concentrating in particular on their relations first with the bishops and secular clergy and second with the other regular orders in the areas in which they settled. This will give practical illustration of the role and standing of the Humiliati within the Church in the localities.

THE PASTORAL FRAMEWORK

A useful framework against which to measure the development of a pastoral structure by the Humiliati is provided by the almost contemporary emergence of the Mendicant orders. In the decades between 1218 and 1250, the Franciscans and Dominicans acquired a range of papal privileges which enabled them to create, in the words of Dal Pino, 'a second pastoral framework, flanking that of the parish clergy and to some extent in competition with it'.[3] This was based on a gradual accumulation of privileges, from the right to preach and hear confessions to authorisation to use portable altars and bury the laity in their churches. A short summary will provide a standard against which to assess the development of the rights of the Humiliati. The brief and

---

[3] Dal Pino, 'L'Evoluzione dell'idea di mendicità nel duecento', p. 26; see also P.-M. Gy, 'Le statut ecclésiologique de l'apostolat des prêcheurs et des mineurs avant la querelle des mendiants', *Revue des sciences philosophiques et théologiques*, 59 (1975), 79–88.

simplified chronology which follows is based in the first instance on the outline given by Dal Pino.[4]

The first step taken by the papacy in supporting the pastoral role of the Mendicants was to exhort the bishops to facilitate their mission and allow them to preach in their dioceses. Honorius III sent letters to this effect on behalf of the Dominicans in February 1218 and for the Friars Minor in June 1219.[5] To this was added the right to use portable altars for the celebration of the office in their communities without first obtaining the consent of the diocesan bishops, a privilege given to the Dominicans in May 1221 and to the Minors in 1224.[6] In March 1222, both orders also obtained licence to celebrate the office in time of interdict.[7] At this date there was little or no delay between the issuing of concessions to the Dominicans and their extension to the Franciscans. In other matters more fundamental to the care of souls, however, including confession and burial, a significant gap developed. This can partly be explained in terms of the relative clericalisation of the two orders, as well as the prohibition in the *Testament* of Francis on petitioning privileges from the Roman Curia.[8] Thus perhaps as early as 1221 and certainly by 1227, Honorius III asked the bishops to allow the Dominicans to hear the confession of the faithful, while the Franciscans received the clear right to hear the confession of those who attended their sermons only in 1237.[9] This was extended to all the faithful by Innocent IV only in 1250, twenty-three years after the acquisition of the same privilege by the Dominicans, and still caused problems. A similar pattern is repeated concerning burial rights: although the Minors were the first to obtain a concession, issued in July 1227, this was limited to the burial of their own brethren.[10] In November of the same year, the Dominicans obtained a far more extensive privilege, allowing them to bury all those who requested it, a freedom granted to the Minors again only in February 1250.[11] Finally, the churches of the order of Preachers were declared *conventuales*, or public, by Gregory IX in 1228, while those of the Minors achieved this status only in 1250.[12] Thus the Dominicans enjoyed the full range of pastoral privileges already by the

---

[4] Dal Pino, 'L'Evoluzione dell'idea di mendicità nel duecento', pp. 26–7.

[5] *BF* I, p. 2; *Historia diplomatica sancti Dominici*, 98.

[6] *BF* I, p. 20; *Historia diplomatica sancti Dominici*, 143.

[7] *BF* I, pp. 9–10.   [8] Francis of Assisi, *Testament*, p. 68.

[9] *BF* I, pp. 214–15; the passage concerning the Dominicans and confession was in the copy of the 1221 letter used by Ripoll and Bremond in the *Bullarium ordinis fratrum praedicatorum*, but has not since been found; see Rusconi, 'I francescani e la confessione nel secolo xiii', p. 270 n. 59; on Franciscans and confession, see Moorman, *A History of the Franciscan Order*, pp. 121–2, 181–3.

[10] *BF* I, p. 31.   [11] Summary, *BF* I, p. 555.   [12] *BF* I, p. 538.

late 1220s, while the Franciscans attained the same standing only in mid-century.

The pattern for the Humiliati, with its three theoretically distinct elements, necessarily strays quite widely from this model and certain steps are missing altogether. Nonetheless, some of the stages are there and the comparison is illuminating. Perhaps most significant is the delay in providing official backing for the Humiliati as preachers. Except for support for Tertiary meetings (*colloquia*), advocated by Innocent III in 1201 and again in 1211 by Gerard *de Sesso*, his legate, it was left to Innocent IV in 1249 to make a universal claim for the Humiliati as preachers, praising their knowledge and eloquence and ordering archbishops and bishops to allow them to preach the word of God publicly in their cities and dioceses.[13] Similarly, the right to use portable altars, given to the Mendicants in the early 1220s, was conceded only in part to the Humiliati, more than a decade later. In January 1236, Gregory IX wrote to the archbishop of Milan and his suffragans, asking them to allow the Humiliati to celebrate the office with portable altars in the regular (*non seculares*) houses of the order which did not have their own churches. This letter, however, was couched in terms which gave the bishops much greater leeway than that allowed them for the Mendicants: the concession was to be made if it appeared fitting and would not damage others (*si videritis expedire . . . sine preiudicio alieni*).[14]

In one area the Humiliati of the First order did precede the Mendicants, but it was a privilege which was more closely related to the internal life of their communities than to the care of souls outside them. In 1201 *Non omni spiritui* authorised them to celebrate the office during interdicts, with members of the Second order present, behind closed doors and in low voices, without ringing bells.[15] As we have seen, the Dominicans acquired this privilege only several years after their approval. The concession to the Humiliati gave permission for the Second order to attend and this was extended later: in 1227 Gregory IX wrote to the 'brothers and sisters of the Humiliati' (without specifying which order), allowing them to attend the office, to make confession and bury their dead during interdicts.[16] This may also have included the Tertiaries, but these were only specifically mentioned in 1246 when, in response to a petition, Innocent IV gave a similar privilege to the Third order.[17] In the same year, Innocent IV's fundamental, reforming decree, *Ex ore domini*, sent to both the First and Second orders, repeated the privilege given to the First order in 1201, allowing them to celebrate the

---

[13] Appendix I, 7, *16, 73.   [14] Appendix I, 47.   [15] Appendix I, 9.
[16] Appendix I, 24.   [17] Appendix I, 57, see also appendix I, *119.

office during interdicts, but made no reference to confession.[18] Presumably, the 1227 privilege allowing them to make confession was still in use.

Although these records suggest the Humiliati were considered preachers, as the accounts of Jacques de Vitry and the letter of Innocent IV of 1249 illustrate, this was not linked to the care of souls and they did not achieve the independent pastoral status of the Friars Minor or Preacher in this period.[19] The care of souls exercised by the Mendicants was imposed by the papacy and gradually extended to the inquisition and control of hospitals, significantly modifying the wider pastoral structure and often excluding the bishops.[20] That of the Humiliati remained to some extent dependent on the bishops. Unless the letters have been lost, which seems unlikely, since copies would undoubtedly have been made, we must assume that they did not officially enjoy the freedom to hear confession and minister to all the faithful from 'public' churches achieved by both Mendicant orders by mid-century.

There are several possible explanations for this difference, though the weight given to each must depend more on personal preference than any clear evidence. The heretically tinged past of the Humiliati may have played a role, as may their apparent lack of a strong, central organisation to focus on such issues early on. Their failure to find a strong supporter in the Curia comparable to Hugolino, whose enthusiasm undoubtedly pushed the Franciscans into the limelight, may also have been important. The first cardinal protector was Otto *de Tonengo*, only appointed in the 1240s.[21] Similarly, the failure of the Humiliati to move into the universities and to attract some of the great minds of their generation, or to spread beyond the boundaries of northern and central Italy, may have been determining factors. Such reflections, however, contribute little to our understanding of the position of the Humiliati themselves. Examination of the situation among the Humiliati in practice will provide a more fruitful approach.

In principle the First order enjoyed greater official freedom than the Second which, as an enclosed order, had no external pastoral role. They were often dependent on the First order or on parish churches for the essential offices of the sacrament, at least until 1246.[22] There is some later evidence to suggest that this distinction was in practice perceived to be important: in 1251 the Dominicans of Milan insisted that the new community of the Humiliati next door must not create a *canonica* of the

---

[18] Appendix I, 59, see also above, pp. 207–8.   [19] On Vitry, above, p. 188.
[20] See Violante, 'Le istituzioni ecclesiastiche nell'Italia centro-settentrionale durante il medioevo: province, diocesi, sedi vescovili', p. 111.
[21] See p. 206.   [22] Appendix I, 63, above, pp. 107, 145.

First or 'greater order' (*maioris ordinis*), presumably because they thought this would bring wider rights and present a greater threat.[23] Several Second order houses did, however, have churches before this date and both the papal letters and the notarial records raise doubts about the comprehensive nature of the distinction between communities in the two orders.[24] Examination of the evidence for the involvement of the Humiliati in the burial of the faithful, one of the most important and best-documented aspects of the care of souls, provides a useful way of illustrating the problems. It will also once more illuminate the dichotomy between idea and practice so often present in the history of religious movements.

THE HUMILIATI AND THE BUSINESS OF DEATH

Burial

The bulls approving the Humiliati in 1201 made no reference to burial, except to decree that members of the Third order were to attend each other's funerals, saying the Lord's prayer twelve times and the *Miserere* for their souls.[25] The privilege for the community of Viboldone, however, issued by Urban III in 1186 and renewing an earlier privilege of Alexander III, had allowed for the free burial of any who might choose to be interred there (*qui se illic sepeliri deliberaverint*), saving only the rights of the Church from which the dead were taken.[26] Whether or not this clause had been included in Alexander's bull, there is some evidence that the practice may have been established at Viboldone in the 1170s. In 1176 Guy *de Porta Orientale* and the brethren of the community arranged compensation to the local priest for the revenues which he might lose because of their presence in his *pieve*.[27] No reference was made to the burial of the dead in this document, but oblations were specifically mentioned and might well be associated with the provision of such a service. What is certain is that by 1186 at least, the Viboldone community was authorised to bury the faithful.

There are a small number of other early references to burial and cemeteries associated with the Humiliati. The community at the Brera in Milan obtained the right to have a cemetery early in their history. In 1201, or soon after, Philip *de Lampugnano*, archbishop of Milan, allowed the house to have an oratory and 'free' cemetery (*liberum*).[28] They may

---

[23] On this dispute see pp. 242–4.   [24] Above, pp. 127, 146–7.   [25] Appendix I, 7.
[26] Appendix I, 3; see also x.3.28, 'De sepulturis'.
[27] On Guy and this agreement, see above, p. 46.
[28] Appendix I, *10.

not, however, have had a cemetery before 1229–30, since there is evidence that their church was not built until that date.[29] Another relatively early reference to a Humiliati cemetery comes from Genoa, where the daughter-house of San Michele in Alessandria requested permission to have an oratory and cemetery in 1228, but no details are as yet known.[30] Finally, in 1236, one of the witnesses in a dispute between the bishop of Lodi and the community of Ognissanti near Lodi recalls the burial in their church of a woman whose status in relation to the community was then in dispute.[31]

It is not clear from these references how 'free' was interpreted, but other documents provide some clues. As we have seen, in 1227 Gregory IX allowed the 'brothers and sisters of the order of the Humiliati' concessions during times of interdict and this included the right to be buried in a church cemetery, though without solemn rites.[32] The same privilege was specifically extended to the Third order in 1246.[33] In the meantime, in 1236 Gregory IX ordered the archbishop of Milan to allow the Humiliati to administer the sacraments to the Second order and to have cemeteries for their own use, but to ensure that any churches in their neighbourhoods (*vicinie*) were not cheated of their customary oblations and other rights.[34] On the basis of these documents it would appear that, in official terms, 'free' meant freely burying their own brethren. The Brera community, however, seems also to have been burying, or expecting to bury, lay members of the parish in which their house stood. This is implicit in the agreement drawn up with the priest of the parish church of Sant'Eusebio about compensation, since the archbishop and his chapter had now authorised any member of the *vicinia* to choose to have themselves interred in the newly built church.[35] The agreement was stipulated in the presence of the archbishop, Henry *de Settala*, and in his palace. Paganus, minister of the Brera, gave 33 lire to William, the priest of Sant'Eusebio, in compensation for any loss which his church might incur and specifically because of the funerals or oblations which the Humiliati might thus take away from the church of Sant'Eusebio. This was done in the presence of five men attested as representatives of the *vicinia* and two members of the Cagapisto family, who held the *iuspatronatus* of the church.[36] The priest

---

[29] Appendix I, *38. See also above, p. 143.
[30] M. Calleri, 'Su alcuni "libri iurium" deperditi del monastero di San Siro di Genova', *Atti della società ligure di storia patria*, new series 34 (1994), 157–84.
[31] See Mercatili Indelicato, 'Per una storia degli Umiliati nella diocesi di Lodi', pp. 482–3.
[32] Appendix I, 24.   [33] Appendix I, 57.   [34] Appendix I, 46.
[35] Appendix I, *38: 'possit se ordinare sepeliendum in ecclesia predicta de Braida, et ibi sepulturum [Tiraboschi = sepulcrum] eligere et habere'.
[36] On the Cagapisto family, see above, pp. 49–50.

of Sant'Eusebio was to be invited to any funerals of members of the *vicinia* and whether he came or not, or wished to come and even if the *vicinus* did not want him there, he was to receive the same oblation as he would have received had he been present. For the burial of members of the *vicinia* who were members of the order (Tertiaries), the rights of the Brera or of their own church were also specifically protected.[37] The laity's desire for association with the new order could thus be expressed not only by joining the Tertiaries, but also by remaining outside the order yet choosing burial in a regular community.

Already in 1230 the Brera community had the right, recognised by the secular hierarchy, to bury the faithful of their parish, even apparently within the walls of their own church. The Brera, however, was a large and powerful community and this is the only such concession for a regular community extant in these years. There are other examples of concessions given for a particular house to have a cemetery: in 1232 the Second order house of Humiliati in Tortona was given a church by the bishop and Berardus I dal Pozzobello, archpriest of Monza (1232–4) allowed the Humiliati of Sant'Agata in the *borgo* to have an oratory and cemetery (c. 1233).[38] The freedom enjoyed by the communities of Viboldone and Brera was not authorised, however, in these cases. In Monza, the cemetery was to be for their own and their household's use and that of members of the order and no others unless they had special permission.[39] In Tortona, the brethren were specifically forbidden to bury any outsiders except members of the First and Third orders and the latter were still to pay the canonical oblations (*canonicorum porcio oblacionum*) to their parish church. Such evidence suggests that distinctions between communities of the order lay between those large and powerful enough to win support, such as Viboldone and the Brera and smaller, less well-placed and therefore less powerful houses such as those in Monza and Tortona.

In 1246 the official position changed. *Ex ore domini* authorised communities of both the First and Second orders to bury freely any who so chose (*qui se illic sepeliri deliberaverint*), unless excommunicate or public usurers.[40] As elsewhere, however, in this case practice did not always follow suit. The details of the gift of a church and cemetery made by the bishop of Acqui to the Humiliati of the city in the 1250s do not survive, but a concession made in 1250 by Arderic *de Soresina*, archpriest of Monza (1245–51), four years after the privilege, allowing

---

[37] See also above, p. 163.   [38] Appendix I, *42, *43.

[39] Appendix I, *43: 'statuentes ut a modo liberum habeat cimiterium nobis [leg. uobis] uestraeque familiae omnibusque ordinis Humiliatorum et non aliis, nisi de nostra speciali licentia'.

[40] Appendix I, 59.

the Humiliati of Mediovico to have a cemetery, used the same limitations, indeed even the same language, as the concession made by his predecessor seventeen years earlier.[41] The Humiliati were to bury only their own, unless with special permission. Even twenty-five years later, in 1275, William, bishop of Ferrara (1274–86) and apostolic legate, who gave all three orders permission to build churches in which to hear the office, specified that they should be without cemeteries.[42] The principle of 'free' burial was clearly not unchallenged and, once more, the dichotomy between idea (as expressed in the papal letters) and local practice is underlined.

Nor is evidence that the Humiliati were actually burying the faithful in these communities easy to find. The implied identification of the practice of burial with references to cemeteries made here is not of course inevitable. Burial was also possible within the area of a church or oratory itself, as the 1230 Brera agreement seems to have recognised and as occurred in Lodi. There is, however, little concrete evidence: the extant churches of the order date from the second half of the thirteenth century or later and no earlier tombs appear to survive.[43] Yet there is some confirmation of this practice late in the century. In February 1293 Grimaldus of Castelvecchio, a *magister lignaminum*, left 100 shillings in his will to the Humiliati of Siena for the construction of their church and asked to be buried at the Humiliati house in Siena.[44] Grimaldus was a Tertiary, but evidence from Lodi suggests that a Humiliati church might also be popular as a burial place with others: on 23 April 1307 the commune of Lodi agreed to pay a yearly sum in times of peace for the repair of the Humiliati church of San Cristoforo and to ensure that the materials for the office were available, because the bodies of many from Lodi were buried there.[45] This was a First order community which had been important in the early history of the movement, and is well documented in the thirteenth century, letting property and pursuing the normal administrative activities recorded by notaries.[46] This agreement suggests, however, that the house had fallen on hard times by the beginning of the fourteenth century. The bodies

---

[41] Appendix I, *86; Savio, *Gli antichi vescovi d'Italia*, I, p. 45, under the dates 1252–8, but with no further details.

[42] *VHM* II, p. 308.   [43] Above, p. 146.

[44] Angelucci, 'Gli Umiliati di Siena e la chiesa del borgo franco di Paganico', p. 266.

[45] *CDL*, II/2, p. 600, 'habentes etiam respectum quod in dicta canonica multa laudensium corpora requiescunt'.

[46] See appendix I, 5, above, pp. 55–6, 69, 107–8, and ASMi 187, Lodi, S. Domenico, 107 (6 September/December 1248), 110 (5 February 1250); one of the witnesses in the second document was Peter *de verdello qui est batitor lane*, a rare reference to links with the wool industry; see now Mercatili Indelicato, 'Per una storia degli Umiliati nella diocesi di Lodi', pp. 440–70.

might be those of their own brethren, as well as those from the Second and Third orders. They may have included benefactors such as Bregundius Denarii, who chose burial there in 1236 (and may have belonged to the order),[47] but they seem no less likely to have been lay citizens, towards whom the commune would perhaps have felt greater obligation.

The evidence of wills

Although documentary evidence for lay burials on Humiliati ground is difficult to find, their members were certainly actively involved in the business of death: as executors and beneficiaries of the wills of lay patrons and receiving legacies which may often have been associated with the expenses of funerals. Use of this sort of evidence is not without difficulties.[48] Wills were constructed using notarial formulations which may have standardised the language and motives of an individual testator. As well as their many implications for religious history, wills are a key means for understanding family, patrimonial and economic history. Testators were motivated by the desire to control the destiny of their property and to avoid conflict, as well as by concerns about the after life. Considering pious bequests in isolation is therefore hazardous as a guide to religious fervour. Moreover, at this date statistical surveys of the numbers of wills and the size of donations are unhelpful, since unknown factors such as an individual's total wealth and personal contacts and the varying rate of survival of documents in different archives distort any result obtained beyond any useful meaning.

Nonetheless, as Severino Polica has noted, death provided the occasion for the expression of cultural traditions,[49] and wills are a record, however imperfect, of that expression. Despite statistical difficulties, wills are also quantitatively one of the best sources for the relations between the laity and religious groups such as the Humiliati or the Friars.[50] We can never be sure who was not receiving money, but at least we have some indication of who was. Appendix III provides a sample of wills recording legacies to the Humiliati or their activities as executors from various north Italian towns. This is not a complete list. In Verona alone, numerous other such documents survive from later in

---

[47] Appendix III, 8.

[48] For an excellent introduction see *'Nolens intestatus decedere'. Il testamento come fonte della storia religiosa e sociale* (Perugia, 1985).

[49] G. Severino Polica, 'Morte e cultura ecclesiastica nel duecento', *Studi Storici*, 21 (1980), 909–14, 914.

[50] See the comment by Bartoli Langeli in the introductory note to *'Nolens intestatus decedere'*, p. xvi.

the century and there is neither space nor benefit to justify a comprehensive survey here.[51] Moreover, in spite of the loss of perspective, bequests to family have been omitted, leaving only pious bequests, because the religious and ecclesiastical context for the Humiliati is thereby underlined. Although small, the sample allows several qualitative points to be illustrated, both about the Humiliati themselves and about their relations with the laity and, indirectly, the local Church.

The first and most obvious point to make is that these wills show the Humiliati benefiting directly from the 'spirituality of beneficence' identified by Vauchez as emerging between 1130 and 1260.[52] As early as 1195, Sotius *de Campo Longo* left 40 shillings for his soul to the Humiliati of San Cristoforo in Lodi, and in December 1198 Albert Niger left a share in tithes from Fançago to the same community.[53] In September 1226, Mannara gave 40 shillings to each Humiliati house in Verona and diocese and 10 lire to the Ghiara.[54] In 1227 a canon of Bergamo left money to the Humiliati of the Galgario, and in January 1229 Bregundius Denarii left land and his house with all pots and other utensils to the Humiliati of Lodi, in which he wished them to establish a community, as well as money for annual masses, while seven years later he added a gift of bedding to San Cristoforo, where he wished to be buried.[55] Other examples can be listed for different areas, though most are later.[56] In some cases it is clear that family ties lay behind the legacies. In 1258 Bonaventure left land to two daughters, one of whom was dedicated (*edidicata*) in the Ghiara house in Verona.[57] His legacy to the Humiliati was intended for his daughter and given to the minister on her behalf. Similar patterns are to be found in wills from Zevio, Porto and Verona, and others may have been inspired by similar motives.[58] All gave money or land to the Humiliati specifically because their children were in their houses, a reminder that charity was bound to family interests, a point also made clear in donations for masses and prayers for the souls of relatives.[59] It is perhaps particularly significant, in the context of Humiliati relations with the local Church, that these legacies included bequests from the clergy. In 1227, 1252 and 1259 the

---

[51] See also Mercatili Indelicato, 'Per una riconsiderazione del lavoro presso gli Umiliati. Il caso di Lodi', appendix.
[52] Vauchez, 'Assistance et charité en occident, xiiie–xve siècles', p. 152.
[53] Appendix III, 1, 2; see p. 56. Albert Niger is perhaps related to members of the *de Nigro* family linked with the Humiliati in 1225 and 1272; Mercatili Indelicato, 'Per una riconsiderazione del lavoro presso gli Umiliati. Il caso di Lodi', p. 147 and n. 120.
[54] Appendix III, 6.   [55] Appendix III, 7, 8.
[56] See appendix III, 11 (1239), 14 (1242), 17 (1250), 19 (1253), 20 (1253/7), 21a–b (1253), 22 (12[56]).
[57] Appendix III, 23.   [58] Appendix III, 9 (c. 1234) 12 (1240), 16 (before 1250).
[59] Appendix III, 22 (12[56]); see also Epstein, *Wills and Wealth in Medieval Genoa*, p. v.

Humiliati of the Galgario in Bergamo received legacies from canons of the city.[60] Some local clergy at least were supportive of the new order, not threatened by their presence.

These legacies are not on the scale of benefactions to the Friars. In Bergamo, for example, of 181 extant wills between 1200 and 1350, 39 from the thirteenth century favoured the Dominicans or Franciscans, while only 7 included bequests for the Humiliati.[61] Yet wills also show the Humiliati engaged in the administration of lay beneficence, acting as executors or distributors of bequests (*errogatari et dispensatores*). Like the Friars, the Humiliati and their co-executors were part of the process which enabled the laity to reconcile the demands of religion with the acquisition of wealth. In particular, they undertook to distribute legacies to the poor. In 1215 Pantanus, Finus and Bartholomew of the Ghiara were chosen to distribute property left by Albertinus amongst the poor, 'as they thought it would be most pleasing to God and most useful to his soul'.[62] Similar duties of distribution, either generically to the poor, or 'as they saw fit', were entrusted to Humiliati in Milan, Vimercate, Marliano, Porto and Bergamo as well as in Verona.[63] No doubt these executors sometimes took advantage of the ear of the dying to win money and legacies for their own houses. The fear that such dealings were going on was to lead to their prohibition among the Friars Minor in the constitutions of Narbonne in 1260 and there is no reason to suppose that the Humiliati were not tempted.[64] Certainly funerals and legacies were important sources of revenue and competition, as witnessed by restrictions in communal statutes such as those from Brescia on any payments to clergy, confraters or priests not living at the church where the body was to be buried.[65] In some wills the Humiliati were both beneficiaries and executors.[66] In 1253 Mucius *de Ferarino* left ploughland to the poor, to be distributed by the minister of the Ghiara, but in 1257 he consented to a change, so that the land would go to the Humiliati themselves 'in place of the poor'.[67] Perhaps such agreements were facilitated by the presence of some of the testators in the houses of the order: in 1258 Bonaventure *de Maga* added a codicil to his will

[60] Appendix III, 7, 18, 24; Brolis, *Gli Umiliati a Bergamo*, pp. 41–7, p. 203 and appendix.
[61] Brolis, *Gli Umiliati a Bergamo*, p. 199; De Sandre Gasparini found a similar gap in Verona, 'Il francescanesimo a Verona. Note dai testamenti', p. 122 and n. 135.
[62] Appendix III, 3.
[63] Appendix III, 4 (1224), 5 (1225), 6 (1226), 10 (1237), 11 (1239), 13 (1241), 14 (1242), 15 (1242), 20 (1253/7).
[64] Constitutions of Narbonne 1260: 'Et cum in testamento interfuerint non procurent sibi vel cognatis suis aliquid erogari'. Bonaventure, *Opera omnia*, VIII, p. 452, see also U. Nicolini, 'I Frati Minori da eredi a esecutori testamentari' in *'Nolens intestatus decedere'*, pp. 31–3.
[65] 'Statuti di Brescia', p. 127 (1277). [66] Appendix III, 6 (1226), 11 (1239), 14 (1242).
[67] Appendix III, 20 (1253/7).

when lying in 'the house of the Humiliati brethren where the sick reside'.[68] This may not have been a hospital, but in other towns the Humiliati were working in hospitals and such contacts with the sick and dying must have added to the benefactions made to them.[69] This need not mean that they wished to defraud the deceased or others with rights to the property. In a failed attempt to prevent disputes, in April 1276 the Humiliati of the Brera in Milan, together with the house of Sta Trinità and the Cistercians of Chiaravalle, as heirs of James Crivelli, a judge, declared themselves ready to restore any property which had been acquired through usury.[70]

On the basis of these wills, it could hardly be argued that the Humiliati enjoyed popularity comparable to the 'philo-franciscanism' recently illustrated in Padua and Vicenza.[71] Nonetheless, they show the lay response to the Humiliati *qua* religious: gifts were given to them for the benefit of souls as they were to other religious. When they were appointed as executors, this was sometimes alongside lay relatives of the testator, but was also sometimes with clerics.[72] Thus in 1242 the executors of Ventura *de Brivio* included the archpriest of San Vincenzo in Novara and the priest of San Prancati as well as the Humiliati and a layman.[73] Such ties may have been imposed by the testators but they also show the context inside which the Humiliati operated.

The legacies in these wills illustrate the other demands on a testator's pious generosity. In 1195 Sotius *de Campo Longo* in Lodi made bequests to the cathedral works, the works on the church of San Biagio in the city and the priest there for masses, the hospital of San Biagio outside and the *canonica* of San Sepolcro beyond the Adda, as well as to the Humiliati of San Cristoforo.[74] In 1224, Ruba *de Balsemo*, whose close links with the Franciscans in Milan have recently been detailed, also gave money to several new groups in the city, including, to name only the most prominent, the Friars Minor, the Dominicans (who had recently arrived at Sant'Eustorgio), the hospital of the Brolo, the poor women of Pontecredario, the ministers of the Humiliati *de Senedogo* and generically, the poor 'who shall appear in greatest need'.[75] Over two

---

[68] Appendix III, 23.   [69] Above, pp. 50–1, 53–4, 165, 171 and appendix I, *104.

[70] *Gli atti del comune di Milano* II/2, 714 (30 April 1276), 733 (17 September 1276); see Caso, *I Crivelli. Una famiglia milanese*, p. 43; Alberzoni, 'L'esperienza caritativa presso gli Umiliati', pp. 208–9.

[71] De Sandre Gasparini, 'Il francescanesimo a Verona', p. 124; see also Rigon, 'Francescanesimo e società a Padova nel duecento', pp. 8–26 and M. Apolloni, 'Testamenti in favore dei Frati Minori di S. Lorenzo a Vicenza tra 1280 e 1348', *Il santo*, 30 (1990), 181–237.

[72] See for example, appendix III, 13 (1241), 14 (1242).

[73] Appendix III, 14.   [74] Appendix III, 1.

[75] Appendix III, 4 (1224); Alberzoni, 'I primi francescani a Milano. Note sul testamento di "Ruba

decades later, the will of a Torinese noble, William Gratapallea, reveals a similarly wide scope; as well as to the Humiliati, he left money to churches in Chiusi and Turin, to hospitals in Turin, including the hospital of San Giacomo, to the Friars Minor and for two knights (*milites*), or more if the pope wished, to be sent to the Holy Land.[76]

The Humiliati were only one of innumerable demands on lay beneficence, but such evidence shows that as a deserving cause they had caught the imagination of the laity and acquired a status paralleling contemporary religious groups. They were also closely involved in the pastoral concerns of the laity. What they achieved could never be termed a secondary pastoral framework flanking that of the parish clergy as constructed by and for the Friars Minor and the Dominicans. There is further evidence, however, which suggests that their impact was not inconsiderable. Other groups, including the Mendicants and the more traditional regular and secular institutions of the Church, do occasionally seem to have seen the Humiliati as competitors and as a threat to their livelihood.

THE HUMILIATI, THE BISHOPS AND THE SECULAR CLERGY

The ground rules for the relationship between the bishops and the new order were drawn out in the papal letters of 1201. By the very act of approving the Humiliati himself, Innocent III, as Maccarrone has noted, implicitly affirmed the new principle that canonical legislation concerning religious was the competence of the Apostolic see and no longer left solely to the care of the diocesan bishops.[77] As in other areas, including canonisation, the papacy was gradually arrogating to itself tasks previously entrusted to the bishops, whether by intention or default. These developments may not have contributed to tension between popes and bishops, since the papacy often simply acted on the advice of prelates, but other factors certainly did so, including the close involvement of both sides in the factional politics of their dioceses.[78] Each was concerned to forward their own policies and interests, which occasionally led to trials of strength, such as that between Innocent III and Philip *de Lampugnano*, archbishop of Milan at the turn of the century (1196–1206). After a series of differences of opinion with the pope, Philip was finally forced or at least strongly encouraged to resign in the

---

de Balsemo" (1224)', 144–62; now also discussed in her *Francescanesimo a Milano nel duecento*, pp. 118–31.

[76] Appendix III, 17 (1250).   [77] Maccarrone, *Studi*, p. 290.

[78] See Andrews, 'Innocent III and evangelical enthusiasts: the route to approval', in *Innocent III and his World*, ed. J. C. Moore ((forthcoming) Hofstra, 1999).

autumn of 1206, a few months before his death.[79] Nor was Philip's case
the only such example. The *Gesta* of Innocent III reports that Innocent
also forced others to go, including the bishops of Asti and Ivrea.[80] His
letters confirm this, for example, bishop John Gagnino of Ivrea,
described by Innocent as 'inadequate and ineffectual,' was deposed in
January 1206.[81]

There were of course bishops who were papal appointees, or at least
enjoyed papal support, as demonstrated by the careers of Albert of
Vercelli and Peter of Lucedio, who replaced John Gagnino in Ivrea.[82]
Nonetheless, in the context of their occasionally tense relations with the
papacy, some bishops may have considered the papally approved
Humiliati as an encroachment on their jurisdiction. Added to this was
their dubious status as previously condemned heretics who, moreover,
had been censured because of their refusal to recognise ecclesiastical
authority over preaching, hardly an attitude likely to endear them to
their bishops. Certainly other groups reconciled to the Church,
including the Catholic Poor of Durand of Huesca, did face episcopal
opposition.[83]

In the letters of 1201 to the First and Third orders, Innocent III and
his delegates had revealed an understanding both of the potential areas
of tension between the bishops and the new order and of the ways in
which this might be expressed. They had made some attempt to forestall
the difficulties, giving the bishops clear authority over some areas of the
new order's activities but limiting it in others. As befitted their office,
the bishops were to be responsible for many of the external and financial
aspects of the new order. *Incumbit nobis* established that they were to
oversee the payment of tithes and first fruits by the Third order.[84] *Non
omni spiritui* gave them control over the First order's right to receive
tithes and to accept or build new churches.[85] It also acknowledged the
need to protect the status of other churches and clergy where the
appearance of a new religious house might prejudice both their prestige
and their revenues from the care of souls.

The bishops therefore had quite strong resources of control in
external affairs, touching upon the revenues of Humiliati churches. In
more fundamental matters concerning their way of life and evangelism
however, they were largely excluded. They were nominally responsible

---

79 See Alberzoni, 'Nel conflitto tra papato e impero: da Galdino della Sala a Guglielmo da Rizolio
(1166–1241)', pp. 234–5.
80 *Gesta*, cols. clxxii–clxxiii: 'induxit vel coegit ad cessionem Mediolanensem archiepiscopum,
Astensem, Iporiensem episcopos'.
81 *Ivrea*, I, pp. 216–17: 'insufficiens et inutilis'; *PL*, 215, cols. 777–91, Potthast, 2672.
82 Above, pp. 83–9.
83 See Grundmann, pp. 107–8.   84 Appendix I, 7.   85 Appendix I, 9.

for licensing the exhortations of members of the Third order, but were specifically warned not to withhold permission, so that their responsibility was reduced to little more than a rubber stamp.[86] Similarly, the election of superiors in the First order was subject to episcopal confirmation, but the bishops were warned not to withhold it maliciously. Moreover, while the First order was normally expected to receive the Chrism, holy oil, consecration of altars and ordination of priests from their diocesan bishop and to obtain his authorisation for their churches, they were also authorised to go elsewhere if the bishop were not catholic and did not offer these services freely, a clause which amounted at least implicitly to a threat to the bishops. Finally, visitation of the communities of the order was to be carried out by the provosts of the main houses themselves, thereby removing the most powerful weapon for intervention and correction from the hands of the diocesan ordinary.

The churchmen responsible for agreeing these regulations in 1201 may have had in mind the hostility shown towards the Humiliati in the area of Verona, which Innocent had attempted to circumvent in his letter to bishop Adelard in 1199 concerning the distinction between incorrigible heretics and the Humiliati.[87] The 1201 approval did not, however, put an end to hostility. Some bishops were far from keen to adopt papal policies at the best of times and the relatively independent status of the new order, combined with a quasi-heretical beginning, may have made the Humiliati difficult for some to accept. In Faenza in 1206, Innocent himself seems to have accepted that individuals using the name of Humiliati were to be condemned as heretics.[88] Apart from the Cerea episode in 1203 and a reference to some 'less than Catholic' practices still observed at the Brera in 1226, there is no other evidence for the heretical associations of the Humiliati after 1201 and, as we have seen, the new order by no means had a monopoly on use of the name. There is therefore no reason to suppose either that the individuals condemned at Faenza formed a splinter group from the orthodox Humiliati or that they had any direct links with the Humiliati approved in 1201. Nonetheless, such problems may have lain behind the decision in 1211 of Gerard *de Sesso*, papal legate, perhaps prompted by James of Rondineto, to remind the bishops and clergy of his legation that the Humiliati order was pleasing to both the pope and his legate. The issue here was clearly the Humiliati's heretical past. Gerard reminded the bishops that the integrity of the Humiliati had been approved by the

---

[86] Appendix I, 7.   [87] Appendix I, 4.   [88] Appendix I, 11.

235

Roman Church and went on to warn them not to hinder their meetings, even exhorting the prelates to attend these themselves.[89]

In spite of such highly placed patrons, relations with the bishops were not always smooth. According to depositions made by a witness in the 1230s during a dispute between the community of Ognissanti near Lodi and the bishop, there was long-standing episcopal opposition to the building of their church. Bishop Arderic (1189–1217) had argued that it should be under his authority, a claim apparently in line with the privileges of 1201, while the Humiliati, led by their provost Lanfranc, claimed a special privilege giving them the right to build a house and church 'wherever he wished, without the consent of the bishop'.[90] The status of Ognissanti was still disputed in the 1230s, but in the meantime the same bishop had given the community a chapel of San Giorgio at Fossadolto, subject to his jurisdiction.[91] On the death of the provost, he had also come to pay his respects.[92]

Violante, working on Brescia, suggested that the Humiliati were never greatly liked by bishops of any diocese and explained this in terms of their 'insolent determination' in enforcing the recognition of their rights of exemption and the contribution they thus made to the existing disorder in the local Church.[93] He based his argument on evidence concerning two episodes in Brescia. The first was a long-running dispute over the church of SS Faustino e Giovitta which the bishops of Brescia refused to give to the Humiliati despite papal instructions; the second was an altercation between bishop Berardus Maggi and the Humiliati of San Luca in the 1270s.[94] Such disputes were sometimes dramatic: in 1277 as part of a dispute partly over revenues bishop Berardus attempted to carry out visitation of the Humiliati of San Luca in the company of some canons of Brescia and members of his retinue. He was met with locked doors and chains. According to his own account, he waited outside for some time, had his *ministrale* John Corvus call out that he was there and wished to carry out visitation and three times ordered the community to open the door. When the episcopal party started to leave, the provost and some of the brethren came out and shouted after them. The bishop then returned and had mass celebrated in the Humiliati church, but none of the brethren

---

[89] Appendix I,*16: 'cum in fidei integritate sancte nostre romane ecclesie per divinas scripturas ab orthodoxis ecclesie probati sint'.

[90] *VHM* II, p. 186 and Mercatili Indelicato, 'Per una storia degli Umiliati nella diocesi di Lodi', p. 479.

[91] Appendix I, 12, 35; see also *ibid.*, 39.

[92] Mercatili Indelicato, 'Per una storia degli Umiliati nella diocesi di Lodi', p. 479.

[93] Violante, 'La chiesa bresciana nel medioevo', p. 1073.

[94] *Ibid.*, pp. 1075, 1095; see now Archetti, 'Gli Umiliati e i vescovi alla fine del duecento', pp. 303–5, 278–85.

attended. The bishop then repeated his right to visit the house and to preach there saying that he had heard that it was in a poor state, but the provost denied his authority to do so. After eight days' warning the bishop placed them under interdict and sentence of excommunication.[95]

This conflict over control may have been particularly bitter against the house which provided the first two Masters General of the order. Such high-profile figures as Beltramus and Peter would certainly appear as an alternative pole of authority to the bishop and be likely to make the bishops more wary.[96] However, this dispute formed part of a wider conflict over visitation and procurations with the combined forces of the bishop of Brescia, the archbishop of Milan, Otto Visconti (1263–95) and another Visconti partisan, bishop William *de Avvogadri* of Como (1275–93). The Humiliati were eventually victorious, obtaining papal exemption from episcopal authority in 1288.[97] Yet this crisis should not be seen as an inevitable dénouement towards which all earlier episodes were moving. These difficulties date largely from the second half of the thirteenth century when the situation was undoubtedly dominated by new tensions about pastoral rights, provoked by disputes with the Mendicants. The dispute had as much to do with the political agenda of the three bishops as with the state of the order. There were signs of difficulties elsewhere early on, but there were also signs of comfortable coexistence, if not outright episcopal enthusiasm.

As has already been argued, the early Humiliati were far more a part of the Church establishment than previous studies have recognised. Some communities received churches from bishops and were accepted as part of the ecclesiastical hierarchy.[98] The settlement made at Viboldone in 1176 with the help of Guy *de Porta Orientale*, between the brothers of the church of San Pietro and the provost of the *pieve*, shows that the community was expected to receive tithes and other

---

[95] Archetti, 'Gli Umiliati e i vescovi alla fine del duecento', pp. 310–12.

[96] See Violante, 'La chiesa bresciana nel medioevo', p. 1076.

[97] *Sua nobis dilectus*, 5 April 1280 (original: ASBr, Fondo dell'Ospedale maggiore, bolle in pergamene, filza AA no 1, copy: ASVat, Registro vaticano 39 fos. 239r–240v no. 21, ed. in Nicholas III, *Les registres de Nicholas III*, 63); *Petitio dilectorum filiorum* 8 January 1285 (ASVat, Registro vaticano 41 fos. 215v–219v no. 61, ed. in Martin IV, *Les registres de Martin IV*, 553); *Exhibita nobis dilectorum* 28 May 1285 (ASVat, Registro vaticano 43 fo. 9v no. 22 ed. in Honorius IV, *Les registres d'Honorius IV*, 24); *Per humilitatis exemplum*, 2 September 1288 (original, Brera, AD XVI 1/54a, purchased 1964, register: ASVat, Registro vaticano 44 fos. 37v–38v, ed. in *VHM* II, pp. 322–9, from a different manuscript), *Etsi quibuslibet ecclesiis* 10 September 1288 (original ASVat, Registro vaticano 44 fo. 38v no. 148, ed. in *VHM* II, pp. 329–32 and Nicholas IV, *Les registres de Nicholas IV*, 265); see now also Archetti, 'Gli Umiliati e i vescovi alla fine del duecento'.

[98] Above, ch. 2.

oblations.[99] Even the bishop of Lodi, who objected to the church at Ognissanti, had given them another chapel and was to pay his respects on the death of the provost. Similarly, the settlement drawn up at the Brera in 1230 with the parish of Sant'Eusebio indicates that the Humiliati and their neighbours were carefully laying out ground rules so as to avoid disputes which the appearance of a new church and cemetery, of whatever order, might provoke.[100] The perceived difficulties concerned revenues, be they tithes and first fruits, or funeral dues and other oblations. In the case of the Brera, they also involved certain rights. The parishioners were to be allowed to choose burial in the Brera if they wished, but the superior of the Brera was to forgo any role in the election of the priest of the *pieve*, thus reaffirming the autonomy of the two institutions. These settlements reveal both the areas which were considered sufficiently difficult to merit written agreement and the awareness on both sides of the need to resolve potential difficulties early on. The fact that they did so does not point to basic hostility on the part of the hierarchy such as that posited by Violante. What they do show is that the local secular clergy and the members of the *vicinia* were determined to protect their own resources and autonomy, and either that they were able to force the Humiliati to pay, or that the Humiliati were willing to accommodate their concerns by means of compensation.

A settlement reached in 1232 in Tortona is at the same time both more generous and more restrictive towards the Humiliati. In the episcopal palace, three Humiliati, the provost of San Michele in Alessandria, Anselm, priest and minister of the newly built house near the *borgo* of Tortona and brother Guy *de Viqueria* founder and benefactor of the house, requested that Peter, bishop of Tortona (1221–55) and his chapter should give them the church of San Marco next to their house.[101] The bishop agreed to their petition, giving them the oratory, where the brethren were to receive 'daily nourishment of their souls'.[102] This generosity also, however, gave the bishop the opportunity to impose certain conditions and restrictions: any nourishment was to be for the brethren living there alone. The Humiliati were not to receive any cleric or lay person, in life or death, to the detriment of any church in Tortona, because no church was to be cheated of its dues. They were particularly ordered not to accept any

---

[99] Above, p. 46. [100] Above, p. 226.
[101] Appendix 1, *42. The provost is here given as Anricus, but in 1228 had been Amicus and was to be Amicus later. It seems likely that either the notary or the modern editors mistook the name. On S. Marco, see also above, p. 213.
[102] *Ibid.*: 'cottidie pabulum animarum'.

married or unmarried woman coming out of childbirth or, as we have seen, to perform any funeral except for the brethren of the First and Third orders. If any Tertiaries chose burial there they were still to pay the canonical portion of the oblation due to their parish church (in this case to be understood as one-third). The new community was also to observe sentences of interdict and excommunication imposed by the Church of Tortona against clerics and laity subject to the bishop (this despite the papal privileges to the contrary). They were to pay tithes on their produce and possessions to the chapter of Tortona and the provost and brethren agreed that they should pay the bishop and his successors a yearly cense on the feast of St Mark in recognition of dominion. Finally, the bishop and chapter absolved the Humiliati and their house from all other pecuniary exactions and agreed not to burden them in any way.

This settlement shows both the Humiliati prepared to accept conditions imposed by local ecclesiastics and a prelate's desire to control their activities, echoing that of bishop Arderic of Lodi. They also, however, show the potential generosity of these authorities. This had already been apparent in the early history of the Humiliati and there are several later examples of the donation of churches and the confirmation or concession of rights to build a church or cemetery or both.[103]

In some cases disputes did arise between the Humiliati and the bishops and secular clergy, yet the order and a bishop and his clergy might well enjoy good relations for decades, interrupted only by brief outbursts of tension. Thus, in Verona the hostility shown by the archpriest in 1199 and 1203 does not seem to have resurfaced and the Humiliati flourished in the city. The clear impression is one of an exceptional interruption of longer-term cohabitation, if not mutual esteem. Individual circumstances and individual reactions to them might upset this balance. In particular, questions of revenue and jurisdiction led to tension. But the case for general hostility inherent in Violante's discussion of the situation seems seriously flawed. The history of relations between the Humiliati and the bishops is a regional one. As we have seen, the sense of a unified identity of the Humiliati in the 1220s and 1230s can be undermined by evidence for regional autonomies.[104] It should not be a surprise, therefore, that while the bishop of Brescia sought the means to avoid giving a church to the Humiliati, others had done so early on. Many bishops saw the Humiliati as a means of improving their resources and filling abandoned churches at the very least, others looked on them as a potential threat to their revenues and

---

[103] See for example, appendix I, *54, *80, *86, *94, *107.   [104] Above, ch. 5.

perhaps to their freedom of action. But between 1211 and the third quarter of the century, the idea that the bishops of northern Italy were generally suspicious of the Humiliati as heretics, or resented their insolence, is not upheld by the documents. Four final examples may help to confirm this view.

In 1217, Hugh, the new provost of Ognissanti, was among the witnesses present at the agreement of peace between Piacenza, Pavia and Milan and was appointed, together with the bishop of Pavia, to take possession of a site at Ruvino, where the Pavians had built a castle which was now to be destroyed.[105] In 1231, certain letters concerning an issue now obscure were to be deposited with the abbots of Tiglieto and Sant'Andrea by brother Bartholomew, a Franciscan and by Sardus, bishop-elect of Alba. Sardus declared, however, that he did not wish to be present if the depositions were to be made with either of these men. Yet, if brother Bartholomew wished to deposit the letters with the provost of the Humiliati of Alessandria, then he wished to attend.[106] The circumstances of this preference are not clear, but in the eyes of one disputant at least, the provost of a major Humiliati house appears as a favourable influence to be preferred to the abbots of two Cistercian monasteries.

The situation in Milan in mid-century once more illustrates the importance of relations between individuals. From 1241 to 1263, the archbishop was Leo *de Perego*, a Franciscan who had been active in the area for some time before his election, having helped prepare anti-heretical statutes for Monza in the early 1230s.[107] Between 1247 and 1251, Innocent IV sent him six letters concerning the taxation of the Humiliati and their involvement in secular office, demanding that the archbishop intervene on their behalf to ensure that they were neither excessively taxed nor forced to undertake secular duties against their will.[108] In 1251 Innocent went so far as to threaten the archbishop with the intervention of the archpriest of Monza should he fail to act.[109] The sequence might be understood to indicate some reluctance on the part of the archbishop to support the Humiliati, though many of the letters, copies of which were also sent to members of the order, read more like letters sent to keep the archbishop informed. Other evidence suggests,

---

[105] *Il 'registrum magnum' di Piacenza*, 468, 499, 605, 704. His predecessor, provost Lanfranc, had died some time before 1217 when bishop Arderic, who paid his respects at his death, also died.

[106] *Documenti intorno alle relazioni fra Genova e Alba*, I, 73 (1231): 'illi deposicioni uolebat interesse'.

[107] Frisi, *Memorie della chiesa monzese*, IV, pp. 8–12; W. R. Thomson, *Friars in the Cathedral: The First Franciscan Bishops 1226–1261*, Pontifical Institute of Mediaeval Studies, Studies and Texts, 33 (Toronto, 1975), pp. 93–101.

[108] See appendix I, 67, 69, 76, 89, 91 and 95. [109] Appendix I, 95.

however, that there was no fundamental ill feeling between Leo and the Humiliati. In 1250 Innocent wrote confirming a donation made by Leo to the Humiliati of the church of Sta Trinità in Porta Cumana and of Sta Maria in campo, which belonged to Sta Trinità. The two churches had belonged to the Benedictines but were now in need of reform and Leo had prescribed that the 'order' of the Humiliati was to be observed there henceforth.[110] Moreover, a letter of 1252 suggests that a member of the order may have been a regular presence in the archbishop's retinue. In May, Leo had three papal letters concerning the Humiliati re-copied, so that they might be kept in perpetual memory.[111] He did this in a room near the church of San Barnaba and the archbishop's palace and in the presence of three witnesses: James *de Besana* and Bartholomew of Padua, both Friars Minor, and brother Ottobellus of Gallarate of the order of the Humiliati'. The names of these three men are followed in the document by the expression *capell. infradicti domini archiepiscopi*. The expansion of the abbreviation *capell.* may be either singular or plural, indicating one or more chaplains (*capellanii*). Whichever is correct, it seems clear that Ottobellus, at least, was a chaplain of the archbishop. The presence of a Humiliati brother on the staff of a Franciscan archbishop need only depend on the personal qualities of the individuals involved, but it once more emphasises the potential for good relations between the Humiliati and the hierarchy.

Finally, documents from 1259 in Pavia show members of various Humiliati houses present and active in the business of both Church and commune. On 23 March William, bishop of Pavia, Rainier *de sancto Naçario*, bishop of Maina in Greece, and the prior of the Franciscans in Pavia, judges delegate of the Apostolic see, had a letter from Alexander IV read in public before witnesses and authenticated. The letter released the city from the interdict imposed in 1239 because of their support of Frederick II, provided that the *podestà* and representatives of the city would swear to obey papal dispositions. Among other ecclesiastical and lay representatives, the witnesses included Guy and Nicholas, respectively provost and prior of the 'new house beyond the Ticino of the order of the Humiliati of Pavia' (Oltreticino) and Lanfranc, a brother there. The role of the Humiliati was not simply one of onlookers, for the text of Alexander's letter shows that the city had used the prior and brother Lanfranc as proctors and special messengers to the pope.[112] In the previous year, a brother Lanfranc of the same house, perhaps the same man, had been appointed to collect the tax imposed on the clergy

---

[110] Appendix I, 84. [111] Appendix I *97.
[112] *Documenti degli archivi di Pavia relativi alla storia di Voghera (929–1300)*, 140–2 (1259).

of the city and diocese.[113] Again in 1259, a brother Peter of the Humiliati appears in the retinue of the bishop of Pavia and in his absence presides at the presentation of a letter from Sigebaldus, bishop of Vercelli.[114] In his will of 1267, another bishop, Rainier of Maina, who had been one of the judges delegate in 1259, was to bequeath to the Humiliati of the Oltre-ticino house in Pavia property to feed and clothe three priests (two Humiliati and one other), who were to reside and officiate in the chapel of Sant' Olderico founded in his home.[115] Such evidence must surely betoken the strength of identity between the Humiliati and the local Church and not mutual hostility. It also reveals that their financial expertise, much appreciated – as Zanoni realised – by the communes, did not go unrecognised by their ecclesiastical colleagues.[116]

THE HUMILIATI AND THE REGULAR ORDERS

In discussing the relationship of the Humiliati with the bishops, one theme has been noticeably lacking: that of preaching. Indeed, the silence of the documents about the preaching of the Humiliati, except in the vivid accounts of Vitry and the papal letters of 1201 and 1249, might be interpreted as an indication that their preaching was not of great import.[117] Arguments from silence, however, are notoriously unreliable, and in this case the reference to a dispute between the Dominicans and the Humiliati in the 1250s highlights the dangers, since it implies that some Humiliati at least were still expected to preach, and with notable success. This dispute has already been discussed in the context of the first Master General's administration of the order, but the details are also informative about a theme constantly repeated through-out the documentation, that of competition between the Humiliati and other regulars present in the north Italian towns.

In June 1251 Innocent IV wrote to the prior and brethren of the order of Preachers in Milan confirming the settlement.[118] The cause of the dispute, as we have seen, had been the arrival of brother Arnold *de Vedano* and eight Humiliati brethren from Monza on a site with a house and other buildings which they had purchased, immediately next to the house of the Dominicans and where they intended to reside perma-nently.[119] The Humiliati were far outnumbered by the Dominicans, who had sixty brethren, all named in the document. Yet their presence

---

[113] Crotti Pasi, 'Gli Umiliati a Pavia', p. 334.   [114] *Ibid.*, p. 336.
[115] See Crotti Pasi, 'Gli Umiliati a Pavia', pp.324–5; *Documenti inediti della chiesa pavese*, pp. 27–33.
[116] Zanoni, pp. 216–43.   [117] See above, pp. 188, 223.
[118] Appendix I, 87 and see above, p. 212.
[119] *Ibid.*: 'in que Domo praedicti Humiliati proposuerunt facere continuam residentiam'.

upset the Friars Preacher, for two reasons. The first of these was that the Humiliati had constructed an unauthorised building with windows and openings which overlooked their house and garden on the south side.[120]

Such worries are not uncommon in the tightly-packed cities of northern Italy: to name but one example, in 1251 the *podestà* of Brescia decreed (perhaps solicited by the Dominicans themselves) that no building was to be put up nor window opened next to their house.[121] The importance of space as well as of privacy is transparent. It is the second ground for dispute between the Dominicans and their neighbours in Milan, however, which is most illuminating here. The Humiliati were not to create a *canonica* of the 'major order' (the First order) and nor were they to arrange public preaching (*convocare praedicationem*). The reason given for this last veto is particularly interesting: because by this means the preaching of the Dominicans would be hindered.[122] The Dominicans argued that preaching was their particular duty (*officium et studium*) and that they had long ago chosen the church of Sant'Eustorgio as their headquarters in Milan. Thus they claimed both a monopoly on preaching and greater rights because of the length of time they had been there. Here we have a community of Dominicans, the thirteenth-century order of professional Preachers *par excellence*, sufficiently concerned by the fact, or the prospect, of Humiliati preachers next door to take action to stop them. The immediate succession in the text of the two vetoes – on establishing a *canonica* and on preaching – may mean that the two were related in the minds of the Dominicans and that a Second order community might not be expected to preach to the public. Either way, the *reputation* of the Humiliati as preachers, if not the substance behind this reputation, would seem to be confirmed by their neighbour's reaction.

The Dominicans had the upper hand because they had been there longer and apparently had the power to revoke the sale of land to the Humiliati.[123] They were also papal visitors to the Humiliati and had good relations with them. This perhaps explains why the Humiliati seem to have capitulated on all points. They agreed to wall up the offending windows and other openings and to make do with roof lights (*luxellos super tecta*). They further accepted that they must not form a

---

[120] *Ibid.*, 'non licere ibi aedificare, nec fenestras habere in ipsa domo, nec quae fiet, vel posset fieri . . . contra Domum, seu hortum ipsorum fratrum praedicatorum a meridiana parte'.

[121] G. Panazza, 'Il volto storico di Brescia fino al secolo xix', *Storia di Brescia*, III (Brescia, 1964), pp. 1011–21, p. 1090 n. 2.

[122] Appendix I, 87: 'cum per hoc praedicationes Praedicatorum Fratrum impedirentur'.

[123] *Ibid.*: 'Quam venditionem dicti fratres Praedicatores dicebant posse revocare, seu revocari facere per dictum superstantem dictae ecclesiae sancti Eustorgii, cum ipsa terra, super qua dicta aedificia sunt, sit illius ecclesiae'.

canonica or arrange preaching there. In return the Dominicans withdrew their threat to have the original sale of land revoked.

The settlement records a localised and apparently quickly resolved conflict of interests; because the Humiliati were vulnerable, but also perhaps because they wished to preserve good relations established with the Dominicans. Nonetheless, the underlying issue of competition was not an easily resolved phenomenon.

Numerous other records of disputes between the Humiliati and regular communities survive: in Brescia in May and July 1253 the Humiliati were once more disputing with the Dominicans, this time over the *fonte di montepiano*.[124] Most surviving records of such disputes are late, however, and involve the other religious communities only as rival claimants to property or rights which a lay entity or individual might equally well represent. It is evidence of competition as a religious order which is more illuminating about the nature of the Humiliati's relationship with the Church and other religious, *qua* religious. Competition over recruits provides just such evidence.

Competition over recruits

All religious houses feared the loss of brethren to other orders, as the disputes caused by the loss of brethren to St Bernard's foundation at Clairvaux (and occasionally vice versa) famously illustrated.[125] The problem lay behind the development of the *nisi arctior* clause restricting transfer unless to a stricter regime inserted in the privileges issued to individual communities and whole orders from the second half of the twelfth century. In 1201 this privilege was applied to the Humiliati of the First order. They were both protected against the loss of brethren to other orders *nisi arctioris religionis* and themselves forbidden to accept communities which came from stricter regimes.[126] No evidence survives for the loss of brethren early on. The first recorded case was, however, significant in scale: in 1239 the whole *domus ferabovis* of Zevio, the house founded by Marchesius and Merida in 1218, passed to the Mantuan order of the canons of San Marco.[127] The surviving agreement, drawn up with the consent of their bishop and with papal authorisation, does not record the reasons for the wholesale transfer of the community. The life and rule of the canons of San Marco, approved by Innocent III in 1206–7, bore some similarities to that of the Humiliati, so we may surmise that the move was dictated by reasons of

---

[124] Violante, 'La chiesa bresciana', p. 1081 and n. 1.
[125] Picasso, 'San Bernardo e il "transitus" dei monaci', pp. 181–200.
[126] Appendix I, 9.   [127] Appendix I, *53.

a contingent, local nature.[128] Nonetheless, this transfer may have prompted a clause in Innocent IV's reforming bull of 1246 *Ex ore domini*, forbidding the passage of houses away from the order.[129] *Post hoc* is not *propter hoc*, but the first years of the new magisterial regime do seem to be marked by greater concern for the loss of recruits (or greater ability to get the pope to act on their behalf). Between 1246 and 1251 Innocent IV issued four important letters concerning the problem.

In December 1246 he wrote an open letter to the abbots and prelates of other churches 'to whom it might reach'.[130] He ordered them to announce publicly the excommunication of fugitives from the Humiliati who had been excommunicated by the Master General of their order and who did not return once warned. The letter specified that this applied to those who had left after making their profession and out of lightness of spirit or for other less reasonable cause.[131] Those who had passed to a stricter regime were presumably to be allowed to remain.

In 1249 Innocent wrote directly to the Brera community.[132] This time the problem was specific and local. In order to avoid the various duties entrusted to them by the apostolic legate and the commune on account of the war (with Frederick II) and the adversity of the times, certain members of the house had transferred to other orders. Innocent ruled that this must not be allowed and that other houses were not to accept them, even if they had indulgences to the contrary. In neither the 1246 letter nor that of 1249 is it clear where the Humiliati brethren were going. Nor is it possible to establish on the basis of these letters what might be considered a stricter regime and therefore a legitimate destination for the fugitives. In 1250, however, a third papal letter reveals that transfer to any of the other major orders was unlikely to be considered legitimate. From *Exhibita nobis vestra* of August 1250 we learn that despite papal prohibition, the Cistercians, Carthusians, Franciscans and Dominicans, as well as others, had been accepting Humiliati brethren, claiming that they could do so because of indulgences.[133] The prohibition was now renewed. Finally, in the following year, Innocent wrote to the abbot and General Chapter of the Cistercians asking them to stipulate in their chapter that no Humiliati brethren should be received into the houses of their order.[134] The immediate impact of such letters is difficult to ascertain. The Dominicans did eventually take action: at the provincial chapter held in Milan in 1261, priors and others

---

[128] *Annales camaldulenses ordinis sancti Benedicti*, IV, appendix 2, cols. 631–8.
[129] Appendix I, 59.   [130] Appendix I, 65.
[131] *Ibid.*: 'animi levitate vel alia de causa minus rationabili'.
[132] Appendix I, 70.   [133] Appendix I, 83.   [134] Appendix I, 92.

were warned not to accept members of the order of the Humiliati (as well as other religious) without the special licence of the provincial prior and the same point was made at the Pisa General Chapter in 1276, where authorisation by a Master General was also acknowledged.[135] Whether any provincial prior or Master General ever gave his permission is not recorded.

This series of letters gives the impression of net loss from the Humiliati to other orders. This was not always the case, however. In 1250 Innocent allowed the Humiliati to release those who joined the order from previous vows forbidding the use of fat. The letter gives no clue to the identity of those transferring, but it is likely that they were from another regular order.[136] Moreover, the Dominicans and Franciscans were not immune to losing brethren, as demonstrated by bulls prohibiting the two orders from accepting each other's brethren.[137] By the same token, the Humiliati were not above accepting a fugitive from the Mendicants. In 1251 Innocent IV wrote to the Master General of the Humiliati concerning brother Salvus whom they had accepted, claiming that he had originally been a member of their order and had left without licence, although he had been with the Friars Minor for more than fifteen years. The case was the more irritating to both sides because Salvus was a desirable catch: he had been given office as a provost among the Humiliati and had brought with him books belonging to the Franciscan order which he had surreptitiously removed. Innocent instructed the Master to force him to return to the Franciscans.[138]

One individual is hardly a tendency in himself, but such moves serve to remind us that the picture is complex. There was a state of flux dictated as much by particular, often transient motives, such as the impact of the war on the Brera or an individual's desire for promotion, as by the demands of the particular form of life of each order or their contemporary success.

CONCLUSIONS

This chapter has illustrated aspects of the ecclesiastical side of the Humiliati: their status as religious, developing a quasi-pastoral structure, sharing in the care of souls, enjoying the patronage of bishops and

---

[135] 'Acta capitulorum provinciae Lombardiae et Lombardiae inferioris', p. 143; *Acta capitulorum generalium ordinis praedicatorum*, ed. B. M. Reichert, *Monumenta ordinis fratrum praedicatorum historica*, I (Rome, 1898), p. 86..

[136] Appendix I, 85.   [137] See for example, *BF* I, pp. 345–6 (1244).

[138] Appendix I, 96.

disputing over jurisdiction, revenues and recruits with both seculars and regulars. This highlights the conformist rather than the reforming side of the movement and, indeed, the compensatory settlements between new communities and the local ecclesiastical hierarchy suggest that many of the Humiliati were keen to win acceptance, not to challenge the status quo.

This was not always successful and occasionally they aroused the hostility of the secular and regular church. The picture is not straightforward, however, and each town, even each house, represents a different reality and a variety of relationships. Bishops were keen to have them under their jurisdiction and undoubtedly the 1270s and 1280s saw a crisis with the bishops of Como, Brescia and Milan, but this atmosphere of tension should not be projected back to the first half of the century. Evidence from elsewhere and earlier suggests that conflict was not necessarily a widespread phenomenon. This same evidence confirms that the Humiliati were perceived by contemporary churchmen as legitimate performers on the ecclesiastical stage, a status which underlay their relationship with the laity in the towns and districts in which they were based.

CONCLUSION

This book has traced the remarkable passage of a movement condemned by pope and emperor in 1184 into an established order within the Church. It has been argued that this was in part possible because the Humiliati were a far more traditional movement than previously recognised and much closer to the establishment of the Church than the condemnation of 1184 might be thought to imply. There were, of course, novel developments, as contemporary observers such as the chronicler of Laon and Jacques de Vitry emphasised. Their attitude to manual work as a source of charity, as well as a blessing to the worker, was one important element. The exhortations of their lay members certainly caught the imagination of contemporary commentators. This preaching without authority and their insistence on holding private meetings and rejecting oaths provoked condemnation. Yet, from the very beginning, the Humiliati behaved and were perceived by contemporaries as members of the Church. Even in the twelfth century they received the support of prelates and legacies from the faithful. Evidence for persecution or hostility is extremely limited and may have been particularly linked to the area of Verona. The earliest commentator, the anonymous chronicler of Laon, who explains the condemnation of the movement in 1184, describes them defending, not attacking, the Catholic faith (*pro fide Catholica se opponentes*). Moreover, examination of the regime of the First and Second orders established in 1201 suggests that the idea behind the new order was very close to the ideas of the long-established orders of the Church. Their rule contained elements of both monastic and canonical life, emphasising the traditional virtues of chastity and obedience. Their attitude to poverty, as has previously been shown, reflected the traditional values of common property, not the absolute poverty associated with the Mendicants.[1]

---

[1] Bolton, 'The poverty of the Humiliati', passim.

Innumerable documents show them purchasing land, consolidating their properties in the tradition of monastic houses. This conservatism in their norms established in 1201 was perhaps predictable, in view of the experience of the two local prelates, Peter of Lucedio and Albert of Vercelli, chosen to examine their case: the former a Cistercian, the latter a regular canon by training. They played a key role in the approval of the new order and aspects of early Humiliati observance certainly reflect their direct intervention: the use of the customs and rule of Mortara, the adoption of Cistercian administrative practices, possibly Cistercian confession and perhaps also the adoption of a liturgy close to that of Ivrea and Vercelli. The solutions they found to the dilemma of the Humiliati's position in 1200 were not, however, simply imposed on the movement. The three-tier structure, with a special 'Tertiary' status for lay members, first experimented with here and later imitated by groups linked to the Mendicants, was very probably established by the Humiliati themselves.

In constructing this picture, notarial and papal sources have been both pitted against each other and exploited in conjunction in order to underline the different perspectives they provide. These two types of record help to expose the dichotomy between the idea established by ecclesiastical legislators (both within the order and outside it) and practice in the localities. There was certainly vagueness on both sides about use of the name Humiliati and who belonged to the order: *umiliatismo* may be a helpful way of describing the satellite groups identified by notaries as Humiliati, inspired perhaps by the same ideals, but not linked with the papally approved movement. One group at Cerea near Verona and another at Faenza in 1206 were condemned with the name Humiliati. There is certainly no need on the basis of such thin evidence to posit a splintering of the order, nor any evidence for an affiliation between disaffected Humiliati and the Waldensians.

As the order developed during the thirteenth century the conflict between these two types of sources, curial and local, continues to be important. The Humiliati acquired the juridical status of an order within the Church in 1201, but if an order is defined as a centrally organised institution based on uniform observance, this took shape only gradually. In papal letters the Humiliati are treated as a coherent institution from the very beginning, in need of supervision and correction, as shown in the response to irregular observances at the Brera in Milan in the 1220s, the introduction of papal visitation, or the usual dispensations allowing relaxation of practice concerning for example the crucial elements of oath-taking and fasting. Such letters reflect the normal activities of the Curia in relation to a religious order: imposing authority, acting as court of appeal, but above all responding to petitions, not often initiating new practices.

Early notarial evidence, in particular concerning the terminology used to describe the houses themselves and their members, reveals still greater fluidity well into the thirteenth century. The distinctions between the different houses of the three orders do not seem to have been as neat as was once assumed. Individuals may have belonged to an order in the sense of acquiring a certain 'status', but houses associated with the First order, for example, may have included members of the Second and Third in their communities. Thus, for example, Ognissanti in Borghetto Lodigiano and Viboldone near Milan accepted married couples. Most remarkably, evidence from Milan reveals that in some houses under-age children were accepted, not as oblates (though some did remain) nor, apparently, for education, but perhaps to allow their adult relatives to pursue a religious vocation.

Professions of faith show that the struggle to achieve unity and uniformity in a movement lacking a single founder was perhaps as acute as it was to be for the Franciscans whose founder's ideals proved so controversial. The representatives of the Humiliati in negotiations with the prelates and Curia in 1200–1 may not have found it easy to have the regulations they agreed on accepted. In the 1220s in Milan there were still problems with observance at the major Brera house and records of profession from the area of Verona suggest that the years around 1230 were a watershed for the introduction of more 'regular' observance. A profession made on Wednesday 5 June 1230 is the first to refer to the rule of Innocent III. Records from the third and fourth decades of the century also allow us to reconstruct regional 'congregations' such as that linking Verona, Vicenza and Mantua led by 'senior professed ministers'. Links with Milan are not strong at this point, but a second turning point is provided by the introduction of the Master General in 1246, intended to bring the order into unity and almost certainly based on the pattern of the Dominican order, some of whose friars had been papal visitors of the Humiliati since the 1250s. The disputes the new Master General faced in the following decade reflect the difficulties of holding such an order together.

It is not easy to establish a clear picture of the Humiliati 'on the ground': the sources are too fragmentary, so that while Verona and district is well documented in the early part of the century, evidence for ties between this area and the 'centre' of the order in Milan after the introduction of the Master General are difficult to find. By contrast, evidence for houses in the area of Tortona and Alessandria is relatively poor early on, but the records of disputes from the 1250s suggest a

Conclusion

flourishing network of houses had long existed. Houses and individuals
are extremely difficult to trace over time. They frequently changed
either name or place or both and it is certainly too early to attempt a
study of settlement like that now possible for most other orders.[2] What
can safely be said is that the figures recorded by Jacques de Vitry and
later Bonvesin da la Riva for the number of houses are not likely to be
wildly exaggerated. The order of the Humiliati had very high numbers
of settlements in some areas. These often included both men and
women in large numbers, but the size of communities frequently
fluctuated. Women acted as superiors, but in double communities were
generally subject to the men, as shown in their acceptance of new
members 'on the order of the minister'. A number of communities
were associated with churches or built their own very early on, but
from mid-century there was a drive to increase the number of churches,
encouraged by the popes, in particular in Second order communities.
This may have increased the similarities between houses of the First and
Second order.

Exploring the framework of the order, the houses, their superiors and
the links between them, reveals that local identity was important.
Recruitment was local and strong, autonomous, regional structures
seem to have developed. Perhaps these clear local identities are one
reason why the shaping of a centrally organised institution (the order)
took so long. Strong, local identities may also have lain behind the
failure of the Humiliati to expand beyond northern and central Italy.
Attempts were made: letters of introduction from pope Alexander IV in
1258 asked the French king Louis IX and his bishops to allow the
Humiliati to settle in the kingdom of France. The pope describes their
praiseworthy life and activities, acquiring food by the labour of their
own hands, giving alms, receiving guests and preaching the word of
God, saying that they have 'especially spread in the province of
Lombardia' (*potissimum dilatati*). The letters lie in the archives of the
Brera in Milan, apparently undelivered.[3]

Some bishops were undoubtedly wary of the Humiliati, as Innocent
III and his delegates had foreseen, but this was based on issues of
jurisdiction and revenue. There was no general or automatic hostility
and many were generous to the Humiliati in their dioceses. The
Humiliati are to be found engaging in some of the quintessential pastoral
activities of the religious: distributing the legacies of the faithful, sometimes benefiting from their largesse themselves. In this they acted

[2] Ambrosioni reports, in her introduction to *Sulle tracce*, p. xiii, that a database of houses is in
preparation.
[3] See Appendix I, 116, 117.

251

alongside the other religious of the towns and *contadi* in which they lived, enjoying the patronage of bishops and disputing with both secular and regular clergy over jurisdictions, revenues and even recruits.

This competition should remind us that the Humiliati were both precursors[4] to, and later competitors with, the Mendicants. Even the disputes in which the Humiliati became embroiled and conflicts over observances, such as clerical precedence, reflect the experience of other established religious orders. Their 'mission to the people', not unlike the Dominican commitment to preaching, was recognised by Gregory IX in a letter sent to the provosts and brothers of the Order which commented on their decision to live in the midst of the people: *uos que proposuistis in medio populi uestri degere . . .*[5] It is with the Dominicans in particular that the Humiliati may have enjoyed a special relationship. It was the Dominicans who visited their houses after 1227 and who surely influenced the decision to adopt magisterial-style government in 1246. Humbert of Romans took a particular interest in the order, addressing two of his sermons to their brethren. Perhaps the most dramatic Milanese Dominican of all, the murdered inquisitor and preacher Peter Martyr (d. 1252) is reported to have especially visited Humiliati nuns who, 'attracted by his sweetness and affability received him with joy and affection'. According to Stephen of Salagnac (or his continuator Bernard Gui), 'this order [of the Humiliati] always greatly loved our order of Preachers, and especially the blessed Peter Martyr, and in like manner did the same Peter Martyr and order of Preachers love them'.[6] Thus had the early Humiliati transformed from condemned heretics in the 1180s to a powerfully acknowledged orthodoxy in the mid-thirteenth century.

---

[4] As previous writers have recognised; see for example, Bolton, 'Innocent III's treatment of the Humiliati', pp. 80–1.

[5] Appendix I, 44 (1235).

[6] Stephen of Salagnac and Bernard Gui, *De quatuor in quibus deus praedicatorum ordinem insignivit*, p. 183: 'Hic ordo [of the Humiliati] multum dilexit semper ordinem nostrum Predicatorum, et specialiter beatum Petrum martyrum, et eodem modo martyr et ipse ordo Predicatorum ipsum'; see also Hinnebusch, *The History of the Dominican Order*, I, p. 387, n. 100, A. Dondaine, 'S. Pierre Martyr', *Archivum Fratrum Praedicatorum, 23* (1953), 66–162, 88–89.

CALENDAR OF PAPAL (AND EPISCOPAL) LETTERS AND PRIVILEGES CONCERNING THE HUMILIATI

PREFACE

This appendix is a working document to accompany the text and to assist future study. It includes letters directed to the Humiliati, others which refer to them and in one case (number 1) a letter the existence of which is known only because it is referred to in a later document. Only brief summaries are given, in particular when a letter is discussed in detail above.

References are given to manuscripts, principal published editions, catalogues (regests) and, on one or two occasions, to translations. Citations are given only where these provide substantial information about the document. Similarly, differences between manuscript and published editions are noted only if they substantially change the meaning of the letter or add details of interest.

An asterisk ★ before the number indicates non-papal documents which are not listed with an *incipit* in order to avoid confusion with papal correspondence. Some letters of the archdeacons of Monza are included as they enjoyed quasi-episcopal status; a decision by the council of experts in Florence illustrating the response to a papal letter is also inserted (★119).

Finally, a distinction is made between extant originals sent to the recipients and Vatican Register copies which may often have been transcribed into the Register some time after the letter was sent and on the basis of *minute* rather than the full text.[1] Differences are very minor, but the wording of an original is always adopted.

ABBREVIATIONS USED ONLY IN APPENDIX I

(See p. ix for other abbreviations.)

Asti	*Le carte dello Archivio capitolare di Asti (1238–72)*, ed. L. Vergano, BSSS, 141 (Turin, 1942)
Auvray	Gregory IX, *Les registres de Grégoire IX*, ed. L. Auvray, 4 vols. (Paris, 1896–1955)
Baluze	Innocent III, *Epistolarum Innocentii libri undecim*, ed. S. Baluze, 2 vols. (Paris, 1682)

---

[1] For the debate about the validity of Register copies, see for example Pasztor, 'Studi e problemi relativi ai registri di Innocenzo III', pp. 289–94.

Appendix I

Berger	Innocent IV, *Les registres d'Innocent IV*, ed. E. Berger, 4 vols. (Paris 1884–1921)
Biancolini	Biancolini, G. B., *Notizie storiche delle chiese di Verona*, 7 vols. (Verona, 1750–66, reprinted Bologna, 1977)
de la Roncière	Alexander IV, *Les registres d'Alexandre IV*, ed. Bourel de la Roncière, J. de Loye and A. Coulon, 3 vols. (Paris, 1895–1959)
Giulini	Giulini, G., *Memorie spettanti alla storia . . . di Milano ne' secoli bassi*, 9 vols. (Milan, 1760–5)
Jordan and Wool	*Inventory of Western Manuscripts in the Biblioteca Ambrosiana*, ed. L. Jordan and S. Wool, Part 1, *A–B Superior* (Notre Dame, 1984)
Odorici	Odorici, F., *Storie bresciane*, 10 vols. (Brescia, 1856)
Palestra	*Regesto delle pergamene dell'Archivio arcivescovile di Milano*, ed. A. Palestra, *Archivio ambrosiano*, 12 (Milan, 1961)
Pressuti	Honorius III, *Regesta Honorii Papae III*, ed. P. Pressuti, 2 vols. (Rome, 1888–95, reprinted Hildesheim, 1978)
Puricelli	Puricelli, G., *Historia ordinis Humiliatorum*, ed. P. P. Bosca (1677) Ambrosiana ms. C 74 inf.
Theiner	*Vetera monumenta slavorum meridionalium*, I, 1198–1549, ed. A. Theiner (Rome, 1863)
Ughelli	Ughelli, F., *Italia sacra sive de episcopis italiae*, ed. N. Coleti, 9 vols. (Venice, 1717–22)

1. Before August 1181

Alexander III gives papal protection to the community of Viboldone near Milan.
    Only source: reference in 3 below.

2. 4 November 1184. Verona

Ad abolendam
At the Council of Verona, Lucius III condemns the Humiliati as heretics together with Cathars, Poor of Lyons, Josephines, Passagines and Arnaldists.
    Edition: *Sacrorum conciliorum nova et amplissima collectio*, XXII, col. 477; X.5.7.9; *Texte zur Inquisition*, ed. Selge, p. 26.
    Cited: Gonnet, 'Sul concilio di Verona', pp. 23–6; P. Diehl, '"Ad abolendam" (X.5.7.9) and imperial legislation against heresy', *Bulletin of Medieval Canon Law*, 19 (1989), 1–11.

3. 29 April 1186. Verona

Religiosam vitam degentibus
Urban III to Ubertus provost of the church of San Pietro in Viboldone and the brothers both present and future, professed to the regular life (*regulari vita professis*).
    In response to a petition and following the example of pope Alexander III, Urban takes the church of San Pietro Viboldone into papal protection and gives certain privileges. In particular, he allows them rights concerning burial (*sepulturam*

quoque ipsius loci liberam esse concedimus, ut eorum devotioni, et extremae voluntati qui se illic sepeliri deliberaverint, nisi forte excommunicati, vel interdicti sint, nullus obsistat, salva tamen iustitia illarum Ecclesiarum, a quibus mortuorum corpora assumuntur).

Edition: *VHM* II, pp. 123–5. From a manuscript then held by Marquis Trivulzio of Milan.

Regest: *Italia pontificia*, VI/1, pp. 125–6.

4. 6 December 1199. Lateran

Licet in agro

Innocent III to Adelard, bishop of Verona (1188–1214).

Concerning the distinction between the Humiliati and heretics guilty of doctrinal error, which Innocent had established in a previous letter, but which an archpriest of the diocese had ignored (*dictus archipresbyter tam contra Humiliatos quam universos hereticos sine distinctione quam posueramus in litteris nostris, excommunicationis sententiam promulgavit; cuius occasione sentente nonnulli quosdam, qui licet inviti a populo Humiliati dicuntur, licet nullam heresim sed fidem sicut dicitur, sapiant orthodoxam et in humilitate cordis et corporis studeant Domino famulari*). He instructs the bishop to re-examine the Humiliati.

Register   ASVat Registro Vaticano 4, fo. 201v.

Edition: *PL*, 214 cols. 788–9; *Register*, II, pp. 424–5.

Regest: Potthast, 891; Baluze, I, 491.

Cited: Alberzoni, 'Gli inizi', pp. 196–200.

5. December 1200. Lateran

Licet multitudini credentium

Innocent III to the provosts L[anfranc] of Viboldone and T[rancherius?] of Vialone, the chapters of Rondineto and San Cristoforo Lodi and all the brethren of the same profession, the chapter of the Brera and all the brethren of the same profession with them and Guy *de Porta Orientale* and all the brethren of his profession with him (*eius professionem cum ipso*).

Concerning their *proposita* and the mechanisms for their consideration.

Register: ASVat Registro Vaticano 5, fos. 16v–17r.

Edition: *PL*, 214, cols. 921–2 (with some mistakes).

Regest: Potthast, 119.

Cited: Theiner I, col. 53, 210; Alberzoni, 'Gli inizi', pp. 201–12.

6. December 1200

Olim causam

Innocent III to the bishop (Otto 1196–1202) and chapter of Tortona

He issues judgement in a dispute between the bishop and the Templars in *Lombardia* concerning a concession made by bishop Hugh of Tortona (1183–93) allowing the Humiliati of Tortona to build a hospital and oratory in *loco Calventiae*. The case had previously been heard by C, a canon of the church of Tortona, the cardinal priest of Sto Stefano in Celio Monte and the cardinal deacon of Sant'Eustachio as auditors and more recently by the abbots of Locedio and Columba. Abbot Peter of Locedio explained part of the case to Innocent *viva voce*.

Appendix I

Edition: *Corpus Iuris Canonici*, ed. A. Friedberg, II (Leipzig, 1881), cols. 285–6 (X.2.13.12).
Regest: Potthast, 1195.
Cited: Zanoni, p. 9 n. 3.

7. 7 June 1201. Lateran

Incumbit nobis
Innocent III to Guy *de Porta Orientale*, C. of Monza, A. of Como, N. of Pavia, G. of Brescia, I. of Bergamo, I. of Piacenza, I. of Lodi, R. of Cremona and the other ministers of the same order and their brothers and sisters.
Setting out the rule or *propositum* for the 'Third' order.

Original: Brera AD XVI I/1–2 (poor condition).
Copy: Brera AD XVI I/1.
Edition: *VHM* II, pp. 128–34 (from authenticated copy); Meersseman, *Dossier*, appendix I.
Translation: Stewart, *'De illis qui faciunt penitentiam'*, appendix I, pp. 365–71.
Regest: Potthast, 1416; Theiner, I, col. 58, 99.
Cited: Zerfaß, *Der Streit um die Laienpredigt*, pp. 202–10; Stewart, *'De illis qui faciunt penitentiam'*, pp. 189–96; Dal Pino, *I frati servi di sta Maria*, I, pp. 560–3. Maccarrone, *Studi*, pp. 287–8.

8. 12 June 1201. Lateran

Diligentiam pii patris
Innocent III to the prelates of the Brera, *Domus nova* Milan, Monza, Marlano, Vico, Zerbeto, *Domus nova* Pavia, Bergamo, Brescia and the other prelates of the same order and their brothers and sisters.
Approval of the rule of the 'Second' order.

Original: Brera AD XVI I/3.
Edition: *VHM* II, pp. 135–8. Reprinted in Mosca, *Alberto Patriarca di Gerusalemme*, appendix 6, pp. 661–3.
Regest: Potthast, 1415; Theiner, I, col. 58, 98.
Note: In the original, *De Vico* and *Zerbet.* are separated by the usual double dots left for the name of the superior, which suggests that *Vico* and *Zerbet[ensis?]* were two separate houses rather than one as in *VHM*.
Cited: Dal Pino, *I frati servi di sta Maria*, I, pp. 560–3; Maccarrone, *Studi*, pp. 285–8.

9. 16 June 1201. Lateran

Non omni spiritui
Innocent III to James of Rondineto, Lanfranc of Viboldone, T[rancherius?] of Mealono [sic – for Vialone], Lanfranc of Lodi and the other provosts of the same order and their brothers, both present and future, *regularem vitam professis in perpetuum*.
Approval of the rule of the 'First' order, with an account of the process leading to approval and the framework for government.

Edition: *VHM* II, pp. 139–48 from Puricelli; reprinted in Mosca, *Alberto Patriarca di Gerusalemme*, appendix 6, pp. 655–9.

Appendix I

Regest: Potthast, 1417; Theiner, I, col. 58, 100.
Cited: Dal Pino, *I frati servi di sta Maria*, I, pp. 560–3; Maccarrone, *Studi*, pp. 288–9.

*10. c. 1201 Milan

Philip, archbishop of Milan, to Iohannibellus and his *confratres* and the whole congregation of the Brera.

He gives the Humiliati permission to build an oratory and have a cemetery in the Brera. They may receive the office from any priest, as long as he is Ambrosian (*dum tamen Ambroxiano*). Philip takes their present and future possessions into the protection of the Milanese church.

Original: Brera AD XVI 1/4.
Regest: Giulini, VII, pp. 189–90.
Cited: *VHM* II, p. 149.

11. 12 December 1206. St Peters

Dolorum urgentium multitudo
Innocent III to the *podestà*, consuls and *consilium* of Faenza.

Concerning the expulsion of heretics and naming the Humiliati among them.

Edition: *PL*, 215, cols. 1042–3.
Regest: Potthast, 2932.

12. 15 June 1208. Anagni

Solet annuere sedes
Innocent III to the provost and brothers of Ognissanti, Fossadolto (Borghetto Lodigiano), of the order of St Benedict.

In response to a petition, Innocent confirms their ownership of the chapel of San Giorgio with all that pertains to it.

Edition: *VHM* II, pp. 151–2 (from Puricelli) but dated 19 June 1210. *CDL*, II/I, 225, p. 250 dated 15 June 1208 from a thirteenth-century authenticated copy in Lodi Archivio Vescovile, Armario VIII.
Regest: Potthast, 4015 (dated 15 June 1210).
Cited: Mercatili Indelicato, 'Per una storia degli Umiliati nella diocesi di Lodi', pp. 369–72.

13. 15 June 1208. Anagni

Causam que
Innocent III to the bishop elect of Vercelli (Aliprand Visconti 1208–13).

The pope instructs the bishop elect to hear and resolve a dispute between the bishop of Tortona, archpriest and chapter of Voghera on one side and the abbess of the monastery of Senatore in Pavia, the priest and *vicini* of the church of Sant'Ilario in Voghera on the other over the parochial rights of the church. At an earlier stage in the dispute, the provost of Rondineto (James) had been involved as a judge-delegate, as requested by the abbess of the Senatore.

Appendix I

Copy: ASMi, Archivio diplomatico, bolle e brevi, cart. 6 n. 19.
Edition: Alberzoni, 'Giacomo di Rondineto', appendix 1, pp. 156–7.

14. 31 December 1208. Lateran

Solet annuere sedes
Innocent III to the brothers of the church of Valle Orianese (Oriano near Cassago Brianza).

In response to a petition, he takes their church, which was built with the licence of Philip, late archbishop of Milan, into papal protection.

Original: Brera AD XVII/5.
Edition: *VHM* II, pp. 150–1.
Regest: Potthast, 3584a.
Cited: Longoni, 'Gli Umiliati in Brianza', p. 805.

15. 25 April 1209. Lateran

Cum B[ertarinus] nuntius
Innocent III to the bishop of Vercelli (Aliprando Visconti 1208–13), the archdeacons of Milan (William *de Rizolio*) and Pavia (Master Robaldus).

Following complaints from the bishop of Tortona and the *pieve* of Voghera the pope instructs Aliprand and the archdeacons to verify whether the previous judges delegated by the holy see, including [James] provost of Rondineto, had allowed irregularities in hearing the case concerning parochial rights disputed between the bishop of Tortona, archpriest and chapter of Voghera and the abbess of the monastery of Senatore in Pavia, priest and *vicini* of the church of Sant'Ilario in Voghera.

Original: ASMi, Archivio diplomatico, bolle e brevi, cart. 6, n. 21.
Edition: Alberzoni, 'Giacomo di Rondineto', appendix 5, pp. 161–2.

*16. 19 April 1211. Trezzo

Gerard, cardinal bishop elect of Albano, apostolic legate and bishop-elect of Novara, to all the archbishops, bishops, priests, deacons, provosts, ministers and rectors of his legation and province.

He reminds them that the Humiliati (*religio, quae Humiliatorum appellatur*), have received official approval for the integrity of their faith, exhorts them to attend the Humiliati meetings (*colloquia sive parlamenta*), from which 'much good by the grace of God proceeds' and in any case warns them not to impede or disturb them. The witnesses include lord James, provost of the church of Rondineto in Como.

Edition: *VHM* II, pp. 154–6 from Puricelli.
Cited: Cipollone, 'Gerardo da Sesso, legato apostolico', pp. 374–6.

17. 4 December 1214. Lateran

Universitatem vestram monendam
Innocent III to the *podestà* and rectors of the cities and other places (*loca*), of *Lombardia*.

He instructs them not to exact either the *fodrum* or any other tax from the Humiliati, whom he describes as leading the common life, firmly rooted in the truth of the catholic faith and praiseworthy in the Roman Church and in their devotion to the pope.

Edition: *VHM* II, pp. 156–7 from Puricelli.
Regest: Potthast, 4944.

18. 8 December 1214. Lateran

Quod abrogantes impietatem
Innocent III to the Humiliati of *Lombardia*, constituted in the Catholic faith and apostolic devotion (*humiliati per Lombardiam in fide Catholica et devotione apostolica constitutis*).

He exhorts them to give up impious and secular desires and to live soberly, justly and piously in order to give joy to the pope, earn merit themselves and provide an example for others. They are not to think of this world but are to seek the world to come.

On verso: 'Admonitio ad ordinem u[b]i iube[t] ea proposito pres[e]v[er]e[n]t'.

Original: Brera AD XVI I/6.
Edition: *VHM* II, p. 157.
Regest: Potthast, 4945.

19. 18 December 1220. Lateran

Diligentiam pii patris
Honorius III to the prelates of the Brera, *Domus nova* Milan, Monza, Marlano, Vico, Çerbeto, *Domus nova* Pavia, Bergamo, Brescia and the other prelates of the same order and their brothers and sisters.

He confirms the bull of Innocent III for the Second order (8 above).

Original: Brera AD XVI I/7.

20. 13 December 1226. Lateran

Ex parte vestra
Honorius III to the rector, brothers and sisters of the Humiliati of Brera.

In reply to a petition concerning fasting. As they live by the labour of their hands, they cannot observe the rule concerning fasting and silence without inconvenience. Honorius therefore allows their rector to dispense from these rules in times of work (*tempore laborandi*).

Original: Brera AD XVI I/8.
Edition: Giulini, VII, p. 578.
Regest: Potthast, 7630; *VHM* II, p. 158; Biancolini, VI, p. 194; Pressuti, II, 6098.

21. 13 December 1226. Lateran

Cum ab exordio
Honorius III to the rector, brothers and sisters of the Brera.

He instructs them to observe the rule approved by Innocent III and releases them from observance of earlier customs.

Original: Brera AD XVI 1/9.
Edition: Giulini, VII, pp. 578–9.
Regest: Potthast, 7630; *VHM* II, p. 158; Giulini, IV, pp. 297–8; Biancolini, VI, p. 194; Pressuti, II, 6098.

22. 24 May 1227. Lateran

Petitiones que nobis
Gregory IX to the brothers and sisters of the order of the Humiliati of Oltreticino, Pavia.

In reply to their petition, because they have fallen on such great poverty that many of them are constrained by lack of necessities and there is no hope of recovery without help from the Apostolic see, he gives them the hospital of Sta Giustina to administer. He also gives them the hospital because there has been little or no hospitality observed there and it should relieve their misery and should provide for the poor and infirm. The bishop and others are to have their rights. He specifically forbids them to alienate or diminish the goods of the hospital; rather, they are to reform it and he trusts that they will give alms and do other pious works (*helemosinis* [sic] *et aliis operibus pietatis*).

Register: ASVat Registro Vaticano 14, fo. 13v 90.
Edition: Auvray, I, 90.

23. 25 May 1227. Lateran

Ex parte vestra
Gregory IX to the brothers and sisters of the order of the Humiliati.

In response to a petition, he allows them to use fat on those days when others use meat, especially because oil is scarce in many of the places where they live (*praesertim cum pleraque locorum, in quibus consistitis, oleo non abundet*).

Original: ACA Milan C/6
Copy: Ambrosiana, A 20 sup. fos. 41r–v (early fourteenth-century).
Edition: *VHM* II, pp. 158–9 from Puricelli.
Regest: Potthast, 7916; Biancolini VI, p. 195; Palestra 14; Jordan and Wool, p. 19.

24. 29 May 1227. Lateran

Ex parte vestra
Gregory IX to the brothers and sisters of the order of the Humiliati.

In response to a petition, he allows them to attend the office, make confession and bury their dead in time of general interdict but without solemn rites.

Original: ACA Milan, C/7.
Copy: Thirteenth century: ASVer Ghiara 2, 118 authenticated by Milanese notaries: Guarmaxius son of the late Forte of *borgo* Vimercate . . . Amicus and Conrad son of the late Anselm *de Vedano* of the city of Milan; early fourteenth century: Ambrosiana, A 20 sup. fos. 39v–41r.

Edition: *VHM* II, pp. 159–60 from Puricelli.
Regest: Potthast, 7921; Palestra, 16; Jordan and Wool, p. 19.

25. 29 May 1227. Lateran

Nobis fuit humiliter
Gregory IX to the ministers of the houses of the order of the Humiliati.
   In response to a petition, he allows them to use mattresses and sheets normally forbidden by the institutions of the order and releases them from the observance of fasts and silence when necessity dictates.

Original: ACA Milan, C/8.
Copy: Ambrosiana, A 20 sup. fos. 41v–3r (early fourteenth century).
Edition: *VHM* II, pp. 160–1 from Puricelli.
Regest: Potthast, 7922; Palestra, 15; Biancolini, VI, p. 194 dates this 25 May; Jordan and Wool, p. 19.

26. 30 May 1227. Lateran

Diligentiam pii patris
Gregory IX to the prelates of the Brera, *Domus nova* Milan, Monza, Marlano, Vico, Zerbeto, *Domus nova* Pavia, Bergamo, Brescia and the other prelates of the same order and their brothers and sisters.
   He re-confirms the bull of Innocent III for the Second order (8 above).

Original: Brera, AD XVI I/10.
Regest: *VHM* II, p. 161; Potthast, 7923.

27. 3 June 1227. Anagni

Incumbit nobis
Gregory IX to the Third order.[2]
   Confirmation/reissue of the letter of Innocent III of 7 June 1201 as a full privilege.

Edition: *VHM* II, pp. 162–3 from Puricelli.

28. 7 June 1227. Anagni

Cum felicis memorie
Gregory IX to the ministers and brothers and sisters of the order of the Humiliati.
   He sends them a copy of Innocent III's corrected rule *Omnis boni principium* which Innocent had taken care to have kept at the Curia. He has had it sealed with his own seal for greater security and so that no one shall be able to corrupt it (*quatenus nulli de cetero sit facultas eandem alicujus fermenti regulam depravare*).

Copy: Late thirteenth-century codex: Ambrosiana D 58 inf.; fourteenth-century copies: ACA Milan, A/2; Ambrosiana A 20 sup. fos. 1r–39v.
Edition: Zanoni, pp. 352–70.
Regest: *VHM* II, pp. 163–4 from Puricelli; Potthast, 7925; Palestra, 17; Jordan and Wool, p. 19.

---

[2] No addressee given.

Appendix I

Cited: Castagnetti, 'La regola del primo e secondo ordine', pp. 181–2.

29. 11 June 1227. Anagni

Propositum vestrum approbatum
Gregory IX to Giovannibellus *de Calvençano*, Manaria of Monza, Peter *de Folcatio*. [sic] *de Carate*, William *de Cerliano* and the other ministers of the order of the Humiliati and their brothers and sisters.
    He confirms Innocent III's bull for the Third order (7 above).
    Original: ACA Milan, B/7.
    Copy: ASMi 638 Domenicani Pavia, 1319 (an authenticated copy drawn up at the orders of the archdeacon of Alessandria).
    Regest: *VHM* II, p. 164 from Puricelli; Potthast, 7929; Palestra, 18.

30. 17 June 1227. Anagni

Proposuisti nuper in
Gregory IX to the bishop of Brescia (Guala *de Roniis* 1229–43/44).
    Confirming the donation of the church of of SS Faustino and Giovitta (which had been damaged in an earthquake), which Gregory, as cardinal legate in *Lombardia*, had given to the Friars Preacher (and was later disputed with the Humiliati).
    Edition: *VHM* II, pp. 165–6 from the archives of San Bartolomeo de Contegnaga, Brescia; Odorici, VII, p. 89, CCLXII.
    Regest: Potthast, 7942.
    Cited: Archetti, 'Gli Umiliati e i vescovi', pp. 303–5.

31. 10 July 1227. Anagni

Dilecti filii fratres
Gregory IX to the archbishop of Milan (Henry *de Settala* 1211–31).
    In response to a petition from the Humiliati, he instructs the archbishop to prevent secular authorities from forcing the Humiliati to take oaths even for small matters, because this contradicts their *propositum*, except in certain conditions (*nisi testimonii, calumpnie, pacis et fidei*) and for urgent and evident need.
    Original: Brera, AD XVI I/11.
    Edition: *VHM* II, pp. 166–7.
    Regest: Potthast, 7961.

32. 4 September 1227. Anagni

Succensa est quasi
Gregory IX to Roger, subprior of Bologna, brother Melioratus of the order of Preachers and the priest John *de Gambara*.
    Concerning the visitation of exempt houses, including the Humiliati, in the cities and dioceses of Cremona, Brescia and Bergamo. If all three cannot participate, two of them are to proceed.
    Original: Brera, AD XVI I/12.
    Edition: *VHM* II, pp. 167–8.

Regest: Potthast, 8028.
Cited: Violante, 'La chiesa bresciana nel medioevo', p. 1073.

33. 4 September 1227. Anagni

Succensa est quasi
Gregory IX to Joachim of Sta Maria and Jordan, priors of the order of Preachers
and Gandulfus, a brother of the same order in Padua.
   Concerning the visitation of exempt houses, including the Humiliati, in the
cities and dioceses of Padua, Venice and Treviso. Formula as in 32 above.
   Register: ASVat Registro Vaticano 14, fo. 43r 152.
   Regest: Auvray, I, 153; Potthast, 8027.

34. 16 December 1227. Lateran

Dilecti filii prepositi
Gregory IX to the archbishop of Milan (Henry *de Settala*).
   In response to a petition from the Humiliati, he instructs the archbishop to fulfil
an earlier mandate, warning all those in *Lombardia* and the March who call
themselves Humiliati to observe the rule or *vivendi formam* approved by Innocent
III; and compelling those who did not wish to do this to give up the name, habit,
place and possessions of the Humiliati and transfer to another approved order. This
is to be done before the following Easter otherwise the task will be undertaken by
Al. Dominican prior in Milan, *Al.* of Parma of the same order and Master
Oldericus, canon of Sto Stefano in Brolo in Milan.
   Original: Brera, AD XVI I/13.
   Edition: *VHM* II, pp. 169–70.
   Regest: Potthast, 8083.

35. 18 December 1227. Lateran

Justis petentium desideriis
Gregory IX to the provost and chapter of the church of Ognissanti Fossadolto
(Borghetto Lodigiano).
   He confirms their possession of the church of San Giorgio given to them by the
bishop of Lodi with the consent of his chapter.
   Edition: *VHM* II, pp. 181–2 from Puricelli (but without details of date so that
               Tiraboschi mistakenly dated it to c. 1231); *CDL*, II/I, 283, p. 294,
               from thirteenth-century authenticated copy in the *mensa* of the
               Archivio vescovile Lodi, with date as above.
   Cited: Mercatili Indelicato, 'Per una storia degli Umiliati nella diocesi di
               Lodi', pp. 366–7.

★36. 10 January 1229. Milan

Justis petentium desideriis
Goffredus, cardinal priest of San Marco and apostolic legate,[3] to Albert and his

---

[3] Goffredus *de Castiglione*, a Milanese churchman, later pope as Celestine IV for three weeks in
   1241.

confratres and the congregation of the house in the Brera which once belonged to Guercius and now belongs to them (*olim de guercio nunc vestra*).

In response to a petition, the cardinal confirms the concession already given by the archbishop of Milan[4] for the building of an oratory with a cemetery (*licentiam et auctoritatem construendi* [*VHM = constituendi*] *oratorium in vestro proprio fundo . . . statuens ut illud amodo liberum habeat cimiterium*), subject only to the payment of one pound of wax on the feast of St Mary in September (8 September) and allowing for the office to be celebrated by any priest as long as using the Ambrosian rite (*dummodo Ambrosianus sit*).

Original: Brera, AD XVII/14.
Edition: *VHM* II, pp. 170–1.
Cited: Giulini, VII, pp. 427–8

*37. 15 July 1229. Cervie

Goffredus, cardinal priest of San Marco and apostolic legate, to Albert, provost of the church of Sto Stefano in Brolo Milan.

In response to a petition from the Humiliati concerning the exemption of the hospital of Sta Giustina in Pavia from money exactions. The Humiliati claimed that the chapter of Pavia had unduly oppressed and molested them, asking for an imposing amount of money. They had therefore appealed to the legate, but in contempt of this, the chapter had unjustly excommunicated them and placed them under interdict. The cardinal instructs Albert to investigate and give judgement. The letter, sealed with wax, was delivered in the canonica of Sto Stefano by brother Beltramus *de Campisio*, brother and syndic of the church of the Humiliati built at Pavia on the Ticino and in the presence of witnesses: Peter Berloccus, son of the late Guifredus, Master Oldericus, son of the late Petribellus, and Aliprand Mazali, son of the late Rubeo, canons of Sto Stefano.[5]

Tiraboschi omitted a line after the date: *actum in canonica sancti stephani mediolanen.*

Original: Brera, AD XVII/15.
Edition: *VHM* II, pp. 171–3.

*38. 20 February 1230. Milan and 27 March 1279. Rome

In 1279 Peter of Milan, vice chancellor of the Roman church, has an authenticated copy drawn up of a settlement originally agreed in 1230 between the Humiliati of Brera and William, priest of the parish church (*parochia*) of Sant'Eusebio, Anselm and Mangiaferre Cagapisto and Goffredus son of the late Anselm Cagapisto [the Cagapisto family held the *iuspatronatus* for Sant'Eusebio] and representatives of the neighbourhood (*vicinia*). This concerned the compensation for the priest of Sant'Eusebio for any loss incurred because of the newly built church of the Brera. The representatives of the *vicinia* were Bellinus *de Greppa*, Anricus (Henry) [*VHM = Anna*] *de Barni*, Otto *de Buixio*, Peter *de Cerro* and Christian *de Muzano* whose status as representatives of the *vicinia* was attested by a document prepared by James, son of Airoldo *de Garbaniate*, notary.

---

⁴ See above, no. *10.   ⁵ On Master Oldericus, see above, no. 34.

This is followed by a second document drawn up in the *parlatorio* of the domus of the Brera. Twenty-one brothers of the Brera, on behalf of the chapter and *universitas* of the house and four of the five representatives of the *vicinia* and James as representative of the Cagapisto family, confirm their consent to the agreement.

On the verso in a contemporary hand: *Privilegium pro ecclesia domui Brayde* [. . .] *licet per dominum Philipum Archiepiscopum predecessorem predicti Henrici suam* [. . .] *buerit licentiam ante anno domini mccviii* and: *Privilegium pro ecclesia domui brayde que hedificata fuit mccxxviiii primo iunii.*

    Original: Brera, AD XVI 1/49.
    Edition: *VHM* II, pp. 173–80.

39. 15 January 1231. Lateran

Libertates ecclesiarum quas
Gregory IX to the provost and brothers of the church of Ognissanti Fossadolto in the diocese of Lodi (Borghetto Lodigiano).

    Confirming the provision made by Gerard *de Sesso*, exempting the church from communal or episcopal taxes, except for a pound of wax each year to the bishop for the confirmation of the provosts and the ordination of clerics. He notes that the community, which included eighty men and women (*pie considerans quod octoginta Religiosae Personae inter Viros et Mulieres in Ecclesia vestra Divinis sunt obsequiis mancipatae*) receive the poor and pilgrims and administer to their needs (*quae passim pauperes et peregrinos transeuntes recipiunt, et eis necessaria subministrant*).

    Edition: *VHM* II, pp. 180–1 from Puricelli; *CDL*, II/I 300, p. 309, from a
                  thirteenth-century authenticated copy in the *mensa* of the Archivio
                  vescovile, Lodi.
    Regest: Potthast, 8650.
    Cited: Cipollone, 'Gerardo da Sesso, legato apostolico', p. 376.

★40. 31 May 1232. Mantua

Goffredus, cardinal priest of San Marco and apostolic legate, to the *podestà* and commune of Pavia.

    He exhorts them not to force the 'brothers of the congregation of the order of the Humiliati' to hold office, or to burden them, nor to make them observe lay statutes and agreements or impose undue collects and exactions upon them.

    Edition: R. Soriga, 'Per la storia degli Umiliati in Pavia', *Bollettino della società*
                  storica pavese di storia patria, 16 (1916), 189–90.

41. 8 July 1232. Spoleto

Devotionis vestre supplicationibus
Gregory IX to the provosts and brothers of the Humiliati of *Lombardia* and the March.

    In response to their petition, he allows them to both give and demand oaths as necessity or utility shall require.

    Original: Brera, AD XVI 1/16.
    Edition: *VHM* II, pp. 182–3.

Regest: Potthast, 8963.

*42. 23 July 1232. Tortona

Peter, bishop of Tortona (1221–55), with the chapter of the cathedral (*maioris ecclesie*) assents to the request of the Humiliati, giving them the church or oratory of San Marco with certain conditions.

Edition: *Carte dello Archivio capitolare di Tortona*, II, 392.
Cited: Goggi, *Per la storia della diocesi di Tortona*, II, p. 24.

*43. 17 October c. 1233 (1232/4)[6]

Berardus I dal Pozzobello, archpriest of Monza (1232–4) to Tuttobellus, minister of the *domus* of Humiliati and Humiliati women of Sant'Agata in the *borgo* and the whole congregation of the house.

In response to a petition and with the counsel of his chapter, he allows them to arrange to have an oratory and cemetery on their land, dedicated to 'God and the ever virgin Mary' for their own use and members of the order and no others, unless with special licence. They may also receive any priest to celebrate the office 'as long as he is catholic'.

Edition: Frisi, *Memorie storiche di Monza e sua corte*, II, 108, p. 100; Giulini, VII, pp. 590–1.
Regest: *VHM* II, p. 195.

44. 1 June 1235. Perugia

Si sub lege
Gregory IX to the provosts and brothers of the order of the Humiliati.

In response to a petition from the Humiliati, he orders that the custom (*consuetudo*) in areas of *Lombardia*, that those who have been robbed openly or secretly may take from the lands where the crime was committed, up to the quantity of property lost, shall not be used as a pretext for molesting the Humiliati. He also recalls the Humiliati's proposal of life amongst the people (*uos que proposuistis in medio populi uestri degere*).

Register: ASVat Registro Vaticano 18, fos. 32v–33r 93.
Regest: Auvray, II, 2602.

45. 15 January 1236. Viterbo

Cum a nobis
Gregory IX to the provosts, ministers and brothers of the order of the Humiliati.

In response to a petition, he decrees that they must not allow the brothers of the Third order who live with their families in their own homes to be forced to go to war, because no one can serve God and Mammon (*cum nemo possit deo mammoneque*

---

[6] The date is given as the 'xv kal nov' but the year is missing. Sormani, who perhaps saw a different copy, dated it to 1233, while Frisi dated it 1232–4.

servire) nor are they to suffer burdens (*onera*) against the concessions of their privileges, or to be taxed more than their fellow citizens.

Register: ASVat Registro Vaticano 18, fo. 115r 407.
Regest: Auvray, II, 2995.

46. 18 January 1236. Viterbo

Congruam officii nostri
Gregory IX to the archbishop of Milan (William *de Rizolio* 1230–41) and his suffragans.

In response to a petition from the provosts and ministers of the Humiliati, Gregory instructs the archbishop to allow them licence to have priests to minister the sacraments to the brothers and sisters of the Second order (*in locis Secundi ordinis habendi religiosos sacerdotes qui fratribus et sororibus eorum ecclesiastica sacramenta ministrent*) and to have cemeteries for their own use (*ad opus*), especially as it is not fitting that religious women should go out in the streets for these reasons (*ut mulieres per vicos hac occasione discurrant*). The only proviso is that the churches of the *vicinia* are not to be cheated of their customary oblations or damaged in their other rights (*consuetis oblationibus non fraudentur et alias sui iuris[7] dispendium non incurrant*).

Register: ASVat Registro Vaticano 18, fo. 115v 410.
Edition: *VHM* II, pp. 196–7 from Puricelli; Auvray, II, 2998.

47. 19 January 1236. Viterbo

Universi prepositi et
Gregory IX to the archbishop of Milan (William *de Rizolio*) and his suffragans.

In response to a petition from the provosts and ministers of the order of the Humiliati, he instructs the archbishop to allow the use of portable altars in those regular houses which do not have churches (*non seculares . . . proprias ecclesias non habentibus*).

Register: ASVat Registro Vaticano 18, fo. 115v 409.
Edition: Auvray, II, 2997.

48. 1 February 1236. Viterbo

Insinuantibus dilectis filiis
Gregory IX to the patriarch of Aquileia (Bertold 1218–51) and his suffragans.

In response to a petition from the provosts and ministers of the order of the Humiliati, he instructs the patriarch not to allow the Humiliati living in religious houses (*in religiosis domibus commorantibus*) or their property to be molested in his and his suffragans' cities and dioceses by those who have in the past attacked them.

Register: ASVat Registro Vaticano 18, fo. 104v 343.
Edition: Auvray, II, 2938.

49. 20 February 1236. Viterbo

A nobis humiliter
Gregory IX to the provosts of the order of the Humiliati.

---

[7] In *VHM* the word 'iuris' is missing here.

He authorises them to give the benefit of absolution to those admitted into the conventual houses of the order (*qui in conventualibus domibus vestri ordinis admittuntur iuxta formam ecclesie*), unless guilty of very grave crime (in which case they are to be referred to the Apostolic see) and as long as they shall have done fitting satisfaction for any damage or injury caused.

    Original: Brera, AD XVI I/17.
    Register: ASVat Registro Vaticano 18, fo. 115r–v 408.
    Edition: *VHM* II, p. 195.
    Regest: Auvray, II, 2996.

*50. 12 October 1236

William, archbishop of Milan to all prelates and clerics.

He gives notice of a letter he has received from Gregory IX (46 above) ordering him to allow the Second order permission to have priests and cemeteries as long as this does not damage the churches of the *vicinie*.

    Edition: *VHM* II, pp. 196–7 from Puricelli.

51. 12 May. 1237. Viterbo

Succensa est quasi
Gregory IX to the provincial prior of *Lombardia* of the order of Preachers.

Concerning the yearly visitation of exempt houses, including the Humiliati, in the provinces of *Lombardia*, Piedmont, Romagna and the Marches of Treviso and Ancona as well as the cities and dioceses of Venice and Genoa.

    Register: ASVat Registro Vaticano 18, fo. 288r 81.
    Edition: Auvray, II, 3668.
    Regest: Potthast 10343.

52. 9 October 1238. Anagni

Cum sicut ex
Gregory IX to the provost and brothers of Rondineto in Como.

In response to a petition, he allows them to swear oaths when reason requires and notwithstanding the rule.

    Register: ASVat Registro Vaticano 19, fo. 53v 273.
    Edition: Auvray, II, 4557.

*53. 25 August 1239

James *de Breganza*, bishop of Verona (1225–54) instructs the Humiliati of the house of Zevio in the *villa* of Furca, founded by Marchesius, to observe the rule of the Canons of San Marco Mantua. He acts at the request of brother Ferabove of Zevio and allows them to build a church dedicated to the Virgin and Sant'Agnese, in which they may have priests and clerics. Among other conditions, they are not to admit parish members either to their services or for burial to the detriment of the parish church, but if any do choose to be buried there, the parish church is to have half the income.

Edition: Biancolini, IV, pp. 808–9.
Regest: *VHM* II, p. 197.
Cited: De Sandre Gasparini, 'Aspetti di vita religiosa, sociale ed economica',
            p. 138.

*54. 26 September 1239

Ardingus, bishop of Florence (1230–47), gives the Humiliati the semi-ruined
church of San Donato alla torre. They are to be subject to the jurisdiction of the
bishop and to pay an annual cense of 30 Pisan shillings.

Original: Archivio di Stato Florence, Commenda Covi (no. 2 is entitled 'Filza
            di scritture diverse appartenente ai Padri Umiliati ed estratti di notizie
            riguardanti il detto ordine 26 Marzo 1404 al 1558', and contains
            twenty *pezzi*, the first twelve of which were flood damaged and have
            not yet been restored).[8]
Edition: *Sanctae ecclesiae florentinae monumenta*, II, pp. 1035–6.
Regest: *VHM* II, p. 197.
Cited: Davidsohn, *Forschungen zur Geschichte von Florenz*, IV, p. 402;
            Benvenuti Papi, 'Vangelo e tiratoi. Gli Umiliati ed il loro
            insediamento fiorentino', 78 (who corrects Lami's edition).

55. 13 October 1246. Lyons

Accepte deo et
Innocent IV to the provosts, prelates, ministers, brothers and sisters of the order of
the Humiliati.

He confirms brother Beltramus, provost of San Luca in Brescia, as Master
General of the order. Following a request for help from the Humiliati, Innocent
had appointed Otto *de Tonengo*, cardinal bishop of Porto, to assist them in making
the appointment. He exhorts them to receive Beltramus *in patrem et pastorem*.

Original: ACA Milan, C/12; C/13.
Register: ASVat Registro Vaticano 21, fo. 330r–v 163.
Edition: *VHM* II, pp. 198–200 from Puricelli.
Regest: Palestra, 22 and 23; Berger, I, 2158; Potthast, 12301.

56. 23 October 1246. Lyons

Cum in vestris
Innocent IV to the Master, brothers and sisters of the order of the Humiliati.

In response to their petition, he allows them to use fat from the feast of the Holy
Cross to the feast of All Saints.

Original: Brera, AD XVII/18; ACA Milan, C/14.
Register: ASVat Registro Vaticano 21, fo. 334r 180.
Edition: *VHM* II, pp. 200–1.
Regest: Palestra, 24; Berger, I, 2175; Potthast, 12320.

---

[8] I am grateful to Dr K. J. P Lowe for this information.

Appendix I

57. 23 October 1246. Lyons

Devotionis vestre precibus
Innocent IV to the brothers and sisters of the Third order of the Humiliati.

In response to their petition, he allows them to hear the office, make confession to priests, receive penance and bury the dead in time of general interdict, as long as they exclude the excommunicate, do not ring bells and say the office in a low voice (*subpressa voce*).

Register: ASVat Registro Vaticano 21, fo. 337v 197.
Edition: Berger, I, 2193.

58. 30 October 1246. Lyons

Experientia instructa laboris
Innocent IV to the Master and brothers of the First order of the Humiliati.

As they have informed him that in the *propositum* conceded to the first fathers of the order by the Apostolic see (*quod propositum nominatim vestri ordinis primis fratribus ab apostolica sedis concesso*), there are things which cause them trouble, Innocent states that they are only held to obey that which will be approved by future General Chapters.

Register: ASVat Registro Vaticano 21, fo. 337v 195.
Edition: Berger, I, 2191.

59. 30 October 1246 (9 November). Lyons

Ex ore domini
Innocent IV to the Master and brothers and sisters of the First and Second orders of the Humiliati, both present and future *regularem vitam professis in perpetuum*.

In response to their petition, he renews the protection of St Peter for the houses of the First and Second orders and then makes a series of provisions, some repeating earlier regulations, others modifying the rule and government of the order.

Three passages are different to the text given in Tiraboschi's edition: sales, exchanges, investitures and mortgages (*impignorationes*) agreed by the Master and chapter of any house [not just of the General Chapter] are to be observed inviolably.[9] Provosts and priests [VHM = *prelati*], with deacons and subdeacons may celebrate solemn mass. No house of their order is to be allowed to transfer to any other profession [this passage is omitted in *VHM*].

---

[9] This reading is confirmed (although the name of one of the notaries is different) by a contract of sale drawn up in Novara in 1296 which refers to the bull and to the clause concerning sales and exchanges as follows: 'privillegio [sic] concesso per Innocentium papam magistro et universsis [sic] fratribus et sororibus primi et secundi ordinis Humiliatorum tam presentibus quam futuris, dato Lugduni per manum magistri Martini sancte Romane ecclesie vicecancellarii, .V. ydus novembris, inditione .V., incarnacionis dominice anno .MCCXLVI., pontificatus vero domini Innocentii pape anno quarto, et autenticato per fratrem Carnevarium de masenago notarium et domus de Braida Guercii Mediolanensis de ordine Humiliatorum professum, continenti inter cetera quod omnes venditiones, commutationes et investituras et pignorationes possessionum que de consilio et magistri et capituli cuiuslibet domus vel maioris aut senioris partis ipsius licite facte fuerint, ratas haberi volumus et inviolabiliter observari.' *L'ospedale della Carità di Novara*, 128.

Appendix I

Original: Brera, AD xvi i/17a (bought from Libreria Antiquaria R. Rizzi 1964); ACA Milan, A/4.

Register: ASVat Registro Vaticano 21, fos. 336r–7r 193.

Copy: Contemporary authenticated copy: Archivio capitolare Asti, carte dal 1238 al 1398, document 40 (prepared by Milanese notaries: James son of the late Servairoldi *de Garbagate de braida guerzii* citizen of Milan, Mainfredus, son of Servairoldi, James *de Gargagniate de braida guerzii* citizen of Milan and James of Magnago, notary, son of the late Pinabellus Pancagnoni *porte Vercelline*); two fourteenth-century authenticated copies: ASVer Ghiara bolle papali 5 (1333) and Novara: Codex vetus cols. 50r–v were drawn up by a notary in the 1330s for the hospital of the Carità in Novara, from an authenticated copy prepared by Caremarius [sic] *de Massenago*, a notary and professed member of the Brera house in Milan.

Edition: *VHM* ii, pp. 201–7 from Puricelli. (The original now in the Brera was presumably unknown to Tiraboschi); Biancolini, vi, p. 214 (apparently from the original now in the Brera); *L'ospedale della Carità di Novara*, 134 (of the fourteenth-century copy: *Ex are* [sic] *domini*); *Asti*, 82.

Regest: Potthast, 12331; Berger, i, 2189; Palestra, 25.

Note: The date of this privilege is not immediately clear. The manuscript now in the Brera, which appears to be the original bull, has no date because the end of the text is lost. However, Biancolini's transcript, which matches it closely, dates it to *iii kalendis novembris* (30 October). Tiraboschi, who did not know the Brera original, thought that Biancolini's transcript was full of mistakes but gave the same date because he took it from Puricelli. This is also the date of another original in the archive of the Curia Arcivescovile in Milan. However, the Vatican register dates the letter to *V idus novembris* (9 November) and the same November date is given in two fourteenth-century authenticated copies in Verona and Novara. It may be that the privilege was issued twice.

60. 30 October 1246. Lyons

Unigenitus dei filius

Innocent IV to the brothers and sisters of the Second order of the Humiliati.

In response to their petition and in order to remove any doubts, Innocent clarifies and modifies certain elements of the rule approved by the Apostolic see for the first brothers, who were inexpert concerning the condition, difficulties, burdens of the order and strengths of the brothers (*si aliquando in alicujus sancte religionis proposito vel regula pro varietate personarum et temporis aliquid immutamus dum vel difficilia ad modum faciliorem reducimus vel gravia mitigamus aut obscura lucidius aperimus, non religionem intendimus diminuere sed augere. Sane in regula vestra olim primis fratribus vestri ordinis adhuc paucis et rudibus conditionem difficultates onera ordinis et vires fratrum parum expertis ab apostolica sede concessa quedam continebantur difficilia et confusa que vos iam per experientiam radio cognitionis plenius illustrati vidistis non posse absque gravi incomodo tolerari*). The modifications concern the election of the superior of each house, the canonical hours, the receipt of donations from the faithful (*pia donationes* [*VHM* = *devotione*] . . . *possitis recipere*), letting out land (*ad fictum terras vestras cum expedire videritis . . . concedentes*), fasting and shaving. All other chapters of the rule are to remain valid.

Register: ASVat Registro Vaticano 21, fo. 337r 194.

Copy: ASVer Ghiara 3, 203 (thirteenth-century authenticated copy by notaries from the *Borgo Porta Nuova* in the city of Milan: John, son of Peter Pillosius, James, son of Bellotus *de Luirate* and Anselm son of Anselm *de Lomovico*.

Edition: *VHM* II, pp. 207–10 from Puricelli.

Regest: Berger, I, 2190; Potthast, 12332.

61. 30 October 1246. Lyons

Cum gratie filiis
Innocent IV to the brothers of the Third order of the Humiliati.

Because of the inexperience of the first brethren to whom the rule approved by the Apostolic see was granted and in view of the experience now acquired of the difficulties of observance (*vos instructos experientia super observantia valde difficili eorumdem aggravent plurimum et molestent*), Innocent modifies their rule concerning the distribution of any superfluous food and property to the poor and fasting: from Pentecost to the feast of All Saints, they are not required to fast, except for the sixth day and the fasts instituted by the Church. From All Saints to Christmas and from Epiphany to Lent (*maiorem quadragesimam*), they are to fast devotedly (*ieiunia deuotius seruaturi*) on the fourth and sixth days, ignoring the different provisions of their original *forma vivendi*.

Register: ASVat Registro Vaticano 21, fo. 337v 196.

Edition: Berger, I, 2192.

62. 8 November 1246. Lyons

Auctoritate vobis presentium
Innocent IV to the Master and provosts of the order of the brothers of the Humiliati.

He allows them to absolve postulants wishing to enter the order unless guilty of very grave crime (*gravis et enormis excessus*), in which case they are to be referred to the Apostolic see.

Register: ASVat Registro Vaticano 21, fo. 340v 231.

Copy   ASVer Ghiara 3, 205 (thirteenth-century notarial copy, drawn up by the same notaries as 60 above).

Edition: *VHM* II, p. 210 from Puricelli.

Regest: Berger, I, 2227; Potthast, 12351.

63. 13 November 1246. Lyons

Multorum relatione fideli
Innocent IV to the Master of the order of the Humiliati.

Having heard that the numbers in the Second order have greatly increased and some houses have quite large congregations, but that many houses do not have churches or priests, he orders the Master to ensure that churches are built in those houses of the Second order which do not yet have one, with the help and consent of the bishops. They are also to procure priests to assist in the office.

Original: Brera, AD XVI 1/19.
Register: ASVat Registro Vaticano 21, fo. 341v 238.
Edition: *VHM* II, pp. 211–12.
Regest: Berger, I, 2234; Potthast, 12358.

64. 13 November 1246. Lyons

Etsi ex iniuncto nobis
Innocent IV to brother Stephen of the order of Preachers, *capellano et penitentiario nostro.*

Concerning the visitation of the exempt houses, including the Humiliati, in the provinces of *Lombardia*, Romagna, the Marches of Treviso and Ancona and the cities and dioceses of Venice and Genoa. He may turn for help in carrying out the visitation, not only to members of his own order but to those of others.

Register: ASVat Registro Vaticano 21, Curiales fo. 420r 34.
Regest: Berger, I, 2950; Potthast, 12357.

65. 4 December 1246. Lyons

Cum sicut dilecti
Innocent IV to the abbots and prelates of other churches whom this letter may reach.

In response to a petition from the Humiliati, he instructs them publicly to announce the excommunication of any professed members of the order of the Humiliati whom the Master and brothers shall inform them have left the order out of lightness of soul, or less reasonable causes and who have been excommunicated by the master.

Copy: Brera, AD XVI 1/20. Contemporary authenticated copy drawn up by Miranus son of the late Peter *de cerro* [*VHM*, petri *de Ro*], Mainfredus son of the late James *de Garbagniate de braida guercii* and James, son of the late Airoldus *de Garbagniate de braida guerzii.*
Edition: *VHM* II, pp. 213–14.
Regest: Potthast 12365.

66. 7 June 1247. Lyons

Devota humilitas a
Innocent IV to the Master and provosts of the order of the Humiliati.

In response to their petition, Innocent decrees that, as the *podestà* and rectors of the cities, *castri* and other places of *Lombardia*, compel brothers of the First, Second and Third orders to carry out secular duties, prejudicing and damaging their order and houses, no secular person shall force them to carry out these duties against their will.

Register: ASVat Registro Vaticano 21, fo. 399r 772.
Edition: *VHM* II, p. 216 from Puricelli.
Regest: Berger, I, 2770; Potthast, 12552.

Appendix I

67. 7 June 1247. Lyons

Devota humilitas dilectorum
Innocent IV to the archbishop of Milan (Leo *de Perego* 1241–63).

He warns the archbishop not to allow the Humiliati to be molested for the reasons given in 66 above. The *arenga* discusses the origins of the name of the order in their pious humility (*Devota humilitas . . . a qua idem ordo denominationem accepit*).

    Register: ASVat Registro Vaticano 21, fo. 399r 773.
    Edition: Berger, I, 2771; *BF*, I, pp. 461–2.
    Regest: Potthast, 12553.

68. 8 February 1248. Lyons

A primordio surgentis ecclesie
Innocent IV to the Master of the order of the Humiliati.

In response to a petition from the Master and provosts and in settlement of a dispute at San Michele in Alessandria, where his judges delegate, the Cistercian abbots of Sant'Andrea and Tiglieto, had ordained that brethren of the community should have precedence according to the date of their entry into the order, Innocent affirms the reverence due to clerics and re-establishes an earlier statute of the order giving clerics precedence over the laity in their houses. This is to be observed in all houses of the order.

    Register: ASVat Registro Vaticano 21, fo. 504r–v 559.
    Edition: *VHM* II, pp. 219–21 from Puricelli.
    Regest: Berger, I, 3608; Potthast, 12836.

69. 14 December 1248. Lyons

Ex parte dilectorum
Innocent IV to the archbishop of Milan (Leo *de Perego*).

In response to a petition from the Humiliati, he instructs Leo to ensure that the Humiliati are not unjustly weighed down by the collectors of taxes imposed *pro rata* on the clergy of *Lombardia* in the name of the Church of Rome.

    Original: Brera, AD XVI I/22.
    Edition: *VHM* II, p. 221.
    Regest: Potthast, 13137.

70. 19 January 1249. Lyons

Intimantibus vobis accepimus
Innocent IV to the minister and brothers of the Brera.

In response to their petition and concerning the transfer of brethren to other orders, done without the licence of their ministers, so as to avoid various duties entrusted to them because of the adversity of the times, both by the Apostolic legate and by the commune of Milan, Innocent decrees that none of their professed members may transfer to another order on account of the current war (*instante presertim guerra durante*), without his or the Master General's licence, nor may anyone else receive them, notwithstanding any indulgence of the Apostolic see.

Appendix I

Original: Brera, AD XVI 1/23.
Edition: *VHM* II, pp. 222–3.

71. 30 April 1249. Lyons

De dilectis filiis

Innocent IV to the bishop of Brescia (Azzo *de Torbiato* 1246–53).

Concerning the church of SS Faustino e Giovitta in Brescia which the Dominicans wish to leave and which Innocent now instructs the bishop to confer, with its garden, on the Humiliati of the Second order of Brescia, whose own house is said to be too small (*habitationem nimis artam habere dicantur*), if it shall seem expedient. The Dominican prior and brothers are first to give account for the amounts spent on the buildings (*faciens ab eisdem prius dicti priori et fratribus satisfactionem de sumptibus quos fecerunt in edificiis exhiberi*).[10]

Edition: *VHM* II, pp. 223–4 from the archives of San Bartolomeo de
              Contegnaga, Brescia; Odorici, VII, 262.
Regest: Potthast, 13330.
Cited: Archetti, 'Gli Umiliati e i vescovi', pp. 303–5.

72. 17 June 1249. Lyons

Sua nobis dilecta

Innocent IV to Baldwin Pennello, a canon of Genova.

In response to a petition from *nobile mulier Iacoba, nata quondam Balirii de Castello* of Genoa concerning the office of minister of the hospital of Rivarolio (diocese of Genoa). Following papal instructions, the provost of the church of Genoa had conferred this on Iacoba after the death of the late minister but it had been falsely disputed by the minister and brothers of the hospital known as Bethleem in Prato Ticino in Pavia, who had obtained a letter from Innocent and sent it to the prior of the Humiliati of porta Vacce in Genova [the role of the Humiliati is not made clear]. Innocent now instructs Baldwin to ascertain the facts and, if the minister had died at the time when the administration was given to Iacoba, to put Iacoba in possession of the hospital and defend her once there, if necessary calling on the help of the secular arm.

Copy: ASVat Registro Vaticano 21a (a copy from the original made in 1763
              by G. Garampi), fo. 317v–8r 640.
Edition: Berger, II, 4630.

73. 11 August 1249. Lyons

De singulorum salute

Innocent IV to the archbishops and bishops whom this letter may reach.

They are to give licence to preach the word of God publicly in their cities and dioceses to the brothers of the order of the Humiliati, whose knowledge of letters and eloquence favour this (*quibus ad hoc litterarum scientia et eloquentia suffragantur*).

---

[10] The documents concerning the moneys spent by the Dominicans are published by Odorici, VII, 262.

275

Appendix I

Original: Brera, AD XVI I/27.
Edition: *VHM* II, p. 224.
Regest: Potthast, 13764.

74. 12 August 1249. Lyons

Licet dilecti filii
Innocent IV to Octavian, cardinal deacon of Sta Maria in Via Lata[11] and Gregory, bishop-elect of Tripoli and legate of the Apostolic see.[12]

As he has heard that the Master, provosts and brothers of the Humiliati live in poverty and acquire the necessary food for life through manual labour (*in paupertate viventes, victui suo necessaria de labore manuum suarum acquirant*), yet they receive the messengers of the Apostolic see kindly and treat them with honour when they happen to visit their houses, Innocent exhorts Octavian and Gregory not to oppress them with procurations and collects, as they have great reverence for the Apostolic see.

Original: Brera, AD XVI I/26.
Edition: *VHM* II, p. 225.
Regest: Potthast, 13765.

75. 12 August 1249. Lyons

Ut fratres vestri
Innocent IV to the Master and provosts of the order of the Humiliati.

He allows them and priests of their order to hear confession, impose penance and minister the other sacraments to the brothers and sisters of the Second order.

Original: Brera, AD XVI I/24.
Edition: *VHM* II, p. 226.
Regest: Potthast, 13766; Biancolini, VI, p. 201.

76. 12 August 1249. Lyons

Dilectorum filiorum magistri
Innocent IV to the archbishop of Milan (Leo *de Perego*).

In response to a petition from the Humiliati, he confirms a statute of Gregory *de Montelongo*, bishop-elect of Tripoli, then his legate, which ordered the *podestà*, rectors and others who preside over the cities and *castra* of his legation to refrain from requiring any *fodrum*, *taglie* or other exactions from churches, prelates, clerics and ecclesiastical persons in his legation. He also instructs the archbishop to ensure that the Humiliati are not unduly molested in this matter.

Original: Brera, AD XVI I/25.
Edition: *VHM* II, pp. 226–8.

---

[11] Octavian degli Ubaldini, a Florentine, or from Mugello near Florence, administrator in the church of Bologna, then cardinal deacon of Sta Maria 1244–68. Died in 1273.
[12] Gregory *de Montelongo*, bishop-elect of Tripoli, then transferred to Aquileia in November 1251. Died 1269.

Appendix I

77. 18 August 1249. Lyons

Cum a nobis petitur
Innocent IV to the Master and brothers of the order of the Humiliati.

In response to their petition he confirms the order of his legate Gregory *de Montelongo* forbidding the *podestà*, consuls and others in his legation to oppress the Humiliati or other ecclesiastics with taxes.

Original: Brera, AD XVI 1/28.

78. 3 November 1249. Lyons

Per sedem apostolicam
Innocent IV to the Master of the order of the Humiliati.

He instructs the Master to ensure that one manner of singing and reading the office is observed in the order, notwithstanding any other custom.

Original: Brera, AD XVI 1/29.
Edition: *VHM* II, p. 228.
Regest: Potthast, 13854.

79. 4 November 1249. Lyons

In tuum honorem
Innocent IV to the *podestà* of Milan.

In response to a petition from the Humiliati. The property of numerous brothers of the Brera was included in the inventory of the city of Milan before they entered the order; the *podestà* has unjustly required and extorted collects after they had made their profession and given their property to the house. Innocent thus appeals to the *podestà*'s nobility and reverence for the Apostolic see, asking him to stop molesting the house on this matter.

Original: Brera, AD XVI 1/30.
Edition: *VHM* II, pp. 229–30.
Regest: Potthast, 13855.

*80. 6 February 1250

At the request of Octavian, cardinal deacon of Sta Maria in Via lata, Philip, bishop of Florence (1249–50) gives the provost of the Humiliati of San Michele in Alessandria the *capella* of Sta Lucia on the Arno. They are to remain subject to episcopal jurisdiction and to pay an annual cense of one pound of wax. The particular reason given is that they will be more comfortable there (*cum ibi habilius et melius valeant commorari quam in praedicta ecclesia S. Donati*). They are also specifically authorised to build a new church if needed (*licentiam ut in eodem fundo dicte ecclesie si necesse fuerit possitis aliam ecclesiam de novo fundare*).

Original: Archivio di Stato, Florence.[13]
Edition: *Sanctae ecclesiae florentinae monumenta*, II, p. 948; Ughelli, III, col. 120.
Regest: *VHM* II, p. 230.

---

[13] See above, p. 269, *54.

Appendix I

Cited: Davidsohn, *Forschungen zur Geschichte von Florenz*, IV, p. 402;
Benvenuti Papi, 'Vangelo e tiratoi. Gli Umiliati ed il loro
insediamento fiorentino', pp. 78–9.

*81. 30 April 1250

Sigebaldus, bishop of Novara (1249–78), renews the confirmation for the Humiliati
of San Clemente in Sizzano first issued by bishop Odemarius (1235–49).

Cited: Balosso, 'Gli Umiliati nel Novarese', p. 73, on the basis of an early
nineteenth-century account in the Archivio di Stato Novara:
Armadio Frasconi, ms. XIV 23.

82. 23 July 1250. Lyons

Sua nobis . . magister
Innocent IV to the bishop of Brescia (Azzo *de Torbiato*).

    In response to a petition from the Humiliati concerning the church of SS
Faustino and Giovitta in Brescia, which Innocent had ordered the bishop to give to
the Humiliati, with its house and garden and with the consent of the prior *si
expedire videris*. The bishop had not wished to give the church to the Humiliati,
because no express mention of it was made in the letter (*pro eo quod de ipsa in eisdem
litteris expressa mentio non fiebat*), so the Humiliati had appealed to the pope, who
now ordered the bishop, if this was the case, to confer the church on the Humiliati,
reserving any cense owed to the church of Brescia in recognition of dominion.

Edition: *VHM* II, pp. 232–3 from the archives of San Bartolomeo de
Contegnaga, Brescia.
Regest: Potthast, 14020.
Cited: Archetti, 'Gli Umiliati e i vescovi', p. 304.

83. 13 August 1250. Lyons

Exhibita nobis vestra
Innocent IV to the Master and brothers of the order of the Humiliati.

    In response to their petition: although Innocent had forbidden any brother to
leave his house without licence after making profession, the Cistercians, Carthusians, Franciscans and Dominicans as well as other orders (asserting that they had an
indulgence of the Apostolic see by which they might receive brethren and absolve
them from excommunication, suspension or interdict), had received their brothers,
causing damage to the Humiliati. Innocent therefore decrees that, after making
their profession, no brother, under the pretext of any indulgence, may dare to leave
without licence and that the Master or his officers may excommunicate them, from
which they may be absolved only by the master or his successors or by a special
mandate of the Apostolic see which makes express reference to this present
document.

Original: Brera, AD XVI 1/31.
Register: ASVat Registro Vaticano 22, fo. 7v 46.
Edition: *BF*, I, p. 551.
Regest: Berger II, 4795; Potthast, 14039 (but under August 12); VHM II,
p. 235.

Appendix I

84. 20 August 1250. Lyons

Cum a nobis petitur
Innocent IV to the Master and brothers of the order of the Humiliati.

He confirms the donation made with the consent of his chapter by the archbishop of Milan (Leo *de Perego*) to the Humiliati of the Benedictine church of Sta Trinità in the suburb of Porta Cumana in Milan and of the church of Sta Maria in Campo, which belonged to Sta Trinità, with all its rights and possessions.

Register: ASVat Registro Vaticano 22, fo. 9r 5.
Edition: *VHM* II, pp. 234–5 from *BF*, I, p. 553.
Regest: Berger, II, 4805.

85. 23 August 1250. Lyons

Tua petitio nobis
Innocent IV to the Master of the order of the Humiliati.

In response to their petition, he allows him to release those who join the Humiliati from previous vows forbidding the use of fat.

Original: Brera, AD XVI 1/32.
Register: ASVat Registro Vaticano 22, fo. 8v–9r 55.
Edition: *VHM* II, 235–6.
Regest: Berger, II, 4804; Potthast ,14047. In Berger it is addressed to the Master 'and his successors', but in the Vatican Register it is addressed to the Master alone.

★86. 2 December 1250. Monza

Arderic *de Soresina*, archpriest of Monza (1245–51), in response to their petition, gives Iunius, minister of the house and congregation of the Humiliati brothers and sisters of Mediovico in Monza, permission to build an oratory and cemetery. The church is to be dedicated to the honour of Almighty God and the blessed Virgin Mary and the church of Monza and St James the Apostle. The conditions are the same as those given by Berardus I dal Pozzobello c. 1233 (★43 above). The witnesses include a Dominican, brother John *de Opreno*.

Original: ASMi Fondo Pergamene 592.
Edition: Longoni, 'Origini degli Umiliati a Monza', 9; Frisi, *Memorie storiche di Monza e sua corte*, II, 137, pp. 122–3, from 'Archivio della Chiesa Di Monza'; Giulini, VIII, pp. 655–6.
Regest: *VHM* II, p. 235.

87. 25 June 1251. Genoa

Cum a nobis
Innocent IV to the prior and brothers of the order of Preachers in Milan.

Confirming the settlement of a dispute between the Dominicans of Sant'Eustorgio and the Humiliati of Sant'Agata in Monza who had recently settled near Sant'Eustorgio, over Humiliati preaching, the status of their houses and the building of windows overlooking the Dominicans' garden.

Appendix I

Edition: *VHM* II, pp. 236–43 from archive of Sant'Eustorgio, Milan and from *Bullarium Ordinis Fratrum Praedicatorum*, I, 195.

88. 4 August 1251. Milan

Favore vestre religionis
Innocent IV to the Master and brothers of the Third order of the Humiliati of Milan.

In response to a petition, he decrees that no *podestà* or commune or *universitas* of any other place may force them or the brothers of their order, who live in their own homes with their families, to take up arms, keep horses, do military service or expeditions on horseback, or to give oaths. Nor may they oppress them more than their fellow citizens in the payment of taxes or loans.

Register: ASVat Registro Vaticano 22, fo. 115v 19.
Edition: Berger, III, 5455.

89. 4 August 1251. Milan

Favore religionis dilectorum
Innocent IV to the archbishop of Milan (Leo *de Perego*) and the bishop of Pavia (Rodobaldus Cipolla, 1230–54).

Innocent instructs them to help the Humiliati, not allowing them to be molested on account of the matters enumerated in 88 above.

Edition: *VHM* II, pp. 243–4 from *BF*, I, pp. 575–6.

90. 5 August 1251. Milan

Solet annuere
Innocent IV to the Master and brothers of the Third order of the Humiliati of Milan.

In response to their petition, he decrees that the Humiliati are not to be forced to pay the *bannum* required according to statute from the residents of a parish in which a murder has been committed.

Original: ASVat Registro Vaticano 22, fo. 115v 20.
Edition: Berger, III, 5456.
Related record: *Gli atti del comune di Milano*, II/1, 555 (1269).

91. 5 August 1251. Milan

Solet annuere
Innocent IV to the archbishop of Milan (Leo *de Perego*) and the bishop of Pavia (Rodobaldus Cipolla).

Innocent instructs them to ensure that the Humiliati are not molested on account of the matters enumerated in 90 above.

Edition: *VHM* II, pp. 244–5, from *BF*, I, pp. 576–7.

92. 23 August 1251. Milan

Ex parte dilectorum
Innocent IV to the abbot and General Chapter of the Cistercians.

In response to a petition from the Humiliati, concerning the Cistercians' acceptance of Humiliati brethren in spite of papal letters to the contrary, he asks them to ordain in their chapter that no brother of the Humiliati should be received into their order.

      Original: Brera, AD XVI 1/36.
      Edition: *VHM* II, pp. 245–6.

93. 25 August 1251. Milan

Insinuastis nobis quod
Innocent IV to the Master and brothers of the order of the Humiliati.

In response to a petition, informing Innocent that the provosts, prelates and brethren of certain houses of the order, after making their profession, honour the habit and observe the rule of the order, yet refuse to obey the Master or to admit him for visitation or correction as do the other houses of the order, to the danger of their souls and the evident detriment of the whole order, Innocent decrees that all the provosts, prelates and brothers of the order shall obey the master and admit him for due correction and visitation, if necessary under the threat of ecclesiastical censure.

      Edition: *VHM* II, pp. 246–7 from Puricelli.
      Regest: Potthast, 14388.

*94. 11 September 1251

John, bishop of Florence (1251–75), transfers the Humiliati of San Donato alla torre to Sta Lucia.

      Edition: *Sanctae ecclesiae florentinae monumenta*, II, p. 1035; Ughelli, III, cols.
                  122–4.
      Regest: *VHM* II, p. 247.

95. 22 September 1251. Brescia

Personis omnibus ecclesie
Innocent IV to the archbishop of Milan (Leo *de Perego*).

He instructs the archbishop to prevent the *podestà* and commune of Milan forcing the Humiliati of the First and Second orders to carry out public offices (*officia publica seu communitatis*) and other duties detrimental to church liberty (*detrimentum libertatis ecclesiastice*) and injurious to the order. If he should be remiss in this, Innocent will write to the archpriest of Monza (Raymond della Torre) in his diocese, to force the archbishop to act, notwithstanding any apostolic indulgence.

      Original: Brera, AD XVI 1/37.
      Edition: *VHM* II, pp. 247–9.

Appendix I

96. 21 November 1251. Perugia

Dilecto filio . . ministro
Innocent IV to the Master of the order of the Humiliati in *Lombardia*.

Innocent had learnt from the minister of the Friars Minor of Genoa that Salvus, a brother of that order who had been *conversatus* for over fifteen years, had given up his habit and transferred to the order of the Humiliati. Innocent had therefore ordered the Master and his order not to keep him and to remove him from the office of provost which he held (*ac removeretis omnino a prepositura eiusdem ordinis quam tenebat*). However, the Master and provosts who were with him had not done so and although the Franciscan minister had excommunicated Salvus, nonetheless they kept him in the order with the books which he had stolen from the Franciscans (*cum libris de ipsorum ordine furtive sublatis*), arguing that he had first been professed in the order of the Humiliati and had left without licence. As it is dangerous to converse with this man who has been justly separated from the communion of the faithful, Innocent instructs the Master to remove Salvus from office as provost, to declare him excommunicate and to avoid him thereafter until he shall return, with the books, to the Friars Minor and live under his minister. Otherwise he will call on the bishop of Tortona to force the Master to do so using the threat of ecclesiastical censure, notwithstanding any indulgence to the contrary.

> Register: ASVat Registro Vaticano 22, fos. 119v–20r 53.
> Edition: *BF*, I, pp. 578–9
> Regest: Potthast, 14419; Berger, III, 5489.
> Cited: Brooke, *Early Franciscan Government*, p. 225.

*97. 13 May 1252. Milan

Leo, archbishop of Milan, in the chamber next to the church of San Barnaba near to the archiepiscopal palace and in the presence of witnesses (brother James *de besana* and brother Bartholomew of Padua, both Franciscans and brother Ottobellus of Gallarate of the order of the Humiliati, *capell. infradicti domini archiepiscopi*) instructs a notary to draw up authenticated copies of three privileges for the Humiliati issued by Innocent IV.

The three bulls are as follows:

> **97a.** 23 August 1251. Milan
>
> *Meritis devotionis*
> Innocent IV to the archbishop of Milan (*Leo de Perego*) and the bishops of Pavia (*Rodobaldus Cipolla*) and Brescia (*Azzo de Torbiato*).
>
> In response to a petition by the Master and brothers of the order of the Humiliati, Innocent has decreed that the members of the First and Second orders should not be required to carry out the common business of the city or other places or to collect tolls (*communia negotia civitatum vel aliquorum locorum exercere, vel pedagia colligere minime teneantur*) and he now instructs the archbishop and bishops to ensure that the Humiliati are not molested in this manner.

97b. 12 February 1250. Lyons

Persone humiles divini
Innocent IV to the archbishop of Milan (Leo *de Perego*).

The master, provosts and prelates of the order of the Humiliati of *Lombardia* have complained to the pope that although the professed members of the order are afflicted by serious injury and expense on account of the evil times, nonetheless, certain *podestà* and communes of *Lombardia* and especially those of Milan, have required loans from the houses of the order in their districts. So, as Innocent does not wish to add insult to injury (*quod afflictis addatur afflictio*), or to allow the Humiliati, under the powerful hand of the Lord to be injured by lay powers (*potentia laicali*), he instructs the archbishop to ensure that the Humiliati are no longer so molested.

97c. 21 August 1251. Milan

Ex parte dilectorum
Innocent IV to the archbishop of Milan (Leo *de Perego*) and the bishops of Brescia (Azzo *de Torbiato*) and Pavia (Rodobaldus Cipolla).

The Master and brothers of the Humiliati have informed the pope that, although the brethren of the Third order have an indulgence that they must not carry arms or go to war, yet the *podestà* and communes of cities and other places exact and extort collects from those who do not go into the army. Innocent, wishing that these brothers should enjoy the fruits of this indulgence (*ut de indulgentia huiusmodi fratribus ipsis fructus proveniat affectatus*), decrees that they are not to be required to pay any collect and the archbishop and bishops are to ensure this.

Original:	Brera, AD XVI I/33. *Ex parte Dilectorum* itself also survives in very poor condition: Brera, AD XVI I/35.
Copy:	Brera, AD XVI I/34 (fourteenth century: 12 September 1334) drawn up by Arasmolus son of the late William *de pirovano* (Asmolus describes the original, including the lead bull and the circumstances of the copying in detail), Bellotolus son of Guiscardus of Desio and Pellegrinus son of Mafeius *de [. . .]*. The copy is sealed by the *dominus vicarius*.
Edition:	*VHM* II, pp. 249–52.

98. 11 August 1252. Perugia

Dilecti filii fratres
Innocent IV to the bishop of Novara (Sigebaldus).

In response to a petition from the brothers of the Second [*VHM* omits *secundi*] order of the Humiliati of Milan, Innocent instructs the bishop to ensure that the *podestà* and commune of Milan stop forcing the Humiliati to hold public office in the city and to lend money to the commune (which, if it is true, damages the liberties of the church). He may use the threat of ecclesiastical censure, but is not to place the whole of Milan under excommunication or interdict unless he receives a special mandate to this effect.

Original: Brera, AD XVI I/38.
Edition: *VHM* II, p. 253.

99. 28 January 1253. Perugia

Cum dilecta in
Innocent IV to the minister and convent of the *domus parva* Cremona.

As Marchisia, sister of B., a servant of Peter [Capocci, 1244–59], cardinal deacon of San Giorgio al Velabro, wishes to live with them according to their rule, he asks them to accept her as their sister and *socia* and treat her with sincere love (*et sincera in domino caritate tractetis*), notwithstanding any privileges which they may have.

Register: ASVat Registro Vaticano 22, fo. 267v 666.
Regest: Berger, III, 6525.

100. 3 April 1253. Perugia

Cum dilecta in
Innocent IV to the provost (sic) of the order of the Humiliati in *Lombardia*.

Concerning Marchisia (99 above), Innocent asks the provost, in so far as it concerns him (*prout ad te pertinet*), to allow her to enter the said house notwithstanding any other provisions.

Register: ASVat Registro Vaticano 22, fo. 267v–8r 667.
Edition: Berger, III, 6526.

101. 20 November 1253. Lateran

Sua nobis dilecti
Innocent IV to William, cardinal-deacon of Sant'Eustachio.

In response to a petition from the Humiliati concerning the use of eggs, milk and cheese on those days on which there is no fast imposed by the Church, Innocent asks William to make arrangements as shall seem fitting to him (*ut super hoc statuas, quod videris expedire*).

Original: Brera, AD XVI I no 39.
Register: ASVat Registro Vaticano 23, fo. 33r 270.
Edition: *VHM* II, p. 257.
Regest: Berger, III, 7093; Potthast, 15168.

102. 13 December 1253. Lateran

Ex parte tua
Innocent IV to the Master of the order of the Humiliati.

In response to a petition from the Master, provosts, prelates and brothers of the First and Second orders of the Humiliati of the city and diocese of Milan, Innocent authorises the master to ensure that the Humiliati are no longer required to exercise the business (*comuni negotia*), of the cities or other places or collect tolls, as he had written in an earlier privilege.

Original: Brera, AD XVI I/40.
Edition: *VHM* II, p. 258.

Appendix I

103. 18 December 1253. Lateran

Cum a nobis petitur
Innocent IV to the provost and convent of the Humiliati of Prato Ticino in Pavia.

In reply to their petition, he confirms all liberties and immunities conceded by his predecessors as well as any liberties and exemptions from secular exactions reasonably given to them by kings, princes and the Christian faithful and their lands and possessions and other goods peacefully obtained.

    Original: Brera, AD XVI 1/41.
    Edition: *VHM* II, p. 259.

*104. 11 February 1254. Milan

In the house of the Brera in Milan, brother Beltramus, Master of the whole order of the Humiliati, stipulates the settlement of a dispute which had arisen between the provosts and convents of the house or church of San Michele in Alessandria and the convent of the church of San Marco in Tortona concerning the election of the prior in the church of San Marco, novices, revenues and property which come to it and the receiving of those in the fraternity who wish to convert for the good of their souls. He first causes letters which he has received concerning the dispute to be recorded in the account of the settlement.

These are as follows:

    104a 13 December 1253. Lateran

    Sua nobis dilecti
    Innocent IV to the Master of the order of the Humiliati.

    In response to a petition from the prior and brothers of the church of San Marco of the Humiliati in Tortona, Innocent instructs the Master to take care to settle the dispute between this house and the provost and convent of San Michele in Alessandria, who claim that the prior and brothers are subject to them and concerning certain other rights, which had been in contention for a long time and which the Master had neglected to settle, to the serious damage of the said prior and brothers.

    *104b No date given

    William, cardinal deacon of Sant'Eustachio (described by Beltramus as protector of the order: *venerabilis patris nostri Ordinis Protectoris*), to the Master of the order of the Humiliati.

    Concerning the dispute between San Marco Tortona and San Michele Alessandria, over the election of the prior of San Marco, the profession of novices, revenues and other monies due to the church of San Marco and on the acceptance of the sick for conversion (*ac infirmis ad conversionem recipiendis*). Lest in fighting they should in a short while consume the substance of their churches, which had been acquired by extended toil (*ne ibi litigando brevi ora consumerent ecclesiarum suarum substantiam longis sudoribus acquisitam*), he does not wish them to dispute this case in the Curia or elsewhere so he instructs the master, together with the minister of the Friars Minor of the Milanese Province, the provosts of Rondineto and Viboldone, brother Tuttobellus of Monza and brother Miranus of the Brera, of the order of the Humiliati, to settle the dispute. If any of these cannot or will not take part, he is to obtain the advice of others.

Beltramus then stated that, as he feared that a similar dispute concerning the same issues (*articulis*) might arise between San Michele and the convents of the churches of Sta Marta in Genoa and Sta Trinità in Asti and wishing to remove cause for dispute, he has carefully discussed the matter with the provosts of Rondineto and Viboldone and with brother Tuttobellus of Monza and brother *Mirabonus* (sic) of the Brera (but without the Franciscan minister because he could not be asked, being absent from these parts: *quia non erat in istis partibus*) and has now ordained the settlement of the dispute as follows:

(i)   The election of the prior is normally to be carried out annually by four brothers of the convent who shall appoint him with the advice and assent of the majority or *sanior pars*, bearing in mind the health of souls and the utility to the church. If they cannot agree, the provost or his messenger or vicar, may appoint a suitable prior for the church. After the election of the prior, the provost or his vicar, with the advice of the prior and the four, shall elect the other officials.

(ii) Concerning the acceptance of brethren in good health, Beltramus determines that three from each of the houses (San Marco, Sta Marta and Sta Trinità) shall come to the house of San Michele in Alessandria and there, with the provost and six of the brothers of San Michele, shall discuss the numbers to be accepted in each of these churches and in San Michele and once agreed, the provost of San Michele, with the consent of his brothers shall receive brothers and sisters up to that number as established.

(iii) On the profession of novices, Beltramus ordains that when there should be any novice in any of these churches who wishes to procede to regular observance (*qui profiteri desideret observantiam regularem*), if the prior and convent shall wish to receive the novice, the provost himself shall go to him personally and carefully enquire into his life and customs, lest while outside the cloister and travelling in various places they should sink back in memory and desire for old pleasures (*ne dum extra ea claustra septa per loca diversa pergentes relabantur in memoriam et desiderium veterum voluptatum*). If the provost cannot go, he is to send the prior of the church to receive the profession in his place.

(iv) On the acceptance of sick brethren, he orders that the prior and convent of the church which they wish to enter, shall inform the provost as soon as possible, humbly requesting permission to receive the sick person. If, however, it is feared that the postulant may soon die, Beltramus gives the prior and convent licence to receive him or her, but warns them not to abuse this privilege. If the provost should be in distant parts so that he cannot be contacted quickly and there is a pressing case (*casus mortis incumbat*), the prior and convent may receive the sick person.

(v)   Donations and other property which comes to any of the churches by any title, except from the customary business (*de mercaturi consuetis*) shall all belong to that same church, for the use of the brothers and sisters living there. The profits from customary and honest business are to be administered by brethren deputed to hold this office (*ad illud officium deputatos regantur fideliter*), are to be kept totally separate from the other goods of the church and are to be used above all to pay immediate debts. He also orders that the priors and convents of these churches must not purchase any property or build anything without the advice and consent of Beltramus himself and the provosts of Viboldone and Oltreticino, until the said debts are fully paid off (*integre persoluta*), after which Beltramus and the provost of San Michele shall decide what shall be done with their profits.

All of these clauses are to be observed inviolate, objectors being subject to excommunication, saving only the duties of subjection, honours, visitation and correction and other rights belonging to the church of San Michele.

Finally, Beltramus reserves to himself and his successors the right to modify, add to, correct and interpret any of the clauses as shall seem best and orders that a public document be drawn up, furnished with his seal.

The witnesses are: James, provost of the church of San Giovanni of the Humiliati of Porta Orientale, brother William *de Sexto*, prelate of the *domus nova*, brother Anricus *de Mascenago* of the same house, brother Peter of the Humiliati house of Sant'Agata (Monza) and *alii plures*.

> Edition: *VHM* II, pp. 260–6.

105. 15 May 1254. Assisi

Petitio dilectorum
Innocent IV to the provost of the church of Rondineto of the order of the Humiliati, in the diocese of Como.

In response to a petition from the archdeacon and chapter of the church of Como, he instructs the provost to investigate and, if possible, to settle a dispute over provision to prebends in the church of Como.

> Register: ASVat Registro Vaticano 23, fo. 92v 661.
> Regest: Berger, III, 7521.

106. 2 September 1254. Anagni

Ex parte dilectorum
Innocent IV to the bishop of Mantua (Martin *de Puzolerio*, 1252–68).

In response to a petition from the Humiliati concerning their transfer to the church of SS Faustino and Giovitta in Brescia, which he is to ensure that the bishop of Brescia (Cavalcane *de Salis* 1253–63) confirms.

> Edition: *VHM* II, pp. 267–8 from the archives of San Bartolomeo de
>   Contegnaga, Brescia.

*107. 10 June 1255

William d'Este, bishop of Adria (fl. 1240–58), authorises the start of work on the church of San Bartolomeo (San Bartolo) by the Humiliati of Rovigo, on land outside the southern gate of the city conceded to brother Agostinus, syndic of the community by brother Paglia in the same year.

> Cited: *Rovigo. Ritratto di una città*, I, p. 153.

Appendix I

108. 4 March 1256. Lateran

Justis petentium desideriis
Alexander IV to the provost and brothers of Rubono (in Register copy identified as *ordinis humiliatorum*) in the diocese of Milan.

In response to their petition, Alexander confirms the directive of the archbishop of Milan and his chapter, subjecting the monastery of the nuns of Rubono in the diocese, then of the order of St Benedict, which had been abandoned in both spiritual and temporal matters (*in spiritualibus et temporalibus desolatum*), to the Humiliati both in temporal and in spiritual things. The Humiliati *ordo* approved by the Apostolic see is to be observed there and visitation is to be the task of the provost of the order; all previous rights belonging to the archbishop and his successors and to the church of Milan are to be reserved. The Humiliati are also to provide for the needs of food and clothing of the nuns from the property of the monastery, for as long as they should be placed in any of the monasteries of the order by the archbishop and his successors.

     Register: ASVat Registro Vaticano 24, fo. 152v 177.
     Edition: *VHM* II, pp. 268–9 from *BF*, II, p. 121; de la Roncière, I, 1214; Potthast, 16278.

109. 23 March 1256. Lateran

Dilectus filius frater
Alexander IV to the Master of the order of the Humiliati.

Following the report of brother Egidius, proctor of the Master and of the Humiliati, Alexander instructs the Master to act upon the order of Innocent IV and have churches built in Second order houses which do not yet have one and to have suitable brothers of the Second order promoted (*promouere facias*) as clerics, subdeacons, deacons and priests, so that they may celebrate the office. If the Master fails to act, the pope will order the provost of Viboldone to force him to do so, using the threat of ecclesiastical censure.

     Original: ACA Milan, C/17.
     Edition: *VHM* II, pp. 270–1 from Puricelli.
     Regest: Biancolini, VI, p. 201; Palestra, 29.

*110. 6 August 1257. Milan

In the *domus nova* and in the presence of witnesses (brother Fichus, minister of the *domus nova* and brother Peter *de Misena* and brother Thomax, prior of Asti (*de Astu*) and brother Thomasus of the house of the Humiliati *de Astu* and brother John Bianchi of the house of the Humiliati of Viboldone and brother Lanfranc, priest and brother James of the house of the Humiliati of San Marco, Tortona), brother Beltramus Master general of the whole order of the Humiliati approves and ratifies the settlement of a dispute between the house and chapter of San Michele in Alessandria, represented by the provost brother Roland and brother William, their syndics and proctors and Ognissanti in Florence, represented by brother Meliorellus and brother Bencivene, their syndics and proctors. The dispute was heard before Conrad, provost of Viboldone of the diocese of Milan and brother Miranus of the

Humiliati of the Brera, delegated by the Apostolic see. The documents concerning the case are then copied out and are as follows:

*110a.

An account of the San Michele case, given by brother Roland provost of San Michele.

*110b.

The sentence of the judges, condemning Ognissanti and ordering them to give obedience to San Michele.

110c. 25 October 1256. Anagni

Sua nobis dilecti
Alexander IV to the provost of the church of Viboldone in the diocese of Milan and brother Miranus of the house of the Brera in Milan.
 He instructs them to hear the case and give judgement.

*110d. Sunday 30 April 1256

Actum in primo Consilio generali
The General Chapter gives authority and consent to the proceedings for settling the dispute.
 In the palace of the church of San Pietro in Viboldone, in the presence of Redulfus Riboldus of Monza and Leo Mantegatius of the city of Milan and brother Roffinus *de Axeno de Concellis* as witnesses, Master Beltramus, with the will of the General Chapter, or the greater and wiser part, so that the dispute may not continue between San Michele of Alessandria, represented by brother Roland provost, brother Gavarrus Buxagus, brother Roffinus *de Solerio* and brother Bernard Buxagus on one hand and Ognissanti in Florence, represented by brother Melioratus, brother Albertinus and brother Donatus on the other, committed the investigation and settlement of the dispute to the provost of Viboldone, brother Miranus of the Brera in Milan, brother Tuttobellus prelate of Sant'Agata in Monza and brother Gabriel of Brescia.[14] If brother Gabriel were unable or unwilling to be present, his place was to be taken by the provost of Sta Croce Novara. The Master, Beltramus, with the consent of brother Lanfranc of Parma, brother James *de Cugnate* of Alessandria, brother Miranus of the Brera, brother Tuttobellus of Monza, brother Guy, provost, brother Conrad, provost of Viboldone, brother Boni, provost of the *Galgario* in Bergamo and brother Stephen, provost of Rondineto in Como,[15] *diffinitores* of the order, set a term of fifteen days for each side to present their case and further ordered that neither side might use any document written after that day or appeal to the pope.

---

[14] This Gabriel may be the man named in 1275 as prelate of San Paolo di Pontevico, Spinelli, 'Gli Umiliati in Emilia-Romagna', p. 140.
[15] Stephen of Rondineto is perhaps the same man who presided at a profession in the hospital of San Vitale, 1249, see Arizza, 'L'ospedale di San Vitale,' 10.

Appendix I

*110e.

On Monday 1 May, in the presence of Guifredus Bazo, notary of the city of Milan, Amizo, provost of Sta Maria which is known as the *domus Fratris Ottatii* of Porta Vercellina and brother Orivabene provost of Rubono, Master Beltramus made some adjustments to the conditions for the hearing and ordered that neither side was to put any dispute between the two houses before any other judge than those named, on pain of excommunication.

*110f.

The documents recording the appointment of the proctors on each side.
> Edition: *VHM* II, pp. 278–89.

111. 17 November 1257. Viterbo

Ex parte dilectorum
Alexander IV to the abbot of San Marciano, Tortona of the order of St Benedict.

In response to a petition by the provost and convent of the *domus Dei* in Asti of the order of the Humiliati and because of their excessive poverty, Alexander instructs the abbot to give them the church of San Michele *de Duducino* in the diocese, whose patrons and clerics gave their consent, if this is indeed the case.
> Register: ASVat. Registro Vaticano 25, fo. 95r 715.
> Edition: de la Roncière, II, 2318.

112. 19 May 1258. Viterbo

Sub religionis habitu
Alexander IV to the bishop of Mantua (Martin *de Puzolerio*).

As Alexander has heard that the Master and brothers of the order of the Humiliati have suffered injury from some who take the name of the Lord in vain (*qui nomen Domini recipere in vacuum*), he instructs the bishop to assist them against the insolence of robbers, thieves and attackers, not allowing them to be molested and punishing transgressors with ecclesiastical censure.
> Original: Brera, AD XVI 1/45.
> Edition: *VHM* II, pp. 289–90.

113. 20 May 1258. Viterbo

Gratiae divinae praemium
Alexander IV to the provosts, prelates and all the brothers of the order of the Humiliati.

As Beltramus, Master of the order had died, the General Chapter of the order came together and elected Peter, provost of San Luca in Brescia as Master of the order. Alexander confirms his election and exhorts the brethren to receive him joyfully and honourably and treat him as their father and pastor of their souls, giving him due obedience and reverence.
> Original: ACA Milan, C/18

Appendix I

Edition: *VHM* II, pp. 290–1 from Puricelli.
Regest: Palestra, 30.

114. 20 May 1258. Viterbo

Dilecti filii praepositi
Alexander IV to the Master of the order of the Humiliati.

In response to a petition from the provosts and brothers of the Humiliati, he instructs the Master to enforce in Milan the statute imposing a uniform manner of singing the psalms and chanting, which had been ordered by Innocent IV (78 above).

Original: *VHM* II, pp. 291–2 from Puricelli.

115. 3 June 1258. Viterbo

Cum a nobis petitur
Alexander IV to the Master and brothers of the house of SS Faustino and Giovitta in Brescia of the Second order of the Humiliati.

In response to their petition, Alexander confirms the episcopal concession of the *locus* and garden of SS Faustino e Giovitta, made on the instructions of Innocent IV.

Edition: *VHM* II, pp. 292–3 from the archives of San Bartolomeo de Contegnaga, Brescia.

116. 13 November 1258. Anagni

Ad ea que animarum
Alexander IV to the king of France (Louis IX).

As the Humiliati, whose merits he underlines (*apud Deum et homines sint ipsorum exigentibus meritis gratiosi et propter eorum conversationem laudabilem, ut pote qui propriis manibus laborando sine aliorum tedio victum querunt, elemosinas tribuunt, recipiunt hospites et predicant verbum Dei, in provincia Lombardie potissimum dilatati*) wish to expand into his kingdom, he asks Louis to give them and their messengers help and advice in establishing and encouraging their religion.

Original: Brera, AD XVI I/44.
Edition: *VHM* II, pp. 293–4.

117. 13 November 1258. Anagni

Ad ea que animarum
Alexander IV to the archbishops, bishops and other prelates of the Church who may read this letter.

He asks these ecclesiastics to support the Humiliati in their attempt to expand into France (116 above).

Original: Brera, AD XVI I/42 and 43 (two copies of same letter).

Appendix I

118. 1258. Viterbo

Alexander IV to the minister and convent of the house of the Humiliati of Parma.
He exempts them from communal taxes and exactions.
    Edition: Affò, *Storia di Parma*, III, pp. 76–8.
    Cited: Spinelli, 'Gli Umiliati in Emilia-Romagna', p. 155.

*119. 16 July 1259. San Salvatore Florence

In the church of San Salvatore in Florence, the council of experts (*Consilium peritorum virorum*) Diedatus, *Abatie Florentie*, Cambius *de Perebola* and Master Accursius, canons of the church of Sto Stefano *ad pontem* in Florence, declare that the provost and convent of the Humiliati brothers of Ognissanti *extra civitatem Florentie*, may receive the men and women of their Third order at the office, during the present general interdict (*tempore etiam huius generalis interdicti*). They do so because there is one Master, provost and prelate of the First, Second and Third orders of the said brothers of the Humiliati and they are all subject to one obedience, visitation and correction (*cum unus sit magister prepositus et prelatus et primi et secundi et tertii ordinis dictorum fratrum humiliatorum et omnes sub una obedientia visitatione et correctione consistant*), as appears in a papal privilege and because there is a special privilege for the Third order, that in times of general interdict, they may hear the office and receive the sacraments unless the interdict specially concerns them. Furthermore, a letter of pope Alexander IV to the bishop of Florence, stated that there was no special or express interdict on the Third order.
    The witnesses were lord Maccius *Abatie Florentie*, the priest James, rector of the church of Sta Lucia at Sant'Eusebio,[16] and brother Thomas of the convent of Ognissanti.
    Edition: *VHM* II, pp. 295–6.

120. 13 December 1260. Lateran

Sua nobis dilecti
Alexander IV to the abbot of San Dionigi, Milan, the archpriest of Fara and the provost of the church of Sterniano in Bergamo in the dioceses of Bergamo and Milan.
    In response to a petition from the minister and convent of the Humiliati of Olginate in the diocese of Milan. A dispute about money and other matters between the Humiliati and Metellus, *dictum Mororium* [*VHM* = *moronum*] a citizen of Milan, had been heard (while the see of Milan was vacant) before Azo, *dicto Ceppo* a canon and vicar of the chapter of Milan, who was not delegated by apostolic authority. Azo had proceeded in the case against the minister and convent giving an incorrect and unjust sentence, so that they had appealed to the pope. Alexander therefore asks the three ecclesiastics to hear the appeal legitimately and to confirm or invalidate the sentence.
    Original: Brera, AD XVI 1/47.
    Edition: *VHM* II, pp. 297–8.

---

[16] Perhaps appointed by the Humiliati who had recently moved from Sta Lucia to Ognissanti.

121. 5 December 1262. Orvieto

Devotionis vestre precibus
Urban IV to the minister, brothers and sisters of the house of the Humiliati of the Ghiara in Verona.

In response to a petition, Urban allows the free (*liberas personas*) of the brethren, after leaving the world and making their profession (*munda relicta vanitate . . . professionem facientium*), to continue to enjoy rights of succession or other just title to property as if they had remained in the world and to freely distribute, receive, ask for or keep such property excluding only *feudalibus rebus*.

Original: ASVer. Bolle papali 12/2.

122. 5 August 1263. Orvieto

Significarunt nobis dilecti
Urban IV to the abbot of San Pietro in Ciel d'Oro Pavia and the provosts of the churches of Ferranea and Baveno in the dioceses of Acqui and Novara.

In response to a petition from the provosts, prelates and brothers of the First and Second orders of the Humiliati of Milan and diocese. They have reported to the pope that the archbishop of Milan (Otto Visconti 1263–95) has claimed that he has received letters from Urban allowing him the faculty of requiring money from the churches and monasteries of the city, diocese and province for his needs (*pro suis necessariis*) and with the pretext of these letters, has ordered them together to produce a large sum of money within a certain period, under threat of excommunication and interdict on their churches. The said provosts and brothers felt themselves unduly oppressed by this, because they humbly requested a copy of the letters but he never had them, so they appealed to the papal audience. Urban therefore instructs the three ecclesiastics to hear the case and give sentence with authority to force witnesses using ecclesiastical censure.

Original: Brera, AD XVI I/47.
Edition: *VHM* II, pp. 299–300.

Appendix II

PROFESSIONS OF FAITH

PREFACE

In 1991 Brolis published transcripts of the profession of vows by postulants in the Bergamo houses of Torre Boldone and the Galgario in 1255 and 1318. She knew of only two other documents of this type, both of which came from Monza and recorded the entry of new members into the *Domus de Carrobiolo* outside the walls and to the Third order *convegno* in the *contrata comuni*. They were dated 1259 and 1349 and had been published by Tiraboschi and Zanoni respectively.[1] Tiraboschi had also published a third document, dated 1253.[2] Nothing before the middle of the century was known to these historians. The Ghiara archive in Verona, however, has a very substantial number of professions of faith dating from 1205 to 1281. Some were published in 1765 by Biancolini and their whereabouts and potential have recently been made clear in the work of De Sandre Gasparini, based on extensive and often fruitful research in the Veronese archives.[3] Another early profession is in the Vatican archive.[4] This appendix gives the first twelve such records in sequence. They are shown in parallel columns and spaced in sections so as to facilitate comparison of the formulae used in each document. Punctuation follows that of the documents, and for the sake of brevity standard abbreviations have not all been expanded. Only personal names have been capitalised to ease comprehension. Otherwise all spellings and capitalisation reflect the practice of the notaries.

---

[1] Brolis, *Gli Umiliati a Bergamo*, pp. 111–13, her appendix 2, 6, 20 with reference to documents in *VHM* II, pp. 296–7, Zanoni, pp. 299–300; the document of 1259 is also in Frisi, *Memorie storiche di Monza e sua corte*, II, no. 149, p. 129.

[2] *VHM* II, p. 13.

[3] Biancolini, *Le chiese di Verona*, III, pp. 258–9 and VI, pp. 265 and 266; see also Zocca, 'La "domus" degli Umiliati di Sta Maria della Giara'; De Sandre Gasparini, 'Per la storia dei penitenti a Verona nel secolo xiii. Primi contributi', pp. 257–83; 'Aspetti di vita religiosa, sociale ed economica di chiese e monasteri nei secoli xiii–xv', pp. 138–42; 'L'assistenza ai lebbrosi nel movimento religioso dei primi decenni del duecento veronese. Uomini e fatti', pp. 25–59, p. 53; 'Movimenti evangelici a Verona all'epoca di Francesco d'Assisi', p. 154.

[4] ASVat, Baldaria 4 (1205). See below, appendix II, 1. Professor De Sandre Gasparini kindly allowed me to consult briefly both a catalogue of the Baldaria documents drawn up by G. Gualdi and the appendix to Zocca's thesis, which are now in her possession. The transcripts used here are my own.

I have used parenthetical dots to indicate omitted material, and dots in square brackets where words are missing or illegible in the original text. Text in square brackets indicates editorial interpolations or suggested readings.

[1] 24 August 1205[5]
die mercurii.

[2] 27 September 1209[6]

[3] 1 January 1210[7]

In domo umiliatorum de Verone. qui sunt in hora glare.

In curia domus humiliatorum de Clara [sic]

In presentia. domini Otolini de Leniaco. domini Pantani. Omneboni. Widoti de Mediolano. domini Stefani de iebeto. domini Çuconis. Magistri Bocasini. et al. rog. tt.

In presentia Riprandi de fossato Firmi. Magistri Boccasini. Martinuci. Francii de Rouredo. Menaboi. fratris Danielis. Federici et aliorum multorum.

In presentia Filipi pistoris. Pantani. Gerardi de milio. Boccadeadam. Ceni. Manfredini. Alberti eius fratris. et al.

Ibique Iema filia Gerardi de milio

Ibique Albertus et Manfredinus fratres. filii condam Rodulfi de Arduino de Ripeclaria et Garscenda soror eorum

Ibique Gisla de Poueiano. Valuina. Sauia de Rodengo de mantuana. Maria de donna Carla.

spontanea voluntate.

isti tres concorditer et spontanea uoluntate.

Item in predicto.

nomine donacionis inter uiuos ut amplius reuocari non possit.

nomine donacionis inter uiuos ut amplius reuocari non possint.

Inuestiuit Boccadeadam et Natalem fratres umiliatorum uice et nomine tocius capituli umiliatorum. et finem. datam. et refutacionem. Accessionem ad proprium fecit In manu iamscripti Boccadeadam et Natalis pro predicto capitulo umiliatorum.

inuestiuere [sic] fratrem Natalem ministrum suprascripte domus humiliatorum. uice et nomine tocius capituli humiliatorum . . .

de omni eo quod habet uel aquirere debet seu aliquo modo ei euenerit. uel haberet tam de proprio quam de aliis rebus. et per

de omni eo quod ipsi habent uel aliquo modo eis euenient uel haberent . . . excepta quadam pecie terre que iacet in curia

[5] ASVat Baldaria 4.   [6] ASVer Ghiara 29.   [7] ASVer Ghiara 29.

eos fratres uice et nomine tocius capituli possidere manifestauit omnia sua bona presencia et futura.

et in super Boccadeadam et Natalem pro uniuerso capitulo umiliatorum elegerunt et receperunt ipsam Iemam per suam sororem in domo umiliatorum.et hoc totum factum fuit presente et consenciente fratribus et sororibus umiliatorum qui ibi aderant

Rupeclarie ubi dicitur Viero

hoc facto statim incontinenti ipse frater Natalis pro uniuerso capitulo humiliatorum qui congregantur ad Glaram et Aicardina ministra sororum ellegerunt eos per suos fratres et Garscenda per sororem in ea domo humiliatorum

secundum condicionem aliorum fratrum et sororum

Notary: Enricus notarius domini regis Henrici. Interfui et rogatus scripsi.

Notary: Enricus notarius domini regis Henrici interfui et Rogatus scripsi

Notary: As no. 2

---

[4] 14 February 1210[8]

(text follows 'Item in predicto' of no. 3)

In presentia Boccasini. Fineti. notarii. Içerini filii Enrici de domino Zucone. Willielmi bacede. Filipi pistoris. Cirioli notarii. Martinuci et aliorum multorum

Ibique Albertus pater fratris Widi. et Clara atque Sauiola Mantuana.

omnes predicte sorores et frater Albertus concorditer et spontanea uoluntate

nomine donacionis inter uiuos ut amplius reuocari non possint

[5] 1 May 1211[9]
In domo humiliatorum de glara.

In presentia domini Pantani. Forçani. Iohannis de tofanello. Firmi. Gerardi de milio et al.

Ibique Albertus de scanna uaca de Porto.

nomine donacionis inter uiuos [. . .] amplius reuocari non possit et sua spontanea uoluntate

[6] [. . .] June? 1211[10]
In curte domus h[umiliatorum]

[. . .] Çuconis. domini Pantani. Firmi. Iohannis. [. . .] Surgo et al. rogat. tt.

Ibique M[aça de] Scanna uaca

nomine donacionis inter uiuos [. . .]

[8] ASVat Baldaria 29.   [9] ASVer Ghiara 35.   [10] ASVer Ghiara 35.

inuestiuere fratrem
Balduinum. ministrum
tocius capituli
humiliatorum. qui
congregantur ad glaram.
uice ac nomine tocius
capituli humiliatorum
predictorum.
. . .

de omni eo quod predicte
sorores et frater habent et
aliquo modo eis euenient.
uel haberent . . .

inuestiuit.
Boccam[deadam].
Riprandi de fossato.
Tugrum calça[. . .]tium.
Iacobum cinciueram.
ministros [. . .]
uniuersitatis et comunitatis
humiliatorum qui
congregantur ad glaram.

de omni eo quod habet
uel aliquo modo ei
euenerit . . .

Item dixit idem Albertus
quod uolebat stare et per
[. . .]are toto tempore sue
uite in domo Porti uel
alibi obedienciam [. . .]d
uolun[tatem] ministrorum
et suorum successorum
secundum uoluntate dei et
stare et ui[. . .].

in omnibus et per omnia
fecit similem . . . in
manibus suprascriptorum
Boccedeadam [sic] et
Iacobi cinciuere recipiente
pro se et uniuersorum
suorum sociorum et dixit
idem per omnia attendere
ut pater eius.

hoc facto. statim
incontinenti predictus
Balduinus pro uniuerso
capitulo humiliatorum et
Aicardina ministra
sororum acceperunt et
ellegerunt per suas sorores
illas et eum Albertum in
domo humiliatorum
secundum modum et
condicionem aliarum
sororum et aliorum
fratrum. Et hoc totum
factum fuit presentibus et
consencientibus fratribus et
sororibus qui ibi aderant.

hoc facto statim
inconti[nen]ti ministri per
uoluntatem qui ibi aderant
ellegerunt ipsum
Albertum Scan[na uaca]
pro suum [. . .] porti
et in osculo fraternitatis
osculati [. . .] eum

et statim [. . .] per
uoluntatem fratrum et
sororum. qui ibi aderant
ellegerunt ipsam Maçam
per sororem in eadem
domo de Glara.
et [. . .] presens Serena
ministra predicte domus
recepit eam per sororem
in [. . .] illa domo et in
osculo fraternitatis eam
osculauit

Actum in domo predicta
Notary: As no. 2

Notary: Enricus notarius
domini regis Henrici

Notary: Enricus notarius
domini regis Henrici

---

[7] 2 January 1212[11]
In domo fratrum de Glara.

[8] 9 June 1224[12]
In Iebeto sub porticu
sororum.

[9] 11 June 1224[13]
In oratorio sororum
humilium [sic] de Glara.

[11] ASVat Baldaria 35.

[12] ASVer Ghiara 92.

[13] ASVer Ghiara 101.

in presentia [. . .] de
runco. Carlaxarii. notarii
qui dicitur Bixolus.
Riprandi de fossato. [. . .]
Iohannis de tofanello.
Alberti mucii. Venture qui
dicitur Rebiço. [. . .]
fratris Gandulfi et al. mlt.
rogat. tt.

in presentia Alberti.
Bonaçonte. Widi. fratris
Bertrami. Spinelli. et al.

In presentia. fratris Fini
presbiteris campi marzii.
domini Forçani de eodem
loco. fratris Rodulfi qui
Baraia uocatur. fratris Frei.
fratris Boniiohanis. fratris
Warienti. et fratris
Octonis qui fuit de Porto
et al. tt.

Ibique Laçarinus qui
[. . .]mone et Luchesa filia
predicti Bixoli. et Ota filia
[. . .] similiter

Ibique Auenante filia
Richelde qui fuit de
Nogara. Ota filia Riçardi
calçarerii.

Ibique Garçeta neptis
domini Iacobi medici.
Veronella filia fratris
Bonaçunte. Karaconsa filia
domini Ubetini de
Cagabisis. Fineta filia
Wilielmi de Caramo. et
Benuegnua filia Asinelli
uclarii. et Bia filia
Lafranci. et Fatina filia
quondam Piçoli qui fuit
de Calavena. et Bonissima
filia Bertoldi de Bulçano.
et Idiadasa filia Octonelli
de bracio de Porto.
et Viuiana filia quondam
Amigi de Cremonese.
Vigolana filia Ubetini
sartorii. et Victoria
Bonacursii filia de
Arcignano. et enGelenda
[sic] filia Iacobine de
çempa. et Martha filia
Gerardi de Mantua. et
Aurilia filia Tarusii de
Calavena. et Iema filia
Bonsegnorii.

misericordiam cum uenia
petens ministris maioribus
et anterioribus comunitatis
humiliatorum et fratribus
et sororibus ibidem
presentibus.

misericordiam cum uenia
petens ministris maioribus
comunitatis humiliatorum
ciuitatis Verone et eius
districtus et fratribus et
sororibus humiliatorum
ibidem presentibus
quatinus eas in sorores sue
fraternitatis reciperent.

nomine donacionis inter uiuos ut amplius re[. . .] [spon]tanea uoluntate

Inuestiuerunt Wiliel[. . .] erçarum. Boccasinum. Guiçardum. Finetum. notarium m[. . .] uniuersitatis et communitatis humiliatorum Verone. et episcopatus. . . recipientes uice ac nomine tocius capituli humiliatorum pro ut dictam est nominatim de omni eo quod ipsi habent uel alio modo eis euenerint tam de proprio quam de aliis rebus. et per ipsos ministros possidere manifestauer[un]t

et uniusquisque [iam]scriptorum dixit suo proprio ore quod uolebat stare et hobedire [sic] illis ministribus [sic] [. . .] successoribus pro capitulo omnium humiliatorum. et stare et uiuere toto [tempore sue uite] [. . .] tate secundum modum humiliatorum.

hoc facto dicti [. . .] insimul cum domino Pantano ministro domus Glare ellegerunt [. . .]

nomine donacionis ut amplius inter uiuos reuocari non possint.

Inuestiuerunt dominum Pantanum et Bartholameum laurudum ministros maiores suprascripte fraternitatis humiliatorum recipientes pro se et pro omnibus aliis suis sociis.

nominatim de omnibus suis bonis mobilibus et immobilibus. que nunc habent uel eis iuste posset euenire.

et insuper suprascripte sorores promiserunt deo et suprascriptis ministris semper in castitatem permanere et sine proprio uiuere et obedienciam et reuerenciam prestare ministris maioribus professis qui nunc sunt uel pro tempore fuerint ministri suprascripte fraternitatis. et specialiter ministro et ministre in qua domus permanserint per uoluntatem ministrorum et secundum quod nunc tenent uel tenebunt deo dante obseruare dixerunt..

et hoc facto statim Imildina ministra dicte domus precepto suprascripti domini

nomine donacionis inter uiuos ut amplius reuocari non possint

Inuestiuer[unt] dominum Pantanum ministrum dicte comunitatis huiliatorum [sic] ciuitatis Verone et eius districtus recipiente[m] pro se et pro omnibus aliis suis sociis

de omnibus suis bonis mobilibus et immobilibus. que nunc habent uel eis iuste possent euenire et. per eum uice comunitatis humiliatorum suprascriptorum possidere manifestauerunt. et

Insuper uouerunt deo perpetuam castitatem. et uiuere sine proprio. et obedientiam ministris maioribus professis qui nunc sunt uel pro tempore fuerint ministri supracripte congregacionis uel comunitatis suprascriptorum humiliatorum. et ministro predicte domus Glare. scilicet fratri Octoni in qua nunc morantur uel alico [sic] tempore per uoluntatem ministrorum maiorum ut suprascriptum est morabantur illo ministro exhibere et seruare promiserunt.

hoc facto statim soror. Biatrisina ministra suprascripte domus per precepto dicti domini

Laçarinum et Luchesem per fratrem et per sororem in eadem domo humiliatorum de Glara. Ota uero in domo Iebeti ellecta fuit. his omnibus adimpletis Tombexana ministra predicte domus de Glara elegit ipsam Luchesem per sororem et in osculo fraternitatis osculate fuer[it]. Laçarinus [re]ceptus fuit per fratrem [a] domino Pantano ministro domus Glare et ab aliis fratribus. Ota uero recepta fuit per Enricum notarium ministrum Iebeti uice et nomine aliarum sororum Iebeti et sic Victoria soror domus Iebeti pro se et [. . .] rum Iebeti osculauit illam Otam per suam sororem in osculo fraternitatis.

Pantani recepit eas per sorores in osculo pacis et signe subiectionis ubicumque eas ponere uoluerint

Pantani ministri eas suprascriptas in sorores et pro sororibus suprascripte fraternitatis in osculo pacis et signo subiectionis recepit ubicumque eas ponere uoluerint

Actum in domo humiliatorum de Glara

Actum est. hoc. in suprascripto. loco;

Notary: Enricus notarius domini regis Henrici

Notary: Enricus notarius domini regis Henrici

Notary: Taurellus sacri palatii notarius

Verso: [. . .] sororum

Verso: Cartam sororis Auenantis [sic] et Ote de domus Iebeto

---

[10] Eodem die et[14] (text follows no. 9)

[11] Wednesday 5 June 1230[15]

[12] Tuesday 10 February 1232[16]

In Iebeto in oratorio sororum.

In Verona in oratorio sororum de domo sancti Pauli.

In oratorio fratrum dictorum humiliatorum domus Glare

in presentia dictorum. testes.

In presentia domini presbiteri Warimberti de ecclesia sancti Vitalis. presbiteri Iohannis de Novaie. Carlaxarii. Bonacursii. fratris Pantani. et aliorum.

In presentia domini Petri diaconi qui fuit de Leniaco et habitat ad sanctum Leonardum. domini Grosii. Vitalis filii Boniiohannis de Braida. fratris Taurelli. notarii.

[14] ASVer Ghiara 101.   [15] ASVer Ghiara 136.   [16] ASVer Ghiara 139.

fratris Ferrarii. notarii.
fratris Nicoleti de hora
sancti Pauli qui fuit de
Cremona. fratris [. . .]ini.
fratris Gerardi qui fuit de
Uicencia. fratris Widi qui
fuit de Legnago et
aliorum.

Ibique Petrus de
cremonese et Finetus filius
Bonitacini notarius. et
Meiorina filia domine
Octe de campo marçio.

Ibique Coram cruce et
suprascriptis sacerdotibus
Bonacursius filius
Omneboni de musio de
Leniaco. Flore filia
Carlaxarii de musio de
Iebeto. Iacobina filia
suprascripti Bonacursii de
Iebeto. Iema neça predicti
domini presbiteri
Warimberti. Mandola filia
quondam Pascalis de pleve
de Sacco.

Ibique Coram cruce et
ipso Petro diaco[no]
Oriebona neça Morbii.
notarii. de Iebeto

fecerunt. idem. in
omnibus et super omnia.
in manu dicti domini
Pantani. ministri dicte
comunitatis. ut superius
continetur.

Isti omnes suprascripti
stantes cum candela
accensa et scripto sue
professionis tenentes in
manibus suis
ita dixerunt unus quisque
pro se ut inferius legitur
Ego do et offero me et res
meas deo et congregationi
humiliatorum Verone et
eius districtus. Mantue et
eius districtus. Vicencie et
eius districtus. et promitto
Obedienciam fratri
Taurello ministro maiori
professo recipiente[m] pro
se et uice ac nomine
suorum sociorum
ministrorum maiorum
professorum qui modo
sunt uel pro tempore
fuerint ministri
suprascripte
congregationis et
specialiter ministro domus
in qua nunc habito uel

cum candela accensa et
scripto sue professionis
tenentes in suis manibus
sic dicens.

Ego soror Oriebona do et
offero me et res meas deo
et congregationi
humiliatorum Verone et
eius districtus. Mantue et
eius districtus. Vicencie et
eius districtus et promitto
obedienciam fratri Otoni
qui fuit de Porto ministro
maiori professo
recipientem pro se et uice
ac nomine suorum
sociorum ministrorum
maiorem professorum qui
modo sunt uel pro
tempore fuerint ministri
iamdicte congregationis et
specialiter ministro domus
in qua nunc habito

pro tempore habitabo per uoluntatem ministrorum maiorum professorum secundum regulam huius congregationis secundi ordinis datam et abprobatam a domino papa Innocencio deo gr[aci]as amen.

hoc facto statim suprascriptus Bonacursius et una queque [sic] suprascriptarum sororum pro se dedit candelam illam accensam et scriptum sue professionis quam et quod in manibus tenebant in manibus eiusdem fratris Taurelli et postea ipse et una queque illarum accepit candellam et scriptum de manibus predicti Taurelli et posuit ante crucem cum uenia et reuerencia.

uel pro tempore habitabo per uoluntatem ministrorum maiorum professorum secundum regulam domini pape Innocencii datam et abprobatam huic congregationi deo gr[aci]as amen.

hoc facto ipsa Oriebona dedit Candelam accensam et scriptum sue professionis in manibus suprascripti Otonis de Porto et postea accepit candelam illam et scriptum de manibus eius et posuit ante crucem.

et frater Octo minister suprascripte domus per precepto dicti domini Pantani.\eos/ in fratres et pro fratribus et dicta Biatrisina ministra eam Meiorinam in sororem et pro sororibus suprascripte fraternitatis in osculo pacis et signo subiectionis receperunt. ubicumque eos uel eam ponere uoluerint.

his omnibus adimpletis frater Bonaçonta minister suprascripte domus Iebeti precepto suprascripti Taurelli ipsum Bonacursium in osculo pacis et signo subiectionis in simul cum aliis fratribus qui tunc ibi aderant recepit. Similiter soror Bonafemina ministra ipsius domi precepto eiusdem fratris Taurelli dictas sorores in osculo pacis et signo fraternitatis et subiectionis in eadem fraternitate recepit et similiter alie sorores que ibi aderant eas receperunt eodem modo ut ministra receperat.

His omnibus adimpletis. Bonafemina ministra suprascripte domus precepto suprascripti fratris Otonis ipsam Oriebonam in osculo pacis et signo subiectionis in eadem fraternitate in serore [sic] et pro sorore recepit ubicumque ministri maiores eam ponere uoluerint.

his omnibus completis
suprascriptus frater
Taurellus precepit
suprascripto Bonacursio et
dictis sororibus ut starent
in eadem domo Iebeti ad
uoluntatem ministrorum
maiorum professorum qui
modo sunt uel pro
tempore fuerint ministri
suprascripte
congregationis.

Item suprascriptus frater
Otonus ibi presens
[prece]pit dicte Oriebone
ut staret in eadem domo
ad uoluntatem
ministrorum maiorum
professorum

Actum. est. hoc. in
suprascripto. loco.
Notary: Taurellus sacri
palatii notarius

Notary: Enricus notarius
domini regis Henrici

Notary: Enricus notarius
domini regis Henrici

Verso: cartam Bonacursii
filii Omneboni de Mu sio
[sic] de Leniaco. et Flore
et Iacobine. Ieme f. neça
domini presbiteri
Warimberti. Mandole.
omnes isti sunt de domo
Iebeti. recepte fuer[unt] in
ministerio fratris
Bonaçonte.
mcc trigesimo. indic.
tercia.

Verso: Cartam sororis
Oriebone neça Morbii.
notarii. de jebeto
millesimo cc. trigesimo
secundo. indic. quinta

303

Appendix III

WILLS

PREFACE

This appendix gives details of a sample of wills involving the Humiliati, as either beneficiaries or executors. In the interests of brevity only 'pious bequests' are included.
References to the Humiliati have been underlined.

KEY

d. − *denari*
t. − *tertiolorum*/terzoli
s. − *solidi*
l. − *libri*
i. − *imperiali*
v. − veronesi

Appendix III *Humiliati wills*

Date (place)	Testator (and motives)	Legacy	Beneficiary	Clauses/executors
[1] 1195[a]	Sotius *de Campo Longo* for his soul	40 s.i.	church of San Cristoforo of the Humiliati	*pro anima mea*
		12 d.i.	San Biagio in Lodi	*laborerio ipsius ecclesie*
		30 d.i.	priest *Teutaldo* of San Biagio *pro missis cantandis*	
		2 s.i.	hospital of San Biagio *fuori*	
		12 i.	*canonica* of San Sepolcro *ultra Abduam*	
		12 i.	*maioris ecclesie de Laude*	*laborerio*
		2 s.i.	Ottabelle	*pro anima mea*
		3 d.i.		*pro maltolto*
[2] 1198[b]	Albert Niger	a share in tithes from Fançago	The *canonica* of San Cristoforo [San Cristoforo shared half the tithes with the poor of the hospital of San Biagio; the other half was to go to the Cathedral works]	

[a] Samarati, 'I primi insediamenti Umiliati', pp. 115–17 (16 March).
[b] ASMi, 182 Lodi, Sta Chiara Nuova (10 December).

Appendix III (cont.)

Date (place)	Testator (and motives)	Legacy	Beneficiary	Clauses/executors
[3] 1215[c] _in porto . . . in domo fratrum humilatorum_	_Albertinus filius condam brunelli testamentum faciendo sua bona hoc modo disposuit_	_Omnibus aliis suis bonis_ [except legacies to relatives]	_Pauperes_	executors: _Dominus Pantanus_, Finus and Bartolomeus [_Ministri of_ Humiliati]: _dispensatores et fideles comissarios in distribuenda predicta hereditate inter pauperes ubi eis visum_ [. . .] _magis placere deo et maiorem utilitatem esse anime ipsius Albertini_ . . .
[4] 1224[d] _actum ad lectum ubi iacebat_	Ser Ruba, _filius quondam ser Petri de Balsemo, civitatis Mediolani, de Pusterla S. Eufimie_ _Deus omnipotens ac redemptor noster animas quas condidit ad studium salutis semper invitat_ . . . _Cum pro Deo omnia alia pauperibus proposuerim disponere_ . . .	12 d.t. 3 l.t. 1 carrum vini and 20 s.t. 3 s.t. every Friday from now until the feast of San Pietro (_die veneris in omni edomada_ [sic])	_cuilibet infirmo de Alcuromano._ _ad laborem fratrum Minorum de domibus que iusta ecclesiam S. Victoris ad Ulmum ediffcantur_ _fratres_ of S. Eustorgio [Dominicans] _fratres_ of S. Eustorgio [Dominicans]	_qui debeant offerri super altarem quando celebrabunt missam ad obsequium meum_ _qui debeant dari in pane frumenti_

(cont.)

[c] ASVer, Ghiara 50 (19 January).
[d] Alberzoni, _Francescanesimo a Milano nel duecento_, appendix 4, 1 (27 March).

306

Appendix III (cont.)

Date (place)	Testator (and motives)	Legacy	Beneficiary	Clauses/executors
		sextam partem ficti on a plot of land [worth 7 s.t.]	*fratres* of S. Eustorgio [Dominicans]	*pro fiendo annuale unum omni anno pro anima mea*
		1 *carrum vini*	*sorores* of S. Eustorgio [Humiliati? see p. 57]	
		30 s.t.	*ad laborem eclesia de Lavepra*	
		10 s.t.	hospital of Brolo	
		1 *sestarium leguminum*	*domine paupere de Pontecredario*	
		and 20 s.t.		if they build a church (*si levaverint ibi ecclesiam*)
		5 l.t.	*Ministri Humiliatorum de Senedogo*	*quas disponere debeant prout eis melius visum fuerit*
		5 l.t.	*domus sororum presbiteri Olderici qui morantur ad Pusterlam Tonsam*	to pay the debts of the house (*in solvendo . . . debito*)
	. . . pro remedio et mercede anime mee	*mantellum meum*	*frater* Carlevarius	
		anything remaining (*et si aliquid superhabundaret . . .*)	*pauperibus personis quibus . . . errogatarii viderint maiorem necessitatem incumbere*	executors: *dominus presbiter* Oldericus, ser Albertonus Saporitus, Beltramus *de Balsemo* [testator's brother] (*errogatari et dispensatores*)
				all *male ablata* to be repaid

Appendix III (cont.)

Date (place)	Testator (and motives)	Legacy	Beneficiary	Clauses/executors
[5] 1225*e*	Iohannes Nazarii *de Burgo Vicomercato*	3 l.t.	church of Sta Maria of Vimercate	for lights during Lent
	Decet unumquemquam ante quam natura solvat debitum taliter faccultates [sic] suas disponere ut post eius migratione nulla lis vel dissensio valeat oriri	1 *libram oleum fixtum* [sic] every year	church of Sta Maria of Vimercate	likewise, for lights during Lent every year
		1 *aliam libram olei fictum* every year	church of Sto Stefano	
		tithes on 2 plots of land	church of Sto Stefano	
		12 d.i. every year	*clerici de Vicomercato*	for office and mass every year *in annali meo*
		up to 25 l.t. (*etiam in vestimentis*)	*pauperibus*	*pro male usurpatis*
		1 *modium de blava . . . in pane* every year on *annuali meo* and on that of his wife Bellixia *similiter*	*pauperibus*	
		3 l.t.	<u>*societas humiliatorum*</u>	which they are to distribute: <u>*ubi fuerit in utilitate illorum qui volunt Deo servire*</u>
		3 d.t.	hospital of St Maria *ad Morianum*	executors: his wife domina Bellixia and the *prepositus et fratibus de Vicomercato, datores et exactores*

e Mambretti, 'Note sugli insediamenti Umiliati nel territorio di Vimercate', appendix 1 (8 May).

308

Appendix III (cont.)

Date (place)	Testator (and motives)	Legacy	Beneficiary	Clauses/executors
[6] 1226[f] Verona in hora illorum de molis in do [sic] domini Bernardi de grassa	*Dominus* Mannara *iacens* de *infirmus et sane mentis* . . .	20 s.	hospital of S. Luca	executors: *In omnibus aliis meis bonis pauperes michi heredes instituto loco et vice quorum reliquo et statuo dominus Baruius de humiliatis, et Wilielmus baçeta et dominus Bernardum de grassa, fideicommissarios, et dispositores et dispensatores*[g]
		6 l.	*sororibus pauperibus minoribus*	
		10 l.	*humiliatis a Glara* [Ghiara]	
		40 s.	*unicuique domorum humiliatorum de Verone et episcopatu*	
		In omnibus aliis meis bonis pauperes michi heredes instituto	*pauperes*	to be distributed to the poor as shall seem best to executors
[7] 1227[h]	a canon of Bergamo	10 s.i.	*illi de Galgare* [Humiliati]	
		12 d.i.	church of Galgario [Humiliati]	
[8] 1229/36[i]	Bregundius Denarii	the house in which he stays in the *vicinia* of San Tommaso with all *vasis et utensilibus et in aliis rebus in it* at the time of his death and a *podere* in Mulazano (1229)	*ordini humiliatorum de laude, sive compagnie humiliatorum de laude*	*in qua domo vel in quo podere debeat fieri quedam mansio humiliatorum* . . . .

(cont.)

[f] ASVer, Ghiara 115 (29 September).

[g] Sewn to the document are 2 records of execution of the will in April 1229 distributing money to relatives.

[h] Brolis, *Gli Umiliati a Bergamo*, p. 203.

[i] *VHM* II, pp. 14–15 (10 January). Will and codicil of 1236 now in Mercatii Indelicato, 'Per una riconsiderazione del lavoro presso gli Umiliati', appendices 1 and 2.

309

Appendix III (cont.)

Date (place)	Testator (and motives)	Legacy	Beneficiary	Clauses/executors
		2 *modios blava* and 1 *modium leguminum*	*mansio sororibus de domus sachi denarii*	
		10 s.i. every year from a fictum of commune	*canonica sancti Christophori*	For office every year for his soul
		10 s.i. every year from a fictum of commune	monastery of Cerreto (Cistercians)	For office every year of his soul
		Remainder of *fictum* of commune	*mansio humiliatorum* to be founded in his house	
		2 *staria frumenti*	monastery of San Bassiano fuori	For office every year for his soul
		100 l.i.	*hospitali omne*	For returning *male ablata*
		10 s.i.	Friars minor	
		1 *modium blave*	hospital of Sant'Antonio	
		1 modium blave	each other mansio of Lodi … *qui sit humiliatorum Laude*	Executors: Include provost of San Cristoforo and six men
		1 modium blave	poor of hospital of San Biagio	
		5 s.i.	poor of hospital of San Bartolomeo	
		5 s.i.		

Appendix III (cont.)

Date (place)	Testator (and motives)	Legacy	Beneficiary	Clauses/executors
		His wife Celsa may stay, if she wishes to remain chaste, in his house and live there with other Humiliati sisters (1236) Bedding (1236) *Omnes panni sui*	The house is to be *in dispositione humiliatorum laude* *canonica sancti Cristofori Pauperibus*	*ubi vult iacere* to be sold and given to the poor for his soul
[9] c. 1234[j] *In Verona in domo fratrum humiliatorum de Glara*	Iohanis *de Rubeo* of Zevio	100 l.d.v. of which 70 l. 6 s. 8 d. are given as 2 pieces of ploughland, the remainder to be paid by his son.	his daughter Flordezia *que vocatur Benedicta (sororem domus fratrum humiliatorum de gebeto)*	executor: Girardus son of testator.
[10] 1237[k] *In suburbio civitatis Verone. In domo humiliatorum domus Glare*	Ubicinus *filius quondam Girardi de Nigrario*	1 plot of ploughland or 12 l.d.v. (if his son wishes to keep the land)		to be sold and price to be given *pro anima mea ubi eis bonum videbitur* executors: *ministris communalibus domui et collegiorum humiliatorum Verone*

[j] ASVer, Ghiara 146 c. 1234: record of the execution of the will.
[k] ASVer, Ghiara 151 (8 May).

311

Appendix III (cont.)

Date (place)	Testator (and motives)	Legacy	Beneficiary	Clauses/executors
[11] 1239¹	Redulfus qui dicitur Gaux de burgo Marliano	1 plot of land [2 perches and 2 tabelle next to church]	church and canonica of Sto Stefano de burgo Marliano and canons of the church	
in burgo Marliano in domo humiliatorum prati de Andam	. . . casum humanae fragilitatis praecogitans utilitatem etiam suae animae et parentium et propinquorum descendentium amicorum providere volens . . .	20 s.t. [on the said plot of land]	frater Pietro Ghislando de congregatione fratrum minorum quae stat ad ecclesiam sancti Georgii de burgo Marliano	
	. . . ad honorem Dei et beati protomartiris Stefani omnium sanctorum Dei, in remisione peccatorum suorum . . .	40 s.t.	congregatione fratrum humiliatorum prati de Andamo	
		20 s.t.	pauperibus personis	to be distributed by fratres William Fiorono and Peter Guarino ministris fratrum humiliatorum de burgo
		20 s.t.	fratres William and Andrew humiliatis de domo humiliatorum domus de Godenti	
		20 s.t.	fratri Perogie d'aroxio ad utilitatem suae congregationis	ad utilitatem congregationis ipsius domus
		10 s.t.	humiliatabus de burgo novo	
		10 s.t.	Beuenudae de Catanio et eius sororibus seu suae congregationis	
		5 s.t.	reclausis quae stant apud ecclesiam sancti Stefani de Marliano	executors: the church and canonica of Sto Stefano

¹ A. Martegani, 'Gli Umiliati di Mariano e i Visconti', pp. 19–20 (18 May).

Appendix III (cont.)

Date (place)	Testator (and motives)	Legacy	Beneficiary	Clauses/executors
[12] 1240*m*	Oto de caliario de porto	60 l.d.v. (two plots of land to be sold)	his daughter *soror* Liadasio, a sister in the *humiliati* house of Porto	Executor: Bonauentura [testator's son]
				all debts to be repaid.
[13] 1241*n* *In porto in domo fratrum humiliatorum*	*Bonacursius de orte* *iacens in lecto sane mentis . . . pro remedio anime mee . . .*	100 l.		*fratres Otonis & Bonadomanis, humiliati* and testator's son, Segnoretus, to distribute *ubi cumque utilius anime mee eos videbitur expedire . . .*
		3 l.	church of Orte	*ad emendam campanam ecclesie*
		11 s.	*ponti calmeçane de orte*	
		5 s.	church of San Romasio	
		5 s.	church of San Vito	
		20 s.	church of San Pietro in Porto	
		10 s.	church of San Bartolomeo	to be distributed as clothing (*in indumentis*)
		100 *brachiapani*	*pauperes*	Executors: *frater* Otonis and *frater* Bonadomanis

m ASVer, Ghiara 170 (22 August) execution of will by testator's son.
n ASVer, Ghiara 177 (28 June).

313

Appendix III (cont.)

Date (place)	Testator (and motives)	Legacy	Beneficiary	Clauses/executors
[14] 1242*o*	*Ser Ventura de Brivio condam speciarius*	40 s.i.	Friars Minor	Executors: the archpriest of S. Vincenzo, *dominus Egydius* priest of S. Prancati, *magister Torussus Sprarius* and several Humiliati: the *prepositus* of the Galgario, minister of the *domus Communis* and *frater Mafeus de humiliatis* of the *domus humiliatorum de rasole*
	... esset bone et sane mentis et eius sanitate sciens bona et facultates suas ...	10 s.i.	to each humiliati house of the city and *virtutis* of Bergamo except the *domus Communis*	
	pro remedio anime sue et pro male ablatis et amore dei	20 s.i.	*domus Communis* of Humiliati in Bergamo	*Communis* and *frater*
		20 l.i. and *vasa que habet in Galgare*	church of Galgario [Humiliati]	
		3 l.i.	church of San Leonardo and its hospital	
		any further property	*pauperes nostre civitatis et episcopatus Pergami*	according to the best and greatest need (*melius et maior necessitatis*)
[15] 1242*p* *In villa Porti in domo habitacionis domini Omneboni de dominicis ...*	*Omnibonus de dominicis de Porto*	5 s.	*laborerio* of church of San Pietro in Porto	Executors: *dominus Oto minister fratrum humiliatorum de Porto et dominus Grandis de Grandis*
	iacens in lecto testamendum faciendo ...	40 s.	hospital of the poor	
	... pro deo et anima sua	95 l.d.v. and 1 *arcam*, 1 *archetam*, 1 *bancam*, 2 *vegetos*, 1 *laram*, 1 *corbam*, 1 *vallum*, 1 *camestrum*, 1 *veolum*, and 1 *vacinam*		at the disposal of the executors

o ASBg, Archivio notarile cartella 1, 189 bis (17 September) regest, Brolis, *Gli Umiliati a Bergamo*, appendix 2 no. 2.
p ASVer, Ghiara 181 (26 September).

Appendix III (cont.)

Date (place)	Testator (and motives)	Legacy	Beneficiary	Clauses/executors
[16] before 1250[q] *In palacio communis verone*	*Pomus de porta sancti Stephani*	25 l.d.v. (land to the value of)	Wiota [his daughter] … *qui est edidicata* [sic] *in dicta domo humiliatorum*	land given to dominus frater Rivabene *minister* of the humiliati of the Beverara, by brothers of the beneficiary who agree that Rivabene has given Wiota *vestes … religionis*
[17] 1250[r]	*Nobilis vir dominus* William Gratapallea *de Clareio*	25 *libras vianensium vel secusiensium*	church of San Michele of Chiusi	He promises obedience to the *ecclesie sancte venerande dei mandatis* for his burial in the church and to be used every year in *commemoratio perpetuo*, for monks to have a meal
		20 s. *secusiensium*	*ecclesie maiori* of Turin	
		5 s. *secusiensium*	each church and hospital of Turin	
		12 *tunicas*	Friars Minor living in Turin	
		100 s. of the same money	*ordini humiliatorum apud Taurinum constituto*	
		1 *modium frumenti*	hospital of S. Giacomo	

(cont.)

[q] ASVer, Beverara busta 1/10 (15 February) execution of the will; also recorded in busta 4 app. 2 no. 4.
[r] *Documenti inediti e sparsi sulla storia di Torino*, ed. F. Cognasso, 200 (20 September) codicil.

Appendix III (cont.)

Date (place)	Testator (and motives)	Legacy	Beneficiary	Clauses/executors
		2 *milites* to be sent *ultra mare in subsidio terre sancte* (and more if the pope wishes) *pro remedio anime sue*		he declared that he had acquired 600 *libras vianensium malo ordine et de rebus male acquisitis* but he did not say who he owed, so he ordered that it should be restored from his own money or *saltim* for his soul through the judgement of the lord pope (his son to go to the pope to arrange this)
[18] 1252[s]	a canon of Bergamo	2 s.i.	church of Galgario [Humiliati]	
[19] 1253[t] *in domo ipsius Artoni*	Artonus Becarius *sive* Calçatus	his house with land and buildings in Moncalerio	monastery of Casanova	*pro anima sua*
	. . . *cum multi casus eciam repentini incidant mortalibus quibus preventi et preocupati* . . .	1 *costarenca* of land	church of Sta Maria *ad opus et pro opere ecclesie*	
	. . . *diem huius vite labentis et extremum cupiens prevenire* . . .	1 *costarenca* of land	*fratribus umiliatis de Moncalerio*	

(cont.)

[s] Brolis, *Gli Umiliati a Bergamo*, p. 203.
[t] *Cartario della abazia* [sic] *di Casanova fino all'anno 1313*, ed. A. Tallone, 357 (26 February).

316

Appendix III (cont.)

Date (place)	Testator (and motives)	Legacy	Beneficiary	Clauses/executors
	... ne posteris pateat copia seu materia litigandi ...	1 costarenca of land	illis de stapharda	pro anima sua
		10 s.	friars minor in Moncalieri	
		2 boconos of land superfluum	hospital iusta reclusum	debeant dare pro eius anima
[20] 1253/1257" In curte humiliatorum Glare et sub porticalia	Mucius de Ferarina sane mentis loquens testamentum faciendo et sua ultimam voluntatem declarando	1½ campi of ploughland	pauperibus [in 1253]	To be sold and money to be distributed ubi melius erit inter pauperes [in 1253]
			Humiliati of Ghiara vice pauperum [in 1257]	with the consent of Mucius who was present so that the Humiliati may do what they wish with it
				Executors: frater Salandinus of humiliati of Ghiara or other minister que pro tempore erit
[21a] 1253" In Verona sub intrata domus humiliatorum a	Nigrelus filius quondam Primafere de Gebeto ... nullam habens corporis	13½ plots of land (omnibus meis bonis) some neighbouring lands of	fratres collegium seu uniuersitatem domus humiliatorum de Gebeto	(cont.)

" ASVer, Ghiara 248 (21 September 1253). On the same parchment is a codicil dated 15 May 1257 when the land goes to the Humiliati, drawn up in ponticello domus humiliatorum glare.

Appendix III (cont.)

Date (place)	Testator (and motives)	Legacy	Beneficiary	Clauses/executors
Glara	*egriditunem* [sic] *set sane mentis precauens casum humane fragilitatis ne de suis rebus oriatur contencio suam ultimam uoluntatem declarant* [sic]	Humiliati of *domus Feraboi in Zevio*	[Zevio] *de qua domo nunc frater Bon[ui]nus est minister*	
[21b] 1253^v Same day, place and witnesses	*Domina Aldematia uxor Nigreli condam Primafere ipso suo marito presente et volente sane menti nullam paciens* [sic] *corporis egritudinem precavent*	*omnibus meis bonis*	*universitatem et collegium fratrum humiliatorum domus de Gebeto de qua domo frater Bonuinus nunc est minister*	
[22] 12[56]^w *in camere Berardi*	Berardus Canossa ... *volens ad honorem Dei et individuae Trinitatis in obsequio ac salute anime sue et ad restaurationem usure, quam suo tempore percepit*	20 s.i. every year 10 s.i. every year 5 s.i. every year 3 s.i. every year	*infirmi* S. Lazeri *pauperes Caritatis* *humiliate* church of S. Nicola	Executors: his heirs legacies to be paid *super bonis sive rebus suis* every year on feast of San Martino for which the priest to celebrate every year on the day of their deaths *pro anima*, for his father, his son Albertus and for Berardus himself . . . *et que anniversaria apponantur in martellorio ipsius ecclesie*

^v ASVer, Ghiara 250 (2 November). Sewn together with the will of his wife and execution of his legacy to the Humiliati (28 February 1260).
^w L'ospedale della Carità di Novara, 176 (13 March). The year is missing in the original.

Appendix III (cont.)

Date (place)	Testator (and motives)	Legacy	Beneficiary	Clauses/executors
[23] 1258ˣ *in domo fratrum umiliatorum a Glara ubi infirmi morantur . . .*	*Dominus* Bonauentura de Maga S Sebastiani *iacens infirmo in lecto volens facere codicillum et non remouendum aliud testamentum set confirmando sic dixit . . .*	half share of 3 plots of land: 2 in Colonie 1 ploughland	Desiderata, his daughter *que est hedidicata* [sic] *in domo humiliatorum a Glara*	the other half of the land to go to her sister Anna Bonauentura then donates the land for Desiderata to the minister of the house, *dominus frater* Bonorus
[24] 1259ʸ	a canon of Bergamo	10 s.i.	church of Galgario [Humiliati]	for the needs of the house and for perpetual office

ˣ ASVer, Ghiara 265 (14 April 1258) codicil.
ʸ Brolis, *Gli Umiliati a Bergamo*, p. 203.

BIBLIOGRAPHY OF PRIMARY SOURCES
AND PRINCIPAL WORKS CITED

MANUSCRIPTS

ADMONT

Stiftsbibliothek
  Ms. 22

BERGAMO

Archivio di Stato
  Archivio Notarile, Cartella 1,1, imbreviature of the notary Bartolomeo Carbonari

BRESCIA

Archivio di Stato
  Ospedale Maggiore, bolle in pergamene, filza AA no 1

COMO

Archivio di Stato
  Ospedale di Sant'Anna, ospedaletti antichi, cartelle 5 and 8

LODI

Archivio vescovile
  Armario VIII, cartella I

Biblioteca comunale
  B 17

MILAN

Archivio della curia arcivescovile
  A/2, A/4
  B/7
  C/6–8, C/12–14, C/17–18

Bibliography

Archivio di stato

    Archivio diplomatico, bolle e brevi, cartella 6
    Fondo pergamene
        182 Lodi, Sta Chiara Nuova
        187 Lodi, San Domenico
        191 Lodi, Sta Maria in Biolo
        385 Sta Caterina alla Chiusa
        435 San Marco
        470 and 471 Sta Maria di Brera
        526 Umiliati di Porta Vercellina
        638 Domenicani, Pavia
        1899 Sta Margherita

Biblioteca ambrosiana (microfilms)

    A 20 sup.
    C 74 inf.
    D 58 inf.
    D 88 inf.
    D 273 inf.
    F 82 sup.
    G 301 inf.
    G 302 inf.
    H 205 inf.
    H 210 inf.
    S 89 sup.
    V 9 sup.

Biblioteca nazionale di Brera

    AD XVI 1
    AE X 10
    AF IX II A2
    AG XI 3

Biblioteca trivulziana, Archivio

    Fondo belgioioso cartella 291

MUNICH

Bayerische Staatsbibliothek

    Clm 3879

PARIS

Bibliothèque nationale

    lat. nouvelles acquisitions 991

Bibliography

VATICAN CITY

Archivio Segreto Vaticano
Registri vaticani 4, 5, 14, 18, 19, 21, 21a, 22, 23, 24, 25, 39, 41, 43 and 44
Archivio della nunziatura Veneta. Fondo del monastero di San Giovanni di
Baldaria

Biblioteca vaticana
Reginense latina 2001
Vat lat. 1377

VERONA

Archivio di Stato
Fondo di Sta Maria della Ghiara
Fondo di Sto Spirito
Fondo di S. Giovanni della Beverara
Bolle papali

VICENZA

Archivio di Stato
Fondo delle corporazioni soppresse. Monastero di Ognissanti buste 1 and 2

PRINTED SOURCES

This list includes secondary works containing substantial editions of documents and
historical studies down to the end of the fifteenth century. Edited works by medieval
authors in this section are listed under the first name of the author.

'Acta capitulorum provinciae Lombardiae et Lombardiae inferioris', ed. T. Kaeppeli,
Archivum fratrum praedicatorum, 11 (1941), 138–72.
Acta pontificum romanorum inedita, ed. J. von Pflugk-Harttung, 3 vols. (Stuttgart, 1881–8,
reprinted Graz, 1958).
Alan of Lille, 'De fide catholica contra haereticos sui temporis', book 2, 'Contra
Waldenses', caps. 15–19, comp. J. P. Migne, *PL*, 210 (Paris, 1855), cols. 390–4.
Alexander IV, *Les registres d'Alexandre IV*, ed. Bourel de la Roncière, J. de Loye and A.
Coulon, 3 vols. (Paris, 1895–1959).
'"Analecta heidelbergensia" varietà', ed. E. Winkelman, *Archivio della società romana di
storia patria*, 1 (1879), 361–7.
Annales camaldulenses ordinis sancti Benedicti, ed. I. Mittarelli and A. Costadoni, 9 vols.
(Venice, 1755–73).
Annales cistercienses, ed. A. Manrique, 4 vols. (Lyons, 1649–57).
'Annales mediolanenses minores', ed. P. Jaffé, *MGH SS*, XVIII (Hanover, 1863) pp. 392–9.
'Annales mellicenses, Continuatio zwetlensis altera', ed. W. Wattenbach, *MGH SS*, IX
(Hanover, 1851), pp. 541–4.
Anonymous, 'Vita de S. Joanne de Meda', ed. C. Suyskens, *AASS*, September VII
(Antwerp, 1760), pp. 358–60.

Bibliography

Anonymous of Laon, *Chronicon universale* (excerpts), ed. G. Waitz, *MGH SS*, xxvi (Hanover, 1882), pp. 442–57.

Gli atti del comune di Milano nel secolo xiii, vol. 1/11, *1217–1250*, vol. 11/1, *1251–1262*, vol. 11/2, *1263–1276*, vol. 111/1, *1277–1300*, ed. M. F. Baroni (vols. 11/1 and 111/1) and M. F. Baroni and R. Perelli Cippo (vols. 11/1 and 11/2) (Milan/Alessandria, 1976–97).

Benedict XI, *Le registre de Benoît XI*, ed. C. Grandjean (Paris, 1883–1905).

Bernard Balbo, 'Vita de S. Lanfranco', ed. D. Papenbroek, *AASS*, June iv (Antwerp, 1707), pp. 620–30.

Bonacursus, 'Vita haereticorum', comp. J. P. Migne, *PL* 204 (Paris, 1855), cols. 775–92.

Bonaventure, *Opera omnia*, ed. the Fathers of the College of St Bonaventure, 10 vols. (Quaracchi, 1882–1902).

Bonvesin da la Riva, *De magnalibus mediolani. Meraviglie di Milano*, ed. and trans. P. Chiesa (Milan, 1998).

The Book of St Gilbert, ed. R. Foreville and G. Keir (Oxford, 1987).

Bullarium ordinis fratrum praedicatorum, ed. T. Ripoll and A. Bremond, 8 vols. (Rome, 1729–40).

Bullarum diplomatum et privilegiorum sanctorum romanorum pontificum, ed. A. Tommassetti, 24 vols. (Turin, 1857–72).

Burchard of Ursberg, *Chronicon*, ed. O. Abel and L. Weiland, *MGH SS*, xxiii (Hanover, 1874), pp. 333–83.

'Capitula monachorum', *Hludowici I capitularia. Constitutiones aquisgranenses*, *MGH Leges*, 1, ed. G. H. Pertz (Hanover, 1835), pp. 200–4.

'Capitulare monasticum 817', *Addimenta ad Hludowici Pii et Hlotharii capitularia*, *MGH Leges*, 1, ed. A. Boretius (Hanover, 1883), pp. 343–9.

Cartario della Abazia [sic] di Casanova fino all'anno 1313, ed. A. Tallone, BSSS, 14 (Pinerolo, 1913).

Carte dello Archivio capitolare di Asti (1238–1272), ed. L. Vergano, BSSS, 141 (Turin, 1942).

Carte dello Archivio capitolare di Tortona 801–1220/1221–1313, ed. F. Gabotto, V. Legé and C. Patrucco, 2 vols., BSSS, 29–30 (Pinerolo, 1905).

Carte dello Archivio vescovile d'Ivrea fino al 1313, ed. F. Gabotto, 2 vols., BSSS, 5–6 (Pinerolo, 1900).

'Le carte di Sta Maria Vecchia di Como', ed. L. Biondi, L. Martinelli Perelli and R. Perelli Cippo, *Studi di storia medioevale e di diplomatica*, 14 (1993), 211–74.

Carte e statuti dell'agro ticinese, ed. R. Maiocchi, BSSS, 129 (Turin, 1932).

Carte inedite e sparse dei signori e luoghi del pinerolese fino al 1300, ed. B. Baudi di Vesme, E. Durando and F. Gabotto, BSSS, 3/2 (Pinerolo, 1909).

Carte varie di Casale e monasteri del Monferrato. Cartari minori, ed. E. Durando, BSSS, 42 (Pinerolo, 1908).

Chrodegang, 'Regula canonicorum secundum Dacherii recensionem', comp. J. P. Migne, *PL* 89 (Paris, 1863), cols. 1058–96.

Chronicon fratris Francisci Pipini ordinis praedicatorum, ed. L. A. Muratori, *RIS*, ix (Milan, 1726), cols. 583–752.

Conciliorum oecumenicorum decreta, ed. J. Alberigo *et al.* (Bologna, 1973).

Constitutiones domini Coelestini legati in Lombardia, ed. L. A. Muratori, *RIS*, viii (Milan, 1726), cols. 1065–8.

Corpus iuris canonici, ed. A. Friedberg, 2 vols. (Leipzig, 1879–81).

The Crusades: A Documentary Survey, ed. J. A. Brundage (Milwaukee, 1962).

Bibliography

'De S. Galdino S.R.E Cardinale', ed. G. Henskens, *AASS*, April II (Antwerp, 1675), pp. 593–9.

Documenti circa la vita e le gesta di San Carlo Borromeo, ed. A. Sala, 3 vols. (Milan, 1851–61).

Documenti degli archivi di Pavia relativi alla storia di Voghera (929–1300), ed. L. C. Bollea, BSSS, 46 (Pinerolo, 1909).

'Documenti del monastero e della canonica di Sant Ambrogio dal xiii al xv secolo', ed. A. Ambrosioni, G. Cariboni, A. Summa and A. Vezzoli, *La Basilica di S. Ambrogio. Il tempio ininterroto*, ed. M. L. Gatti Perer, 2 vols. (Milan, 1995), II, pp. 559–65.

Documenti inediti della chiesa Pavese, ed. G. Bosisio (Pavia, 1859).

Documenti inediti e sparsi sulla storia di Torino, ed. F. Cognasso, BSSS, 65 (Pinerolo, 1914).

Documenti intorno alle relazioni fra Genova e Alba, vol. I, *1141–1270*, vol. II, *1270–1321*, ed. A. Ferretto, BSSS, 23 and 50 (Pinerolo, 1906–10).

'Documenti relativi a monasteri padani nel fondo "Morbio" della biblioteca universitaria di Halle an der Saale (DDR)', ed. F. Menant and G. Spinelli, *Centro storico benedettino, Bollettino informativo*, 7 (Rome, 1979), 5*–10*.

Francis of Assisi, *Testament*, ed. and trans. B. Fahy, *St Francis of Assisi: Writings and Early Biographies*, ed. M. A. Habig (London, 1973), pp. 67–70.

Galvano Fiamma, *Chronicon extravagans et chronicon maius (ad an. 1216)*, ed. A. Ceruti, *Miscellanea di storia italiana* (Turin, 1869), VII, pp. 506–773.

Manipulus florum sive historia mediolanensis ab origine urbis ad annum circiter 1336, ed. L. A. Muratori, *RIS*, IX (Milan, 1727), cols. 533–740.

Giacomo Filippo Foresti, *Supplementum supplementi chronicarum* (Milan, 1483).

Goffredus da Bussero, *Chronicon*, ed. L. Grazioli, 'La cronaca di Goffredo di Bussero', *ASL*, 33 (1906), 211–45.

Gregory the Great, *Regula pastoralis*, ed. F. Rommel and C. Morel, trans. and notes B. Judic, *Grégoire le grand, Sources chrétiennes* 381 (Paris, 1992).

Gregory IX, *Les registres de Grégoire IX*, ed. L. Auvray, 4 vols. (Paris, 1896–1955).

'Guglielmo Cassinese (1190–1192)', ed. M. W. Hall, H. C. Krueger and R. L. Reynolds, *Notai liguri del secolo xii*, II (Genoa, 1938).

Heresies of the High Middle Ages, trans. W. L. Wakefield and A. P. Evans (New York/ London, 1969).

Heresy and Authority in Medieval Europe, ed. E. Peters (London, 1980).

Historia diplomatica sancti Dominici, ed. M. H. Laurent, *Monumenta historica sancti Dominici*, I, *Monumenta ordinis fratrum praedicatorum historica*, XV (Paris 1933).

Honorius III, *Regesta Honorii Papae III*, ed. P. Pressuti, 2 vols. (Rome, 1888–95, reprinted Hildesheim, 1978).

Honorius IV, *Les registres d'Honorius IV*, ed. M. Prou (Paris, 1888).

Humbert of Romans, *Sermones ad humiliatos*, comp. Zanoni (Milan, 1911), pp. 261–3 from *Maxima bibliotheca veterum patrum*, 25 (Lyons, 1677), pp. 456–567.

Innocent III, *Acta*, ed. T. T Haluszynskyi (Vatican City, 1944).

Epistolarum Innocentii libri undecim, ed. S. Baluze, 2 vols. (Paris, 1682).

Opera omnia, comp. J. P. Migne, *PL*, 214–17 (Paris, 1855).

Selected Letters of Pope Innocent III Concerning England (1198–1216), ed. C. R. Cheney and W. H. Semple (London, 1953).

Innocent IV, *Les registres d'Innocent IV*, ed. E. Berger, 4 vols. (Paris 1884–1921).

Institutio canonicorum aquisgranensis, ed. A. Werminghoff, *MGH Leges*, III/II, *Concilia aevi karolini*, part I (Hanover/Leipzig, 1906), pp. 308–421.

Bibliography

Inventory of Western Manuscripts in the Biblioteca Ambrosiana from the Frank M. Folsom Microfilm Collection, ed. L. Jordan and S. Wool, part 1 *A–B Superior;* part 2 *C–D Superior;* part 3 *E Superior* (Notre Dame, 1984, 1987, 1989).

Italia pontificia. Regesta pontificum romanorum, ed. P. F. Kehr, W. Holtzmann *et al.*, 10 vols. (Berlin, 1906–75).

Jacques de Vitry, *The 'Historia occidentalis' of Jacques de Vitry: A Critical Edition*, ed. J. F. Hinnebusch, *Spicilegium Friburgense*, 17 (Freibourg, 1972).

Lettres de Jacques de Vitry (1160/70–1240) évêque de Saint-Jean-d'Acre. Edition critique, ed. R. B. C. Huygens (Leiden, 1960).

Johannis Teutonici apparatus glossarum in compilationem tertiam, ed. K. Pennington (Vatican City, 1981)

John of Brera, *Chronicon ordinis Humiliatorum* (1419), ed. G. Tiraboschi *VHM* III, pp. 229–86.

Excerptum (1421), ed. Zanoni (Milan, 1911), pp. 336–44.

Jordan of Saxony, *Libellus*, ed. H. C. Scheeben, *Monumenta ordinis praedicatorum historica*, 16 (Rome, 1935), pp. 1–88.

Landulf of St Paul, 'Historia mediolanensis', ed. L. Bethmann and P. Jaffé, *MGH SS*, xx (Hanover, 1868), pp. 17–49.

Marco Bossi, *Chronicon sui Humiliatorum ordinis anno domini 1493 Conditum*, ed. Zanoni (Milan, 1911), pp. 345–52.

Martin IV, *Les registres de Martin IV (1281–85)*, ed. F. Olivier-Martin (Paris, 1901–35).

'I necrologi eusebiani', ed. G. Colombo, *Bollettino storico-bibliografico subalpino*, 6 (1901), 1–15.

Nicholas III, *Les registres de Nicholas III (1277–1280)*, ed. M. Gay (Paris, 1898–1938).

Nicholas IV, *Les registres de Nicholas IV (1288–92)*, ed. E. Langlois, 2 vols. (Paris, 1886–1905).

L'ospedale della Carità di Novara: il Codice vetus. Documenti dei secoli xii–xiv, ed. M. F. Baroni (Novara, 1985).

Le pergamene degli Umiliati di Cremona, ed. V. D'Alessandro (Palermo, 1964).

Pergamene milanesi dei secoli xii e xiii conservate presso l'Archivio di stato di Milano, VI, ed. R. Perelli Cippo (Milan, 1988).

Pergamene milanesi dei secoli xii e xiii conservate presso l'Archivio di stato di Milano, XII, ed. L. Martinelli (Milan, 1994).

Peter the Chanter, 'Verbum abbreviatum', comp. J. P. Migne, *PL*, 205 (Paris, 1855), cols. 23–370.

Quellen zur Geschichte der Waldenser, ed. A. Patschovsky and K.-V. Selge, *Texte zur Kirchen- und Theologiegeschichte*, 18 (Gutersloh, 1973).

'Die Regesten des Kaiserreiches unter Heinrich VI 1165(1190)–1197', ed. G. and K. Baaken, 2 vols. *Regesta imperii*, IV/3 (Cologne/Vienna, 1979).

Regesto delle pergamene dell'archivio arcivescovile di Milano, ed. A. Palestra, *Archivio ambrosiano*, 12 (Milan, 1961).

I registri del monastero di s. Abbondio in Como: secolo xiii, ed. R. Perelli Cippo (Como, 1984).

Il 'registrum magnum' del comune di Piacenza, ed. E. Falconi and R. Peveri, 4 vols. and index (Milan, 1984).

La règle du Maître, ed. A. de Vogüé, 3 vols. *Sources chrétiennes*, 105 (Paris, 1964–5).

Robert of Saint-Marien, *Chronicon*, ed. O. Holder-Egger, *MGH SS*, xxvi (Hanover, 1882), pp. 219–87.

Sacrorum conciliorum nova et amplissima collectio, ed. J. D. Mansi, 25 vols. (Venice, 1759–82).

Bibliography

Salimbene de Adam, *Chronicon. Nuova edizione critica*, ed. G. Scalia, *Scrittori d'Italia*, 232 (Bari, 1966).

Sanctae ecclesiae florentinae monumenta, ed. G. Lami, 4 vols. (Florence, 1758).

Smaragdus, 'Expositio in regulam sancti benedicti', ed. A. Spannagel and P. Engelbert, *Corpus consuetudinum monasticarum*, 8 (Siegburg, 1974).

Statuta capitulorum generalium ordinis cisterciensis ab anno 1116 ad annum 1786, ed. J. M Canivez, 8 vols. (Louvain, 1933–41).

'Statuti di Brescia', ed. F. Odorici, *Storie di Brescia*, VII (1856), pp. 104–39.

'Statuti rurali veronesi', ed. C. Cipolla, *Archivio veneto*, 37–8 (1889), 81–107 and 341–80.

Stephen of Salagnac and Bernard Gui. *De quatuor in quibus deus praedicatorum ordinem insignivit*, ed. T. Kaeppeli, *Monumenta ordinis fratrum praedicatorum historica*, 22 (Rome, 1949).

Texte zur Inquisition, ed. K.-V. Selge, *Texte zur Kirchen- und Theologiegeschichte*, IV (Gutersloh, 1967).

Thomas of Celano, *Vita prima sancti Francisci*, ed. Quaracchi Fathers, *Analecta franciscana*, X (1926–41), pp. 1–126.

Udalric, 'Consuetudines cluniacenses', comp. J. P. Migne, *PL* 149 (Paris, 1882), cols. 635–778.

Vetera monumenta slavorum meridionalium, ed. A. Theiner, 2 vols. (Rome, 1863–75).

'Vita beati Joachimi abbatis', ed. H. Grundmann, 'Zur Biographie Joachims von Fiore und Rainers von Ponza', *Deutsches Archiv*, 16 (1960), 437–546, 528–46.

'Vita prima sancti Bernardi', comp. J. P. Migne, *PL*, 185 (Paris, 1833), cols. 273–80.

'Vita S. Alberti', ed. D. Papenbroek, *AASS*, April I (Antwerp, 1675), pp. 769–99.

'Vita secunda sancti Bernardi', comp. J. P. Migne, *PL*, 185 (Paris, 1833), cols. 469–524.

SECONDARY WORKS

L'Abbazia di Viboldone (Milan, 1990).

Adami, F. E., 'La "domus sancti Bartholomei de Rodigio". Contributo alla storia degli Umiliati', *Il monastero di S. Bartolomeo di Rovigo, Accademia dei concordi di Rovigo. Studi e ricerche*, I (Rovigo, 1979), pp. 9–41.

Affò, I., *Storia di Parma*, 4 vols. (Parma, 1792–5).

Alberzoni, M. P., 'I primi francescani a Milano. Note sul testamento di "Ruba de Balsemo" (1224)', *Ricerche storiche sulla chiesa ambrosiana*, 10 (Milan, 1981), 144–62.

'Chiesa e comuni in Lombardia. Dall'età di Innocenzo III all'affermazione degli ordini mendicanti', *La Lombardia dei comuni* (Milan, 1988), pp. 33–52.

'Il monastero di Sant Ambrogio e i movimenti religiosi del xiii secolo', *Il monastero di S. Ambrogio nel Medioevo, Convegno di studi nel xii centenario 784–1984* (Milan, 1988), pp. 165–213.

'L'esperienza caritativa presso gli Umiliati. Il caso di Brera (secolo xiii)', *La carità a Milano nei secoli xii–xv*, ed. M. P. Alberzoni and O. Grassi (Milan, 1989), pp. 201–23.

'Nel conflitto tra papato e impero: da Galdino della Sala a Guglielmo da Rizolio (1166–1241)', *Diocesi di Milano*, I, Storia religiosa della Lombardia, 9 (Brescia/ Gazzada, 1990), pp. 227–57.

Francescanesimo a Milano nel duecento (Milan, 1991).

'Gli inizi degli Umiliati. Una riconsiderazione', *La conversione alla povertà nell'Italia dei*

Bibliography

secoli xii–xv, Convegni del Centro di studi sulla spiritualità medioevale, 27 (Todi, 1991), pp. 187–237.

'Un mendicante di fronte alla vita della chiesa nella seconda metà del duecento. Motivi religiosi nella cronica di Salimbene', Salimbeniana. Atti del convegno per il VII centenario di fra Salimbene, Parma 1987–1989 (Bologna, 1991), pp. 7–34.

'Innocenzo III e la riforma della chiesa in "Lombardia". Prime indagini sui visitatores et provisores', Quellen und Forschungen aus italienischen Archiven und Bibliotheken, 73 (1993), 122–78.

'San Bernardo e gli Umiliati', San Bernardo e l'Italia, ed. P. Zerbi (Milan, 1993), pp. 96–124.

' "Sub eadem clausura sequestrati". Uomini e donne nelle prime comunità Umiliate lombarde', Uomini e donne in comunità. Quaderni di storia religiosa, 1 (1994), 69–110.

'Giacomo di Rondineto. Contributo per una biografia', Sulle tracce, pp. 117–62.

Ambrosioni, A., 'Controversie tra il monastero e la canonica di Sant'Ambrogio alla fine del secolo xii', Rendiconti. Classe di lettere e scienze morali e storiche dell'Istituto lombardo di scienze e lettere, 105 (1971), 643–80.

'Monasteri e canoniche nella politica di Urbano III', Istituzioni monastiche e istituzioni canonicali in occidente 1123–1215, Atti della settima settimana internazionale di studio, Mendola 1977, Miscellanea del centro di studi medioevali, IX (Milan, 1980), pp. 601–30.

'Umiliate/Umiliati', DIP, IX (Rome, 1997), cols. 1489–1507.

Andenna, G., 'Una famiglia milanese di "cives" proprietari terrieri nella pieve di Cesano Boscone. I Cagapisto', Raccolta di studi in onore di S. Mocha Onory. Contributi dell'Istituto di storia medioevale, II (Milan, 1972), pp. 641–86.

Andrews, F. E., 'Principium et origo ordinis: the Humiliati and their origins', The Church Retrospective, ed. R. Swanson, SCH, 33 (Oxford, 1997), pp. 149–61.

'The second generation of the "Sambin Revolution": new writings on the Humiliati', Journal of Ecclesiastical History, 49 (1998), 140–8.

Angelucci, P. 'Gli Umiliati di Siena e la chiesa del borgo franco di Paganico', Chiesa e società dal secolo iv ai nostri giorni. Studi storici in onore del P. Ilarino da Milano, Italia sacra, 30 (Rome, 1979), pp. 261–89.

Archetti, G., 'Gli Umiliati e i vescovi alla fine del duecento. Il caso bresciano', Sulle tracce, pp. 267–314.

Arizza, A. and M. Longatti, 'Gli Umiliati in diocesi di Como', Periodico della società storica comense, 53 (1989), 131–52.

Baldi Cammarota, F., 'Origine della "domus" degli Umiliati di San Cristoforo in Verona', Studi storici veronesi Luigi Simeoni, 24 (1974), 1–28.

Baldwin, J. W., 'The intellectual preparation for the canon of 1215 against ordeals', Speculum, 36 (1961), 613–36.

Balosso, G., 'Gli Umiliati nel Novarese', Novarien, 12 (1982), 42–90.

Barbieri, G., 'La funzione economica degli Umiliati', Economia e storia, 21 (1974), 159–81.

'Un insediamento dell'ordine degli Umiliati', Chiese e monasteri nel territorio veronese, ed. G. Borelli (Verona, 1981), pp. 197–208.

Bascapè, G. C., 'Insegne e sigilli dell'ordine degli Umiliati', Studi di letteratura. Storia e filosofia in onore di Bruno Revel (Florence, 1965), pp. 93–4.

Benvenuti Papi, A., 'Una città e un vescovo. La Firenze di Ardingo (1230–1247)', L'ordine dei servi di Maria nel primo secolo di vita. Atti del convegno storico, Firenze 1986 (Florence, 1988), pp. 55–152.

Bibliography

'Vangelo e tiratoi. Gli Umiliati ed il loro insediamento fiorentino', *La 'Madonna di Ognissanti' di Giotto restaurata. Gli Uffizi: studi e ricerche*, 8 (Florence, 1992), 75–84.

Besozzi, L., 'Le case degli Umiliati nell'Alto Seprio', *Rivista della società storica varesina*, 16 (1983), 42–73.

'L'ultimo preposito degli Umiliati di Cannobio', *Verbanus* 5 (1984), 413–40.

Biancolini, G. B., *Notizie storiche delle chiese di Verona*, 7 vols. (Verona, 1750–66, reprinted Bologna, 1977).

Bolcati, L. and F. Lomastro Tognato, 'Una *religio nova* nel duecento vicentino: gli Umiliati della città e del contado (sec. xiii)', *Religiones novae. Quaderni di storia religiosa*, 2 (1995), 149–79.

Bolton, B. M., 'Innocent III's treatment of the Humiliati', *Popular Belief and Practice*, ed. G. J. Cuming and D. Baker, SCH, 8 (Cambridge, 1971), pp. 73–82.

'Tradition and temerity: papal attitudes towards deviants 1159–1216', *Schism, Heresy and Religious Protest*, ed. D. Baker, SCH, 9 (Cambridge, 1972), 79–91.

'Sources for the early history of the Humiliati', *The Materials, Sources and Methods of Ecclesiastical History*, ed. D. Baker, SCH, 11 (Oxford, 1974), pp. 125–33.

'The poverty of the Humiliati', *Poverty in the Middle Ages*, Franziskanische Forschungen, 27, ed. D. Flood (1975), 52–9.

The Medieval·Reformation (London, 1983).

'Via ascetica: A papal quandary', *Monks, Hermits and the Ascetic Tradition*, ed. W. J. Sheils, SCH, 22 (Oxford, 1985), pp. 161–91.

'For the see of Simon Peter: the Cistercians at Innocent III's nearest frontier', *Monastic Studies*, 1 (Bangor, 1990), 146–57.

'A show with a meaning: Innocent III's approach to the Fourth Lateran Council 1215', *Medieval History*, 1 (1991), 53–67.

Bondioli, P., *Storia di Busto Arsizio*, 2 vols. (Varese, 1937/54).

Boyle, L. E., 'Innocent III and vernacular versions of scripture', *The Bible in the Medieval World*, ed. K. Walsh and D. Wood, SCH Subsidia, 4 (Oxford, 1985), pp. 97–107.

Brentano, R., 'Italian ecclesiastical history: the Sambin revolution', *Medievalia et Humanistica*, new series 14 (Ottawa, 1986), 189–97.

Brett, E. T., *Humbert of Romans: His Life and Views of Thirteenth-century Society*, Pontifical Institute of Mediaeval Studies, Studies and Texts, 67 (Toronto, 1984).

Broggi, M. M., 'Il catalogo del 1298', *Sulle tracce*, pp. 3–44.

Brolis, M. T., ' "Superstantes pontis de Lemen". Un'inedita testimonianza sugli Umiliati a Bergamo nel secolo xiii', *Archivio storico bergamasco*, 14 (Bergamo, 1988), 9–16.

Gli Umiliati a Bergamo nei secoli xiii e xiv (Milan, 1991).

"Quibus fuit remissum sacramentum". Il rifiuto di giurare presso gli Umiliati', *Sulle tracce*, pp. 251–65.

Brooke, C. N. L., 'Monk and canon: some patterns in the religious life of the twelfth century', *Monks, Hermits and the Ascetic Tradition*, ed. W. J. Sheils, SCH, 22 (Oxford, 1985), pp. 109–29.

'Priest, deacon and layman: from St Peter Damian to St Francis', *The Ministry: Clerical and Lay*, ed. W. J. Sheils and D. Wood, SCH, 26 (Oxford, 1989), pp. 65–85.

Brooke, R. B., *Early Franciscan Government: Elias to Bonaventure* (Cambridge, 1959).

The Coming of the Friars (London, 1975).

Brundage, J. A., *Medieval Canon Law* (London/New York, 1995).

Brune, P., *Histoire de l'ordre hospitalier du Saint-Esprit* (Lons-le-Saunier/Paris, 1892).

Bull, A., 'Canonici regolari di Sta Croce di Mortara', *DIP*, II (Rome, 1975), cols. 145–7.

Bibliography

Bull, M., *Knightly Piety and the Lay Response to the First Crusade* (Oxford, 1993).

Campi, P. M., *Dell'historia ecclesiastica di Piacenza*, ed. P. M. Campi the Younger, 3 vols. (Piacenza, 1651–62).

Caraffa, F. (ed.)., *Monasticon Italiae*, I, *Roma e Lazio* (Cesena, 1981).

Caselli, G., *La via romea 'cammino di dio'* (Florence, 1990).

Caso, A., *I Crivelli. Una famiglia milanese fra politica, società ed economia nei secoli xii e xiii*, Biblioteca della "nuova rivista storica", 38 (1994).

Castagnetti, D., 'La regola del primo e secondo ordine dall'approvazione alla "regula benedicti" ', *Sulle tracce*, pp. 163–250.

Castiglioni, C., 'L'ordine degli Umiliati in tre codici illustrati dell'Ambrosiana', *Memorie storiche della diocesi di Milano*, 7 (Milan, 1960), pp. 7–36.

Chenu, M.-D., 'Moines, clercs, laïcs, au carrefour de la vie évangélique (xiie siècle)', *Revue d'histoire ecclésiastique*, 49 (1954), 59–89.

Nature, Man and Society in the Twelfth Century: Essays on New Theological Perspectives in the Latin West, ed. and trans. J. Taylor and L. K. Little, preface by E. Gibson (Chicago/London, 1968).

' "Fraternitas." Evangile et condition socio-culturelle', *Revue d'histoire de la spiritualité*, 49 (1973), 385–400.

Cicconetti, C., *La regola del Carmelo. Origine-natura-significato*, Textus et studia historica carmelitana, 12 (Rome, 1973).

Cipollone, M., 'Gerardo da Sesso vescovo eletto di Novara, Albano e Milano', *Aevum*, 60 (1986), 223–39.

'Gerardo da Sesso, legato apostolico al tempo di Innocenzo III', *Aevum*, 61 (1987), 358–88.

Cipriani, R., *Codici miniati dell'Ambrosiana. Contributo a un catalogo* (Milan, 1968).

Constable, G., *Monastic Tithes from their Origins to the Twelfth Century* (Cambridge, 1964).

Corsi, M. L., 'Note sulla famiglia da Baggio (secoli ix–xiii)', *Raccolta di studi in memoria di Giovanni Soranzo, Contibuti dell'Istituto di storia medioevale*, I (Milan, 1968), pp. 166–204.

Coulton, G. C., *Five Centuries of Religion*, 4 vols. (Cambridge, 1927).

Cracco, G., 'Premessa', *Minoritismo e centri veneti nel duecento, nel ottavo centenario della nascita di Francesco d'Assisi (1182–1982)*, separate edition of *Civis studi e testi* 19–20, ed. G. Cracco (Trento, 1983).

Cremascoli, L., 'La regola degli Umiliati in un codice del secolo xiii', *Archivio storico lodigiano*, 69 (1950), 49–55.

Crosara, F., ' "Jurata voce". Saggi sul giuramento nel nome dei re e degli imperatori dall'antichità pagana al medio evo cristiano' 3, *Annali della facoltà giuridica dell'Università di Camerino*, 28 (1962), 269–337.

Crotti Pasi, R., 'Gli Umiliati a Pavia nei secoli xii e xiii', *Bollettino della società pavese di storia patria*, new series 46 (1994), 11–32; now reprinted in *Sulle tracce*, pp. 317–42.

da Bergamo, M., 'Beltramo da Brescia', *DBI*, VIII (Rome, 1996), pp. 78–9.

da Milano, I., 'L'eresia di Ugo Speroni nella confutazione del maestro Vacario', *Studi e Testi*, 115 (1945), 456–66.

'Il "Liber supra stella" del piacentino Salvo Burci contro i Catari e altre correnti ereticali', *Aevum*, 17 (1948), 90–146.

'Umiliati', *Enciclopedia cattolica*, XII (Rome, 1954), cols. 754–6.

Dal Pino, F., *I frati servi di sta Maria dalle origini all'approvazione (1233–c. 1304)*, 2 vols. (Louvain, 1972).

Bibliography

Il laicato italiano tra eresia e proposta pauperistico-evangelica nei secoli xii–xiii (Padua, 1984).

'L'Evoluzione dell'idea di mendicità nel duecento', *Esperienze minoritiche nel Veneto del due-trecento. Atti del congresso di Padova 1984, Le Venezie francescane*, new series, 2 (1985), 11–36.

Davidsohn, R., *Forschungen zur Geschichte von Florenz*, 4 vols. (Berlin, 1896–1908).

d'Avray, D. L., *The Preaching of the Friars: Sermons Diffused from Paris before 1300* (Oxford, 1985).

Deroux, M. P., 'Les origines de l'oblature bénédictine', *Revue Mabillon*, 17 (1927), 1–16, 81–113, 193–216 and 305–51.

de Saint-Marthe, D. and the Fathers of the Congregation de St Maur, *Gallia christiana*, 14 vols. (Paris, 1715–1865).

De Sandre Gasparini, G., 'Per la storia dei penitenti a Verona nel secolo xiii. Primi contributi', *Il movimento francescano della penitenza nella società medievale*, ed. M. d'Alatri (Rome, 1980), pp. 257–83.

'Aspetti di vita religiosa, sociale ed economica di chiese e monasteri nei secoli xiii–xv', *Chiese e monasteri nel territorio veronese*, ed. G. Borelli (Verona, 1981), pp. 133–94.

'Movimenti evangelici a Verona all'epoca di Francesco d'Assisi', *Le Venezie francescane*, new series 1 (1984), 151–62. First published in *Note mazziane*, 17/2 (1982), 53–7.

'L'assistenza ai lebbrosi nel movimento religioso dei primi decenni del duecento veronese: uomini e fatti', *Viridarium floridum. Studi di storia veneta offerti dagli allievi a Paolo Sambin*, ed. M. C. Billanovich, G. Cracco and A. Rigon, *Medioevo e umanesimo*, 54 (Padua, 1984), 25–59.

'Il francescanesimo a Verona. Note dai testamenti', *Esperienze minoritiche nel Veneto del due-trecento. Atti del congresso di Padova 1984, Le Venezie francescane*, new series 2 (1985), 121–41.

La Vita religiosa nella marca veronese-trevigiana tra XII e XIV secolo (Verona, 1993).

De Stefano, A., 'Le origini dell'ordine degli Umiliati', *Rivista storico-critica delle scienze teologiche*, 2 (1906), 851–71.

'Delle origini e della natura del primitivo movimento degli Umiliati', *Archivum Romanicum*, 11 (1927), 31–75. Republished in *Riformatori ed eretici del medio evo* (Palermo, 1938), pp. 127–208.

Riformatori ed eretici del medio evo (Palermo, 1938).

Diehl, P., 'Overcoming reluctance to prosecute heresy in thirteenth-century Italy', *Christendom and its Discontents: Exclusion, Persecution and Rebellion, 1000–1500*, ed. S. L. Waugh and P. D. Diehl (Cambridge, 1996), pp. 47–66.

Dizionario biografico degli italiani, ed. A. M. Ghisalberti *et al.* (Rome, 1960–) I–.

Dizionario degli istituti di perfezione, ed. G. Pelliccia (1962–68) and G. Rocca (1969–) (Rome, 1974–), I–.

Doran, J., 'Oblation or obligation? A canonical ambiguity', *The Church and Childhood*, ed. D. Wood, SCH, 31 (Oxford, 1994), pp. 127–41.

Dubois, J., 'Les ordres religieux au xiie siècle selon la curie romaine', *Revue Bénédictine*, 78 (1968), 283–309.

'Ordo', *DIP*, vi (Rome, 1980), cols. 806–20.

Du Cange, C., *Glossarium ad scriptores mediae et infimae latinitatis*, 6 vols. (Paris, 1733–6).

Les 'ecclesiastica officia' cisterciens du xiie siècle, ed. and trans, D. Choisselet and P. Vernet (Reiningue, 1989).

Bibliography

Epstein, S., *Wills and Wealth in Medieval Genoa 1150–1250* (Cambridge Mass./London, 1984).

Wage Labour and Guilds in Medieval Europe (Chapel Hill/London, 1991).

Erba, A. M., 'Chierici regolari di S. Paolo', *DIP*, II (Rome, 1975), cols. 945–74.

Evans, G. R., *Alan of Lille: The Frontiers of Theology in the Later Twelfth Century* (Cambridge, 1983).

Fonseca, C. D., 'Arnolfo', *DBI*, IV (Rome, 1962), pp. 284–5.

Freed, J. B., *The Friars and German Society in the Thirteenth Century* (Cambridge Mass., 1977).

Frisi, A. F., *Memorie della chiesa monzese*, 4 vols. (Milan, 1774–80).

Memorie storiche di Monza e sua corte, 2 vols. (Milan, 1794).

Gatti Perer, M. L., 'Gli affreschi trecenteschi', *L'Abbazia di Viboldone*, pp. 103–213.

Giulini, G., *Memorie spettanti alla storia al governo ed alla descrizione della città ed della campagna di Milano ne' secoli bassi*, 9 vols. (Milan, 1760–5).

Giunta, F., 'Gli Umiliati di Cremona', *Bollettino storico cremonese*, 3 (1948–9), 201–24.

Giussani, A., 'Il sarcofago di san Giovanni da Meda', *Rivista archeologica della provincia e dell'antica diocesi di Como*, 59–61 (1910), 93–114.

Goggi, C., *Per la storia della diocesi di Tortona. Raccolta di notizie storiche*, II (Tortona, 1964).

Gonnet, G., 'Sul concilio di Verona', *Bollettino della società di studi valdesi*, 140 (1976), 21–30.

Gratien De Paris, *Histoire de la fondation et de l'évolution de l'ordre des frères mineurs au xiiie siècle*, reprinted with bibliography by M. D'Alatri and S. Gieben (Rome, 1982).

Gribomont, J., 'Le formule di professione in occidente', in 'Professione', *DIP*, VII (Rome, 1983), cols. 934–9.

Gruber, E., 'Die Humiliaten im alten Tessin', *Zeitschrift für schweizerische Geschichte*, 18 (1938), 268–304.

Guerrini, P., 'Gli Umiliati a Brescia', *Miscellanea Pio Paschini*, II (Rome, 1948), pp. 187–214.

Guidoni, E., *La città dal medioevo al rinascimento* (Rome/Bari, 1981).

Hinnebusch, W. A., *The History of the Dominican Order*, 2 vols. (New York, 1973).

Hueck, I., 'Le opere di Giotto per la chiesa di Ognissanti', *La 'Madonna d'Ognissanti' di Giotto restaurata. Gli Uffizi. Studi e ricerche*, 8 (Florence, 1992), 37–50.

Iriarte, L., *Storia del francescanesimo* (Naples, 1982).

Kaeppeli, T., *Scriptores ordinis praedicatorum medii aevii*, 4 vols. (Rome, 1970–93).

Lambert, M. D., *Medieval Heresy: Popular Movements from the Gregorian Reform to the Reformation* (Oxford, revised edition, 1992).

Leff, G., *Heresy in the Later Middle Ages: The Relationship of Heterodoxy to Dissent c. 1250–c. 1450*, 2 vols. (Manchester, 1967).

Little, L. K., *Religious Poverty and the Profit Economy in Medieval Europe* (London, 1978).

Longoni, V., 'Gli Umiliati in Brianza', *Archivi di Lecco*, 8 (1985), 797–824.

'Origini degli Umiliati a Monza', *Studi monzesi*, 3 (1988), 19–45.

Maccarrone, M., 'Riforma e sviluppo della vita religiosa con Innocenzo III', *RSCI*, 16 (Rome, 1962), 29–72.

Studi su Innocenzo III, Italia Sacra, 17 (Padua, 1972).

Maiolino T. M. and C. Varaldo, 'Diocesi di Genova', *Liguria Monastica, Italia Benedettina*, II (Cesena, 1979), pp. 93–151.

Maleczek, W., 'Ein Brief des Kardinals Lothar von SS. Sergius und Bacchus (Innocenz III.) an Kaiser Heinrich VI', *Deutsches Archiv*, 38 (1982), 564–76.

Bibliography

Pietro Capuano, patrizio amalfitano, cardinale, legato alla quarta crociata, teologo (†1214), trans. F. Delle Donne, rev. and updated by the author (Amalfi, 1997); originally published as *Petrus Capuanus. Kardinal. Legat am Vierten Kreuzzug, Theologe* (†1214) (Rome/Vienna, 1988).

Mambretti, R., 'Prime ricerche per una storia delle case religiose in Monza. La "Domus Caputiarum" di Piro (secolo xiv)', *Aevum*, 61 (1987), 398–407.

'Note sugli insediamenti Umiliati nel territorio di Vimercate', *ASL*, 115 (1989), 329–41.

Manni, D. M., *Osservazioni sopra i sigilli antichi de' secoli bassi*, 30 vols. (Florence, 1739–86).

Manselli, R., 'Gli Umiliati, lavoratori di lana', *Produzione, commercio e consumo dei panni di lana (nei secc. xii–xviii). Atti della seconda settimana di studio, Prato, 1970*, ed. M. Spallanzani, ii/2 (Florence, 1974), pp. 231–6.

Il secolo xii. Religione popolare ed eresia (Rome, 1983).

Marrucci, R. A., 'Il territorio e il complesso di Viboldone', *L'Abbazia di Viboldone*, pp. 63–101.

Martegani, A., 'Gli Umiliati di Mariano e i Visconti', extract from *ASL*, 95 (1968), 3–23.

Meersseman, G. G., *Dossier de l'ordre de la pénitence au xiiie siècle* (Fribourg, 1961).

'Ordo fraternitatis'. *Confraternite e pietà dei laici nel medioevo*, 3 vols., Italia Sacra, 24–6 (Rome, 1977).

Menant, F., 'Les monastères bénédictins du diocèse de Crémone. Répertoire', *Centro storico benedettino italiano. Bollettino informativo*, 7 (Rome, 1979), 11*–67*.

Mercati, G., 'Due ricerche per la storia degli Umiliati', *RSCI*, 11 (1957), 168–94.

Mercatili Indelicato, E., 'Per una riconsiderazione del lavoro presso gli Umiliati: il caso di Lodi', *Il lavoro nella storia della civiltà occidentale. Atti del xvii convegno del centro di studi avellanti*, ii (Urbino, 1994), pp. 111–75.

'Per una storia degli Umiliati nella diocesi di Lodi. Le case di S. Cristoforo e di Ognissanti nel XIII secolo', *Sulle tracce*, pp. 343–492.

Merlo, G. G., *Tensioni religiose agli inizi del duecento. Il primo francescanesimo in rapporto a tradizioni eremitico-penitenziali, esperienze pauperistico-evangeliche, truppi eretricali e istituzioni ecclesiastiche* (Torre Pellico, 1984).

'Minori e Predicatori nel Piemonte del duecento: gli inizi di una presenza', *Piemonte medievale. Forme di potere e della società, Studi per G. Tabacco* (Turin, 1985), pp. 207–26.

'Tra "vecchio" e "nuovo" monachesimo (metà xii–metà xiii secolo)', *Studi storici*, 28 (1987), 447–69.

Eretici ed eresie medievali (Bologna, 1989).

Miccoli, G., 'La storia religiosa', *Storia d'Italia*, ii/1, *Dalla caduta dell'impero al secolo xviii* (Turin, 1974), pp. 431–1079.

Minghetti, L., 'L'episcopato vercellese di Alberto durante i primi anni del xiii secolo', *Vercelli nel secolo xiii. Atti del primo congresso storico vercellese, Vercelli, 1982*, ed. R. Ordano *et al.* (Vercelli, 1984), pp. 99–112; reprinted with minor changes as 'Alberto vescovo di Vercelli (1185–1205). Contributo per una biografia', *Aevum*, 59 (1985), 267–304.

Moore, J. C., 'Lotario dei conti di Segni (pope Innocent III) in the 1180s', *Archivum Historiae Pontificiae*, 29 (1991), 255–8.

Moore, R. I., *The Birth of Popular Heresy*, Documents of Medieval History, 1 (London, 1975).

Bibliography

'New sects and secret meetings: association and authority in the eleventh and twelfth centuries', *Voluntary Religion*, ed. W. J. Sheils and D. Wood, SCH, 23 (Oxford, 1986), pp. 47–68.

Moorman, J., *A History of the Franciscan Order from its Origins to the Year 1517* (Oxford, 1968).

Mornacchi, N., 'Aspetti della vita comune presso i canonici regolari mortariensi in Genova', *La vita comune del clero nei secoli xi e xii, Atti della settimana di studio, Mendola 1959*, Miscellanea del centro di studi medioevali, II (Milan, 1962), pp. 154–62.

Morris, C., *The Papal Monarchy: The Western Church from 1050 to 1250* (Oxford, 1989).

Mosca, V., *Alberto Patriarca di Gerusalemme*, Textus et studia historica Carmelitana, 20 (Rome, 1996).

Murray, A., 'Piety and impiety in thirteenth-century Italy', *Popular Belief and Practice*, ed. G. J. Cuming and D. Baker, SCH, 8 (Cambridge, 1971), pp. 83–106.

Neel, C. L., 'The historical work of Burchard of Ursberg, 4: Burchard as historian', *Analecta praemonstratensia*, 59: 3/4 (1983), 221–57.

'The historical work of Burchard of Ursberg, 6: Burchard's life and his historiographical achievement', *Analecta praemonstratensia* 61: 1/2 (1985), 5–41.

'*Nolens intestatus decedere*'. *Il testamento come fonte della storia religiosa e sociale*, Archivi dell'Umbria. Inventari e ricerche, 7 (Perugia, 1985).

Odorici, F., *Storie bresciane*, 10 vols. (Brescia, 1856).

Oltrona Visconti, G. D., *Conventi Umiliati nel Gallaratese* (Gallarate, 1958).

Paolini, L., 'Domus e zona degli eretici. L'esempio di Bologna nel xiii secolo', *RSCI*, 35 (1981), 371–87.

'Gli eretici e il lavoro. Fra ideologia ed esistenzialità', *Lavorare nel medio evo: rappresentazioni ed esempi dall'Italia dei secoli X–XVI*, Convegni del centro di studi sulla spiritualita medievale, 21 (Todi, 1983), pp. 111–167.

'Le Umiliate al lavoro. Appunti fra storiografia e storia', *Bullettino dell'Istituto storico italiano per il medio evo e archivio muratoriano*, 97 (1991), 229–65.

Pasztor, E., 'Studi e problemi relativi ai registri di Innocenzo III', *Annali della scuola speciale per archivisti e bibliotecari dell'università di Roma*, 2/2 (1962), 287–304.

'Humiliaten', *Lexikon des Mittelalters*, 5/1 (Munich/Zurich, 1991), cols. 210–11.

Pellegrini, L., 'Gli insediamenti degli ordini mendicanti e la loro tipologia. Considerazioni metodologiche e piste di ricerca', *Les ordres mendiants et la ville en Italie centrale (v.1200–v.1350)*, special issue of *Mélanges de l'école française de Rome. Moyen age, temps modernes*, 89 (1977), 563–73.

Insediamenti francescani nell'Italia del duecento (Rome, 1984).

Pennington, K., *Pope and Bishops: The Papal Monarchy in the Twelfth and Thirteenth Centuries* (Pennsylvania, 1984).

Pezza, F., *L'ordine mortariense e l'abbazia mitrata di Sta Croce* (Mortara, 1923).

Piacitelli, C., 'La carità negli atti di ultima volontà milanesi del xii secolo', *La carità a Milano nei secoli xii–xv*, ed. M. P. Alberzoni and O. Grassi (Milan, 1989), pp. 167–86.

Picasso, G., 'San Bernardo e il "transitus" dei monaci', *Studi su S. Bernardo di Chiaravalle nell'ottavo centenario della canonizzazione* (Rome, 1975), pp. 181–200.

Pittura bolognese del '300. Scritti di Francesco Arcangeli, ed. P. G. Castagnoli (Bologna, 1978).

Poole, R. L., *Lectures on the History of the Papal Chancery down to the Time of Innocent III* (Cambridge, 1915).

Bibliography

Puccinelli, P., *Chronicon insignis abbatiae SS Petri et Pauli de glaxiate mediolani* (Milan, 1655).

Puricelli, P., *Ambrosianae mediolani basilicae ac monasterii, hodie cistertiensis, monumenta*, 1 (Milan, 1645).

Racine, P., *Plaisance du $x^{ème}$ à la fin du $xiii^{ème}$ siècle. Essai d'histoire urbaine*, 2 vols. (Paris, 1980).

Rigon, A., 'I laici nella Chiesa padovana del Duecento. Conversi, oblati, penitenti', *Contributi alla storia della chiesa padovana nell'età medioevale*, 1, Fonti e ricerche di storia ecclesiastica padovana, 11, ed. C. Bellinati, G. De Rosa, A. Gambasin, A. Rigon, P. Sambin, F. Sartori, S. Stella and A. Vecchi (Padua, 1979), pp. 11–81.

'Penitenti e laici devoti fra mondo monastico-canonicale e ordini mendicanti: qualche esempio in area veneta e mantovana', *Ricerche di storia sociale e religiosa*, new series 17–18 (1980), 51–73.

'Francescanesimo e società a Padova nel duecento', *Minoritismo e centri veneti nel duecento, nell'ottavo centenario della nascita di Francesco d'Assisi (1182–1982)*, separate edition of *Civis studi e testi*, 19–20, ed. G. Cracco (Trento, 1983), pp. 8–26.

Ripamonti, G., *Historiarum ecclesiae mediolanenses*, 3 vols. (Milan, 1617–28).

Robinson, I. S., *The Papacy 1073–1198: Continuity and Innovation* (Cambridge, 1990).

Rocca, G., 'La triade di obbedienza, povertà e castità', in 'Professione', *DIP*, VII (Rome, 1983), cols. 884–971, 939–41.

Romagnoli, P., 'Gli Umiliati a Modena (xiii/xiv sec.)', *RSCI*, 46 (1992), 489–526.

Ronchetti, G., *Memorie istoriche della città e chiesa di Bergamo*, 7 vols. (Bergamo, 1805–39).

Rouse, R. and Rouse, M., 'The schools and the Waldensians: a new work by Durand of Huesca', *Christendom and its Discontents: Exclusion, Persecution, and Rebellion, 1000–1500*, ed. S. L. Waugh and P. D. Diehl (Cambridge, 1996), pp. 86–111.

Rovigo. Ritratto di una città, Centri storici del Polesine, 1 (Rovigo, 1988).

Rusconi, R., 'I francescani e la confessione nel secolo xiii', *Francescanesimo e vita religiosa dei laici nel '200. Atti dell'viii convegno internazionale della società internazionale di studi francescani, Assisi, 1980* (Assisi, 1981), pp. 251–309.

Samarati, L., 'Dalla fondazione di Lodi Nuova alla riforma Tridentina', *Diocesi di Lodi*, Storia religiosa della Lombardia, 7 (Brescia/Gazzada, 1989), pp. 47–66.

'I primi insediamenti Umiliati nella diocesi di Lodi. Problemi', *Archivio storico lodigiano*, 112 (1993), 85–117.

Samaritani, A., 'Gli indirizzi di Innocenzo III nei riguardi dei monasteri benedettini emiliani', *Ravennatensia* 9, *Atti del convegno di Bologna nel XV centenario della nascita di San Benedetto, 1980* (Cesena, 1981), pp. 225–55.

Savio, C. F., *Gli antichi vescovi d'Italia dalle origini al 1300 descritti per regioni*, I, Piemonte, II, Lombardia, Milano (Turin, 1898–Florence, 1913), no more published.

Scott Davison, E., *Forerunners of Saint Francis and Other Studies*, ed. G. R. B. Richards (Boston/New York, 1927).

Selge, K.-V., *Die ersten Waldenser, mit Edition des 'Liber Antiheresis' des Durandus von Osca*, 2 vols. (Berlin, 1967).

'Die Armut in den nichtrechtgläubigen religiösen Bewegungen des 12. Jahrhunderts', *La povertà del secolo xii e Francesco d'Assisi. Atti del II convegno internazionale, Assisi 1974* (Assisi, 1975), pp. 179–216.

et al., 'Verbali delle sedute', *La povertà del secolo xii e Francesco d'Assisi, Atti del II convegno internazionale, Assisi 1974* (Assisi, 1975), pp. 7–81.

'Humiliaten', *Theologische Realenzyklopädie*, 15 (Berlin, 1986), pp. 691–6.

Bibliography

Sormani, N., 'L'origine de'laici regolari, cioè Umiliati, nobili mercatanti nel secolo XI', *La Gloria dee santi milanesi che ne' piu torbidi secoli produssero l'ordine de' cherici regolari e quello anche de' laici, nobili mercatanti* (Milan, 1761).

Spinelli, G., 'Gli Umiliati in Emilia-Romagna (appunti per una ricerca)', *Ravennatensia 9. Atti del convegno di Bologna nel XV centenario della nascita di san Benedetto, Bologna, 1980* (Cesena, 1981), pp. 133–74.

'Nota sul problema dell'ubicazione delle "domus" degli Umiliati', *La presenza dei benedettini a Bergamo e nella Bergamasca*, Fonti per lo studio del territorio bergamasco, 4 (Bergamo, 1984), pp. 154–8.

'La diffusione del culto di San Bernardo in alta Italia', *San Bernardo e l'Italia*, ed. P. Zerbi (Milan, 1992), pp. 193–215.

Stewart, R. M., *'De illis qui faciunt penitentiam': The Rule of the Secular Franciscan Order: Origins, Development, Interpretation*, Bibliotheca Seraphico-Capuccina, 39 (Rome, 1991).

Storti, G., *Arena Po. Lineamenti di storia medioevale* (Pavia, 1972).

Sulle tracce degli Umiliati, ed. M. P. Alberzoni, A. Ambrosioni and A. Lucioni (Milan, 1997).

Tabacco, G., 'La storia politica e sociale', *Storia d'Italia* II/1, *Dalla caduta dell'impero al secolo xviii* (Turin, 1974), pp. 5–427.

The Struggle for Power in Medieval Italy: Structures of Political Rule, trans. R. Brown Jensen (Cambridge, 1989).

Tagliabue, M., 'Gli Umiliati a Viboldone', *L'Abbazia di Viboldone*, pp. 9–33.

Thomas, A. H., 'La profession religieuse des Dominicains. Formule, cérémonie, histoire', *Archivum fratrum praedicatorum*, 39 (1969), 5–52.

Thouzellier, C., *Catharisme et valdéisme en Languedoc à la fin du xiie et au début du xiiie siècle* (2nd edn, Louvain/Paris, 1969).

Tocco, F., 'Il processo dei Guglielmiti', *Rendiconti della reale accademia dei Lincei, Classe di scienze morali, storiche e filologiche*, 5th series, 8 (1899), 309–42, 351–84, 407–32, 437–69.

Ughelli, F., *Italia sacra sive de episcopis Italiae*, ed. N. Coleti, 9 vols. (Venice, 1717–22).

Vacandard, E., *Vie de saint Bernard*, 2 vols. (Paris, 1895).

Valentini E., 'Gli Umiliati a Vercelli nel 1271', *Bollettino storico vercellese*, 18–19 (1982), 31–56.

Vauchez, A., 'Assistance et charité en occident, xiiie-xve siècles', *Domanda e consumi, livelli e strutture (nei secoli xiii–xviii). Atti della sesta settimana di studio, Prato, 1974*, ed. V. Barbagli Bagnoli (Florence, 1978), pp. 151–62.

Vicaire, M. H., *St Dominic and His Times* (London, 1964).

Violante, C., 'Arnolfo', *DBI*, IV (Rome,1962), pp. 281–2.

'La chiesa bresciana nel medioevo', *Storia di Brescia*, I (Brescia, 1963), pp. 1001–124.

'Hérésies urbaines et hérésies rurales en Italie du 11e au 13e siècle', *Hérésies et Societés dans l'europe préindustrielle: XIe-XVIIIe siècles*, ed. J. Le Goff (Paris, 1968), pp. 171–202. Reprinted as 'Eresie nelle città e eresie nel contado in Italia dal xi al xiii secolo', in *Studi sulla cristianità medioevale, società; istituzioni, spiritualità*, ed. P. Zerbi (Milan, 1972), pp. 349–79.

'Le istituzioni ecclesiastiche nell'Italia centro-settentrionale durante il medioevo: province, diocesi, sedi vescovili', *Forme di potere e struttura sociale in Italia nel medioevo*, ed. G. Rossetti (Bologna, 1977), pp. 83–111.

'L'Organizzazione ecclesiastica per la cura d'anime nell'Italia settentrionale e cen-

Bibliography

trale', *Pievi e parrocchie in Europa dal medioevo all'età contemporanea*, ed. C. D. Fonseca and C. Violante (Galatina, 1990), pp. 203–24.

Volpe, G., *Movimenti religiosi e sette ereticali nella società medievale italiana (secoli xi–xiv)* (Florence, 1922).

Webb, D. M., 'The pope and the cities: anticlericalism and heresy in Innocent III's Italy', *The Church and Sovereignty c. 590–1918: Essays in Honour of Michael Wilks*, ed. D. Wood. SCH Subsidia, ix (Oxford, 1991), pp. 135–52.

Wickham Legg, J., 'The divine service in the sixteenth century illustrated by the reform of the Breviary of the Humiliati', *The Divine Service in the Sixteenth Century* (London, 1890), pp. 273–95.

Wickstrom, J., 'The Humiliati: liturgy and identity', *Archivum fratrum praedicatorum*, 62 (1992), 195–225.

Zerbi, P., 'La rinascita monastica nella bassa milanese dopo l'anno 1000', *Ricerche storiche sulla chiesa ambrosiana*, 9 (Milan, 1980), 55–81.

Zerfaß, R., *Der Streit um die Laienpredigt. Eine pastoralgeschichtliche Untersuchung zum Verstandnis des Predigtamtes und zu seiner Entwicklung im 12. und 13. Jahrhundert* (Vienna/Basle/Freiburg, 1974).

UNPUBLISHED WORKS

Andrews, F. E., 'Innocent III and evangelical enthusiasts: the route to approval', in *Innocent III and his World*, ed. J. C. Moore (forthcoming, Hofstra, 1999).

'The early Humiliati; the development of an order c. 1176–c. 1270', doctoral thesis, University of London, 1994.

Arizza, A., 'L'ospedale di S. Vitale in Como (secc. xiii–xiv)', dissertation, Università Cattolica, Milan 1983–4.

Morelli, F., 'La casa di Rondineto in Como (secc. xiii–xiv)', dissertation, Università Cattolica, Milan 1985–6.

Zocca, V., 'La "domus" degli Umiliati di Sta Maria della Giara in Verona dalle origini alla fine del secolo xiv e panorama sulla diffusione dell'ordine nel distretto veronese, con una silloge di 107 documenti inediti dal 1152 al 1399', dissertation, Università degli Studi, Padua 1969–1970.

GENERAL INDEX

Hum. indicates individuals or communities named as Humiliati in contemporary sources, but does not necessarily indicate affiliation to the official order. *d.* is an abbreviation for *domus*. The appendices have not been included in this index.

Index

Index

Odo, bishop of Paris, 81
Oggiono, Humiliati in, 149
Ognissanti (Florence, originally at San Donato alla torre, then Sta Lucia) (*Hum.*), 143, 145n, 146, 171, 214, 215, 216
Ognissanti (Fossadolto, Borghetto Lodigiano) (*Hum.*), 73n, 74, 141, 142, 143, 148, 151, 153, 158, 159, 160, 164, 226, 236, 240, 250; conflict with bishop, 236, 238
Oldericus, canon of Sto Stefano in Broilo (Milan), 204n
Oliverius (*Hum.*), minister of *d. de S. Salvario* (Vicenza), 170
Olona (river), 52
Oltreticino (Pavia) (*Hum.*): *see d. de Ultra Ticinum/*Oltreticino
Omnis boni principium: see rule of *in* Humiliati
Oriano (nr. Cassago Brianza): *see d. de Orliano*
Ota (*Hum.*), sister at Zevio, daughter of Rizardus, 177, 179, 190
Otto *de Brezia*, brother in fraternity at Borgovico (Como), 164
Otto *de Casteliono*, minister of the Brera (Milan), 79
Otto *de Tonengo*, cardinal bishop of Porto, First Cardinal Protector of Humiliati, 206, 224
Otto Visconti, archbishop of Milan, 237
Otto, *veglone* of Sta Maria *Yemalis*, 49
Ottobellus (*Hum.*), of Gallarate, chaplain to archbishop of Milan, 241
Ottobonus *de Lazate*, of Senago, 194, 195, 196
Oulx, 84

Padua, 204, 205, 232
Paganico (nr Siena): *see* San Michele (Paganico)
Paganus (*Hum.*), minister of the Brera (Milan), 226
Pagliate, 159
Pantanus (*Hum.*), minister of Ghiara, 153, 179n, 231; senior minister in Verona, 168
Paolini, Lorenzo, 32, 35
papacy, 220, 233
papal bulls/correspondence, 221, 242, 249
  Ad abolendam (1184), 39–40, 41, 43, 47, 57, 62, 63, 64, 65, 67
  Bullarium Humiliatorum, 6
  Cum felicis memorie (1227), 109, 110–11, 124
  Diligentiam pii patris (1201, to the Second Order), 66, 72, 96, 105–6, 107, 110, 147, 181
  Ex ore domini (1246), 135, 207–8, 223, 227, 245
  Exhibita nobis vestra (1250), 245
  Incumbit nobis (1201, to the Third order), 52, 66, 74, 100, 101–5, 106, 108n, 110, 126–7, 137, 147, 165–6, 234

Licet in agro (1199), 66, 67
Licet multitudini credentium (1200), 66, 69–72, 73, 78, 80, 124
Non omni spiritui (1201, to the First order), 48, 66, 72–3, 90, 105, 106–8, 109, 110, 126, 129n, 136, 147, 160, 162–3, 223, 234
Olim causam (1200), 53, 64, 73
Quemadmodum solicitus pater (1571), 3, 16n
Religiosam vitam degentibus (1186), 47, 225
Unigenitus dei filius (1246), 134
Parabiago, 160
Paris, 90n, 93
Parma, 76, 86, 93; Humiliati in, 167, 171
Passagines, 40
Patarines, 26, 28, 40, 49, 50, 61, 63, 188
Patrologia Latina, 23, 69
Pavia, 51, 75, 84, 94, 155, 156, 240, 241, 242; bishop of, 94, 132, 240; Humiliati in, 52, 59, 62, 148, 149, 155, 156, 158, 166, 168, 197, 241, 242; *see also d. de porci/porcorum, d. de Ultra Ticinum/*Oltreticino, *d. nova, mansio de Cadrona, mansio fratris Ardenghi,* Sta Maria in Pertica, Sta Maria Maddalena
Paxinus Polvale (*Hum.*), of Viboldone, 193, 196n
Pellegrini, Luigi, 35
penitents, 130n
Pense (*Hum.*), novice of Zevio, 185
Perugia, 210n
Peter, bishop of Tortona, 238
Peter (*Hum.*), brother in retinue of bishop of Pavia, 242
Peter Cabacia (*Hum.*), 51, 57
Peter Capuanus, 92; as auditor of the Humiliati, 94–5; career of, 93, 96; involvement in the fourth crusade, 93; writings of, 93–4
Peter *de Brissia* (*Hum.*), Second Master General of the Humiliati, 143n, 186, 218, 237
Peter *de Bussero*, archpriest of Monte Velate, 77
Peter *de Madio*, 184
Peter *de Misenti* (*Hum.*), brother at *d. nova* (Milan), 155
Peter *de Sologno*, 49
Peter *de verdello qui est batitor lane*, 228n
Peter Martyr, Dominican inquisitor, 252
Peter of Blois, *Tractatus de fide*, 40
Peter of Cuniolo, 55
Peter the Chanter, *Verbum abbreviatum*, 130n
Peter, Cistercian abbot of Lucedio, 66, 73, 81, 234, 249; as auditor of the Humiliati, 83, 86, 89, 91, 111, 112, 116, 122, 123, 125; career of, 86–7, 88, 97; as patriarch of Antioch, 88–9
Peter, cardinal priest of Sta Cecilia, 92
Petra (*Hum.*), sister in Senago, daughter of Leo Borrinus, 193, 195

Index

Index

Index

Cambridge Studies in Medieval Life and Thought
Fourth series

★ *Also published as a paperback*